Centering Transparency and Trust in Data and AI Ecosystems

Otmane Azeroual
https://orcid.org/0000-0002-5225-389X
University of Hagen, Germany

IGI Global
Scientific Publishing
Publishing Tomorrow's Research Today

Vice President of Editorial Melissa Wagner
Director of Acquisitions Mikaela Felty
Director of Book Development Jocelynn Hessler
Production Manager Mike Brehm
Cover Design Jose Rosado

Published in the United States of America by
IGI Global Scientific Publishing
701 East Chocolate Avenue
Hershey, PA, 17033, USA
Tel: 717-533-8845 | Fax: 717-533-7115
Website: https://www.igi-global.com E-mail: cust@igi-global.com

Library of Congress Cataloging-in-Publication Data

LCCN: 2025044738 (CIP Data Pending)
ISBN13: 9798337367613
Isbn13Softcover: 9798337367620
EISBN13: 9798337367637
British Cataloguing in Publication Data
A Cataloguing in Publication record for this book is available from the British Library.

Table of Contents

Detailed Table of Contents

compliance, including issues of algorithmic transparency, data security, & mitigation of inherent biases within AI systems. Subsequently, it will explore role of AI in enhancing compliance, detailing its application in automated data audits, real-time breach detection, & managing user consent. It will also discuss critical function of AI in Data Loss Prevention (DLP) and use of ML for anomaly detection in security systems. It aims to provide a definitive guide for organizations and policymakers seeking to leverage AI's potential while upholding the highest standards of data protection and individual privacy.

This paper analyses data governance frameworks in mergers and acquisitions (M&A) with specific focus on India and the European Union. It examines how India's Digital Personal Data Protection Act, 2023, addresses privacy and cross-border data transfer challenges, contrasting it with the EU's comprehensive regime under the GDPR, Data Governance Act, Data Act, and AI Act. Using comparative doctrinal analysis and stakeholder insights, the paper evaluates mechanisms such as Standard Contractual Clauses and Binding Corporate Rules, highlighting gaps in India's enforcement capacity, data ownership principles, and valuation. It further assesses the EU's emerging contractual fairness obligations and AI liability standards influencing M&A transactions. The study finally proposes statutory reforms and harmonisation pathways to align India's legal framework with EU benchmarks for transparent, accountable, and sustainable data governance in cross-border corporate transactions.

Artificial intelligence is transforming accounting practice, taking over tasks from bookkeeping to forecasting with a speed that once seemed impossible. Yet

This chapter per the authors aims to advance transparency and trust in data and AI ecosystems by examining explainability, evaluation, and continuous monitoring for classical machine learning models and large language models. The target groups include researchers, AI practitioners, policymakers, and governance professionals seeking operational and regulatory guidance. The chapter adopts a lifecycle-based analytical approach, synthesizing recent literature, governance frameworks, and practical transparency artifacts such as model cards, evaluation metrics, and monitoring pipelines. The findings highlight that transparency-by-design, coupled with robust evaluation and post-deployment monitoring, significantly improves accountability, risk mitigation, and stakeholder trust. The chapter concludes that integrating technical, human-centered, and governance perspectives is essential for deploying trustworthy and sustainable AI systems at scale.

This chapter examines Human-in-the-Loop (HITL) and participatory approaches for trustworthy AI, emphasizing human oversight, stakeholder engagement, and ethical alignment across the AI lifecycle. It discusses implementation challenges, best practices, and case studies, highlighting iterative feedback loops that enhance accuracy, transparency, and legitimacy. Future directions focus on scalable HITL, inclusive governance, interdisciplinary collaboration, and adaptive policies to ensure socially responsible AI.

As artificial intelligence systems proliferate across critical industry sectors, the imperative to build platforms that are simultaneously capable and trustworthy has grown urgent. This chapter examines five cross-sector case studies—spanning financial services, healthcare, manufacturing, public administration, and retail—to surface the governance architectures, transparency mechanisms, and accountability structures that distinguish trustworthy AI deployments from opaque, high-risk alternatives. Drawing on responsible AI governance frameworks, the Digital Trust Ecosystem Framework (DTEF), NIST AI RMF, and the EU AI Act, the chapter synthesises recurring patterns: layered data governance, explainability-by-design, fairness auditing pipelines, and human oversight protocols.

This chapter presents a comprehensive analysis of global AI governance, focusing on balancing innovation, ethical responsibility, and regulatory oversight. It examines the roles of governments, industry, academia, and civil society within complex AI ecosystems, highlighting technological drivers, open versus proprietary AI, and economic and societal impacts. The chapter explores regulatory approaches, including the EU AI Act, US soft law, and global coordination models, and discusses the integration of standards and ethics-by-design. Future scenarios for AI governance, adaptive regulation, and public-private partnerships are analyzed to provide actionable

Preface

INTRODUCTION

The accelerating integration of data and artificial intelligence into nearly every sector of society has brought unprecedented opportunities for innovation, efficiency, and insight. Yet, alongside these advancements, concerns surrounding transparency, accountability, and trust have become increasingly urgent. As AI systems grow more complex and influential, stakeholders—from policymakers and researchers to industry practitioners and civil society—are called upon to ensure that these technologies are not only powerful but also understandable, fair, and aligned with human values. This volume, Centering Transparency and Trust in Data and AI Ecosystems, emerges in response to this critical need.

Transparency and trust are not peripheral considerations; they are foundational to the sustainable development and adoption of AI systems. Without clear governance structures, explainable mechanisms, and participatory approaches, AI risks reinforcing opacity and undermining public confidence. This book positions transparency as both a technical and sociotechnical imperative—one that spans data pipelines, algorithmic design, regulatory compliance, and organizational culture. By centering these themes, the contributions in this volume collectively explore how trust can be cultivated, measured, and maintained across diverse AI ecosystems.

This edited collection brings together interdisciplinary perspectives from law, computer science, governance, and industry practice. The chapters reflect a global outlook, incorporating insights from different regulatory regimes, economic contexts, and application domains. Together, they provide a comprehensive examination of how transparency can be operationalized and how trust can be institutionalized in data-driven environments. The aim is not only to diagnose current challenges but also to offer actionable frameworks and forward-looking strategies.

CHAPTER OVERVIEWS

Chapter 1 establishes the conceptual and governance foundations of transparency in AI ecosystems. It examines accountability, responsibility, and liability through an end-to-end governance lens, emphasizing traceability, reproducibility, and organizational clarity in roles and oversight mechanisms.

Chapter 2 explores the intersection of AI, data privacy, and regulatory compliance. It analyzes global frameworks such as GDPR, CCPA, and PIPL, while also demonstrating how AI can serve as both a compliance challenge and a powerful tool for enhancing data protection through automation and real-time monitoring.

Chapter 3 provides a comparative legal analysis of data governance in mergers and acquisitions, focusing on the European Union and India. It highlights regulatory gaps, cross-border data transfer challenges, and the need for harmonization to support transparent and accountable corporate transactions.

Chapter 4 introduces MSME financial standards as a practical governance framework for trustworthy AI in accounting. It bridges traditional accounting principles with modern AI ethics, offering a grounded approach for smaller enterprises navigating digital transformation.

Chapter 5 delivers a comprehensive treatment of explainable artificial intelligence (XAI), covering both classical machine learning models and large language models. It presents key methodologies and critically evaluates their role in making AI systems interpretable and auditable.

Chapter 6 advances the concept of transparency-by-design by focusing on evaluation, explainability, and continuous monitoring across AI lifecycles. It underscores the importance of integrating technical tools with governance artifacts such as model cards and monitoring pipelines.

Chapter 7 centers on human-in-the-loop and participatory approaches, emphasizing the role of human oversight and stakeholder engagement in building trustworthy AI systems. It highlights iterative feedback mechanisms and inclusive governance practices.

Chapter 8 presents industry case studies that illustrate how trustworthy AI platforms are designed and governed in practice. It identifies recurring patterns such as layered governance, fairness auditing, and explainability mechanisms across sectors.

Chapter 9 concludes the volume by examining future directions in global AI governance. It explores the balance between innovation and regulation, emphasizing human-centered AI, adaptive policy frameworks, and the importance of international collaboration.

CONCLUSION

As the chapters in this volume collectively demonstrate, transparency is not a singular solution but a multifaceted commitment that must be embedded across technical, organizational, and regulatory dimensions. Building trustworthy AI systems requires more than compliance; it demands a proactive alignment of values, practices, and incentives that prioritize clarity, accountability, and inclusivity. The frameworks and case studies presented here offer pathways for translating these principles into actionable strategies.

Equally important is the recognition that trust is dynamic and context-dependent. It evolves alongside technological advancements, societal expectations, and regulatory developments. Therefore, fostering trust in AI ecosystems requires continuous engagement, evaluation, and adaptation. The integration of explainability, participatory governance, and lifecycle monitoring highlighted throughout this book provides a foundation for such ongoing efforts.

We hope this volume serves as both a scholarly resource and a practical guide for advancing transparency and trust in data and AI ecosystems. By bringing together diverse perspectives and insights, we aim to contribute to a more responsible and human-centered future for AI—one in which innovation and integrity progress hand in hand.

Chapter 1
Accountability, Responsibility, and Liability in AI and Data Ecosystems:
Centering Transparency Through End-to-End Governance

Oindrilla Ghosh
http://orcid.org/0000-0001-9609-0781
Christ University, India

Ananya Pandey
http://orcid.org/0000-0002-2419-6314
Christ University, Bangalore, India

ABSTRACT

Accountability, responsibility, and liability in AI and data ecosystems require governance that centers transparency. Organizations map data flows, model lifecycles, and decision points from data collection to user outcomes. Accountability assigns roles: data scientists, engineers, operators, and sponsors share duty for accuracy, fairness, and safety. Responsibility creates practices, risk assessments, and change management that prompt timely correction when biases or errors emerge. Liability clarifies legal exposure for misuses or breaches, aligning incentives with user trust. Transparent governance builds trust by publicly articulating standards, and oversight mechanisms across developers, vendors, and customers. End-to-end transparency enables traceability, reproducibility, and continual improvement. Mechanisms like independent audits, explainable outputs, and red-teaming strengthen resilience.

DOI: 10.4018/979-8-3373-6761-3.ch001

A culture of openness, well-defined escalation paths, and measurable metrics ensures that accountability remains practical, not aspirational, across technical and organizational layers.

INTRODUCTION

In the rapidly evolving landscape of AI and data ecosystems, accountability, responsibility, and liability are central pillars for trustworthy innovation. This triad operates as a framework to ensure that organizations, developers, users, and other stakeholders can anticipate, explain, and justify decisions that affect individuals and society (Ansell et al., 2024). Accountability focuses on the obligation to explain actions and outcomes, to provide recourse when harm occurs, and to answer to applicable governance structures. Responsibility denotes the assignment of duties to specific actors within the data lifecycle, data collection, curation, labeling, model development, deployment, monitoring, and maintenance so that each step has clear ownership (Babacan, 2025). Liability concerns the legal and financial consequences that arise from harms or non-compliance, including who bears the costs and how remedies are provided. When these elements are aligned, AI systems become more transparent, auditable, and ultimately more resilient to misuses and failures (Broadhurst & Gray, 2022).

Centering transparency through end-to-end governance means designing governance that spans the entire lifecycle of data and models, from data provenance and collection practices to deployment, monitoring, and decommissioning. End-to-end governance requires explicit policies, measurable controls, and auditable traces that enable third parties regulators, customers, civil society, and internal risk teams to verify compliance, assess risk, and hold the appropriate actors accountable (Hinterleitner et al., 2024). Transparency is not merely disclosure of outcomes; it is about revealing the processes that generate those outcomes. This includes model cards and data sheets that document purpose, training data sources, performance metrics across diverse populations, limitations, and potential biases. It also encompasses impact assessments that anticipate social, ethical, and environmental effects, and governance mechanisms that empower redress, explanation, and red-teaming of systems before and after deployment (Salvador & Sancho, 2023).

A practical governance approach recognizes the distributed nature of AI and data ecosystems. Roles may include data stewards, model evaluators, product managers, legal/compliance officers, and external auditors. It requires cross-functional collaboration to align business objectives with ethical norms, regulatory requirements, and user rights. For organizations, this translates into implementing robust risk management frameworks, incident response protocols, and escalation paths for emerging harms (Kumi & Hayman, 2025). For individuals, it means enhanced rights to understand how algorithms affect them, access to recourse, and assurance that their data is treated with care. Ultimately, the aim is to create systems that can explain decisions, justify actions, and be held to consistent standards across different contexts and jurisdictions (Bolleyer, 2021).

In practice, end-to-end governance integrates technical measures (data lineage, versioning, model monitoring, interpretable design) with organizational controls (policies, training, governance committees, internal audits) and legal remedies (liability allocation, consumer protection mechanisms). The result is not a one-size-fits-all blueprint but a modular, adaptable framework that can scale with evolving technologies while preserving core values such as fairness, safety, privacy, and accountability (Bravim et al., 2025). By centering transparency, organizations can build greater trust with users and society, accelerate responsible innovation, and reduce the likelihood or severity of harms associated with AI and data-driven systems.

HISTORICAL EVOLUTION

The concepts of accountability, responsibility, and liability in AI and data ecosystems have evolved from traditional governance of human decision-making to a complex, multi-stakeholder regime shaped by technological, legal, and social forces. Early governance focused on data protection and ethical use in the wake of growing information systems (Nair, 2024). As organizations began to deploy automated decision-making, questions about accountability emerged: who is responsible for a biased loan denial, an incorrect medical suggestion, or a discriminatory advertisement? Initial responses relied on high-level ethics guidelines and voluntary industry codes, coupled with liability concepts rooted in consumer protection and product liability law. However, the speed and opacity of automated systems necessitated more concrete mechanisms for traceability, auditability, and remedy (Moya & Goenechea, 2022).

A notable shift occurred as data governance matured into more formalized data stewardship and model governance practices. Data provenance, quality control, and documentation longstanding concerns in data-intensive domains gained renewed attention. The movement toward responsible AI introduced practices such as model cards, data sheets for datasets, and impact assessments that sought to foreground context, limitations, and potential harms (Ansell & Torfing, 2022). These tools aimed to operationalize accountability by making the assumptions and trade-offs behind AI systems visible to stakeholders. Simultaneously, academic and industry research advanced methods for explainability, fairness, and robustness, offering technical pathways to clarifying how decisions are made and where biases may originate.

Regulatory developments marked a watershed moment in liability and accountability. General data protection regulation (GDPR) in the European Union enshrined rights to explanation and user control over personal data, while consumer protection and financial services frameworks began to address algorithmic decision-making more explicitly (Chen, 2023). In the United States, a patchwork of sector-specific regulations, antidiscrimination laws, and emerging state-level privacy rules influenced organizational practices. International cooperation began to emphasize harmonization of standards for transparency, risk management, and governance, even as enforcement varied by jurisdiction (Mizrak, 2024).

The rise of end-to-end governance reflects a convergence of these strands. Organizations started mapping data flows, model lifecycles, and decision points to identify who should be accountable at each stage. They built governance bodies with cross-functional representation and instituted ongoing monitoring, incident response, and redress mechanisms (Pitidis et al., 2024). The decentralization of data ecosystems where data is sourced globally, models are deployed across contexts, and automated decisions affect diverse groups generated new challenges: cross-border data transfers, transfer of liability across service providers and users, and the need for interoperable standards. The current landscape seeks to balance innovation with responsibility by embedding transparency into technical design, organizational processes, and legal infrastructures (Broadhurst & Gray, 2022). As AI systems become more autonomous and embedded in critical sectors, the push toward end-to-end governance is likely to intensify, evolving alongside advances in data ethics, governance tooling, and regulatory expectations.

THEORETICAL FRAMEWORKS

Accountability, responsibility, and liability are interrelated yet distinct concepts that must be reconciled within AI and data ecosystems. A robust theoretical framework starts by clarifying roles, expectations, and consequences across the lifecycle of data- and AI-powered systems from data generation and collection to deployment, maintenance, and impact assessment (Chen, 2023). Four pillars help structure this inquiry: governance theory, moral philosophy of responsibility, legal-economic liability models, and sociotechnical systems thinking.

Governance theory provides the scaffolding for who has authority, how decisions are made, and how incentives align with public values. End-to-end governance emphasizes that accountability cannot be a single bottleneck (e.g., a developer or a firm) but a distributed process spanning data provenance, model development, deployment, monitoring, and remediation (Wojczewski et al., 2023). This view encourages traceability, auditable decision trails, and clear escalation paths. It also supports the creation of joint accountability mechanisms among stakeholders data subjects, data processors, platform operators, regulators, and end users through contracts, policy instruments, and transparent governance artifacts.

Moral philosophy of responsibility helps distinguish intention, outcome, and foreseeability. Responsibility-taking can be voluntary (accountability for decisions and harms one caused or could have prevented) or ascribed (liability for failures due to systemic conditions) (Cook, 2021). In AI, we often distinguish upward responsibility (designers and managers), downward responsibility (operators implementing the system in practice), and horizontal responsibility (collaborators across teams and organizations). A nuanced framework recognizes moral responsibility even when outcomes arise from complex, distributed interactions, while also acknowledging limits to control (Levine et al., 2023). This leads to practices like responsibility mapping, where stakeholders identify who should own decisions at each stage, who should be held to account for harms, and how to allocate remedial duties.

Legal-economic models of liability bring structure to risk allocation, ensuring that incentives promote safer, more transparent systems. Traditional tort or product-liability notions may be insufficient for AI due to autonomy, uncertainty, and scale (Nasibov, 2021). Therefore, hybrid models that blend contractual accountability (who bears risk under a contract) with ex ante risk allocation (e.g., liability caps, insurance, or mandatory disclosure requirements) can be more effective. These models may introduce "responsibility as dynamic liability," where liability follows learning and adaptation: as a system learns or is retrained, new liability boundaries emerge (Syal et al., 2021). Insurance markets, standardized risk assessments, and mandatory disclosures about model capabilities, data provenance, and performance in diverse contexts can operationalize these ideas.

Sociotechnical systems thinking emphasizes that technologies do not operate in a vacuum; social, organizational, and technical components co-create outcomes. Accountability emerges through alignment among incentives, culture, governance processes, and technical design (Krogh & Lo, 2023). This approach supports transparent decision-making, shared mental models among stakeholders, and the embedment of ethical and legal considerations into design choices (privacy-by-design, fairness-by-design, safety-by-design). It also acknowledges ambiguity and the need for ongoing governance adaptation as systems evolve.

CHALLENGES AND OPPORTUNITIES

End-to-end governance seeks to embed transparency across the entire lifecycle of AI and data ecosystems. While conceptually appealing, this approach faces practical, normative, and operational challenges that must be navigated to realize meaningful accountability, responsibility, and liability.

One core challenge is provenance and traceability. Data and models often pass through multiple hands, transformations, and sub-processors. Achieving auditable provenance requires principled data lineage, versioning, and standardized metadata practices (Kolmodin, 2024). Technical hurdles include handling large-scale training data with privacy safeguards, tracking lineage through model updates, and ensuring that traces remain interpretable to non-technical stakeholders. Governance mechanisms mandatory data and model cards, disclosure of data sources, and standardized evaluation benchmarks can promote transparency, but they must be implemented in accessible language and complemented by independent audits to avoid greenwashing (Stupak et al., 2021).

A second challenge concerns explainability and user comprehension. Transparency is not just about revealing inputs and outputs; it is about ensuring stakeholders understand how decisions are made, the uncertainties involved, and the potential biases (Ibones et al., 2024). This demands layered explanations: technical rationales for developers, policy-relevant summaries for regulators, and contextualized disclosures for data subjects. End-to-end governance should incorporate explainability requirements at each stage, with metrics that are auditable, such as calibration of confidence scores, fairness indicators across groups, and robustness to distribution shifts (Smidt et al., 2025). However, there is a risk of overwhelming stakeholders with complexity. Solutions include providing tiered transparency: high-level disclosures for the public, detailed technical logs for trusted auditors, and on-demand explanations for affected individuals.

A third challenge is balancing transparency with proprietary considerations and security. Firms may fear that full disclosure of models or datasets could erode competitive advantage or expose vulnerabilities (Damiyano, 2024). The governance framework must reconcile openness with legitimate protections through mechanisms such as secure external audits, redacted datasets, synthetic data proxies, license-based access, and governance-level guarantees rather than full public disclosure. This often necessitates trusted intermediary bodies (regulators, third-party auditors, or standards organizations) to verify claims without compromising sensitive information (Garcia et al., 2023).

Liability implications are tightly coupled with governance design. Clear accountability mappings, defined in governance documents and contracts, help determine who bears risk for specific harms. Transparency aids this by making decision pathways inspectable (Bua & Bussu, 2023). Yet liability is contingent on foreseeing harm, demonstrating negligence or fault, and causal linkages dactors that are difficult to prove in complex AI systems. End-to-end governance can mitigate this by mandating risk assessments, impact analyses, and pre-emptive remediation plans, thereby reducing the likelihood or magnitude of harms and creating a framework for prompt corrective action.

Opportunities abound when transparency becomes an operational norm. Organizations can build trust with users and regulators, reduce compliance costs through standardized disclosures, and improve system design via feedback loops from audits and stakeholder input (Van Wessel et al., 2021). A well-structured end-to-end governance regime also supports ongoing learning updating policies as technologies evolve, refining risk models with new data, and clarifying liability frontiers as capabilities expand. Cross-sector collaboration on common standards, data stewardship best practices, and independent oversight can further strengthen transparency.

ROLE OF AI IN ACCOUNTABILITY, RESPONSIBILITY, AND LIABILITY IN AI AND DATA ECOSYSTEMS

Artificial intelligence shapes decisions, models, and systems across industries, making accountability, responsibility, and liability central concerns for governance. The role of AI here is both a vehicle and a target: it is the engine that enables more informed decisions and the element whose faults and biases demand clear governance (Williamson et al., 2022). A robust accountability framework recognizes AI as a socio-technical artifact an assemblage of data, models, human actors, and organizational processes and seeks to ensure that responsibility for outcomes is clearly assigned, explainable, and enforceable.

First, AI amplifies the need for explicit responsibility across stages of the lifecycle. Data collection, labeling, model training, deployment, monitoring, and maintenance each create opportunities for error, bias, or harm (Bolton et al., 2023). End-to-end governance requires mapping owners and operators for every stage, with defined duties: data stewards for input quality; model developers for design choices and bias mitigation; deployment teams for context awareness and risk controls; and governance bodies for oversight and escalation. Clear delineation of roles helps prevent diffusion of responsibility, where decisions are insulated from accountability due to complexity or organizational silos (Willems, 2021).

Second, accountability hinges on transparency and explainability. AI systems should provide intelligible rationales for decisions, along with information about data provenance, feature influences, and confidence levels. This transparency enables stakeholders users, regulators, auditors, and affected communities to understand why a decision occurred and whether it aligns with applicable norms and laws (Bravim et al., 2025). Accountability is not merely about post-hoc justification; it is embedded in the design: interpretable models where feasible, auditable pipelines, and documentation that traces data lineage, model iterations, and decision rules.

Third, governance mechanisms must address liability in a nuanced way. Liability frameworks need to attribute responsibility across organizations and individuals involved in AI-enabled decisions (Arnaouti et al., 2022). This includes considering third-party data, outsourced components, and external service providers. Liability also entails preemptive risk-sharing arrangements, such as contractual obligations for bias testing, safety verifications, and post-deployment monitoring. A mature approach links liability to governance metrics: traceable decision logs, anomaly detection, and incident response playbooks that demonstrate due diligence and timely remediation (Annan et al., 2021).

Fourth, accountability practices require measurable governance outcomes. Key performance indicators include the rate of bias mitigations, time-to-detect and time-to-respond to failures, completeness of data provenance records, and the availability of decision explanations to affected users (Riboldi, 2024). Independent audits, red teams, and model risk reviews promote objective assessment, complementing internal governance. A culture of accountability transparent incentives, whistleblowing channels, and equitable remediation processes ensures that accountability is not a checkbox but an ongoing practice.

Fifth, end-to-end governance is essential to align AI-driven accountability with broader ethical and legal norms. It integrates data governance, model governance, deployment governance, and impact assessment (Njoku, 2022). It also requires stakeholder participation, including communities whose interests are affected by AI decisions, to ensure that governance reflects diverse values and mitigates disproportionate harms.

USE OF AR, VR, AND MR

Augmented Reality (AR), Virtual Reality (VR), and Mixed Reality (MR) offer immersive, immersive visualization and interaction capabilities to enhance governance of AI and data ecosystems. Their value lies in translating complex, abstract governance constructs into tangible, experiential tools that improve transparency, training, and oversight across the end-to-end lifecycle.

First, AR/VR/MR can visualize data lineage and model governance in interactive formats. Auditors and governance teams can "walk" through data flows, observe influence diagrams, and inspect lineage with spatial representations that reveal how data moves, transforms, and propagates through models (Samaratunge & Alam, 2021). Immersive dashboards can illustrate compliance checkpoints, bias risk surfaces, and decision rationales in a comprehensible, intuitive manner. This spatial framing helps stakeholders grasp interdependencies and identify gaps that textual reports may miss.

Second, immersive simulations support risk testing and scenario planning. VR environments can recreate deployment contexts, enabling teams to test how AI systems respond to edge cases, data shifts, or adversarial inputs. By simulating consequences in a safe, controlled space, organizations can refine control mechanisms, error budgets, and escalation protocols. AR overlays during live operation can alert operators about data anomalies, model drift, or broken governance checks in real time, enhancing situational awareness without interrupting workflows (Njoku, 2022).

Third, AR/VR/MR enhances training and accountability culture. Immersive training modules teach developers, operators, and decision-makers about bias, fairness, safety, and regulatory obligations. Learners can engage with consistent, repeatable exercises that embed governance norms, making accountability practices tangible rather than abstract (Chaudhry, 2022). This experiential learning strengthens the understanding of responsibilities across roles and fosters organizational alignment around end-to-end governance principles.

Fourth, these technologies support transparent incident response and post-incident analysis. In AR, responders can visualize incident timelines, accountable owners, and remediation steps overlaid on real-world environments or data ecosystems. VR can reconstruct incidents to facilitate root-cause analysis and collaborative reviews among diverse stakeholders. MR enables cross-functional teams to co-create remediation plans with shared, interactive models of the system's state and the decisions that led to the outcome (McKeague & Bies, 2025).

Fifth, AR/VR/MR can democratize governance by making complex policies accessible to non-experts. Immersive explainability tools translate multi-layered governance requirements into digestible experiences, helping users understand how data, models, and decisions affect them. This transparency supports informed consent, stakeholder trust, and acceptance of AI-driven outcomes (Mir et al., 2024).

CASE STUDIES

Case Study 1: COMPAS and Criminal Justice Risk Assessment

Overview and Context

The Correctional Offender Management Profiling for Alternative Sanctions (COMPAS) is a risk assessment tool used in multiple jurisdictions to predict the likelihood of reoffending. It aggregates disparate data sources, including prior convictions, demographics, and behavioral indicators, to generate a risk score used in bail, sentencing, and parole decisions. The case raises core questions about who bears responsibility when a machine-guided decision adversely affects a person's liberty, and how courts and administrators can verify, contest, and improve such systems through governance that centers transparency.

End-to-End Governance in Practice

Data governance: Source data quality, representativeness, and potential biases must be audited. Sensitive attributes (e.g., race) must be handled carefully to avoid discriminatory impact.

Model governance: Version control, audit trails, model documentation, and performance monitoring across demographics. Regular bias/variance analysis and recalibration are essential (Ansell et al., 2024).

Decision governance: Clear mapping from risk score to decision, with predefined thresholds, discretionary review, and appeal mechanisms for defendants and lawyers.

Transparency and explainability: Stakeholders need intelligible explanations of how inputs influence scores and how decisions are made, without compromising proprietary safeguards.

Liability and accountability: Institutions deploying COMPAS must articulate accountability lines developers, deployers (courts), and oversight bodies. Redress mechanisms for misclassification or unjust outcomes should exist.

Liability, Accountability, and Lessons

Liability is shared: developers are responsible for model design and validation; deploying agencies are responsible for how outputs are used; oversight bodies (courts, public defender offices) ensure lawful application and remedy.

Accountability gaps arise when decision-making relies on opaque proxies or when human review is delegated without adequate checks. End-to-end governance must require human-in-the-loop review where risk scores trigger substantial decisions (Babacan, 2025).

Lessons emphasize robust impact assessments, public reporting of accuracy metrics by subgroup, and independent audits. When transparency is limited due to security concerns or risk of gaming, governance should emphasize explainability to the extent feasible and provide decision-makers with verifiable evidence rather than raw weights.

Governance Recommendations

Establish independent risk-audit teams to review model inputs, features, and outputs for bias and fairness before deployment.

Implement standardized, auditable documentation (model cards) detailing data provenance, training regimes, performance by demographic groups, and decision logic boundaries.

Create external oversight mechanisms: judicial or parliamentary reviews, public dashboards on model performance, and a clear process for redress (Broadhurst & Gray, 2022).

Enforce robust human-review protocols for high-stakes decisions with explicit liability allocation among stakeholders.

Promote continuous improvement: post-deployment monitoring, feature revalidation, and sunset clauses for models with planned decommissioning.

Case Study 2: GDPR Accountability in Data-Driven Credit Scoring

Overview and Context

A European bank deploys an AI-driven credit scoring system to assess loan applicants. The system ingests transactional data, credit histories, utility payments, and alternative data. The case examines how end-to-end governance can satisfy GDPR requirements for data subject rights, transparency, purpose limitation, and the accountability principle (Article 5(2)) in a high-stakes financial context.

End-to-End Governance in Practice

Data governance: Data minimization, purpose specification, and lawful bases for processing. Data lineage traces for data sources, transformations, and model outputs.

Model governance: Documentation of model choice, training data, performance metrics, and process for ongoing monitoring. Documentation of risk of disparate impact and mitigation steps (Hinterleitner et al., 2024).

Transparency and accountability: Automated explanations to applicants about why they were approved or denied, with avenues to contest decisions and request human review.

Data subject rights: Mechanisms to access, rectify, erase, or port data, and to object to automated decision-making with meaningful human involvement where required.

Liability: Clear allocation of responsibility across data controllers (bank), data processors (vendors), and governance bodies in case of breaches or unfair outcomes.

Liability, Accountability, and Lessons

Liability for incorrect credit decisions can fall on the bank for the automated decision, especially if human oversight is lacking or ineffective.

GDPR requires accountability: the bank must implement technical and organizational measures to demonstrate compliance (data protection by design and by default, DPIAs, etc.).

Lessons emphasize proactive impact assessments, explicit consent where necessary, and robust human review processes for automated decisions affecting creditworthiness (Salvador & Sancho, 2023).

Governance Recommendations

DPIA (Data Protection Impact Assessment) conducted early and updated with model changes.

Transparent score explanations, clear thresholds, and right to human review for adverse decisions.

Audit trail of data sources, feature engineering, model versioning, and decision logs.

Regular bias testing and impact analyses across protected classes; remediation where discrimination is detected.

Incident response and breach notification protocols aligned with GDPR requirements (Kumi & Hayman, 2025).

Case Study 3: Healthcare AI – IBM Watson for Oncology and the Liability of Automated Medical Guidance

Overview and Context

IBM Watson for Oncology aimed to assist clinicians with evidence-based cancer treatment recommendations. The case explores healthcare accountability for clinical outcomes, patient safety, and the interplay between machine guidance and physician judgment within structured governance that supports transparency.

End-to-End Governance in Practice

Data governance: Use of high-quality clinical data, de-identification, and patient consent where applicable.

Model governance: Documentation of treatment recommendations, evidence bases, confidence levels, and limitations. Versioning tied to clinical guidelines.

Clinical integration: Clear delineation of roles physician decision-making remains primary, with AI as a support tool. Documentation of AI-derived suggestions in the patient record (Bolleyer, 2021).

Transparency: Clinicians and patients should understand the rationale behind recommendations, the evidence base, and uncertainties.

Liability: Responsibility for clinical outcomes remains with the healthcare provider; liability may extend to developers if negligence in design or validation is proven.

Liability, Accountability, and Lessons

Blurred boundaries: When AI guidance is wrong, questions arise about whether liability rests with clinicians who relied on it, institutions, or developers.

Lessons highlight the necessity of human-in-the-loop processes, conservative deployment with strong validation, and explicit disclaimers about AI limitations (Bravim et al., 2025).

Governance Recommendations

Clinical governance: Multidisciplinary oversight committees to review AI tools and ensure alignment with guidelines.

Evidence-based evaluation: Rigorous clinical trials or prospective studies demonstrating safety and efficacy.

Documentation: Transparent reporting of confidence, limitations, and contraindications.

Patient consent and disclosure: Clear communications about AI-assisted recommendations.

Liability frameworks: Clear allocation of responsibility with insurance coverage that reflects AI-assisted care.

Case Study 4: Public Safety and Facial Recognition

Overview and Context

Public safety deployments of facial recognition (FR) systems for policing or crowd management raise concerns about privacy, accuracy, and civil liberties. The case emphasizes the need for governance that centers transparency and accountable use in sensitive public contexts.

End-to-End Governance in Practice

Data governance: Minimization of biometric data collection, retention limits, and robust encryption.

Model governance: Validation of FR performance across demographics, post-deployment monitoring, and red-team testing.

Transparency: Public disclosure of where and how FR is used, with accessible explanations for decisions influenced by FR matches (Nair, 2024).

Accountability: Clear roles for developers, operators, and oversight bodies; mechanisms for complaints and redress.

Liability: Potential liability for misuse or wrongful arrests; require governance measures to prevent harm.

Liability, Accountability, and Lessons

Potential for civil liberties violations if used without adequate safeguards. Transparent, auditable processes reduce risk.

Lessons underscore the need for independent audits, sunset clauses, and legal oversight (Moya & Goenechea, 2022).

Governance Recommendations

Public-facing governance frameworks outlining permissible use, data retention, and oversight.

Independent audits and impact assessments on accuracy, bias, and civil rights impacts.

Clear escalation paths for false positives and wrongful detentions.

Case Study 5: AI Hiring Tools – Amazon's Discontinued Recruiting Tool and the Liability of Automated Talent Decisions

Overview and Context

In 2018–2019, Amazon discontinued an AI-powered recruiting tool due to biased performance against female candidates. The case examines accountability, bias remediation, and governance in automated hiring systems.

End-to-End Governance in Practice

Data governance: Training data reflecting historical biases. Mitigation requires diverse, representative data and bias-aware feature engineering.

Model governance: Documentation of model objectives, evaluation metrics, de-biasing techniques, and monitoring for drift.

Hiring process governance: Transparent decision criteria, rule-based overrides, and human-in-the-loop for critical hiring decisions (Ansell & Torfing, 2022).

Transparency: Clear explanations to applicants about automated decision processes, with recourse options.

Liability: Employers bear responsibility for discriminatory outcomes; vendors may share liability if negligent in design or validation.

Liability, Accountability, and Lessons

Case demonstrates that unchecked automation can perpetuate bias. Accountability requires robust governance, external audits, and redress mechanisms.

Lessons emphasize the necessity of human oversight, diverse training data, ongoing monitoring, and the ability to halt or modify tools that create unfair outcomes (Chen, 2023).

Governance Recommendations

Mandated bias testing across protected classes prior to deployment.

Transparent decision criteria and human review for sensitive roles.

Continuous monitoring and rapid decommissioning processes for biased tools.

External audits and governance bodies to assess fairness and compliance.

IMPLEMENTATIONS OF REGULATORY FRAMEWORKS IN AI AND DATA ECOSYSTEMS

Regulatory frameworks are increasingly shaping how organizations design, deploy, and monitor AI and data-driven systems. Effective implementations require a mix of legally grounded principles, practical standards, and adaptive governance that can keep pace with rapid technological change (Mizrak, 2024). The core objective is to embed accountability, risk management, and transparency into end-to-end workflows from data collection to model deployment and ongoing operation.

Key Components and Approaches

Legislative Baselines: Adopt and harmonize core AI/ML laws (e.g., data protection, non-discrimination, consumer protection, safety standards) with sector-specific requirements (healthcare, finance, critical infrastructure). This creates a predictable regulatory floor that reduces compliance ambiguity for cross-border deployments (Pitidis et al., 2024).

Risk-Based Regulation: Regulate AI systems according to risk tiering (unacceptable, high, limited, minimal). High-risk systems such as those affecting safety, fundamental rights, or critical decision-making receive stricter controls: pre-deployment impact assessments, continuous monitoring, and independent conformity assessment. Lower-risk systems benefit from lightweight governance and voluntary codes of practice (Broadhurst & Gray, 2022).

End-to-End Governance Standards: Require organizations to demonstrate governance across data lifecycle and model lifecycle. This includes data provenance, data quality controls, bias detection, model documentation (model cards, data sheets), versioning, and change management. Standards should emphasize traceability from data intake to outcome.

Independent Oversight and Accountability Mechanisms: Establish independent bodies (regulatory agencies, accredited third-party assessors) to audit compliance, investigate incidents, and enforce penalties. Consider mandatory incident reporting, post-market surveillance, and public dashboards for transparency.

Technology-Neutral, Outcome-Focused Rules: Design regulations that emphasize outcomes (accuracy, fairness, safety) rather than rigid technical prescriptions. This allows innovation while maintaining core protections and enables updates as techniques evolve (Chen, 2023).

Data-Impact Assessments and Safety Certification: Require systematic impact assessments that identify potential harms, data biases, privacy risks, and security gaps. For high-risk systems, mandate third-party safety or fairness certifications before market release.

Transparency and Explainability Provisions: Define permissible levels of explainability for different use cases, ensure disclosure of senior-level system responsibilities (who built, who owns, who can audit) and publish high-level system characteristics without compromising proprietary methods.

Privacy by Design and Data Governance: Enforce data minimization, purpose limitation, consent management, and robust security practices. Encourage federated learning, differential privacy, and data lineage tracking to preserve privacy while enabling insights (Wojczewski et al., 2023).

International and Cross-Border Cooperation: Promote harmonization through international standards bodies and mutual recognition of conformity assessments to facilitate cross-border AI deployment while maintaining safeguards.

Enforcement Tools: Leverage licensing regimes, mandatory accreditations for organizations handling high-risk systems, and liability frameworks that hold entities accountable for failures or harms. Use penalties, corrective actions, and remediation requirements to deter non-compliance (Cook, 2021).

Implementation Roadmap and Best Practices

Stakeholder Involvement: Involve regulators, industry, civil society, and the public early in standard-setting to reflect diverse concerns and expectations.

Incremental Rollout with Sunset Provisions: Phase in requirements, with periodic reviews and sunset clauses to adapt to new evidence and technology changes.

Open Standards and Shared Repositories: Develop open datasets for compliance testing, model cards, bias benchmarks, and audit trails to enable independent verification without compromising IP (Levine et al., 2023).

Capacity Building: Invest in regulator and industry training to understand models, data practices, and risk indicators. Build technical literacy for meaningful oversight.

Redress and Remedies: Ensure accessible channels for individuals to seek redress when harms occur, including clear complaint processes and speedy remediation.

Data and Model Portability: Promote interoperability of governance tools (e.g., lineage tracking, audit logs) to ease audits and transitions between providers (Nasibov, 2021).

ETHICAL CONSIDERATIONS AND END-TO-END TRANSPARENCY IN GOVERNANCE

Ethical considerations in accountability, responsibility, and liability within AI and data ecosystems require embedding transparency throughout the entire lifecycle data collection, model development, deployment, and ongoing operation. End-to-end governance ensures that ethical commitments translate into verifiable actions, with clear delineation of duties and recourses in case of harm or failure (Syal et al., 2021).

Core Ethical Principles

Accountability: Establish explicit ownership of outcomes, with clear roles for data stewards, model developers, operations teams, and organizational leadership. Accountability must extend beyond "compliance" to tangible responsibility for harms and unintended consequences.

Responsibility: Define who is responsible for each lifecycle stage (data governance, model training, evaluation, monitoring, and decommissioning). Assign responsibility for fairness, safety, privacy, security, and human oversight (Krogh & Lo, 2023).

Liability: Clarify civil and regulatory liability, including joint and several liability where multiple parties contribute to risk. Create mechanisms for redress that align incentives to prevent harm rather than merely respond to it.

Transparency: Promote openness about data sources, model capabilities, limitations, decision logic where feasible, and the chain of responsibility. Public-facing explanations should be accurate, accessible, and not reveal sensitive or proprietary information (Kolmodin, 2024).

End-to-End Transparency and Governance Practices

Data Provenance and Quality: Maintain chain-of-custody records for data inputs, transformations, and labeling processes. Implement data quality metrics and bias assessment results that are auditable and shareable with stakeholders.

Model Documentation and Provenance: Use model cards, data sheets for datasets, and algorithmic impact assessments to articulate the intended use, performance across diverse groups, and potential risks. Versioning and change logs are essential to track updates that could affect behavior (Stupak et al., 2021).

Observable Decision-Making: Where possible, provide explanations or rationale for decisions, especially in high-stakes scenarios. For opaque models, offer surrogate explanations, local interpretability, and auditing capabilities without compromising security.

Human-in-the-Loop and Oversight: Design mechanisms for human review, override capabilities, and escalation procedures for critical decisions. Define triggers for human intervention and ensure operator training to understand system limits (Ibones et al., 2024).

Bias and Fairness Audits: Conduct ongoing audits for disparate impact, representation gaps, and outcome quality across demographic groups. Publicly report findings and remediation plans, with timelines.

Privacy and Security by Design: Integrate privacy-preserving techniques (de-identification, minimization, encryption) and robust security controls from the outset. Ensure data minimization aligns with governance objectives and stakeholder rights.

Incident Reporting and Remediation: Establish transparent, timely incident reporting frameworks. Provide root-cause analysis, corrective actions, and measurable improvements. Communate learnings to affected communities and regulators (Smidt et al., 2025).

Stakeholder Engagement: Involve affected communities, users, and workers in governance discussions. Use participatory approaches to address ethical concerns, especially for systems with potential societal impact.

Accountability Mechanisms: Create formal accountability pathways, including internal escalation routes, external audits, and independent oversight where appropriate. Align incentives to prioritize ethical outcomes rather than mere compliance (Damiyano, 2024).

Centering Transparency

Public Accountability Dashboards: Publish high-level metrics on system performance, fairness indicators, incident counts, and remediation progress. Ensure dashboards balance transparency with legitimate security and IP protections.

Documentation as a Living Artifact: Treat governance documents, risk assessments, and audit reports as living artifacts that evolve with the system. Ensure updates are timestamped and publicly or accessibly available where appropriate (Bolton et al., 2023).

Clear Responsibility Maps: Publish clear responsibility maps showing who is accountable for data, models, operations, and governance outcomes. This clarity helps stakeholders know where to seek recourse.

Economic and Social Justification: Explain the societal value of deployments, including benefits, harms avoided, and alignment with ethical norms. This helps build trust and legitimacy (Bravim et al., 2025).

CONCLUSION

In thc evolving terrain of AI and data ecosystems, accountability, responsibility, and liability are not mere legal abstractions; they are operational imperatives that shape trust, adoption, and societal outcomes. End-to-end governance defines clear ownership at every stage of the lifecycle. It assigns responsibility for data provenance, quality, consent, and usage restrictions; it clarifies the accountability for model design choices, risk assessment, bias mitigation, and performance monitoring; and it designates liability pathways for harms arising from AI systems, including cascading effects in interconnected data ecosystems. This clarity reduces ambiguity, enables timely decision-making, and fosters a culture of continuous improvement. It also supports a proportional approach to accountability and liability, recognizing that different stages carry varying levels of risk and control. For instance, data governance practices address privacy and consent, model governance handles robustness and fairness, and deployment governance manages real-world risk and user impact.

In terms of liability, a robust governance regime differentiates between fault lines where negligence, malfeasance, or misreporting occur and systemic risk that arises from the compound effects of interdependent systems. Liability models must account for shared responsibility among data providers, model developers, platform operators, and downstream users. This implies contracts and regulatory frameworks that specify duty of care, risk allocation, and remedies, including remediation costs, insurance mechanisms, and compensatory schemes. A proactive approach to liability emphasizes redressability: the capacity to detect, explain, and rectify harms quickly, rather than merely assigning blame after the fact.

Suggestions: Practical Steps to Strengthen Accountability, Responsibility, and Liability through End-to-End Transparency

A robust approach to accountability, responsibility, and liability in AI and data ecosystems begins with precise lifecycle ownership and systematic transparency, embedded directly into technical and organizational processes. First, map the entire data–model lifecycle end-to-end and assign explicit ownership at each stage from data collection, cleaning, consent management, and provenance to model development, evaluation, deployment, monitoring, and post-deployment impact assessment. Document decision rights, control points, and escalation paths in governance charters, contracts, and service-level agreements so that responsibilities are traceable and enforceable. This clarity must be complemented by unified transparency dashboards that illuminate data lineage, feature provenance, model versions, performance across subgroups, drift indicators, and decision rationales in a manner accessible to internal teams, auditors, and, where appropriate, the public, all while preserving privacy. Implementing modular governance controls allows different layers data governance for privacy and consent, model governance for fairness and interpretability, and deployment governance for risk management and rollback capabilities to operate in concert, with policy-as-code enabling automated compliance checks and rapid remediation when issues arise. To translate transparency into trust, organizations should adopt explainability and interpretability mechanisms that deliver user-facing explanations, system-level rationales, confidence scores, and mechanisms for appeal, tailored to diverse audiences including data subjects, operators, and regulators.

Proactive risk assessment and testing regimes must be ordinary course: formal pre-deployment risk assessments, ongoing red-teaming, stress testing, and scenario planning that anticipate real-world harms and inform preemptive mitigations. A rigorous remediation pipeline should be established, enabling timely redress for harms, with clear channels for reporting, remediation timelines, and post-incident reviews that feed back into governance updates and product design. Cultivating an ethics-informed culture and continuous training across disciplines data science, legal, policy, design, and user advocacy helps sustain accountability as teams evolve and as AI systems scale. Aligning governance with legal norms requires mapping to applicable data protection, consumer protection, and sector-specific frameworks, maintaining auditable decision trails, and preparing for regulator scrutiny. External scrutiny should be welcomed through independent audits, third-party assessments, and participation in standards development, with opportunities to publish anonymized datasets or model cards where possible to bolster public confidence while protecting sensitive information. Finally, governance must be adaptable and iterative, incorporating feedback loops that measure governance effectiveness, user trust, and actual social impact, with continuous policy refinement and investment in scalable, repeatable processes that mature as technology evolves.

Future Research Directions: Exploring New Frontiers in End-to-End Governance for AI and Data Ecosystems

Future research should advance provenance formalization and lineage reasoning across heterogeneous and evolving data landscapes, focusing on scalable capture, verification, and interpretation of data provenance and model lineage, plus the development of interoperable schemas and ontology standards that enable cross-platform trust. Investigations into multi-stakeholder accountability are needed to design governance models that balance rights and responsibilities among data subjects, providers, developers, platforms, and regulators, including incentive-compatible mechanisms and dispute-resolution frameworks that remain practical in fast-moving ecosystems. Liability research must address emergent harms indirect, long-tail, or systemic harms arising from complex, interconnected models by exploring joint and several liability constructs, insurance mechanisms, and probabilistic risk transfer tailored to AI contexts. Dynamic explainability in production environments poses another frontier: developing explanations that remain meaningful as models adapt through online learning and data drift, and that scale across diverse user expertise. Privacy-preserving transparency strategies such as synthetic data, differential privacy, and secure multiparty computation should be advanced to enable effective audits without compromising individual privacy. Auditing at scale demands automated, scalable assurance across distributed AI systems, including standardized audit trails, certification regimes, and alignment with evolving standards. Governance metrics and benchmarking require standardized measures to evaluate transparency, accountability, and trust, culminating in benchmark datasets and evaluation methodologies that enable meaningful cross-organizational comparisons. Responsible data collaboration, including data trusts and consent frameworks, warrants deeper study to balance openness with consent and rights preservation, while regulatory foresight research can help policymakers design adaptable, future-proof regimes that accommodate rapid AI progression. Human-centric governance invites exploration of mechanisms for meaningful human oversight and autonomy protection, ensuring governance intersects with human values and dignity. Interoperability and standardization efforts are crucial for cross-domain compatibility, with milestones in data schemas, model cards, risk templates, and reporting formats that facilitate governance across sectors. Environmental and social governance implications of AI systems should be integrated, measuring sustainability and social impact as governance criteria. Finally, education and tooling for governance must evolve to empower engineers, managers, and policymakers with practical tools, curricula, and enablement to implement end-to-end governance at scale, bridging theory and practice. Collectively, these research directions aim to operationalize transparent governance that scales with technology, harmonizes with law, and aligns with evolving social expectations.

REFERENCES

Annan, N., Beseng, M., Crawford, G., & Kewir, J. K. (2021). Civil society, peacebuilding from below and shrinking civic space: The case of Cameroon's 'Anglophone'conflict. *Conflict Security and Development, 21*(6), 697–725. DOI: 10.1080/14678802.2021.1997454

Ansell, C., Sørensen, E., Torfing, J., & Trondal, J. (2024). *Robust governance in turbulent times*. Cambridge University Press. DOI: 10.1017/9781009433006

Ansell, C., & Torfing, J. (2022). Introduction to the Handbook on Theories of Governance. In *Handbook on theories of governance* (pp. 1–16). Edward Elgar Publishing., DOI: 10.4337/9781800371972.00007

Arnaouti, M. K. C., Cahill, G., Baird, M. D., Mangurat, L., Harris, R., Edme, L. P. P., Joseph, M. N., Worlton, T., & Augustin, S.Jr. (2022). Medical disaster response: A critical analysis of the 2010 Haiti earthquake. *Frontiers in Public Health, 10*, 995595. DOI: 10.3389/fpubh.2022.995595 PMID: 36388301

Babacan, H. (2025). From crisis to policy action: Tackling climate change through SDG 13. *The International Journal of Community and Social Development, 25166026251351370*(2), 205–221. Advance online publication. DOI: 10.1177/25166026251351370

Bolleyer, N. (2021). Civil society, crisis exposure, and resistance strategies. In *Routledge handbook of illiberalism* (pp. 939–956). Routledge. DOI: 10.4324/9780367260569-68

Bolton, D., Landells, T., & Habib, M. (2023). Collaborating and Competing in Development Agendas: State—Civil Society Tensions in Achieving SDGs. In *The complexities of sustainability* (pp. 77-120).

Bravim, J. M., de Carvalho, A. C. V., Segatto, A. P., & Morais-da-Silva, R. L. (2025). Are there key characteristics of social enterprises that foster relationships with government, universities and civil society? *Social Enterprise Journal, 21*(5), 864–889. Advance online publication. DOI: 10.1108/SEJ-08-2024-0136

Broadhurst, K., & Gray, N. (2022). Understanding resilient places: Multi-level governance in times of crisis. *Local Economy, 37*(1-2), 84–103. DOI: 10.1177/02690942221100101

Bua, A., & Bussu, S. (Eds.). (2023). *Reclaiming participatory governance: Social movements and the reinvention of democratic innovation*. Taylor & Francis. DOI: 10.4324/9781003218517

Chaudhry, S. (2022). The assault on civil society: Explaining state crackdown on NGOs. *International Organization, 76*(3), 549–590. DOI: 10.1017/S0020818321000473

Chen, X. (2023). Understanding the role of Civil Society Organizations (CSOs) in the "central government-local government-society" framework: A case study on public crisis management during the pandemic in China. *International Public Management Journal, 26*(4), 570–588. DOI: 10.1080/10967494.2022.2115595

Cook, A. D. (2021). Humanitarian diplomacy in ASEAN. *Asian Journal of Comparative Politics, 6*(3), 188–201. DOI: 10.1177/20578911211019247

Damiyano, D. (2024). Sustainable Social Services Financing for Local Governments. In *Financial Sustainability of Local Governments in Southern Africa* (pp. 198–214). Routledge. DOI: 10.4324/9781003498230-11

Garcia, S., Carrigan, C., & Wiepking, P. (2023). Global civil society response to the COVID-19 crisis. *Voluntas, 34*(6), 1310–1321. DOI: 10.1007/s11266-023-00589-5

Hinterleitner, M., Knill, C., & Steinebach, Y. (2024). The growth of policies, rules, and regulations: A review of the literature and research agenda. *Regulation & Governance, 18*(2), 637–654. DOI: 10.1111/rego.12511

Ibones, K. A., Enero, J. V., Jore, J. S., Mamhot, V. I., Matheu, C. M., Pacaldo, H. B. B., & Jardin, R. A. (2024). Enabling role of civil society organizations (CSOs) in local environmental management in the Philippines: A systematic review. *Journal of Civil Society, 20*(4), 359–379. DOI: 10.1080/17448689.2024.2381826

Kolmodin, S. (2024). Collaboration to support refugees: The importance of local-level relations among civil society organizations. *Journal of Civil Society, 20*(2), 130–149. DOI: 10.1080/17448689.2024.2319357

Krogh, A. H., & Lo, C. (2023). Robust emergency management: The role of institutional trust in organized volunteers. *Public Administration, 101*(1), 142–157. DOI: 10.1111/padm.12894

Kumi, E., & Hayman, R. (2025). Can domestic resource mobilisation by civil society organisations (CSOs) open up civic space in the Global South? *Development in Practice, 35*(4), 669–687. DOI: 10.1080/09614524.2025.2487791

Levine, A. C., Park, A., Adhikari, A., Alejandria, M. C. P., Bradlow, B. H., Lopez-Portillo, M. F., Mutwafy, S., Zumbyte, I., & Heller, P. (2023). The role of civil society organizations (CSOs) in the COVID-19 response across the Global South: A multinational, qualitative study. *PLOS Global Public Health, 3*(9), e0002341. DOI: 10.1371/journal.pgph.0002341 PMID: 37708149

McKeague, L. K., & Bies, A. L. (2025). Nonprofits and Interest Groups in Crisis Management. In *Oxford Research Encyclopedia of Politics*. DOI: 10.1093/acrefore/9780190228637.013.1530

Mir, G., Durrani, N., Julian, R., Kimei, Y., Mashreky, S., & Doan, T. D. (2024). Social inclusion and sustainable development: Findings from Seven African and Asian contexts. *Sustainability (Basel)*, *16*(11), 4859. DOI: 10.3390/su16114859

Mizrak, K. C. (2024). Crisis management and risk mitigation: Strategies for effective response and resilience. *Trends, challenges, and practices in contemporary strategic management*, 254-278. DOI: DOI: 10.4018/979-8-3693-1155-4.ch013

Moya, J., & Goenechea, M. (2022). An approach to the unified conceptualization, definition, and characterization of social resilience. *International Journal of Environmental Research and Public Health*, *19*(9), 5746. DOI: 10.3390/ijerph19095746 PMID: 35565141

Nair, J. (2024). Reconfiguration and transformation for resilience: Building service organizations towards sustainability. *Journal of Services Marketing*, *38*(4), 404–425. DOI: 10.1108/JSM-04-2023-0144

Nasibov, M. (2021). Civil Society and Pro-Democracy Social Movements: Troubled Relations Within Authoritarian Regimes? *Frontiers in Political Science*, *3*, 708872. DOI: 10.3389/fpos.2021.708872

Njoku, E. T. (2022). Strategic exclusion, co-option and containment: Towards an integrative theory of state-CSOs relations. *Critical Studies on Terrorism*, *15*(4), 917–944. DOI: 10.1080/17539153.2022.2111776

Pitidis, V., Coaffee, J., & Lima-Silva, F. (2024). Advancing equitable 'resilience imaginaries' in the Global South through dialogical participatory mapping: Experiences from informal communities in Brazil. *Cities (London, England)*, *150*, 105015. DOI: 10.1016/j.cities.2024.105015

Riboldi, M. (2024). The Loci of Power and Connection: A framework for exploring the democratic relationships of civil society organisations. *Interest Groups & Advocacy*, *13*(2), 244–263. DOI: 10.1057/s41309-024-00209-7

Salvador, M., & Sancho, D. (2023). Local governments facing turbulence: Robust governance and institutional capacities. *Social Sciences (Basel, Switzerland)*, *12*(8), 462. DOI: 10.3390/socsci12080462

Samaratunge, R., & Alam, Q. (2021). Accountability and transparency in emerging countries: Governance, democratic currents and change. *Public Administration and Development*, *41*(4), 147–156. DOI: 10.1002/pad.1963

Smidt, H., Johansson, J., & Richter, T. (2025). Civil society under attack: The consequences for horizontal accountability institutions. *Studies in Comparative International Development*, *60*(1), 81–110. DOI: 10.1007/s12116-023-09423-x

Stupak, I., Mansoor, M., & Smith, C. T. (2021). Conceptual framework for increasing legitimacy and trust of sustainability governance. *Energy, Sustainability and Society*, *11*(1), 5. DOI: 10.1186/s13705-021-00280-x PMID: 33758740

Syal, R., van Wessel, M., & Sahoo, S. (2021). Collaboration, co-optation or navigation? The role of civil society in disaster governance in India. *Voluntas*, *32*(4), 795–808. DOI: 10.1007/s11266-021-00344-8

Van Wessel, M., Naz, F., & Sahoo, S. (2021). Complementarities in CSO Collaborations: How working with diversity produces advantages. *Voluntas*, *32*(4), 717–730. DOI: 10.1007/s11266-020-00227-4

Willems, J. (2021). Accountability and transparency: cornerstones of civil society governance. In *Research handbook on nonprofit governance* (pp. 46–70). Edward Elgar Publishing., DOI: 10.4337/9781788114912.00012

Williamson, A. K., Kingston, K. L., & Bennison, L. (2022). Similar or different? Downward accountability across civil society organisational forms. *Voluntas*, *33*(5), 1002–1014. DOI: 10.1007/s11266-021-00441-8

Wojczewski, S., Grohma, P., & Kutalek, R. (2023). Risk communication and community engagement with vulnerable groups: Perceptions of social-services CSOs during Covid-19. *International Journal of Disaster Risk Reduction*, *94*, 103817. DOI: 10.1016/j.ijdrr.2023.103817 PMID: 37360248

Chapter 2
AI for Compliance and Data Privacy

Aryan Vasa
Ajeenkya D.Y. Patil University, India

Sunil Sankathala
http://orcid.org/0009-0004-7809-7647
Ajeenkya D.Y. Patil University, India

Krutika Patre
http://orcid.org/0009-0001-7969-4409
Ajeenkya D.Y. Patil University, India

Kritikka Kunte
Ajeenkya D.Y. Patil University, India

Devanshi Soni
Ajeenkya D.Y. Patil University, India

Susanta Das
http://orcid.org/0000-0002-9314-3988
Ajeenkya D.Y. Patil University, India

ABSTRACT

Rapid integration of AI across various sectors has created a complex challenge at the nexus of data privacy & regulatory compliance. This chapter will provide a comprehensive analysis of how AI can be both a threat & a solution to modern data protection challenges. It will first examine fragmented global regulatory landscape, focusing on key frameworks like the GDPR, CCPA, & PIPL, and complexities they introduce for organizations. We will delve into the challenges of ensuring compliance, including issues of algorithmic transparency, data security, & mitigation of inherent biases within AI systems. Subsequently, it will explore role of AI in enhancing compliance, detailing its application in automated data audits, real-time breach detection, & managing user consent. It will also discuss critical function of AI in Data Loss Prevention (DLP) and use of ML for anomaly detection in security systems. It aims to provide a definitive guide for organizations and policymakers seeking to leverage AI's potential while upholding the highest standards of data protection and individual privacy.

DOI: 10.4018/979-8-3373-6761-3.ch002

1. INTRODUCTION

Nowadays, in the era of digitalization, Artificial Intelligence (AI) is a powerful force that is transforming the way businesses and organizations manage or control their cybersecurity, compliance, and data privacy. Organizations are progressing towards AI-centric culture and upgrading their work-potential with the assistance of AI and Machine Learning (ML) algorithms-based models, often to automate their processes, improve decision-making, and protect extensive digital ecosystems. Deep Learning (DL) architectures, ML, predictive analytics, and automation systems used as AI to detect and respond to threats have improved detection capability protection by enabling enterprises to discover vulnerabilities and reduce risk streams quicker than conventional methods. AI also facilitates proactive methods of defense, which develop in tandem with the dynamically evolving characteristics of cyber-attacks, since it can be both adaptively intrusion-detected and real-time anomaly-monitored (Maddali, 2024; Talati, 2022). Nevertheless, as much as such advances are of tremendous benefits, new regulatory and ethical complexities are presented. The AI systems often handle vast amounts of sensitive and personal data, and it is a fine line between innovation, security, and privacy that organizations have to walk (Arora, 2015).

Since companies have been immersing themselves in AI integration as a part of their cybersecurity infrastructure, the boundaries between technology, governance, and compliance have been becoming more and more interconnected. Unless such AI algorithms are governed, the same AIs that improve operational efficiency can accidentally put organizations at risk of data privacy or non-compliance. It has increased the awareness that AI should be designed, implemented, and operated in a responsible manner to guarantee compliance with moral principles and legal regulations without compromising technological advances. To achieve success, organizations should make sure that the AI systems are built with good governance measures and are compliant with international privacy laws like General Data Protection Regulation (GDPR) and California Consumer Privacy Act (CCPA), encompassing ethical protection and risk-reduction strategies across the lifecycle of the AI (Ijaiya, 2024; Kakarala & Rongali, 2025; Talati, 2022).

The spread of AI has enhanced the regulation of online businesses. New rules that govern the collection, processing, and storage of personal data by organizations have been made highly restrictive by regulations like the General Data Protection Regulation (GDPR) in Europe, the California Consumer Privacy Act (CCPA) in the United States, and the Health Insurance Portability and Accountability Act (HIPAA) (Gajbhiye et al., 2024; Mbah, 2024). These frameworks focus on the principles of transparency, accountability, consent, and the right to the protection of their data, as well as they have control over their personal information. Nevertheless, AI-enabled systems can be complex deep-learning models, which will generate output based on unstructured, opaque decision-making processes that are impossible to interpret or explain. This non-transparency jeopardizes the principles of regulation like accountability, minimization of data, and the right to recognition, which may necessitate legal adaptability that can respond to the risk of automated decision-making (Arora, 2015; Lukács & Váradi, 2023).

Furthermore, the use of AI by organizations is met with a disjointed regulatory environment as organizations implement AI solutions all over the world. Although GDPR is considered a good privacy standard in the EU, healthcare data is regulated by HIPAA, and consumer data by CCPA in the United States, and localization and data sovereignty requirements are strictly followed in the Personal Information Protection Law (PIPL) in China. This clutter of laws presents business complications to global companies that handle international data migrations (Mbah, 2024). Indicatively, an AI system that handles both EU and U.S. data will be required to simultaneously adhere to the GDPR data minimization requirements and the HIPAA privacy regulations of the relevant patients. Consequently, the concept of compliance has become more of a strategic priority than a mere legal requirement, and this strategic compliance demands smart automation and responsive governance to tackle the various regulatory landscapes. AI integration into the organizational processes brings forth serious compliance issues of the General Data Protection Regulation (GDPR) especially given the scope of the big data processing and inference of the AI systems (Dewitte, 2025; Gajbhiye et al., 2024; Maddali, 2024).

The introduction of AI-compliance technologies has changed the manner in which organizations comply with these regulatory requirements. The conventional models of compliance that use manual reviews and fixed questionnaires are no longer adequate to handle the dynamism and the data-intensive aspects of AI-driven activities. In response, the businesses are turning to AI compliance tools- systems that use machine learning, natural language processing and predictive analytics to identify and enforce compliance and record compliance in real time (Gajbhiye et al., 2024). These tools are able to identify anomalies automatically, identify non-compliant activities, revise policies based on new regulations, and create reports that are readable during audits. Continuous monitoring of internal policy by using AI-driven Governance, Risk, and Compliance (GRC) applications is now a possibility, because such tools can compare inner policies with the changing legal requirements to make sure that data handling operations are in line with regulations like GDPR and PCI DSS. As an example, AI compliance systems are used in financial institutions to identify suspicious transactions when using anti-money laundering (AML) regulations, and in healthcare to ensure that access to patient data is in accordance with HIPAA regulations (Maddali, 2024). The automation is efficient and minimizes the possibility of a human factor error, which reduces the cost of compliance and increases transparency. However, the use of AI in compliance management poses new problems. Design Automated systems should be developed in a responsible manner to avoid the possibility of algorithmic bias, interpretability, and overreliance on machine decisions. It is thus recommended that organizations implement compliance by design - entailing the incorporation of principles of compliance and human controls into AI processes. A successful AI adherence involves ethical leadership, ongoing regulation, and the implementation of explainable AI to hold themselves responsible and reduce bias, as well as ensure customer confidence (Arora, 2015; Ijaiya, 2024; Mirishli, 2024).

The Data Loss Prevention (DLP)-protecting the sensitive information against unauthorized access, leak, or misuse is one of the most common and applicable fields of AI use in cybersecurity. As an AI-based DLP system, predictive analytics, pattern recognition, and behavioral analysis are used to track data flow across the networks and identify possible threats before it could develop into breaches. In contrast to the classical systems of DLP, which are usually static and do not learn new data interactions, AI-based tools learn new insights to change their detection models to detect new risks (Talati, 2022; Gajbhiye et al., 2024). As an illustration, AI systems will be able to detect abnormal file transfers, insider threats, and predict malicious exfiltration attempts with improved detection performance. These systems are also useful during the process of automatic enforcement of compliance rules, e.g. whether confidential information is encrypted in transmission, or whether access control is applied in accordance with regulatory guidelines. According to industry reports, AI-powered surveillance and DLP systems can decrease the risk of breach of data, but available empirical data is still scarce and differs in terms of organizational environments. Moreover, combining Privacy-Enhancing Technologies (PET) that includes federated learning and homomorphic encryption with AI-based DLP makes security more secure and privacy intact. These technologies enable keep sensitive data encrypted or stored locally and at the same time do analytics with AI systems. Consequently, companies can comply with the requirements and at the same time retain the operational flexibility needed in the contemporary cybersecurity (Talati, 2022; Mbah, 2024).

In addition to technical protection, privacy and ethics in AI-driven systems have turned out to be a fundamental element of organizational governance. AI models, in particular, generative and predictive, require massive, sensitive data sets, which predetermines the importance of privacy protection and ethical design at the initial phases of development (Arora, 2015). Privacy-by-design focuses on deploying data protection channels, including anonymization, encryption, privacy-enhancing technologies in the AI life cycle in order to reduce risks without compromising the usefulness of the data (Awwal-Bolanta & Anakanire, 2024; Sresth et al., 2021). Recent privacy-saving methods such as differential privacy, federated learning, and secure multiparty computation can help organizations to collectively prepare AI models without revealing raw data. As an example, federated learning can help hospitals to build diagnostic models based on distributed data without breaching HIPAA rules, and financial institutions can use differential privacy to anonymize customer data to meet the GDPR requirement (Mbah, 2024). On the same note, secure multiparty computation enables two or more parties to run joint analysis without disclosing their respective data inputs hence confidentiality and legal compliance. Ethical AI governance models focus on fairness, accountability, transparency, and explainability-concepts that will ensure the sustainability of the trust of the population in AI technologies. As Arora (2015) points out, responsible AI systems should not only conform to the requirements of the law but prioritize the values of the society, avoiding bias, discrimination and misuse of data. In this regard, companies should develop cooperation between cybersecurity experts, data scientists, legal professionals, and ethicists and create a set of governance models that would enable alignment between innovation and privacy and regulatory compliance (Talati, 2022).

In the current research, bibliometric analysis is used to survey the research trends in the area of the integration of AI to ensure compliance and privacy. The data that is required in the analysis is found in Lens.org database. The graphical maps of the keywords and research topics are drawn up with the assistance of VOSviewer software, but the development of publications, the input of the countries, and the most active publishers are condensed in the form of graphs and tables. All these approaches provide a great summary of the ways which the research in this sphere transformed and evolved.

This chapter is a conceptual and narrative review that summarizes the existing literature to discuss the role of Artificial Intelligence in regulatory compliance and data privacy. The identification of relevant academic literature to support the methodological transparency was achieved by a systematic search of major scholarly databases (such as Lens.org and PubMed) with the add-ons of a specific search in Google Scholar. The search was limited to 2018 -2025 to include recent trends in AI-compliance, privacy engineering, and regulatory technology. Such keywords and search combinations comprised "AI compliance," RegTech, AI governance, data privacy, data protection, GDPR, HIPAA, and privacy-preserving machine learning.

Peer-reviewed journal articles, conference papers, technical frameworks and legal or regulatory analysis were prioritized as the selection criteria based on substantive methodological or conceptual illumination of AI-enabled compliance systems. To sustain academia rigor, vendor marketing information, blogs, promotional literature and non-traceable sources of information in the industry were omitted. After the screening of relevancy and quality of publications using title, abstract, and full-text, approximately 80 to 120 were then used in the thematic synthesis. The chosen articles were helpful in informing the discussion of regulatory frameworks, AI methods, implementation issues, case examples, and new research directions that are discussed throughout the chapter. Based on the selected literature, the chapter examines about regulatory requirements and AI compliance tools, introducing readers to regulations, frameworks, and data privacy laws as well as giving an overview of challenges in manual compliance, giving a basic idea about the significance of AI for compliance and data privacy, roles of AI and different AI compliance tools and platforms. The chapter will also give overview of case studies and illustrative examples with techniques of maintaining privacy in AI-powered security systems, as well as outlining the impact of AI on compliance and data privacy. Moreover, the legal and ethical considerations along with future research directions based on given frameworks, regulations and techniques have been elaborated. Figure 1 depicts the general flow of the chapter.

Figure 1. Flowchart of the chapter, displaying the general flow.

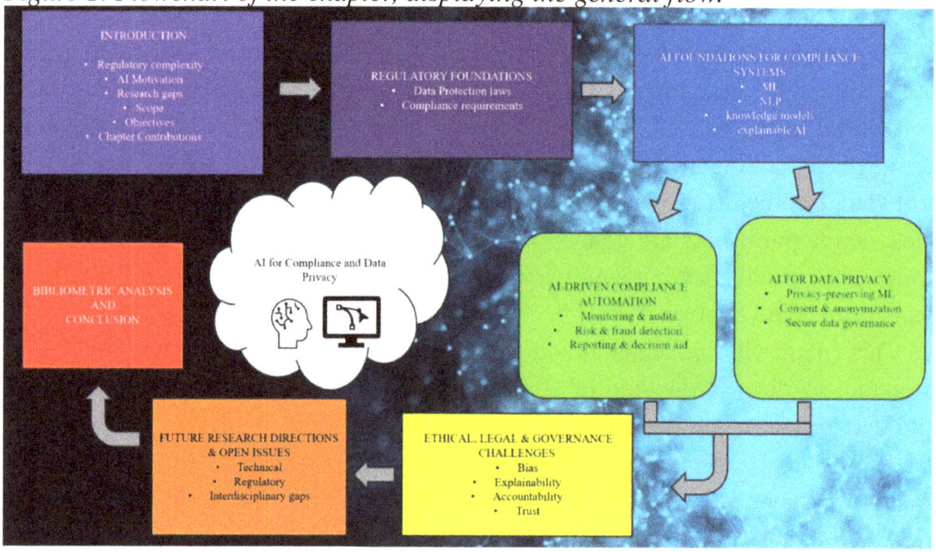

2. REGULATORY REQUIREMENTS AND AI COMPLIANCE TOOLS

The speed of deployment of Artificial Intelligence (AI) and Machine Learning (ML) in all industries, including the financial and health care industries, as well as government services, has provided a multifaceted overlap between innovation and regulatory need. With the adoption of cloud computing environments by organizations to process their data, the problem of adhering to the requirements of global data protection laws has become a significant area of operation (Samant, 2024). This has not only shown the weaknesses of the conventional manual compliance activities but also led to the development of advanced AI-powered applications to oversee and guarantee regulatory compliance in digital ecosystems (Reis et al., 2023).

2.1. Overview of Global Data Privacy Regulations

2.1.1. Foundational Data Privacy Law

In the European Union (EU), the General Data Protection Regulation (GDPR) is widely regarded as one of the most comprehensive data protection frameworks, establishing obligations related to lawful processing, transparency, accountability, and data subject rights, which ensures far-reaching rights to data subjects and imposes some penalties on non-observation, the fine is up to EUR20 million or 4% of the global annual turnover (Samant, 2024). The requirements under the GDPR are strict regarding the legal grounds of processing, the access requests made by the subjects of a data, and the principle of Privacy by Design, which presupposes that organizations should include the protection measures into the initial stages (Sangaraju, 2025). The laws that promote compliance in the United States are sector and state-specific. Formed in the healthcare industry, the Health Insurance Portability and Accountability Act (HIPAA) requires high security requirements and privacy regulations to protect the privacy of the Protected Health Information (PHI) (Sangaraju, 2025). In the meantime, California Consumer Privacy Act (CCPA) with amendments by the California Privacy Rights Act (CPRA) gives its residents strong rights to access their personal information, such as the right to know, the right to delete, or the right to opt-out of selling and sharing their data, which sets an example in other states of the USA (Samant, 2024; Chintoh et al., 2025).

2.1.2. Having Frameworks and Standards

In addition to the required legislation, compliance assurance is frequently based on the internationally accepted standards according to which best practices in information security are set. An international standard, ISO 27001, defines the principles of how to create, install, manage, and improve an Information Security Management System (ISMS), necessitating the systematic method of addressing the security threats of an organisation. The industrial guidance suggests that the System and Organization Controls 2 (SOC 2) framework is a highly popular tool in North America, and the organizations are obligated to engage in controls to cover the five Trust Services Criteria (TSC) that include Security, Availability, Processing

Integrity, Confidentiality, and Privacy. On the same note, other cybersecurity and privacy models provided by the National Institute of Standards and Technology (NIST), e.g., the Cybersecurity Framework (CSF), focus on a risk-management model with five fundamental functions: Identify, Protect, Detect, Respond, and Recover (NIST, n.d.; Security Scientist, 2024). Adoption of such standards is typically driven by contractual, industry, or risk management requirements rather than statutory enforcement.

2.1.3. New AI-Specific Regulation

Another level of regulation is being developed that will control the technology itself. The EU AI Act is the first global legal framework of AI, and it takes a risk-based approach, classifying systems as either unacceptable, high, limited, and minimal risks (KPMG, 2024). The European Union Artificial intelligence act provides a regulatory model on AI systems that is risk-based. According to the Act, four classifications of applications are distinguished, including unacceptable risk (prohibited systems, including social scoring, AI in healthcare, employment, or critical infrastructure), high-risk systems, limited risk, and minimal risk. High-risk AI systems are prone to certain requirements such as risk management processes, data control systems, technical documentation, transparency, human supervision, and post-deployment controls. These provisions have great consequences to organizations using AI in compliance and surveillance or decision-support scenarios. The systems that are considered unacceptably risky, including universal social scoring, are prohibited, whereas high-risk systems in the employment and healthcare sector must be highly governed in terms of data, transparency, and human responsibility (European Parliament, 2025; IBM, n.d.). Alongside these legislative activities, the OECD AI Principles have become the first inter-governmental standard allowing innovative, trustful, and human rights-respecting AI. The OECD AI Principles provide non-binding international guidance promoting transparency, accountability, robustness, and human oversight in AI systems (OECD, n.d.). These values focus on human management and control, openness, understandability, resilience, and responsibility in the overall AI system lifecycle (OECD, n.d.). These privacy regulations, security standards, and AI-specific laws combine to form a very dynamic and complicated compliance environment that AI systems must be developed to find their way through (Chintoh et al., 2025).

One should also differentiate between legal and non-legal regulations and voluntary standards in the environment of compliance guidelines. Legal requirements that are enforced through statutory requirements like the GDPR, HIPAA, and CCPA are legally binding and enforceable by regulators. Standards and frameworks like ISO/IEC 27001, SOC 2 and the NIST Cybersecurity Framework, in contrast, are best-practice guidance and are often adopted on a voluntary basis or mandated by a contract or industry expectation as opposed to legislatively.

The distinct categorization of statutes, regulations and standards are depicted in Table 1.

Table 1. Distinction between statutory regulations and voluntary standards in AI and data privacy compliance

Category	Examples	Legal Status
Statutes	GDPR, HIPAA, CCPA	Legally binding
Regulations	EU AI Act	Binding (when enforced)
Standards	ISO 27001, NIST CSF, SOC 2	Voluntary / contractual

2.2. Challenges in Manual Compliance:

2.2.1. Difficulty and Changeability of Regulatory Amendments

Organizations are under operation in many jurisdictions and with varying and changing legal requirements. The time and cost incurred to manually trace, process, and project these diverse and hefty regulatory documents to the internal operations policies is resource-intensive (Samant, 2024). Moreover, compliance teams are supposed to observe not only existing laws, such as GDPR and HIPAA, but also to keep up with the appearance of new ones, as the EU AI Act and new state privacy laws, which makes the issue of policy interpretation in real-time nearly impossible as a manual job (Chintoh et al., 2025).

2.2.2. Expensive and Intensive Characteristics of Compliance Audits

Conventional and manual compliance procedures in their nature are resource intensive and expensive. Audits and risk assessments are processes that are dependent on human operators who can slow down major processes and provide inefficiencies (Lore et al., 2023). Such operations require full-time workers like compliance officers or legal representatives who, review large volumes of regulatory and operational documents, procedures, and technologies, take away much financial and human resources (Reis et al., 2023). This method is usually reactive, being concerned with demonstrating the compliance after the fact, instead of being proactive and actively emphasizing it (Lore et al., 2023).

2.2.3. Human Errors and Data Silos

Human error is prone in manual processes, and it may also vary in terms of misunderstanding a regulatory provision to misclassification of sensitive information (OneTrust, n.d.). Besides, during large digital ecosystems, data is usually created and stored in large volumes and volume with high speed, outpacing conventional compliance strategies that tend to be mostly disjointed and compliance-focused as opposed to privacy-first (Reis et al., 2023). Such fragmentation creates data silos, where the sensitive data is not regulated or secured consistently, so it is highly challenging to perform an overall data discovery and prevent risk monitoring in a continuous manner, and this circumstance elevates the chances of breaches and non-compliance fines (Samant, 2024).

2.3. Role of AI in Compliance Management

AI is quickly turning compliance into a not only expensive but also reactive and not a proactive and automated and ongoing business service. AI technologies exploit advanced algorithms to address the shortcomings of manual procedures, providing improved speed, accuracy and predictability in regulatory risk management.

2.3.1. Artificial Intelligence to Interpret and Map Policies

Natural Language Processing (NLP) in the analysis and interpretation of regulatory texts is one of the most useful AI compliance applications. NLP algorithms may digest large masses of legislature and statutes, buy out particular compliance needs, and automatically overlay these demands against internal policies, controls, and data processing operations of an organization (Samant, 2024). As an example, the INTREPID framework is an AI-based system that was created to process linguistic resources and machine learning to verify non-compliant documents related to the GDPR in the Italian Public Administration, a task that was previously performed manually at high costs (Lore et al., 2023). This automation significantly reduces processing time, the initial configuration and continuous adjustment of compliance programs to changes in the law (OneTrust, n.d.). Practically, AI-based compliance is implemented as a multi-step processing pipeline, which combines the regulatory interpretation, mapping the controls, and human control. The process of an average AI compliance involves the following steps:

i. **Regulatory text ingestion:** Legal and regulatory documents are collected and processed using Natural Language Processing (NLP) techniques.

ii. **Requirement extraction:** Named Entity Recognition (NER) and classification models identify obligations, controls, and compliance conditions.
iii. **Control mapping:** Extracted requirements are mapped to internal policies, data assets, and control frameworks using predefined compliance ontologies.
iv. **Risk scoring:** Machine learning models assess the likelihood and impact of potential non-compliance based on system logs, data flows, and user activity.
v. **Human validation loop:** Compliance officers review high-risk alerts, resolve ambiguities, and approve or override automated decisions.
vi. **Audit log generation:** All actions, model outputs, and human interventions are recorded to support regulatory audits and accountability.

Despite increasing automation, AI-based compliance systems are subject to false positives and false negatives. Organizations typically implement risk thresholds that determine when alerts require human review, ensuring that critical compliance decisions remain subject to expert oversight.

2.3.2. A Machine Learning-Risk Scoring / Compliance Monitoring

Continuous compliance monitoring requires AI and, specifically, Machine Learning (ML) in order to be automated. ML models have an opportunity to map data in real time automatically labelling it by sensitivity (e.g., PHI, PII) and jurisdiction, which becomes essential to address the global regulations on data protection (Samant, 2024). Besides, ML is applied to score risks, assigning a probability or a degree of severity to different compliance vulnerabilities, including identifying suspicious or non-compliant access profiles and controlling user consent on digital services (Samant, 2024; Reis et al., 2023). AI models are incredibly efficient in identifying anomalies, indicating possible non-compliance cases or security breaches according to the abnormalities of a normal organizational activity (Samant, 2024).

2.3.3. Non-Compliance Detection Predictive Models

Predictive models hold a pivotal change in reactionary auditing to prevention of risks. These models process historical compliance data, audit outcomes, and system activities to predict non-compliance areas in the future or the areas of possible vulnerable before an incident takes place (Chintoh et al., 2025). This predictive compliance capability enables organizations to deploy remedial controls and distribute resources strategically, which helps to support an algorithmic accountability and CIA risk prevention on a real-time basis as part of complex AI-driven processes (Chintoh et al., 2025). In a strictly regulated sector, such as healthcare, AI is also used to enforce compliance by privacy-preserving AI (PPAI), federated learning, and encryption where models can be instructed with sensitive data and (v) does not necessarily expose the underlying personal data, so compliance without any violation of the laws such as HIPAA for GDPR can be achieved (Sangaraju, 2025).

2.4. AI Compliance Tools and Platforms

2.4.1. OpenPages: IBM Watson Compliance

IBM OpenPages including Watson combines the GRC features with AI towards offering advanced compliance monitoring. The platform uses the natural language processing of Watson to deliver regulatory insights, automated audit works, and enforce risk and control management (IBM, n.d.). It assists companies in overseeing regulatory risks and ascertains transparency in AI decision-making through the utilization of advanced analytics and enterprise-level scalability to handle compliance in the large corporations (DevOps School, 2025).

2.4.2. Microsoft Purview and Compliance Manager

Commercial platforms such as Microsoft Purview provide automated classification and policy enforcement capabilities; however, independent empirical evaluations of their effectiveness and false-positive rates are limited in the academic literature, which offers Data Security Posture Management (DSPM) dedicated to AI (Microsoft, 2025). It utilizes the available security measures such as data classification and labelling and Data Loss Prevention (DLP) to oversee and enforce interactions with AI applications including proprietary systems such as Microsoft Copilot (Microsoft, n.d.). The Insider Risk Management of Purview has the ability to distinguish and alleviate internal risks like data leakage or IP theft through the use of the ML models thus ensuring that the use of AI does not violate the security and ethical policies of the organization (Microsoft, 2025).

2.4.3. OneTrust

OneTrust is a well-known privacy and compliance automation support. The AI Governance module assists companies in integrating compliance throughout the AI lifecycle. The newest inventions are an AI model inventory and risk mapping, an automated Data Subject Access Request (DSAR) processing, and consent and preference management orchestration across jurisdictions (DevOps School, 2025). OneTrust employs regulatory intelligence of a network of researchers all over the world to deliver current compliance guidance and save a substantial amount of manual work spent on research and documentation (OneTrust, n.d.).

2.4.4. BigID

BigID is a data-specific platform paying significant attention to the automated data recognition and categorization, which underlies AI conformity. The platform is an AI-based tool, which pinpoints and identifies the location of sensitive and regulated data within an enterprise, including AI/ML training data (BigID, n.d.). BigID enables the organization to enhance data hygiene and detect potential risks linked to accessing data by AI models, as well as implement strategies of data minimization to enhance compliance with concepts such as the principle of purpose limitation, directly with the assistance of concepts like purpose limitation (DevOps School, 2025).

2.4.5. TrustArc

Another site is TrustArc, which provides AI-based compliance platforms that are aimed at assisting businesses in proving their responsibility. It also includes the features of AI Impact Assessment, which is required by the new regulations, and data inventory, mapping data flows, and consent lifecycle management (DevOps School, 2025). It is mainly valuable as it creates audit-ready reports and allows customizable compliance workflow, which facilitates the compliance with numerous regulatory bodies throughout the world (DevOps School, 2025).

3. ILLUSTRATIVE USE CASES FROM REPORTED IMPLEMENTATIONS

All the examples used in this section have been synthesized using published literature and documented organizational implementation. They are supposed to demonstrate typical application patterns of AI in compliance and data privacy and not to be controlled experimental evaluations. Operational use cases have been described in most of the existing sources, and no standardised performance measurement or independent comparative studies are available.

3.1. AI-Driven Compliance in the Financial Sector

Artificial intelligence has become a key element in the financial sector, with institutions required to adhere to stringent rules and regulations, including the SOX, GLBA, and AML standards, to automate compliance and integrity of data. A large financial institution across the world introduced an artificial intelligence-based compliance auditing program, which employed machine learning in its cross-checking of millions of transactions to internal and international regulations. The system was developed to substitute manual auditing and reducing the amount of human error, also enhanced the identification of anomalies, unauthorized transactions and the possibility of compliance violations. The AI tool was constantly learning and creating real-time audit reports, as well as identifying high-risk activities to be investigated (Onoja et al., 2021).

NLP also helped to augment this structure by interpreting policy documentations, communications with customers, and regulatory filings to identify discrepancies and risky provisions. NLP tools enabled compliance officers to pick high priority issues by automating the interpretation of the complex compliance requirements which enhanced efficiency and accuracy. Users of these AI systems in institutions claimed that they were finding more irregularities, paying less to comply, and improving privacy- protection- because artificial intelligence made people less inclined to needless access to sensitive data. All in all, this example shows that AI-based compliance solutions can help to enhance regulatory compliance and protect financial data privacy at the same time (Onoja et al., 2021).

3.2. Cloud-Based Compliance and Data Privacy in Business Operations

The inclusion of AI in cloud-based Knowledge Management Systems (KMS) has undergone changes in the way organizations are able to guarantee compliance and safeguard sensitive data. A multinational enterprise implementation described in prior studies introduced an AI-powered hybrid cloud KMS to store information base of the enterprise in a way that is compliant with GDPR and CCPA. The system sorted the documents automatically based on the sensitivity, encrypted documents, and generated audit reports to ensure lawful data manipulations in accepted jurisdictions (Moyo et al., 2023).

The AI was able to track user behaviour in real-time using machine learning and identify anomalies (unauthorized access or unusual data transfers) and send notifications to security teams. Additional control was also achieved through Natural Language Processing (NLP) that considered documents containing personal identifiers or confidential information and blocked uploading to the cloud, which enhanced proactive data security. Also, adaptive encryption, which is powered by AI, dynamically scaled the protection level based on the sensitivity of data, with consideration of both security and efficiency. Such innovations allowed to improve the preparedness of audits, reduce the number of errors in human oversight, and improve the principles of data governance on a global scale-an example of how AI-based cloud compliance systems contribute to improve operational efficiency and privacy protection (Moyo et al., 2023).

3.3. Real-Time Monitoring With NLP-Based Tools

The implementation of Natural Language Processing (NLP) technologies has transformed the compliance management process as it allows conducting constant and real-time monitoring rather than regular audits. One multinational business service company installed an AI-driven NLP system to scan internal communications, including emails, chat logs, and transaction notes, to identify possible breaches of the policy. The system identified risks based on linguistic context, sentiment, and intent, which enabled the system to detect minor infractions of the system such as sharing data without authorization or mismanagement of sensitive information (Onoja et al., 2021). In addition to detection, NLP tools also helped to comply with privacy by automatically redacting all the personally identifiable information (PII) within communications and records. Such a monitoring and privacy protection are two capabilities that can help organizations protect their integrity and ensure compliance with the international data protection regulations with AI-based NLP applications (Moyo et al., 2023).

3.4. AI in Healthcare: Enhancing HIPAA Compliance and Patient Privacy

When dealing with healthcare, it is crucial to ensure that the data of the patient remains confidential according to the Health Insurance Portability and Accountability Act (HIPAA). A healthcare organization case reported in the literature introduced a deep learning-based system that tracks electronic health record (EHR) access in real-time, automatically identifying an unusual activity or any attempt at unauthorized access. The AI models determined the suitable access level of the staff according to the clinical roles and made alerts in case of deviations to provide the opportunity to investigate the situation immediately (Maguluri, 2024).

Also, NLP tools facilitated the privacy of data because sensitive data in clinical records were identified and de-identified during data sharing. The system also tracked the communications with the external entities to avoid infringement of privacy. In addition to regulatory compliance, AI-based solutions helped the hospital to advance ethical data governance, i.e., algorithms to assess the fairness of diagnostic models and identify possible biases. These explainable and automated audit trails not only improved the transparency and confidence but also indicated how AI can support HIPAA standards and ethical and privacy-conscious healthcare practices (Maguluri, 2024).

3.5. AI-Driven Compliance Auditing in a U.S. Financial Institution

One of the leading financial institutions in the U.S. introduced an AI-driven compliance auditing solution to address privacy regulations in the CCPA and GLBA laws. The company had problems integrating various state-level data privacy needs, which it has handled with the integration of machine learning and NLP. Its AI system was used to automatically correlate privacy rules to internal compliance structures, check internal data logs and communication on non-compliance, and analyze regulatory updates to suggest policy changes in real-time. This automation minimized the amount of audit work by hand, enhanced reporting accuracy and created a uniform compliance standard in all the states (Chintoh et al., 2025).

Moreover, models of AI-based anomaly detection were used to track financial transactions to detect possible privacy violations and fraud. The system provided instant alerts in the case of unauthorized access or abnormal data transfer, which allowed making a corrective decision in time and reducing risks. The institution showed that compliance efficiency and data privacy protection could be improved by means of ethical AI governance by aligning its algorithm with fairness, transparency, and accountability principles in the financial industry (Chintoh et al., 2025).

3.6. AI for Real-Time Privacy Compliance in U.S. Healthcare Systems

One of the largest U.S. medical groups adopted AI-based compliance models to fulfill the HIPAA and GDPR policies and protect patient privacy. Hospitals trained AI models locally without moving the raw patient data through the application of federated learning and differentiated privacy, which guaranteed privacy by design. The gradients were encrypted and identifiers anonymized to ensure a safe collaboration between sites to support compliance as well as medical research. To supplement this, NLP-based surveillance systems automatically analyzed HIPAA laws, searching audit records and EHR systems in search of unauthorized access or abuse of data. These instruments facilitated the real-time realization of non-compliance and justified AI reporting when auditors were employed by the federal government. This allowed the consortium to mitigate risks associated with regulation and enhance patient trust in the ethical use of AI in healthcare because privacy-preserving learning is combined with automated compliance oversight (Sangararaju, 2025).

3.7. AI-Driven Approaches to Compliance and Data Privacy

The INTREPID framework was created in Italy and implemented in the public administration to facilitate the compliance of GDPR by analyzing documents with AI. The system detects personal data and raises possible privacy breaches in administrative records using NLP and machine learning algorithms like Named Entity Recognition (NER) and automated text classification. The automation has led to the minimization of manual auditing work and mitigated the risk of data leaks, as well as provided uniformity in the process of managing the privacy of the government departments (Lore et al., 2023). Also in the financial sector, AI based compliance solutions are used to detect regulatory violations of transactions, communications and documents under a regulatory framework such as the GDPR, HIPAA and AML. With these models, suspicious activity is identified, sensitive data is anonymized, and real-time audit reporting is available, and the operational activities of the organization are in line with the changing data protection requirements. All these AI-driven solutions emphasize the way automation changes the compliance as a responsive requirement to an active data security and governance procedure (Lore et al., 2023).

Despite such examples showing how AI-enabled compliance systems might become practical, the majority of reported cases are descriptive and do not have standardized evaluation parameters, including precision, false-positive, cost-benefit analysis, or longitudinal performance evaluation.

4. MAINTAINING PRIVACY IN AN AI-POWERED SECURITY SYSTEM

AI has altered the coexistence of privacy and security of data in enterprise ecosystems. It allows auditing real-time compliance, automated risk detection, and predictive analytics that are advanced and enhances governance and data protection. Nevertheless, since AI systems require significant data volume to be trained efficiently and perform effectively, they present the new issues of personal data exposure, security breach, and privacy risk. The need to balance the effectiveness of AI-based insights and ethical data usage with compliance is thus a key issue in the contemporary cybersecurity systems (Misra & Tiwari, 2022; Folorunso et al., 2024; Reis et al., 2023).

4.1. The Privacy–Security Paradox

Firms in AI-intensive settings must trade-off privacy versus security, i.e. guarantee adequate data access to smart analytics and maintain the legislative mandate of data minimization. Security and threat-detection tools frequently rely on big and heterogeneous data to draw anomalies and new dangers and regulatory systems, including GDPR and HIPAA, state minimal data-gathering, narrowing of the purpose, and defense of personal data. The over-centralization of data can enhance model functionality and at the same time elevate the propensity of abuse, breaches and non-compliance of regulatory standards. Hence, privacy-sensitive AI systems should include the following features, which allow to support effective analytics without sharing sensitive information: selective data sharing, anonymization, differentially-private, and controlled access control (Ijaiya, 2024; Sresth et al., 2021; Awwal-Bolanta and Anakanire, 2024; Folorunso et al., 2024; Reis et al., 2023). In addition to the exposure of data, AI models at times spill over and can leak private data unintentionally. Such attacks as model inversion allow attackers to infer training data, such as facial image or health records, based on model outputs, and re-identification attacks match anonymized datasets with external sources to reveal individual identities. It demonstrates that it is not enough to protect the raw data and additionally, organizations should protect trained models, API endpoints, and query patterns against abuse. These risks can be mitigated by proper governance, privacy testing, and allowed access to models (Mbah, 2024; Maddali, 2024; Talati, 2022; Gajbhiye et al., 2024).

4.2. AI Techniques for Privacy Preservation

To minimize privacy risks, researchers and practitioners have come up with several privacy preserving AI methods that do not compromise the utility of the model. Differential Privacy (DP) adds statistically atypical noise to data sets or a model in such a way that the impact of any single record can never be recovered and this makes a formal mathematical privacy guarantee. Organizations like Apple and Google have extensively used the method in large-scale data analytics and recommendation systems. Differential privacy will help to further address the regulatory requirements and enhance the trust in data-driven systems by eliminating the risk of re-identification even in case of large-scale data processing (Misra & Tiwari, 2022; Ijaiya, 2024; Awwal-Bolanta and Anakanire, 2024). Federated Learning (FL) is a technology that allows the joint training of AI models in decentralized devices or data centers without centralizing raw data. The model is trained on each node and encrypted model updates are shared with the other nodes to be aggregated. It is also a way that organizations, including hospitals or banks, can enjoy the benefits of shared intelligence without transferring sensitive information across borders without violating laws such as HIPAA or GDPR. FL helps to reduce the possibilities of data leakages and regulatory non-conformity (Sangaraju, 2025; Maguluri, 2024; Misra & Tiwari, 2022).

Homomorphic Encryption (HE) enhances data privacy because it enables a computation on encrypted data. This guarantees that the plaintext cannot be accessed by even the service providers or cloud processors, which keeps the end-to-end secret in the process of running AI applications. Computationally, HE is applicable to limited analytical tasks but remains computationally expensive for large-scale real-time deployment (Onoja et al., 2021; Reis et al., 2023; Misra & Tiwari, 2022). Synthetic Data Generation (SDG) generates artificial data which replicates the format and distribution of actual data but which does not include any information that can be recognized. Artificial data also enables companies to develop, test and verify AI models without using actual user data. Once validated appropriately, it can be an essential privacy-safe AI research tool and a system development that is compliant (Moyo et al., 2023; Misra & Tiwari, 2022; Samant, 2024).

4.3. Privacy by Design in AI Systems

One of the fundamental principles forming the basis of privacy protection is Privacy by Design (PbD), which guarantees the privacy protection during the entire lifecycle of AI development, including data collection and model training, deployment, and decommissioning. As opposed to considering privacy as a secondary consideration, PbD considers such architectural protection as the minimization of data, pseudonymization, and the use of robust control mechanisms. Encryption, anonymization, consent management are some of the techniques that need to be included in AI pipelines to meet regulatory obligations, such as Article 25 of the GDPR (Maddali, 2024; Talati, 2022).

The strategy is also supported by the ongoing Privacy Impact Assessment (PIA) and artificial intelligence-based risk analysis. Those mechanisms assist in revealing sensitive data flows, analyzing risks of misusing models, and provide mitigation strategies, i.e., differential privacy or federated learning. The compliance dashboards of the future, operating on AI, would be able to track the privacy indicators constantly and make dynamic changes in the controls based on the changes in the regulatory needs. This proactive integration makes compliance a self-governing and ongoing governance process, but not a responsive requirement (Awwal-Bolanta & Anakanire, 2024; Folorunso et al., 2024; Samant, 2024; Lore et al., 2023).

4.4. AI for Privacy Compliance Monitoring

With privacy laws becoming more complicated, companies are now implementing AI to use automated compliance scanning. NLP algorithms and machine learning can automatically find, categorize, and label personal data throughout databases, e-mails, and cloud systems, and allow organizations to keep detailed data books. These AI systems have the ability to identify sensitive identifiers, enforce retention policies, and enforce compliance to the principles of access control such as least privilege. Real-time monitoring also helps to facilitate automated breach detection and timely notification, which are mandated by the reality of privacy laws of the world (Reis et al., 2023; Moyo et al., 2023; Talati, 2022). The other area that AI can bring a lot of value to Data flow governance is the other area which can be enhanced by AI. It may enhance and visualize personal data flow across and within organizational units and partner networks. Data transfers become transparent to the auditors and regulators due to the continuous monitoring and visualization, and they can quickly intervene in the event of policy breaches. These systems also improve accountability with unchangeable audit trails, in addition to improving documentation and reporting. In such a way, AI helps to make compliance dynamic, intelligent, and adaptive (Ijaiya, 2024; Javed, 2025; Gajbhiye et al., 2024; Folorunso et al., 2024).

4.5. Case Example: Federated Learning in Healthcare

One of the most notable applications of privacy-preserving AI would be the healthcare industry, in which institutions need to secure patient information under laws such as the HIPAA and GDPR. In the United States, federated learning was implemented in a group of hospitals to create diagnostic models on the basis of medical imaging data. The model was trained locally on patient records in each hospital and the encrypted model updates were sent to an aggregator centrally. The aggregator fused these updates to enhance the accuracy of the diagnoses without having to access raw data of the patients. Even the aggregated updates reduce the risk of data exposure, although privacy guarantees depend on the implementation of encryption and differential privacy mechanisms. Such a collaborative model made it possible to adhere to the laws of data protection and improve clinical results and promote the ethical development of AI (Sangararaju, 2025; Maguluri, 2024; Misra & Tiwari, 2022).

5. IMPACT OF AI ON COMPLIANCE AND DATA PRIVACY

ML and AI are transforming the way organizations tackle the issue of compliance, privacy, and data governance. Such an effect is compliance auditing automation and real-time risk detection, which is among the most important effects that will enable organizations to operate within a variety of intricate frameworks, such as GDPR, HIPAA, and CCPA. AI-based applications will enable systems to track privacy breaches and sort sensitive information automatically and produce compliance reports with minimal human effort. This automation will ease the task of manual audits and also provide compliance checks that are being conducted in a routine manner and accurately. Folorunso et al. (2024) states that this automation strengthens the resistance of the organization to cyber-attacks and provides a high level of timely compliance with the requirements of the regulations by actively monitoring the organization and anticipating actions (Folorunso et al., 2024). The processing of large amounts of data and learning through patterns has also enhanced the protection of data privacy by AI. Machine learning models are able to identify abnormal access patterns or data flows that can potentially indicate an invasion of privacy and thus intervene immediately. These systems can be used to scan user behavior, network traffic and system logs to detect anomalies that can be used to stop data misuse before it happens to compliance teams. Organizations can improve the risk of data leakage by monitoring data in real-time by replacing reactive systems with a proactive AI meeting. Yet, as observed, this increased reliance on AI brings with it new problems, especially that the AI models might inadvertently retrieve and share personal data trained on their data, which also increases the privacy risks of themselves (Misra & Tiwari, 2022).

The other role of AI in the field that is significant is the improvement of predictive compliance and threat modeling. AI systems will be able to predict potential privacy breach or regulatory non-conformity before it occurs through predictive analytics. Indicatively, AI can detect a trend of data abuse that can result in a subsequent breach or compliance failure, which organizations can use to enact protective measures beforehand. Predictive AI is also finding use in helping regulators and auditors to detect gaps in systemic compliance and enhance governance practices. Practically, it implies that organizations are shifting toward dynamic compliance models, in which AI adjusts its policies and monitoring standards dynamically, with the regulated changing (Folorunso et al., 2024). The privacy assurance and risk assessment have also been significantly affected with the introduction of AI. Such tools as the ML Privacy Meter which Misra and Tiwari (2022) explain enable practitioners to measure the privacy risks that AI models pose by modeling possible attacks that could lead to the deduction of personal information using the training data. These tools allow organizations to assess whether their AI models may accidentally disclose sensitive data and take measures to enhance and have more robust protection, including federated learning or differential privacy. This strategy does not only enhance privacy protection, but it also helps to comply with such regulatory requirements as Article 35 of the GDPR that implies carrying out Data Protection Impact Assessments (DPIAs) on the systems involving the usage of such advanced technologies as AI (Misra & Tiwari, 2022).

In cybersecurity compliance, AI helps to respond faster to the incident and make fewer human errors. There are automated Artificial Intelligence systems that can identify violations and immediately sent a pre-programmed reaction, like isolating accounts that have been compromised or preventing unauthorized access. This reduces the time frame of attacks and assists in fulfilling regulatory requirements of prompt notification of breach according to GDPR and other laws about data protection. Moreover, AI-supported Security Information and Event Management (SIEM) tools will be capable of processing large amounts of compliance logs and detecting concealed risks that cannot be detected by human auditors. This enhances data management operations in terms of transparency, auditability, and accountability (Folorunso et al., 2024). The other significant consequence is the development of Privacy-Preserving Machine Learning (PPML) approaches, that are supposed to ensure the safety of user information and preserve the accuracy of AI. Different methods such as differential privacy, homomorphic encryption and federated learning enable AI systems to be trained on decentralized or anonymized data without invading personal privacy. Such solutions assist companies to be within the global data protection regulations and to be able to innovate using AI. Misra and Tiwari (2022) point out that PPML offers a model of striking a balance between innovation and compliance the organization can train models collaboratively with sensitive data remaining confidential and private (Misra & Tiwari, 2022).

Accountability and transparency in compliance are also enhanced by AI. The current AI-based system of governance can trace the nature of the data processing, storage, and sharing among various departments, providing a comprehensive audit trail. Besides the trust that is also developed among stakeholders as a result of such transparency, it is also easier to show compliance to regulators by the organizations. Meanwhile, AI systems assist in ensuring continuous compliance, which is an evolving model, as compliance status does not remain the same but is constantly re-evaluated because of automated validation and anomaly detection. Reported performance metrics in the literature include precision, recall, false-positive rate, and processing latency, although standardized benchmarking across organizations remains limited. Folorunso et al. (2024) emphasize that the same approach is crucial when businesses engage in large-scale cross-border data processing, as it would be unfeasible to glean compliance with the manual inspections (Folorunso et al., 2024). Although these benefits are present, the introduction of AI in compliance and privacy systems is not risk free. The issue of adversarial AI, i.e. the use of AI by malicious actors to either circumvent AI-adopted security measures or to compromise sensitive data, is currently an urgent concern. Both articles emphasize the role of ethical AI development, transparency in AI decision-making and human control to reduce these risks. It is also important to make AI systems explainable and auditable so regulators can have confidence in AI and hold human accountable under the law. In addition, privacy issues because of model memorization or inference attacks are subject to continuous research and regulatory actions to ensure safe and responsible AI systems. Despite increasing adoption of AI-based compliance tools, empirical evidence on their long-term effectiveness, cost-benefit performance, and failure modes remains limited, highlighting the need for standardized evaluation and independent benchmarking (Misra & Tiwari, 2022; Folorunso et al., 2024).

6. INTEGRATION AND SYNERGY: UNIFIED AI COMPLIANCE ARCHITECTURE

The rising magnitude and use of AI systems have posed new governance issues and necessitated coordinated international regulation solutions to guarantee responsible and trustworthy use of AI (Ye et al., 2024). This is a necessary practice since AI models are becoming more and more reliant on large-scale datasets that raise the issue of algorithmic transparency and data usage ethics that can only be mitigated by making sure that the concept of data protection principles is directly incorporated into the design of the system (Mbah, 2024). When all these functions are deployed on the same platform, an organization becomes sure that protection of data is part of its operations, not a post-facto audit; and hence the complexity and fragmented legal demands are easily managed. This integrated architecture has a conceptual model that commences with Regulatory Input that is directed to the AI Compliance Engine. Regulatory Input phase includes constant introduction of new and modified legal requirements across various jurisdictions, which is automatically processed and described by the AI Compliance Engine, which employs sophisticated technologies, such as Natural Language Processing (NLP) and machine learning (Gajbhiye et al., 2024). This engine is the center processing unit, which by default maps these complicated regulations to the internal organizational policies and system settings. This will enable the AI Compliance Engine to automatically perform tedious processes like regular risk assessment and creating comprehensive audit trails, which will decrease the operational load and provide greater compliance of applications to ever-changing security requirements (Utomi et al., 2024).

After generating the policies, the system proceeds to implement Data Privacy Controls, which get input in the AI-driven DLP layer. Data Privacy Controls stage implies the implementation of Privacy-Enhancing Technologies (PETs) into the data processing environment with the adoption of such techniques as differential privacy and federated learning to ensure sensitive data protection in the context of training and implementation of AI models (Arora, 2015). The next AI-based DLP system serves as the enforcement layer, which goes beyond mere key-word matching to run advanced anomaly detection algorithm to bar illegal data transfers, suspicious access patterns or data exfiltration attempts in real-time (Devineni, 2024). Such a synergistic operation helps in the fact that not only the processes are carried out with the security of privacy concerns but also with the constant monitoring of the processes in case of malicious or accidental cases of data loss. Continuous Monitoring is the last stage, which is essential to complete the feedback mechanism keeping the system agile and responsive. This phase uses AI to offer real-time auditing and reporting where the flows of data, application behavior, and compliance measures are continually evaluated against the set policies (Mbah, 2024). In case a breach or non-compliance event happens, the Continuous Monitoring component immediately marks the problem, which will be essential data in responding to the incident right away and automatic remediation, which is fed back into the AI Compliance Engine, to be refined. This continual monitoring will make the whole architecture a self-regulating, dynamic mechanism of ensuring fairness, transparency and accountability in their AI implementations, to turn compliance into an operational requirement that shows a continued level of due diligence to regulatory institutions (Gajbhiye et al., 2024). To clarify the operational structure of the proposed unified architecture, Table 2 summarizes the key components, their primary inputs and outputs, and the associated governance controls required for regulatory accountability.

Table 2. Operational components of a unified AI compliance architecture and associated governance controls

Component	Input	Output	Governance
Regulatory Engine	Legal texts	Control rules	Legal review
Risk Model	Logs, metadata	Risk score	Human override
DLP Layer	Data flows	Alerts	Audit trail
Monitoring	System events	Compliance reports	Versioning

Even though automation helps in sustaining continuous monitoring and risk identification, accountability of organization is also necessary. Human control, audit trails, and model version control controls are needed to make the decision process makeable to any court and to handle any possible failures or unintended consequences of an automated decision-making process.

7. ETHICAL AND LEGAL CONSIDERATIONS

The emergence of AI in compliance and data privacy systems has many opportunities and complicated ethical and legal issues. On the one hand, AI enhances the efficiency of operations, the ability to risk detect, and the effectiveness of decisions, whereas, on the other hand, it creates significant issues associated with human rights, accountability, and equity. These issues are not limited to technical performance but also focus on the matters of public trust, ethical accountability, and regulatory integrity (Mbah, 2024). The main problem is that AI functions must be adjusted to the global standards of data protection, including general data protection regulation (GDPR), California consumer privacy act (CCPA), and health insurance portability and accountability act (HIPAA) so that AI systems could be rendered legally correct, transparent, responsible, and just and with high protection of personal data (Mirishli, 2024; Maddali, 2024). Ethical and legal regulations are of special concern in those areas like healthcare and finance where personal data can be easily misused, biased/ discriminated. Artificial intelligence can also fail to counter the presence of biases within a training dataset, which brings up the issue of fairness and non-discrimination within the context of the GDPR (Dewitte, 2025). Even compliance-oriented AI will provide a new regulatory threat and privacy threat without a robust ethical control (Dewitte, 2025; Reis et al., 2023; Maguluri, 2024; Utomi et al., 2024).

7.1. Transparency and Explainability in AI Compliance Tools

Transparency is one of the key ethical pillars of AI-driven compliance. Current AI systems, especially deep learning systems and complex machine learning structures, tend to be less interpretable, thereby presenting difficulties to regulatory auditability and other accountability standards and difficult to learn how particular compliance or security decisions are obtained (Devineni, 2024; Misra & Tiwari, 2022). The ambiguity of sophisticated models is one of the most important conflicts between Al and GDPR because the regulation demands transparency and substantial information regarding automated decision-making (Dewitte, 2025). This interpretability makes it very difficult to regulate, and such data protection regulations as the GDPR require transparency and accountability, as well as the right of a person to gain meaningful explanations of automated decisions that influence him or her (Lukács & Váradi, 2023). As an example, the companies that employ AI to check on the access control or find violations in their policies should be capable of explaining their systems to internal auditors and external regulators. The absence of interpretability, in addition to a lack of trust, is an action that is against the law, in terms of transparency in automated processing (Moyo et al., 2023; Gajbhiye et al., 2024). To solve this problem, Explainable AI (XAI) is no longer considered as a theoretical study but a regulatory requirement (Arora, 2015; Talati, 2022). XAI frameworks allow people to reason humanly during compliance choices, which can allow organizations to audit and justify the results of algorithms. Explainability has also been a legal requirement of regulators like the Information Commissioner's Office (ICO) in the UK when it comes to automated decision-making (Samant, 2024). It is not always a statutory requirement and often a regulatory expectation. Such applications as the INTREPID system of automated auditing of GDPR documents prove that AI systems are capable of generating clear and auditable compliance histories (Lore et al., 2023). In practice, transparency ought to be strengthened by policy governance, i.e. organizations should issue transparent statements about how they handle AI data, and by technical means, i.e. model interpretability layers or explainable dashboards, which display the effect of data on outcomes. Collectively, these actions make AI-driven compliance cease to be a passive system but rather an auditable and reliable governance system (Chintoh et al., 2025; Folorunso et al., 2024; Sangaraju, 2025).

7.2. Bias and Fairness in Compliance Decisions

The increasing presence of AI in compliance-related decisions puts the nagging problem of algorithmic bias into the spotlight. Since AI systems are learning the patterns in historical data, they tend to replicate or even enhance any biases present in society in historical data (Arora, 2015; Onoja et al., 2021). This may cause discriminatory results, including the unequal risk rating or unequal data labeling by demography, which disrupts both fairness and the principles of lawful processing expressed in privacy legislation, including the GDPR (Lore et al., 2023). Indicatively, in the case of healthcare compliance, an AI controlled by biased training may often call patients of a particular socioeconomic group as being at high risk, breaching ethical and data protection requirements (Utomi et al., 2024; Sangaraju, 2025). Such bias can only be mitigated through active lifecycle governance. Ethical control should be instituted on the design level, and dataset should be carefully maintained, bias should be identified during training, and audit of the models should be performed periodically after implementation (Mbah, 2024). To monitor the discriminatory trends of the various user groups, fairness measurements and adversarial testing would be required (Maddali, 2024; Folorunso et al., 2024). The general principle is to make sure that the AI systems do not foster inequity, but ensure its absence instead, so fairness is one of the pillars of responsible compliance automation (Devineni, 2024; Maguluri, 2024).

7.3. Accountability: Who Is Responsible for AI's Compliance Failures?

The legal issues with AI-based compliance are one of the most urgent ones, which concern accountability. It is also a contested domain of the existing legislation to define who is to be held responsible in case an AI system misclassifies, violates data, or infringes one of the regulations (Maddali, 2024; Samant, 2024). This has been dubbed as the responsibility gap- a scenario where the mainstream legal frameworks do not hold complex and autonomous systems liable (Chintoh et al., 2025). The process of AI development and implementation incorporates several participants, including developers, auditors, and organizational teams, so it is challenging to identify the liability in situations when a tool of AI compliance leads to harm (Lore et al., 2023). In this regard, organizations need to have robust internal governance systems that outline the chain of responsibility, introduce compulsory AI Privacy Impact Assessments (PIAs) and record risk management protocols (Onoja et al., 2021; Talati, 2022). On the outside, governments and regulators have to communicate with the industry to design ethical principles that ensure reliable AI, with everyone bearing responsibility in the process of developing to applying AI (Arokun, 2025; Mbah, 2024). Not only do such structures ensure the protection of the rights of users but also provide developers with motivation to create AI systems that are transparent, fair and auditable. Finally, there should be a multi-stakeholder accountability model that is proactive and which bridges the gap in the law to ensure that AI-driven compliance is both legal and moral (Folorunso et al., 2024; Sangaraju, 2025).

8. FUTURE DIRECTIONS AND RESEARCH CHALLENGES

8.1. Adaptive Compliance Under Dynamic Regulations

Compliance AI systems should no longer be a set and forget. The future systems would require the automatic update of rules and constant reading of laws to be done in order to adapt to any amendment of a privacy rule by the states or to a new law. In practice, it is the construction of regulatory knowledge bases (NLP pipelines to process legal text), rule engines that are modular and constant learning cycles to ensure that the models update their behavior without disrupting operations. The issues of research work are, how to demonstrate that such systems are auditable and legally defensible in case they alter their behavior automatically, and how to update them safely (without causing regressions or introducing bias) (Chintoh et al., 2025).

8.2. Cross-Border AI Governance Harmonization

Since businesses are moving between jurisdictions, a major future trend is having a single compliance layer that can map and reconcile conflicting regulations (e.g. CCPA vs. GDPR). The standardized ontologies and interoperability formats should be investigated to allow AI to convert the local legal requirements into a global compliance plan and mechanisms to mark and deal with the cases that are unavoidable (e.g., when local law mandates that data be localized, and a foreign law permits the transfer). The tough challenges are language translation (finding subtlety), preserving provenance of interpretations of law and developing processes of governance that will be credible to regulate in other jurisdictions. (Chintoh et al., 2025).

8.3. Integration With Blockchain for Auditability

Tamper-evident ledgers such as blockchain can be combined with AI to generate auditable records of decision-making in data-processing: what data was fed into a model, what model version arrived at a decision and what remedial action was taken. This would be encouraging in an attempt to prove compliance during audits and during post incident forensic analysis. Privacy tradeoffs (i.e. what is on-chain and what is off-chain) and scalability and the way to enforce GDPR/CCPA rights (such as deletion) should also be researched in the case of immutable logs. The most important gaps in research are to design hybrid architectures (private channels, pointers to encrypted off-chain records) and legal patterns accepting blockchain evidence. (Chintoh et al., 2025).

8.4. Emerging "RegTech" Innovations

RegTech Software enabling compliance automation — more and more will rely on LLMs, explainable AI, automation of rights-request fulfillment, and real-time dashboard monitoring applications. The second generation of RegTech must go beyond alerting to automatic remediation (such as automatically quarantining suspect data) but with human supervision. Concerns that have been raised in research are proving the correctness of automated remediations, avoidance of amplification of bias by automated systems, and the development of common metrics/regulatory SLAs to evaluate the performance of RegTech. Then there is business/UX challenge: to make RegTech accessible not only to data scientists, but also to legal groups (Chintoh et al., 2025).

9. BIBLIOMETRIC ANALYSIS AI FOR COMPLIANCE AND DATA PRIVACY

The section analyses the connection between Artificial Intelligence Compliance and Data Privacy through a bibliometric analysis provided using research records accessed in Lens.org database. The analysis uses VOSviewer to represent and analyse bibliometric networks, such as the co-occurrence of essential terms, prevailing topics of study and how they change over time. Furthermore, Lens.org dataset is also analysed in a systematic manner in order to determine the patterns in publications, geographical distribution of the production of research articles, and patterns of document type, major publishing company and the coverage of the field in terms of discipline. Graphs and tables are used to outline the findings to have a broad overview of the research on AI with respect to compliance and data privacy.

In Figure 2, the visualization of the network of co-occurring keywords of the PubMed database is provided with the help of the VOSviewer, which analyses the keywords on the basis of research themes connected to the idea of AI compliance and data privacy. In this visualization, the nodes depict common occurrence keywords and the size of the node reflects how common that occurrence is and the lines between the nodes denote how strongly the words co-occur. The thematic clusters are represented by different colours, which can be used to find out the key directions of research and how they are connected to each other.

As can be observed in Figure 2, the highest occurrence and central keywords are artificial intelligence and humans, meaning that the bulk of the publications revolves around the practical uses of humans. Intimately related to them is terminology of AI methodology, including such terms as deep learning, algorithms, convolutional neural networks, and large language models, which demonstrate that the most complex machine learning methods are applied in compliance-sensitive settings, in particular, in healthcare.

The most notable cluster in Figure 2 on the right-side shows topics concerning clinical governance and safe healthcare delivery, which include such keywords as "clinical decision support," quality of health care, security, governance, and algorithmic bias. This cluster is an indication of the importance of regulatory compliance, fairness, and accountability that are on the rise in AI-driven medical systems. The feature of the existence of algorithmic bias also implicates some concern over ethical compliance and the necessity of clear and fair AI models.

The other important cluster focuses on data protection and privacy engineering, which includes such keywords like: data privacy, confidentiality, computer security, privacy-preserving, legal compliance, GDPR, and homomorphic encryption. It means that policy discussions on AI privacy are not exclusive but rather combined with significant technical endeavours to establish secure AI models based on privacy enhancing technology. Also, Figure 2 demonstrates a cluster associated with digital health systems, such as such terms as electronic health records, telemedicine, mobile health, wearable electronic devices, and remote patient monitoring. This indicates the growing compliance and privacy concerns outside of hospitals into larger connected healthcare systems.

In general, Figure 2 proves that the study on AI in PubMed is highly influenced by the junction of clinical practices, privacy regulation, regulatory compliance, and controlling, and thus compliance and data privacy are two key priorities in AI application.

Figure 2. VOSviewer network visualization of keyword co-occurrence on AI for compliance and data privacy, generated using the PubMed database

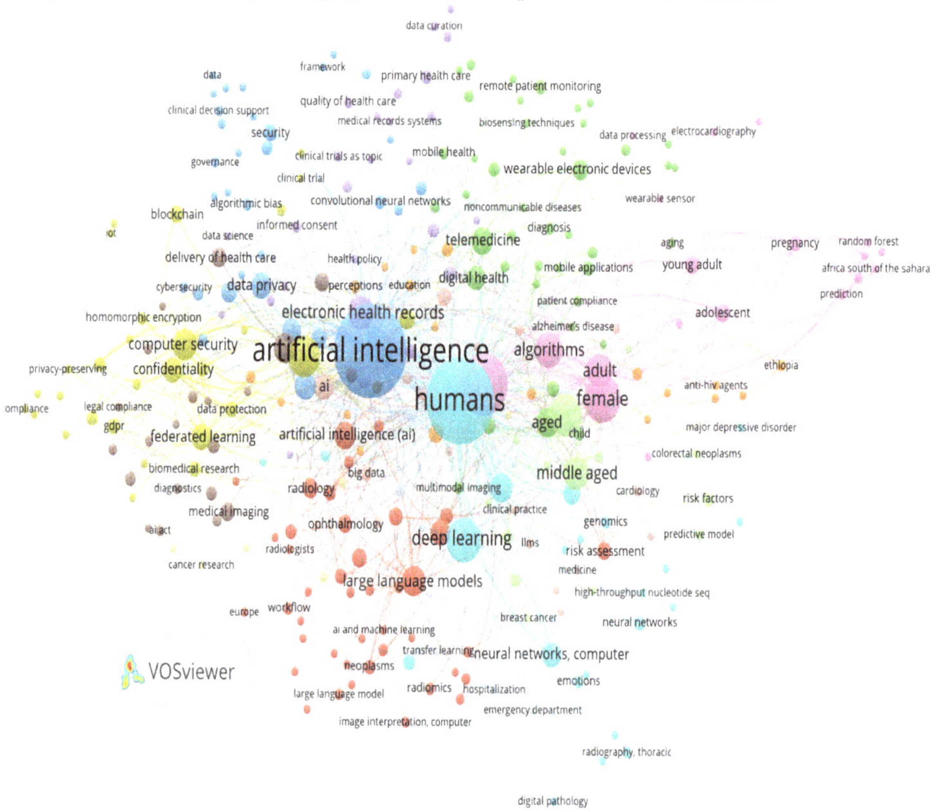

(visualized using VOSviewer) (Data may vary slightly).

Figure 3, the VOSviewer overlay representation, demonstrates the development of the research trends in the area of AI use in compliance and data privacy in accordance with the co-occurrence data regarding the keywords retrieved in the PubMed database. It is a visualization of a network unlike a regular network graph, in that it introduces a time dimension to the map, with the coloration of the nodes being the average year of publication of the keyword used. The time range is denoted by the colour bar on the bottom, with topics that are older being darker and the ones that are newer being lighter/yellow. This is useful in determining the change in the research focus over time.

As Figure 3 shows, the keywords that are the most central and most common are the terms artificially intelligence and humans, which proves the fact that the majority of the publications focus on real-life AI applications that engage human beings and involve sensitive and regulated areas of life such as healthcare. Intimately related to them are such fundamental methodological terms as deep learning, algorithms, neural networks, and large language models, which points to the increased use of current AI methodologies in research on compliance.

One of the greatest lessons of Figure 3 is the prevalence of privacy- and compliance-related terms including: data privacy, confidentiality, computer security, legal compliance, GDPR, and privacy-preserving. These terms constitute a highly user networked area, demonstrating that regulatory and ethical demands are more deeply entrenched into the development of AI systems. The emergence of more sophisticated concepts in security like the homomorphic encryption concept and the federated learning concept suggests that recent discoveries are gravitating towards privacy-sensitive AI designs as opposed to just talking privacy at policy level.

Besides that, Figure 3 shows a close connection between AI privacy studies and digital healthcare infrastructure. Such keywords as electronic health records, telemedicine, mobile health, wearable electronic devices, and remote patient monitoring are recurrent and have a newer trend. This is indicative of the fact that AI-based healthcare systems are moving out of the conventional clinical care setting to interconnected real-time digital ecosystems, where privacy compliance is increasingly more difficult because of the distributed data gathering.

Figure 3. VOSviewer overlay visualization of keyword co-occurrence on AI for compliance and data privacy, generated from the PubMed database using VOSviewer (Data may vary slightly).

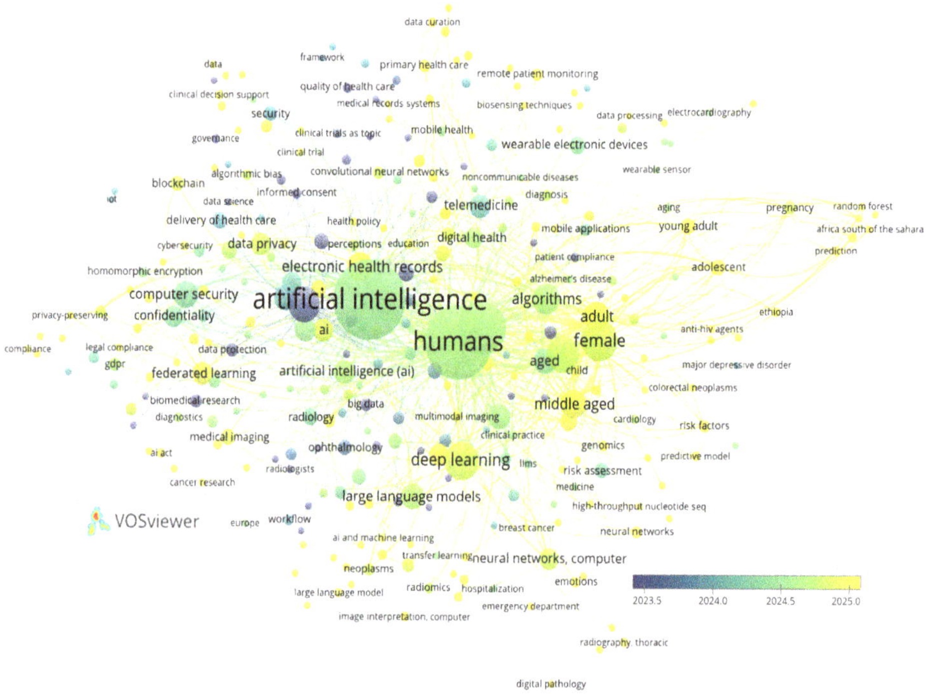

The other significant trend that can be seen in Figure 3 is the increasing focus on fairness, trust, and governance. Such keywords as algorithmic bias, governance, clinical decision support, and quality of health care indicate that compliance research currently considers not just the protection of data, but also responsible AI implementation, transparency, and accountability of clinical decision-making. Generally, Figure 3 shows that the research environment is shifting towards the newer AI approaches to privacy-conscious and regulation-oriented AI practices especially in the healthcare context. The overlay visualization makes it evident that compliance and privacy are no longer the concerns of the second order but become the key aspects of AI research and implementation.

The keyword co-occurrence structure of the research on Artificial Intelligence (AI) and compliance and data privacy in the case of bibliographic data obtained in the PubMed database has been shown on the VOSviewer density view (Figure 4). A density visualization, unlike a network or overlay map, pays emphasis on how much and where the research themes are concentrated. The brighter yellow areas of this map reflect key words with the most frequency and strongest connectedness whereas the darker blue areas are those with weaker frequency and connectedness with other key words.

The largest hot spot, as seen in Figure 4, is the one with the keywords "artificial intelligence" and "humans," which confirms that AI studies in the domain of compliance and privacy are mostly human-driven and are used in sensitive fields, specifically healthcare. The high concentration of the core terms demonstrates the fact that the vast majority of the studies are organized around the human application of real-world data, in which compliance issues and privacy laws play a crucial role.

Very nearby the central hotspot, there are strictly interrelated technical and methodological concepts like deep learning, algorithms, neural networks, and large language models. They are quite active, which means that the recent compliance-based research on privacy starts to embrace more complex AI-related approaches instead of emphasizing the theoretical models of privacy. This implies a switching to more practical implementation, where AI models have to comply as well as perform exceptionally well.

A second significant area of high density, which is observable in Figure 4, is connected with healthcare and digital systems. The keywords that include electronic health records, telemedicine, mobile health, wearable electronic devices, and remote patient monitoring clustering well. This emphasizes the idea that one of the most active fields of AI compliance and privacy research is the field of healthcare. Being a highly regulated industry, these themes represent the necessity to have safe data processing, conscientious clinical practices, and privacy-conscious AI implementation.

Keywords related to privacy and governance including data privacy, confidentiality, computer security, data protection, legal compliance, GDPR, and privacy-preserving are also highly presented. The fact that they are near the central AI terms suggests that the privacy and compliance are no longer discussed separately but are becoming embedded into the design of AI systems. Other more sophisticated privacy-enhancing techniques, including federated learning and homomorphic encryption, can also be found on the map, which indicates the modern privacy-saving AI strategies are receiving more research impetus.

Also, the emerging topics, such as algorithmic bias, governance, and informed consent, are added to Figure 4. These themes show that compliance studies are growing to include beyond technical aspects of privacy to also encompass trust, responsibility, and governance of AI.

In general, Figure 4 is a clear indication that the area of research is very much focused on the human-centred AI use and, specifically, in the healthcare field with high concerns about privacy, security, and regulatory compliance. The density visualization proves that compliance and data privacy are emerging as the main pillars of AI implementation and not as supplementary factors.

Figure 4. VOSviewer density visualization of keyword co-occurrence on AI for compliance and data privacy, generated from the PubMed database using VOSviewer (Data may vary slightly).

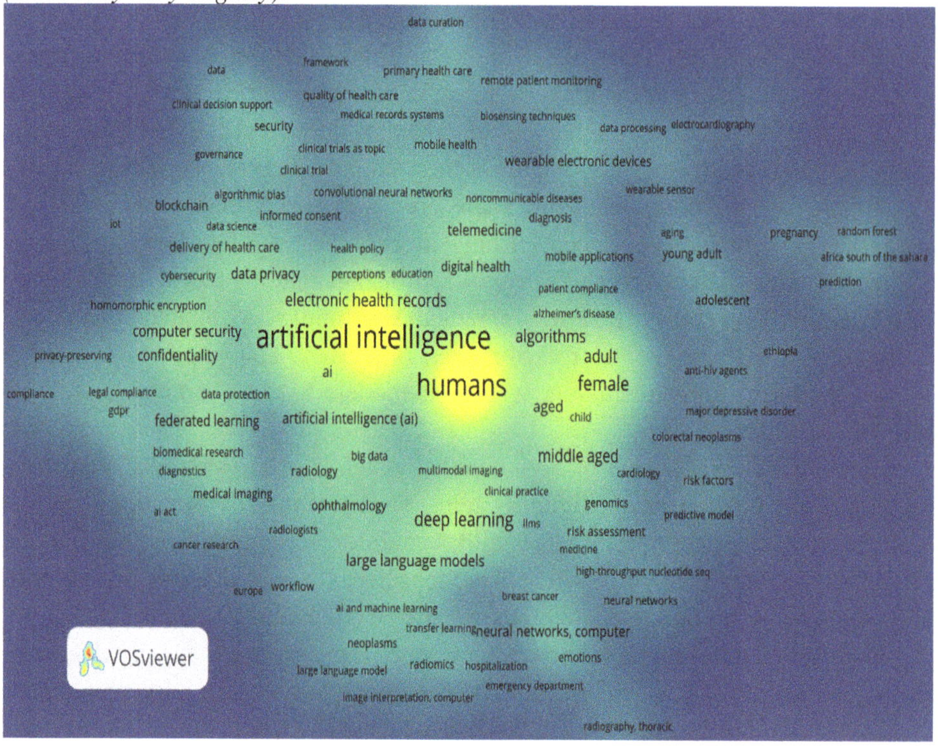

Figure 5 shows the annual rise of academic articles about AI in compliance and data privacy, which was retrieved in Lens.org database. The findings suggest that the activity in the field was exceedingly low before 2019 which can be explained by the fact that the topic of AI-driven privacy and regulatory conformity was not discussed on a large scale in previous scholarly sources.

Another positive indicator of expansion in this research area is a progressive growth in the volume of publications between 2019 and 2022, which was the first stage of expansion within this field. Studies during this time period were more focused on the emerging issues of data governance, data confidentiality, cyberspace security, ethical AI, and regulatory standards, especially in digital and healthcare settings.

A considerable rising trend is observed since the year 2023 when the number of publications starts to rise drastically. This wave underscores the increased global concern over the privacy threats posed by the massive use of AI and, particularly, in sensitive uses that deal with electronic health records, telemedicine, wearable health devices, and data-driven decision-support systems. The trend only grows stronger in 2024 and 2025, with the last case recording the maximum number of publications in the dataset. Such a swift expansion indicates that AI compliance and privacy has now been a massively studied research topic, probably due to a more restrictive legal framework (e.g., GDPR and similar policies across the world), a growing implementation of AI into the real world, and the growing issues of algorithmic bias, consent, and secure data processing.

One can see a slight decrease in 2026 that can be explained by the fact that the year has not been fully indexed yet because of unfinished publication. On the whole, Figure 5 indicates a robust and increasing research trend, which proves that AI as a compliance and data privacy tool is a fast-growing and influential research field.

Figure 5. Year-wise publication trend on AI for compliance and data privacy

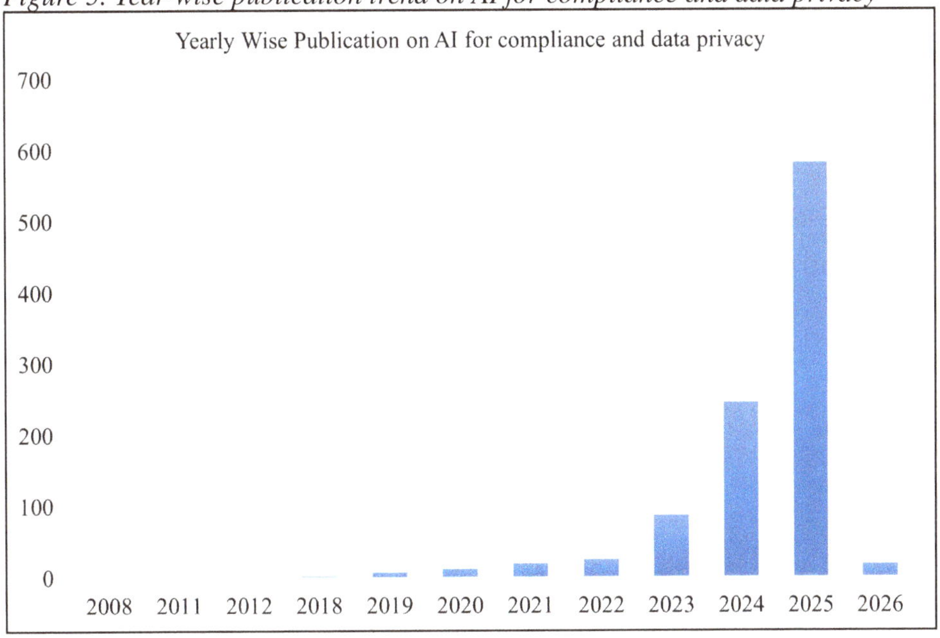

(Source: Lens.org database) (Data may vary slightly).

Figure 6 presents a choropleth (thematic) world map with the country-based publication distribution on the topic of the research article on AI and Compliance and Data Privacy. The countries are marked with various colours of green in which darker the colour, the more the research is produced and lighter the colour, the relatively lower the number of publications.

Based on the visualization, it can be seen that the largest number of publications on the topic of compliance systems based on AI, privacy-preserving AI, and regulatory frameworks are made by the United States. This has been noted to be an outcome of the robust research interest in the US concerning data governance, cybersecurity, AI ethics, and technologies that ensure adherence to the law.

Euromonitor also has a marked publication presence in some countries within Europe especially in the United Kingdom and in certain western states in Europe. This has been anticipated as a result of large impact of regulations like GDPR which has spurred much academic and industrial studies in privacy, consent management and safe deployment of AI.

India and China contribute to publications moderately in Asia, which is also evidenced by the increasing interest in AI governance, digital health privacy, and safe data-sharing systems. Still, there are numerous areas, particularly in Africa and a part of South America, which are lowly qualified which means that the research yield in this field is rather scarce.

In general, Figure 6 gives us a clear overview of the place of the research on AI in compliance and data privacy in the entire world. It also brings out opportunities that may be used to develop research in the future and international partnerships in the underrepresented areas.

Figure 6. Country-wise publication distribution on AI for compliance and data privacy

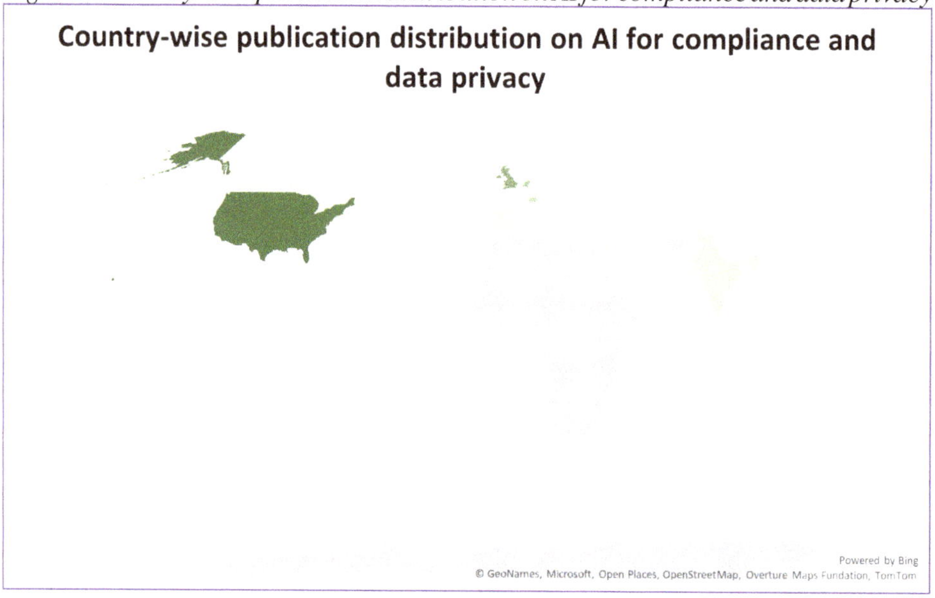

(Source: Lens.org Database; visualized using geographic mapping tools) (Data may vary slightly).

Figure 7 provides a heatmap on publication type that is related to the research area "AI for compliance and data privacy", extracted from the Lens.org database. The heatmap shows visually the distribution of research outputs in several document categories, with darker colours showing greater publication volumes and lighter colours showing lower numbers of publications.

The results indicate that journal articles prevail in the literature by having 14,748 documentations and thus are the most important document type in this domain. This means that the communication about AI-based compliance, privacy protection, and governance research is mostly shared in academic journals, which is peer-reviewed and thus signifies that this is a mature and high credibility field.

The second major categories are book chapters (773) and books (668), which may indicate that the topic is likewise widely addressed in academic books, policy-driven compilations and edited volumes-which are often centred on legal frameworks, ethical AI and regulatory governance.

Other notable contributions include preprints (609), which highlight the fast-growing and rapidly evolving nature of AI privacy research, in which authors tend to share their findings prior to formal journal publication. Similarly, dissertations (601) can be seen as strong academic involvement and more and more doctoral-level research into privacy-preserving machine learning, compliance automation and data governance.

Conference-related publications also play a part in the literature, with 488 conference proceedings articles and lesser numbers in conference proceedings, suggesting that innovation and early-stage technical work being developed are being presented at conferences.

In contrast, other categories such as datasets (18), clinical trials (4) and journal issues (22) occur at a minimum with this research area appearing to be largely theoretical, computational, policy-oriented and system-based as opposed to clinical trial-driven.

Overall, Figure 7 validates the research on AI for compliance and data privacy is highly concentrated in journal publications, with supporting academic books, dissertations, and emergent preprint research, indicating depth as well as growth in the research.

Figure 7. Heatmap showing publication-type distribution for AI for compliance and data privacy

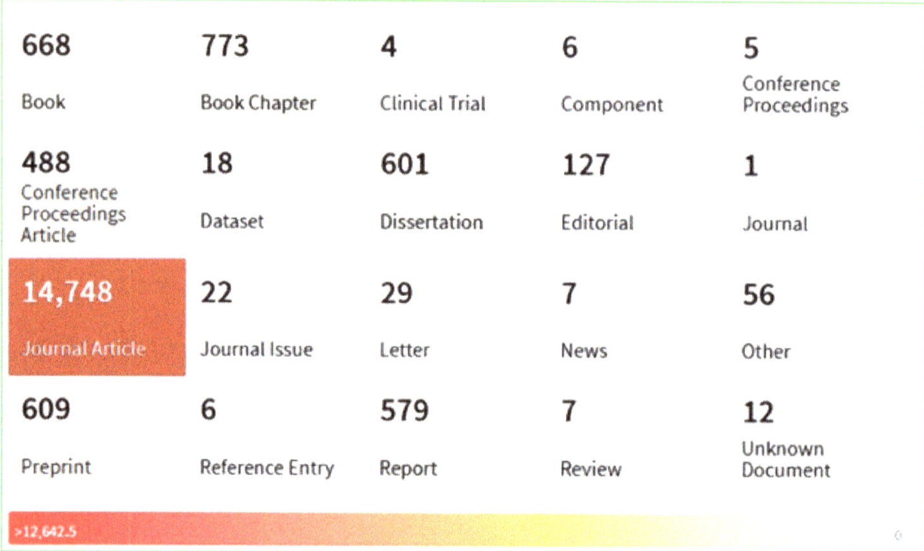

(Source: Lens.org Database) (Data may vary slightly).

Table 3 shows the top 15 publishers that have made contributions to the research field AI in compliance and data privacy, as per the record of publications retrieved in the Lens.org database. The publishers will have ranking based on the number of documents indexed in this topic of research.

Table 3. Top 15 publishers contributing publications on AI for compliance and data privacy (Source: Lens.org Database) (Data may vary slightly).

Publishers	**Count**
GSC Online Press	68
IGI Global	61
MDPI AG	45
IGI Global Scientific Publishing	35
Elsevier BV	23
Springer Science and Business Media LLC	23
Edtech Publishers (OPC) Private Limited	22
Science Research Society	18
International Journal for Multidisciplinary Research (IJFMR)	18
Henry Stewart Publications	17

continued on following page

Table 3. Continued

Publishers	Count
Technoscience Academy	16
Sciencedomain International	16
European Centre for Research Training and Development	15
IEEE	14
International Journal for Research in Applied Science and Engineering Technology (IJRASET)	14
Anfo Publication House	13
Al-Kindi Center for Research and Development	12
Fair East Publishers	12
RADemics Research Institute	11
CRC Press	11

These findings reveal that the GSC Online Press (68 publications) is the most prolific in the field, which demonstrates a substantial amount of research production regarding the automation of compliance, the protection of privacy by AI, the regulatory system, and the provision of applications in the field of regulation. After that comes IGI Global (61 publications), which is well-established in publishing works in the field of artificial intelligence, information systems, cybersecurity, and digital governance, which are heavily overlapping with the research of compliance and privacy.

MDPI AG (45) and IGI Global Scientific Publishing (35) are other top publishers, which demonstrates the increased interest of open-access and interdisciplinary publishers in publishing new findings concerning AI-driven privacy protection, legal-tech systems, and data security structures. Such leading international publishers as Elsevier BV (23) and Springer Science and Business Media LLC (23) are also represented in the list, which confirms that AI-based compliance and privacy studies are now being published in high-impact and globally-recognized scientific journals.

Moreover, engineering and computing focus of this field of research is also emphasized by publishers like IEEE (14) and technical journals like IJRASET (14), especially in domains like privacy-enhancing technologies, secure AI architecture, risk-based compliance monitoring, and regulatory technology (RegTech).

Generally, Table 1 shows that the literature on AI and compliance and data privacy is spread in a blend of technology-driven publishing companies, open-access journals, and large scientific publishing firms, which reflects both the interdisciplinary nature and speed of the field.

10. CONCLUSION

The quick adoption of Artificial Intelligence in today's digital landscape has changed how organizations protect data, meet regulations, and maintain user privacy. This review shows that AI offers strong tools for threat detection, automated auditing, data classification, and real-time governance. However, it also brings complex challenges that need innovative solutions. As companies rely more on AI security systems, they must find a balance between using abundant data for reliable AI insights and protecting fundamental ideals of data minimization and individual privacy. This challenge highlights the need for privacy-focused AI methods like differential privacy, federated learning, homomorphic encryption, and synthetic data generation, which together help lower risks while keeping analytical value. Creating trustworthy AI systems requires integrating privacy-by-design principles throughout all stages of development. From early risk assessments to ongoing monitoring of data flows, organizations must make sure AI models are transparent, understandable, and guided by strong ethical and regulatory standards. Privacy Impact Assessments, automated compliance checks, and AI-driven data discovery have become key tools for maintaining accountability in complex environments. Real-world examples, such as federated learning in healthcare and AI-assisted compliance in financial institutions, show that AI can improve both privacy and security when used responsibly. The effectiveness of AI-enabled compliance systems is highly dependent on data quality, governance practices, and human oversight. Overall, the future of compliance and data privacy depends on balancing technological progress with responsible governance. AI will keep evolving as both a driver of innovation and a protector of regulatory standards if organizations invest in secure systems, strong privacy tools, and ongoing oversight. By taking a balanced and proactive approach, companies can turn AI from a potential risk into a valuable asset that enhances security, builds public trust, and ensures lasting regulatory strength in a fast-changing digital environment.

REFERENCES

Arokun, E. (2025). Complexities of AI trends: Threats to data privacy legal compliance. *Seattle Journal of Technology, Environmental & Innovation Law*, *15*(2), 8. https://digitalcommons.law.seattleu.edu/sjteil/vol15/iss2/8

Arora, A. (2015). Developing generative AI models that comply with privacy regulations and ethical principles. *International Journal of Research in Electronics and Computer Engineering*, *3*(2), 269–277.

Awwal-Bolanta, O., & Anakanire, O. C. (2024). Artificial intelligence and data Privacy: evaluation of the innovations, legal frameworks and technological protection. In *IIARD – International Institute of Academic Research and Development, Journal of Law and Global Policy* (pp. 36–49). JLGP., DOI: 10.56201/JLGP.v9.no2.2024.pg36.49

Chintoh, N. G. A., Segun-Falade, N. O. D., Odionu, N. C. S., & Ekeh, N. a. H. (2025). Cross-Jurisdictional data Privacy Compliance in the U.S.: Developing a new model for managing AI data across state and federal laws. *3*(2), 537–548. https://doi.org/DOI: 10.51594/gjabr.v3i2.96

Chintoh, N. G. A., Segun-Falade, N. O. D., Odionu, N. C. S., & Ekeh, N. a. H. (2025). Developing a conceptual framework for U.S. data privacy compliance in AI systems: Integrating CCPA and HIPAA Regulations. *International Journal of Frontline Research and Reviews, 4*(1), 011–019. https://doi.org/DOI: 10.56355/ijfrr.2025.4.1.0034

Devineni, S. K. (2024). AI in data privacy and security. *International Journal of Artificial Intelligence and Machine Learning*, *3*(1), 35–49. DOI: 10.17605/OSF.IO/WCN8A

Dewitte, P. (2025). AI meets the GDPR. In Cambridge University Press eBooks (pp. 133–157). https://doi.org/DOI: 10.1017/9781009367783.010

Folorunso, A., Adewumi, T. O., Adewa, A., Okonkwo, R., & Olawumi, T. N. Capella University, University of Florida, Ohio University, North Carolina Agricultural and Technical State University, & Ekiti State University. (2024). Impact of AI on cybersecurity and security compliance. *Global Journal of Engineering and Technology Advances, 01–01*, 167–184. https://doi.org/DOI: 10.30574/gjeta.2024.21.1.0193

Gajbhiye, B., Khan, S., & Goel, O. (2024). Regulatory compliance in application security using AI compliance tools. *International Research Journal of Modernization in Engineering Technology and Science*, *6*(8). Advance online publication. DOI: 10.56726/IRJMETS61241

Ijaiya, H. (2024). Harnessing AI for data privacy: Examining risks, opportunities and strategic future directions. *International Journal of Science and Research Archive, 13*(2), 2878–2892. DOI: 10.30574/ijsra.2024.13.2.2510

Javed, A. (2025). Data Privacy and Security in AI-Driven Customer Platforms: A Cloud Computing Perspective. *European Journal of Computer Science and Information Technology, 13*(44), 84–95. DOI: 10.37745/ejcsit.2013/vol13n448495

Kakarala, M. K., & Rongali, S. K. (2025). Data privacy and security in AI. *World Journal of Advanced Research and Reviews, 25*(3), 2517–2523. DOI: 10.30574/wjarr.2025.25.3.0564

Lens database (retrieved in 2025). *Scholar search: AI for compliance and data privacy* https://www.lens.org/lens/search/scholar/list?q=ai%20for%20compliance%20and%20data%20privacy

Lore, F., Basile, P., Appice, A., De Gemmis, M., Malerba, D., & Semeraro, G. (2023). An AI framework to support decisions on GDPR compliance. *Journal of Intelligent Information Systems, 61*(2), 541–568. DOI: 10.1007/s10844-023-00782-4

Lukács, A., & Váradi, S. (2023). GDPR-compliant AI-based automated decision-making in the world of work. In *Elsevier Ltd* (Vol. 50, p. 105848). Computer Law & Security Review. [Journal-article], DOI: 10.1016/j.clsr.2023.105848

Maddali, R. (2024). AI-powered data security frameworks for regulatory compliance (GDPR, CCPA, HIPAA). *International Journal of Engineering Technology Research & Management*, 1–22. https://doi.org/DOI: 10.5281/zenodo.15072096

Maguluri, K. K. (2024). Advancing Patient Privacy in the Era of Artificial Intelligence: A Deep Learning Approach to Ensuring Compliance with HIPAA and Addressing Ethical Challenges in Healthcare Data Security. https://doi.org/DOI: 10.47059/IJMTLM/V27I5/030

Mbah, N. G. O.Geraldine O Mbah. (2024). Data privacy in the era of AI: Navigating regulatory landscapes for global businesses. *International Journal of Science and Research Archive, 13*(2), 2040–2058. DOI: 10.30574/ijsra.2024.13.2.2396

Mirishli, S. (2024). Ethical Implications of AI in Data Collection: Balancing Innovation with Privacy. *ANCIENT LAND, 6*(8), 40–55. DOI: 10.36719/2706-6185/38/40-55

Misra, P., & Tiwari, N. Georgia Institute of Technology, & Bansal Institute of Science and Technology. (2022). Impact of machine learning techniques in Privacy compliance. *Turkish Journal of Computer and Mathematics Education*, 746–760. https://www.researchgate.net/publication/365519178

Moyo, T. M., Tafirenyika, S., Tuboalabo, A., Taiwo, A. E., Bukhari, T. T., & Ajayi, A. E. (2023). Cloud-Based knowledge management systems with AI-Enhanced compliance and data privacy safeguards. *ESIC Market Economics and Business Journal*, *4*(2), 67–77. DOI: 10.54660/IJMFD.2023.4.2.67-77

Onoja, J. P., Hamza, O., Collins, A., Chibunna, U. B., Eweja, A., & Daraojimba, A. I. (2021). Digital Transformation and Data Governance: Strategies for regulatory compliance and secure AI-Driven business operations. *ESIC Market Economics and Business Journal*, *2*(1), 43–55. DOI: 10.54660/.IJFMR.2021.2.1.43-55

PubMed. *Scholar search: AI for compliance and data privacy* https://pubmed.ncbi.nlm.nih.gov/?term=ai+for+compliance+and+data+privacy&sort_order=asc

Reis, O., Okpeke, F., Attipoe, V., & Oluoha, O. M. (2023). A Privacy-First framework for data protection and compliance assurance in digital ecosystems. *Iconic Research and Engineering Journals*, *7*(4), 620–621. https://www.researchgate.net/publication/395415430

Samant, P. S. (2024). Leveraging ai for enhanced compliance with global data protection regulations in cloud computing environments. *International Research Journal of Modernization in Engineering Technology and Science*. Advance online publication. DOI: 10.56726/IRJMETS53514

Sangaraju, V. V. (2025). AI and Data Privacy in Healthcare: Compliance with HIPAA, GDPR, and emerging regulations. *International Journal of Emerging Trends in Computer Science and Information Technology*, 67–74. https://doi.org/DOI: 10.56472/ICCSAIML25-108

Sresth, V., Srivastava, A., & Tiwari, S. (2021). Balancing innovation and security: Advancing data privacy in the age of artificial intelligence and machine learning. *World Journal of Advanced Research and Reviews*, *9*(3), 377–390. DOI: 10.30574/wjarr.2021.9.3.0079

Talati, N. D. V.Dhruvitkumar V Talati. (2022). Enhancing data security and regulatory compliance in AI-driven cloud ecosystems: Strategies for advanced information governance. *World Journal of Advanced Research and Reviews*, *15*(3), 579–594. DOI: 10.30574/wjarr.2022.15.3.0905

Utomi, N. E., Osifowokan, N. S., Donkor, N. A., & Yowetu, N. I. A. (2024). Evaluating the Impact of Data Protection Compliance on AI Development and Deployment in the U.S. Health sector. *World Journal of Advanced Research and Reviews*, *24*(2), 1100–1110. DOI: 10.30574/wjarr.2024.24.2.3398

VOSViewer. (https://www.vosviewer.com/)

APPENDIX

List of Abbreviations

AI: Artificial Intelligence
ML: Machine Learning
DL: Deep Learning
GDPR: General Data Protection Regulation
CCPA: California Consumer Privacy Act
HIPAA: Health Insurance Portability and Accountability Act
PIPL: Personal Information Protection Law
GRC: Governance, Risk, and Compliance
AML: anti-money laundering
DLP: Data Loss Prevention
PET: Privacy-Enhancing Technologies
EU: European Union
PIH: Protected Health Information
ISMS: Information Security Management System
SOC 2: System and Organization Controls 2
TSC: Trust Services Criteria
NIST: National Institute of Standards and Technology
CSF: Cybersecurity Framework
OECD: Organisation for Economic Co-operation and Development
IBM: International Business Machines
NLP: Natural Language Processing
PPAI: privacy-preserving AI
DSPM: Data Security Posture Management
DLP: Data Loss Prevention
DSAR: Data Subject Access Request
SOX: Sarbanes-Oxley Act
GLBA: Gramm-Leach Bliley Act
KMS: Knowledge Management Systems
PII: Personally Identifiable Information
HER: Electronic Health Record
XAI: Explainable AI

Chapter 3
Strategizing EU and Indian Personal Data Governance in Mergers and Acquisitions:
Legal Insights and Corporate Accountability

Lekha Goyal
http://orcid.org/0009-0003-2755-3190
KLE Law College, Bengaluru, India & KLE Technological University, India

Vishnu Prasad
KLE Law College, Bengaluru, India & KLE Technological University, India

ABSTRACT

This paper analyses data governance frameworks in mergers and acquisitions (M&A) with specific focus on India and the European Union. It examines how India's Digital Personal Data Protection Act, 2023, addresses privacy and cross-border data transfer challenges, contrasting it with the EU's comprehensive regime under the GDPR, Data Governance Act, Data Act, and AI Act. Using comparative doctrinal analysis and stakeholder insights, the paper evaluates mechanisms such as Standard Contractual Clauses and Binding Corporate Rules, highlighting gaps in India's enforcement capacity, data ownership principles, and valuation. It further assesses the EU's emerging contractual fairness obligations and AI liability standards influencing M&A transactions. The study finally proposes statutory reforms

DOI: 10.4018/979-8-3373-6761-3.ch003

and harmonisation pathways to align India's legal framework with EU benchmarks for transparent, accountable, and sustainable data governance in cross-border corporate transactions.

1. INTRODUCTION

Data Governance, particularly in Mergers and Acquisitions (hereinafter referred as "M&A") has become a pivotal point for both regulatory bodies and corporations in recent years. Ever since, there is an acceleration in data transformation, there has also been a significant rise in exchanging of sensitive and proprietary data during M&A transactions, raising concerns about the data privacy, protection and compliance. The complexity of M&A transactions often involves combination of not only financial and operational assets but also vast amount of digital data. In India, where the regulatory frameworks such as the Information Technology Act, 2000 and the Companies Act, 2013 govern corporate transactions, ensuring data security is a challenge. Businesses must gear up to navigate risks related to data privacy, especially with introduction of new data protection law such as Digital Personal Data Protection Act, 2023, (hereinafter referred as "DPDP Act") which marks a significant step forward in regulating the data privacy. However, detailed rules and guidelines under this Act, is awaited, the principles concerning data protection, especially in the complex and often high-stakes environment of M&A transactions, remains largely undefined. Moreover, government notifications, reports from regulatory bodies and evolving standards from international practices continue to influence how corporations prepare for M&A transactions, particularly in relation to data governance. Therefore, the research aims to address gaps in India's current data governance framework, specific challenges that emerge during M&A transactions and navigation through these provisions require a fine balance between regulatory compliance and business necessities.

The three main frameworks that govern M&A in India are the Information Technology Act, 2002, the Companies Act, 2013 and the Competition Act, 2002, each of which address specific aspects of corporate transactions. However, these laws lack comprehensive provisions for safeguarding data privacy during M&A or any other corporate transactions for that matter, leaving the businesses defenceless to regulatory uncertainties. For instance, the Information Technology Act, 2002, provides limited guidance on data protection in contexts where data transfer is integral to corporate restructuring processes. This gap has been, however, only partially addresses by the Digital Personal Data Protection Act, 2023, which introduces modern principles of data protection such as purpose/usage limitation, lawful processing and data minimization. Yet, the absences of detailed rules under the DPDP Act, 2023 renders its practical application in M&A ambiguous, creating challenges for companies attempting to align their operations with emerging standards.

M&A transactions fundamentally involve complex combinations of data systems, where due diligence exposes sensitive information to potential vulnerabilities. The absence of explicit regulatory guidance during such process has been emphasized in cases like Verizon's acquisition of Yahoo, where the disclosure of pre-existing data breaches resulted in reputational damage and financial losses for the latter (Securities and Exchange Commission v. Yahoo, 2018). It highlights the need for robust data governance frameworks to protect stakeholders' interests and ensure compliance with privacy standards.

This paper focuses on critically examining the present landscape of data governance in M&A transactions within India, particularly in light of Digital Personal Data Protection Act, 2023. It aims to address the gaps in existing legal frameworks and assess how businesses can steer through the compliance challenges amidst regulatory uncertainties. The paper also evaluates the interplay between the DPDP Act and other statutory frameworks, emphasizing the necessity for coherent legal mechanisms to handle data-related complexities in high-stakes transactions.

2. EVOLUTION OF DATA GOVERNANCE IN MERGERS AND ACQUISITIONS

The concept of data governance in mergers and acquisitions has evolved significantly over the years, transitioning from mere rudimentary practices to complex regulatory framework. With the increase in digitalization of businesses, data has become a central asset in corporate transactions. This transformation necessitated vigorous governance mechanisms to address the unique challenges posed by data integration, security and compliance during M&A.

2.1 Early Phase: Partial Oversight

Initially, M&A transactions focused mainly on financial and operational due diligence with minimal attention to data governance. However, the absence of comprehensive digital frameworks led to fragmented approaches, where data handling practices varied significantly across industries and other jurisdictions. Thus, even in India, the Companies Act, 1956 and its successor, the Companies Act, 2013, provided the basics of legal structure for mergers, amalgamation and acquisitions (Companies Act, 1956; Companies Act, 2013). However, this statute did not account for complexities introduced by the digital age, where the data exchange and privacy concerns began to emerge as critical aspects of corporate transactions (Sundaram, 2004).

2.2 Rise of Privacy Concerns

The advent of digital technologies and the proliferation of personal data transformed the M&A landscape in the late 20th and early 21st centuries. Global incidents such as AOL-Time Warner Merger, where the data management failures led to operational inefficiencies, highlighted the need for structured data governance (Malone & Turner, 2010). In response, the jurisdictions worldwide began enacting data protection laws, with the European Union's Data Protection Directive (1995) marking the beginning (Data Protection Directive, 1995).

In India, the introduction of the Information Technology Act, 2000 marked the country's initial venture into the digital governance. Section 43A of the Act, which mandates compensation for failure to protect sensitive personal data, laid the base for privacy-focused regulations (Information Technology Act, 2000). Despite this, the IT Act remained insufficient for addressing the multifaceted challenges of data governance in M&A transactions such as data privacy and security concerns, data valuation, consent and risk management etc.

2.3 GDPR: A Global Influencer

The adoption of General Data Protection Regulation by the European Union in 2018, represented a shift in data governance. GDPR's extraterritorial application and stringent principles, such as accountability and data minimization, influenced corporate governance practices globally (General Data Protection Regulation, 2018). In India, The GDPR amongst other reasons such as rate of digitalization, *KS Puttaswamy v. Union of India* judgment etc, spurred discussions on modernizing domestic data protection laws, culminating in the drafting of the Personal Data Protection Bill, 2019 and its successor, the Digital Personal Data Protection Act, 2023 (Justice K.S. Puttaswamy v. Union of India, 2019).

2.4 Current Phase: Regulatory Integration

At present, data governance in M&A is characterized by attempts to integrate data protection principles into corporate law. The Companies Act, 2013 introduced provisions for amalgamations and mergers but did not explicitly address data governance (Companies Act, 2013). Similarly, the Competition Act, 2002 focused on preventing anti-competitive practices without considering the role of data in establishing market dominance (Competition Act, 2002).

Digital Personal Data Protection Act, 2023, too, though marks significant step forward, emphasizing lawful processing, purpose limitation and consent, its bare provisions lack clarity on implementation during M&A, particularly regarding data sharing and cross-border transfers. The absence of detailed rules under the DPDP Act has led to regulatory uncertainty, prompting businesses to rely on piecemeal interpretations of existing laws. Thus, the absence of a unified framework that integrates data protection with corporate and competition laws is a significant hurdle. Moreover, the lack of clear guidelines on cross-boarder data flows, data ownership post- merger and accountability during due diligence underscores the need for further reforms.

3. LEGAL CHALLENGES IN DATA GOVERNANCE WITH SPECIAL EMPHASIS ON CASE STUDIES AND EMERGING STRATEGIES FOR CORPORATE DATA ETHICS IN MERGERS AND ACQUISITIONS

The legal tests related with data governance in M&A arise from overlapping regulatory framework, ambiguous and uncertain statutory provisions and the absence of clear implementation of mechanisms. These challenges not only complicate compliance but also creates significant risks for business navigating M&A transactions. Data today, has emerged as both a strategic asset and a critical area of legal and ethical scrutiny. As corporate transactions involve extensive exchange and integration of data, the need to have robust mechanisms to address ethical, regulatory and operational challenged has intensified.

3.1 Ethical Complexities

M&A transactions involve the integration of vast amounts of data, encompassing customer information, operational records and intellectual property. However, without the comprehensive data governance frameworks, these transactions expose companies to significant ethical risks.

The Facebook-Whatsapp Merger is a case at point. The acquisition faced scrutiny for its implications on user privacy. Facebook initially assured users that Whatsapp's data sharing policies would remain unchanged only to alter them post-acquisition, enabling data integration without explicit user consent. This change attracted fines from regulators including 110 million euros from the European Commission for providing misleading information during the merger notification process (European Commission, 2017). However, India has made its stance clear and restricted Whatsapp from sharing data with other Meta entities (Mandayam, 2024). Thus, this case illustrates how insufficient transparency and deviation from commitments can result in regulatory backlash and reputational damage.

3.2 Regulatory Division

One of the foremost challenges is that of fragmentation of regulatory frameworks central to M&A in India. The Companies Act, 2013, that governs mergers, amalgamations and demergers, mainly focuses on procedural and structural aspects of corporate restructuring (Companies Act, 2013). Thus leaving out critical issues such as data sharing, retention etc to be addressed by the companies in their policies and agreements at their discretion. Similarly, the Information Technology Act, 2000 that includes provisions on data security and compensation for breaches, do not cater to the unique risks posed by M&A transactions. Furthermore, the Competition Act, 2002, which regulates anti-competitive practices fails to recognise data as one of the causes of market dominance (Information Technology Act, 2000; Competition Act, 2002). As a result, transactions involving the consolidation of data assets, especially those in digital economy, are not effectively examined. For example, cases like the Google-DoubleClick merger highlights the competitive risks posed by unregulated data consolidation (Case COMP/M.4731 – Google/DoubleClick, 2008).

3.3 Cross Border Data Transfers in M&A

The DPDP Act, 2023 doesn't clearly regulate cross-border transfers in the context of M&A, potentially leading to conflicts with foreign jurisdictions privacy laws. The Act should integrate provisions specifying permissible cross-border data transfer mechanisms, such as standard contractual clauses or binding corporate rules. Regulatory omission could be enhanced by requiring acquires to demonstrate compliance with these mechanisms as part of the court or tribunal approval process.

Cross-border data transfers remain one of the most contentious issues in M&A, particularly in transactions involving jurisdictions with divergent data protection laws. The Flipkart-Walmart acquisitions raised concerns about foreign access to sensitive consumer data, prompting debates on data localization (Saraswathy, 2019). This highlights the limitations of the then-existing legal frameworks such as the IT Act, 2000, in addressing cross-border data flows.

In Google-Fitbit case too, the parties faced regulatory scrutiny for its potential to exploit health data (Case M.9660 – Google/Fitbit, 2020). The European Commission raised concerns about Google leveraging Fitbit's data to strengthen its dominance in the digital advertising market. The merger was eventually approved but only under strict data protection commitments, illustrating the growing importance of such data ethics in mitigating antitrust risks.

3.4 Role of Data Ethics in Due Diligence and Data Breaches

The due diligence phase of M&A involves the allocation of sensitive data between parties revealing it to risks of unauthorised access or breaches. The DPDP Act, under Sections 4 and 5 mandates principles of purpose limitation and lawful processing but does not address the specificities of protecting data during due diligence. For instance, issues such as anonymization, secure data sharing protocols and breach notification requirements remain undefined (Srikrishna Committee, 2018). The inadequacy of safeguarding during due diligence has had a significant repercussion over the years, one of which is seen in Yahoo-Verizon case, where undisclosed data breaches reduced Yahoo's valuation by $350 million. Despite, the DPDP Act, the absence of provisions on mandatory breach notification adds to the challenge, leaving stakeholders exposed to financial and reputational risks (Securities and Exchange Commission v. Yahoo, 2018).

Due diligence phase of M&A is critical for identifying potential risks related to data breaches, unauthorised access or non-compliance. However, several high-profile mergers have demonstrated failures in this regard, underscoring the need for ethical diligence protocols.

For instance, the Marriott-Starwood merger case (Case M.7902 – Marriott International/Starwood Hotels & Resorts Worldwide, 2016). The merger saw a massive data breach that exposed the personal information of over 500 million guests, largely due to vulnerabilities inherited from Starwood's systems (Federal Trade Commission, 2024). This case emphasized the importance of evaluating the cybersecurity posture of both entities during due diligence.

3.5 Challenges in Valuation of Data Assets

The valuation of data as an asset in M&A transactions remains underdeveloped area in Indian law. Unlike the tangible or financial assets, data is inherently intangible and its valuation depends on various factors such as volume, quality and potential for monetization. Indian regulatory framework, currently, do not provide guidance on methodologies for such data valuation leaving companies to rely on subjective assessments. This leads to inconsistent practices and potential undervaluation or overvaluation, affecting stakeholders and regulatory oversight.

3.6 Lack of Clarity in Handling Voluntary Undertakings during M&A

The DPDP Act allows for voluntary undertakings under Section 32, enabling organisations to propose actions to address breaches and demonstrate compliance (Digital Personal Data Protection Act, 2023, s. 32). However, the Act does not clarify the status of such undertaking during corporate transactions like M&A. For instance, if an acquired company has an ongoing voluntary undertaking with the Board, ambiguity exists on whether the acquiring company inherits the obligations.

3.7 Emerging Strategies for Ethical Data Governance

AI and machine learning have become indispensable in managing the complexities of data governance. These technologies enable companies to perform comprehensive due diligence by identifying risks such as data breaches, compliance gaps and also the anomalies within datasets. AI tools can automate the categorization of sensitive data and assess its alignment with privacy laws, including principles of lawful processing and data minimization under the DPDP Act. Moreover, predictive analytics powered by AI can help assess the potential impact of integrating data assests on consumer privacy and regulatory compliance. Ethical AI frameworks ensure that these tools are used transparently and are free from algorithmic biases, aligning with corporate practices with the broader objectives of fairness and accountability.

Blockchain technology offers a decentralised and an immutable ledger system, thus making it a powerful tool for enhancing data integrity in M&A. By creating verifiable records of data transfers and access during transactions, blockchain ensures that data handling is both transparent and secure. This approach aligns with key data protection principles under the DPDP Act, such as ensuring accountability for data controllers. Blockchain also facilitates compliance with cross border data transfer requirements by providing an auditable trail of data movements. This is particularly relevant in jurisdictions where regulators demand real time oversight of data flows. By embedding compliance protocols in blockchain systems, companies can enhance their transparency and mitigate legal risks.

The use of secure sandboxing environments allows parties in M&A transactions to share data without exposing sensitive information to unauthorised access or breaches. Sandboxing involves creating isolated virtual environments where data can be assessed, processed, or analysed under strict controls. Advanced encryptions and anonymization techniques are applied to ensure that original data remains protected. This strategy not only mitigates risks but also enables complaints with the DPDP Act's requirement for data minimization and purpose limitation. Sandboxing also supports risk free data exploration, allowing companies to evaluate the value and risks of data assets without compromising security.

The establishment of complete governance framework that embed ethical principles into decision making processes is a growing trend in corporate data ethics. These frameworks are designed to provide a roadmap for managing data responsibly with the focus on transparency, accountability and stakeholder meeting. Corporate leadership plays a essential role in implementing these frameworks. By appointing chief data officers or data ethics officers, organisations can centralise responsibility for data governance and ensure that ethical considerations remain a priority. These leaders are tasked with integrating ethical standards into all phases of M&A from due diligence to post merger integration ensuring that data handling aligns with both regulatory requirements and public expectations. This has been done by Vistara and made know to please via a public notice published in newspaper (Gandhi & Nagpal, 2024).

Engaging with regulators early in M&A process has emerged as a proactive strategy for mitigating risks and ensuring compliance. This involves submitting detailed regulatory impact assessments, outlining how the transaction aligns with existing laws and addressing potential conflicts. By fostering open communications with authorities, companies can resolve ambiguities and streamline the approval process. This strategy also includes adopting industry standard mechanisms for cross border transfers such as, binding corporate rules or standard contractual clauses, which can be pre-approved by regulators to facilitate smoother integration processes.

Human centric governance prioritises the rights and interests of individuals affected by corporate data practises. This strategy emphasises user consent, Transparency and participatory approaches to decision making. By adopting human centric principles companies demonstrate a commitment to respecting privacy and fostering trust among stakeholders. Under this model, Companies may implement robust user education initiatives. Furthermore, integrating grievance at redressal mechanisms into corporate policies allows individuals to report misuse or violations effectively.

4. COMPARATIVE EU–INDIA REGULATORY FRAMEWORK FOR DATA GOVERNANCE IN MERGERS AND ACQUISITIONS

4.1 EU Regulatory Architecture and Comparative Analysis with India

The European Union has established a comprehensive regulatory ecosystem governing data protection and governance substantially surpassing India's current maturity level. The General Data Protection Regulation (GDPR), enforceable since

May 2018, applies extraterritorially to organisations processing personal data of EU residents regardless of establishment location. Non-compliance carries fines up to €20 million or four percent of annual global turnover, whichever is higher.

Complementing the GDPR, the EU Data Governance Act (2023) and the recently enacted EU Data Act (2024) establish mandatory data-sharing obligations and contractual fairness requirements unprecedented in global frameworks. The Data Act creates affirmative rights for users to access and share data from connected products, requiring data holders to enable third-party access in machine-readable formats. The EU AI Act (2024) introduces risk-based classification distinguishing prohibited AI systems, high-risk systems requiring conformity assessments, and minimal-obligation systems, with non-compliance exposing acquirers to fines up to €35 million or seven percent of turnover.

The GDPR's Chapter V explicitly regulates international data transfers through mechanisms including Standard Contractual Clauses (SCCs) and Binding Corporate Rules (BCRs). India's DPDP Act, 2023, by contrast, grants the central government broad discretionary authority under Section 16 to restrict cross-border transfers with minimal guidance on acceptable mechanisms or restriction criteria (Digital Personal Data Protection Act, 2023, s. 16). This ambiguity creates substantial compliance uncertainty for Indian multinational companies.

Binding Corporate Rules represent the "gold standard" for intra-group data transfers, approved by supervisory authorities and binding corporate entities to uniform protection standards worldwide. Standard Contractual Clauses provide alternatives for independent entities without requiring supervisory approval, accelerating transaction timelines. However, post-Schrems II requirements demand Transfer Impact Assessments evaluating importing countries' legal frameworks, particularly government surveillance laws. India's absence of comprehensive data localisation protections or surveillance safeguards equivalent to EU standards necessitates supplementary technical measures such as encryption or pseudonymisation (Schrems II, 2020).

The DPDP Act mandates data fiduciary consent for processing under Section 4 with limited exceptions, creating practical M&A challenges. During due diligence, buyers require customer and employee data access for business assessment; however, sharing without fresh data subject consent potentially violates Section 4. The GDPR's legitimate interests exception (Article 6(1)(f)) and contractual necessity framework provide greater clarity, extensively interpreted through Data Protection Authority guidance.

4.2 EU Data Act and AI Act: Implications for M&A Data Governance

The Data Act introduces unprecedented contractual fairness obligations in global B2B regulation. Article 13 prohibits unilaterally imposed contractual terms concerning data access, use, and liability that "grossly deviate from good commercial practice" and are "contrary to good faith and fair dealing." The Act establishes both automatically unfair terms (blacklist) and presumptively unfair terms (greylist).

Traditional M&A agreements allocate data-related liabilities exclusively to sellers with buyer indemnification. Under the Data Act, such allocation may be deemed unfair if excluding data holder liability for inadequate data quality. M&A confidentiality clauses preventing disclosed data disclosure to third parties conflict with Data Act switching obligations requiring data holders enable users to share data with competing service providers. For technology acquisitions, if an acquirer purchases an Indian SaaS platform processing EU user data, the Data Act mandates acquirer-enabled data access and platform switching—negating exclusive data control motivating many acquisitions.

The EU AI Act distinguishes providers (AI system developers), deployers (AI system users), and importers/distributors by lifecycle role. High-risk AI systems—including those for employment decisions, credit assessments, and critical infrastructure—require both providers and deployers to implement stringent obligations. Providers must conduct conformity assessments, maintain technical documentation, and implement quality management systems. Deployers must assign human oversight, monitor operation, ensure input data quality, and maintain logs for at least six months.

Unlike the GDPR's controller liability allocation, the AI Act shifts burden-of-proof through rebuttable causality presumptions. Under the proposed AI Liability Directive, if victims establish compliance failures with likely causal links to harm, courts presume non-compliance caused damage. This reverses traditional tort law, requiring defendants disprove causality rather than plaintiffs proving it—substantially expanding corporate exposure. M&A due diligence requires comprehensive AI system audits identifying high-risk systems and verifying compliance; post-closing liability exposure necessitates explicit indemnification covering AI Act obligations and Directive-based liability.

4.3 Enforcement Landscape: GDPR vs Indian Regulatory Maturity

The GDPR's Data Protection Authorities possess expansive investigatory powers: unannounced inspections, documentation demands, employee interviews, and binding corrective orders. DPAs proactively initiate investigations based on complaints, media reports, or independent initiatives—not merely responding to formal complaints. Twenty years of DPA enforcement establish extensive jurisprudence, guidance, and predictable treatment patterns. Precedent fines demonstrate massive exposure: Meta €1.2 billion (2023), Amazon €746 million (2021), TikTok €530 million (2025). Even de minimis compliance lapses generate substantial financial exposure affecting large user populations; M&A acquirers inherit target companies' historical violations, with investigations commencing years post-acquisition, rendering representations and warranties ineffective.

India's nascent Digital Personal Data Protection Authority, pending establishment, will eventually possess comparable powers but lacks operational precedents and detailed procedural rules. This uncertainty contrasts sharply with GDPR's established framework enabling organisations predict regulatory treatment.

The DPDP Act lacks explicit provisions addressing post-merger data ownership, valuation methodologies, and liability allocation for pre-acquisition breaches discovered post-closing (Digital Personal Data Protection Act, 2023). Absent clear mechanisms for data transfer documentation and audit trails—mandated by GDPR through processing records and Data Processing Agreements—Indian companies remain vulnerable to regulatory challenges. Section 32's Voluntary Undertakings enable breach-correction proposals avoiding enforcement, but the Act fails clarifying whether undertakings bind acquiring companies or whether buyers inherit pre-acquisition undertakings. The GDPR provides extensive guidance on successor liability and corporate restructuring, establishing clear frameworks for assigning data protection obligations during mergers.

Neither jurisdiction explicitly regulates data valuation methodologies—a critical gap affecting M&A transactions. The Data Act implicitly addresses valuation through fair-value pricing: Article 6 requires remuneration reflecting "fair and reasonable" compensation covering only direct costs plus proportionate profit, prohibiting monopolistic rent extraction. The DPDP Act provides no valuation guidance, leaving companies reliant on subjective assessments. Data valuation frequently represents material purchase price adjustments; post-closing determinations of non-compliance or restrictions create significant write-downs.

5. DATA ANALYSIS AND INTERPRETATION

For this research, both qualitative and quantitative mode of data collection has been identified. For qualitative mode, structured interviews and case studies are used whereas for quantitative mode, web-based survey via google forms is used. It serves as a practical and insightful data collection method, especially for exploring nuanced perspectives on data governance in mergers and acquisitions under the DPDP Act, 2023. Key stakeholders are corporate lawyers, data privacy experts, compliance officers, judicial officers and law students who can offer real- time insights into the impact and limitations of the Act's bare provisions in the absence of concrete rules. This approach aligns well with the research objectives, as it enables us to explore gaps in compliance, understand stakeholder concerns, and gather empirical data, which will support the development of recommendations tailored to the Indian corporate context.

The analysis of the data collected from 69 stakeholders regarding data governance in mergers and acquisitions in the context of the Digital Personal Data Protection Act, 2023, reveals a multifaceted landscape of understanding of data governance in M&A, compliance challenges and gaps, and recommendations.

5.1 Understanding Data Governance in M&A

Relevant questions integrated and response trend/key responses:

1. *On a scale of 1 to 5, how critical do you think data governance is in M&A transactions?* Response Trend: 85% rated it as 'five-extremely critical' with a minimal share below 'four'.
2. Which aspect of data governance do you find most challenging in M&A transactions?

   Response Trend: 40% cited "integration of data systems" as the top challenge.
3. Are you familiar with the concept of data governance and corporate transactions such as M&A?

Response Trend: 90% confirmed familiarity, with 10% having partial knowledge.

Data governance has emerged as a cornerstone of successful mergers and acquisitions in today's data driven world. As business is increasingly rely on digital assets, managing sensitive data effectively during M&A transactions is no longer optional, it is an operational and legal necessity.

The overwhelming consensus among respondents highlights that the data governance is critical in M&A transactions. It encompasses the policies, procedures and systems used to manage and protect data assets throughout the deal lifecycle. In particular, the stakeholders pointed to its importance in mitigating risks such as data breaches, ensuring compliance with legal framework and facilitating seamless integration of digital infrastructure.

Figure 1.

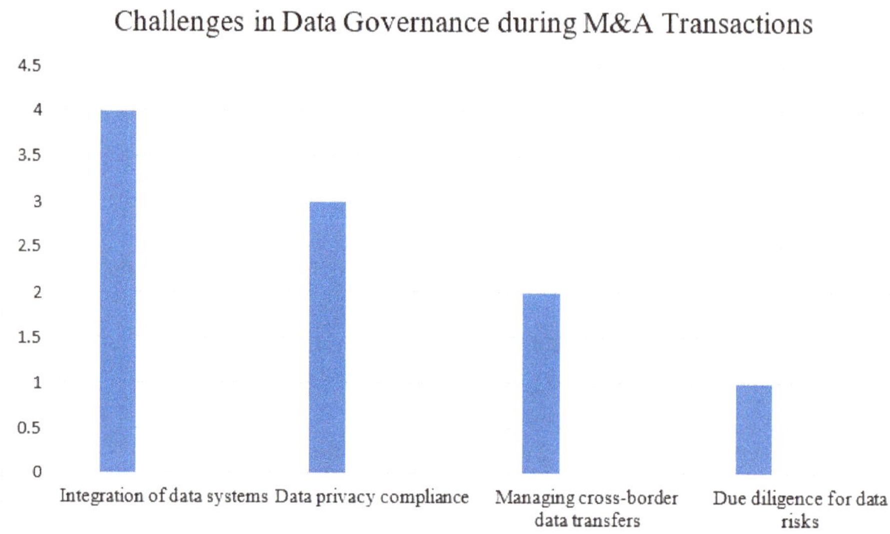

The integration of desperate data systems was identified as the most significant challenge, especially in deals involving entities with different technological architectures and privacy protocols. Merging systems often exposes vulnerabilities, including outdated cyber security measures or incompatible IT structures, which can jeopardise the success of the transaction.

Ensuring compliance with data privacy laws, such as the DPDP Act 2023 in India is a precious issue. Respondents emphasised the high stakes involved in adhering to legal requirements, particularly during the due diligence phase, where the risk of exposing sensitive information is greatest. Absence of clear regulatory guidance under the DPDP Act exacerbates these concerns.

Managing cross border data transfer is another complex area, especially in transactions involving multinational entities. Regulatory disparities between jurisdictions complicate the legal transfer of data, requiring meticulous planning to avoid penalties and operational delays.

Conducting thorough due diligence to identify and address data risks before finalising a transaction is crucial. Respondents highlighted that robust due diligent practises ensured that data governance challenges are identified early, enabling companies to develop strategies for integration and compliance.

5.2 Compliance Challenges and Gaps

Relevant questions integrated and response trend/key responses:

4. Do you think the absence of rules under the DPDP Act impacts data governance in M&A transactions?

Response Trend: 70% agreed it significantly impacts compliance.

5. What specific challenges do you foresee for companies in aligning with the DPDP Act during M&A transactions?

Key Responses: Ambiguity in legal obligations (50%), lack of enforcement mechanisms (30%)

6. In your opinion, do existing laws (for example, IT Act, Companies Act) sufficiently address data protection during mergers and acquisitions transactions?

Response Trend: 65% rated them as "insufficient"

The complaints landscape for data protection in M&A transactions remains fraught with challenges and gaps, stemming from regulatory ambiguity and insufficient enforcement mechanisms. These issues play significant burdens on businesses attempting to navigate complex legal and operational requirements.

The absence of detailed rules under the DPDP Act has left companies struggling to interpret its provisions. This regulatory vacuum has introduced uncertainties about how the Act's principles such as purpose limitation, lawful processing and cross border data transfer will apply during M&A transactions. Respondents expressed concerns over lack of clarity, particularly regarding the operationalization of these principles in high stake deals.

India's existing legal landscape, comprising the Information Technology Act, 2000, the Companies act 2013 and the Competition Act 2002, fails to offer an integrated approach to data governance in M&A. For instance, firstly, the IT Act while addressing cyber security provides limited guidance on handling sensitive data during corporate restructuring. Secondly, the Company Act focuses on procedural aspects of mergers without considering data privacy or integration complexities. And thirdly, The Competition Act does not adequately account for the competitive risks possessed by the data consolidation. This fragmented regulatory environment compels businesses to adapt piecemeal strategies, increasing compliance burden and risks.

Respondents highlighted the absence of robust enforcement mechanisms under the DPDP Act as a critical challenge. Without the clear guidelines or penalties, businesses face difficulties ensuring accountability for data governance failures this gap also complicates the assessment of compliance risks during due diligence as of now.

M&A transactions often involve reconciling differing data governance policies between the merging entities. The incompatibility between India's emerging regulatory standards and existing frameworks such as GDPR and cross border deals further complicates compliance efforts. For example, multinational deals must navigate overlapping get desperate obligations such as data localization under the DPDP Act versus data transfer requirements under GDPR.

Figure 2.

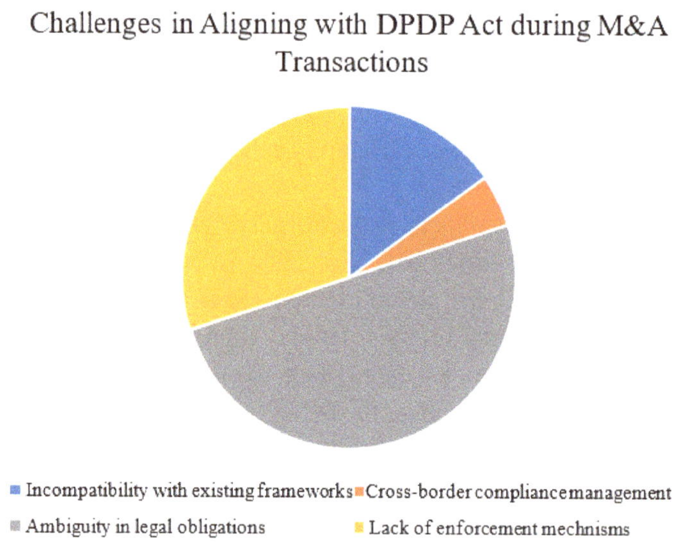

5.3 Stakeholder Recommendations

Relevant questions integrated and response trend/key responses:

7. What measures do you believe companies can proactively take to mitigate data governance risks before the DPDP Act rules are framed?

Key Responses: Conducting data audits (40%) and enhancing contractual safeguards (25%)

8. How can due diligence and data governance strategies be enhanced in M&A transactions to prevent incidents like Marriott Starwood data breach?

Key Responses: Cross-functional teams, risk assessments, robust frameworks.

9. Based on your experience, how can the DPDP Act be practically implemented in M&A transactions to balance corporate accountability and business efficiency?

Key Responses: Clear operational guidelines and continuous monitoring mechanisms.

The recommendations provided by respondents in the questionnaire focus on practical measures that businesses can take to mitigate data governance risks during mergers and acquisitions transactions, particularly amidst the evolving regulatory landscape.

Figure 3.

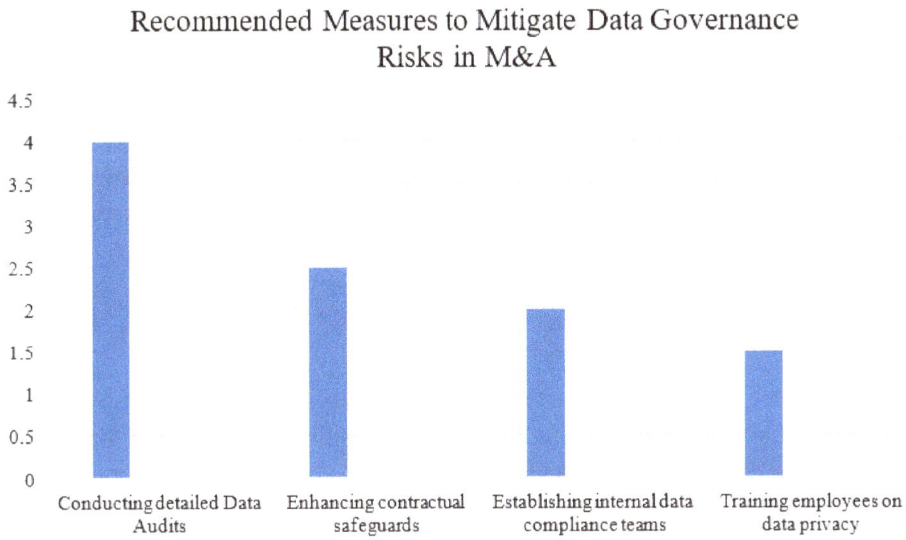

The most widely recommended measure was performing comprehensive audits of data assets before and during M&A transactions. Respondents emphasized that these audits should identify sensitive data, evaluate protection mechanisms, and assess compliance risks, particularly for cross-border data transfers. Audits also help ensure companies are aware of the data they are acquiring, along with associated liabilities.

Strengthening contractual agreements between merging parties is critical for ensuring clarity and accountability in data governance. Recommendations included incorporating clauses to, define ownership of data assets post-merger; establish responsibilities for data protection; and include penalties for data breaches or non-compliance. Such safeguards provide a structured framework for managing data governance expectations and mitigating risks.

Respondents highlighted the importance of forming dedicated compliance teams to oversee data governance during M&A transactions. These teams are tasked with coordinating across legal, IT, and operational divisions to ensure a consistent approach to regulatory compliance

and risk management. While particularly relevant for larger corporations, smaller organizations could benefit by outsourcing these roles temporarily during critical transactions.

Respondents stressed that employee awareness is crucial for maintaining compliance. Training programs should focus on understanding basic data protection laws, including the DPDP Act; recognizing risks like phishing or unauthorized access during M&A; and adopting best practices for handling sensitive data securely.

For effective due diligence, respondents suggested creating cross-functional teams comprising legal, IT, compliance, and security experts. These teams can evaluate risks associated with the target company's data systems, ensuring vulnerabilities are identified and addressed before integration.

Respondents recommended that companies develop clear guidelines to align their operations with data governance requirements under the DPDP Act. Establishing mechanisms for continuous monitoring of compliance efforts post-merger was also emphasized to maintain accountability.

5.4 Findings

The responses lighten a dynamic yet challenging interplay between data governance practices and the complexities of mergers and acquisitions. It is evident that while stakeholders acknowledge the transformative potential of robust data governance, the practical application often falls short due to systemic and regulatory constraints. One of the most striking observations is the reactive nature of many organizations' approaches, prioritizing data audits and compliance measures only after issues arise during M&A transactions. This approach indicates a broader gap in strategic foresight, where businesses are often unprepared to integrate comprehensive data governance frameworks into their core operational planning before engaging in high-stakes transactions. Additionally, the fragmented regulatory environment, particularly in India, creates a labyrinth of legal obligations that companies must navigate. The absence of detailed rules under the Digital Personal Data Protection Act, 2023 leaves organizations in a precarious position, relying heavily on interim interpretations of the Act's provisions. This regulatory uncertainty not only hampers compliance but also diminishes the ability of companies to foster trust among stakeholders during deal-making.

Equally significant is the disparity between larger, resource-rich organizations and smaller enterprises when it comes to preparedness for data governance. Larger entities with established

compliance teams and access to advanced technologies have the upper hand in addressing data governance challenges, leaving smaller firms to grapple with basic measures that often fail to address the complexities of cross-border transactions, legacy system integrations, and data privacy compliance. Furthermore, a noticeable gap exists in the emphasis on cultural integration alongside technological and legal considerations. Respondents often pointed to the challenges of merging not just systems but also differing organizational attitudes toward data governance. This cultural disconnect exacerbates vulnerabilities, especially in multinational transactions where regional regulatory nuances demand a nuanced approach. Thus, the responses emphasize the urgent need for a paradigm shift, one where organizations view data governance as a proactive and strategic imperative, supported by collaborative efforts between regulators, industries, and stakeholders to create a cohesive, forward-looking compliance ecosystem.

6. CONCLUSION

It follows from the above discussion, that the critical intersection of data governance and mergers and acquisitions in India, particularly in light of the evolving regulatory landscape marked by the Digital Personal Data Protection Act, 2023. As corporations navigate and strategize the complexities of M&A transactions, the absence of comprehensive guidelines under this new legislation presents significant challenges. The findings reveal that while the DPDP Act lays a foundational framework for data protection, its current provisions lack the specificity required to address the multifaceted nature of data governance in corporate transactions.

The paper establishes that the hypothesis, asserting that the bare provisions of the Digital Personal Data Protection Act, 2023 are insufficient to address data governance challenges in mergers and acquisitions, holds true. Through critical analysis and stakeholder insights, it answers the research questions by identifying gaps in current frameworks like the IT Act, the Companies Act, and the Competition Act, and their alignment with DPDP Act principles, thus revealing ambiguities and compliance challenges in M&A transactions. The objectives have been met by evaluating the alignment of existing laws with data governance requirements, highlighting challenges such as cross-border data transfers and valuation of data assets, and proposing practical measures for compliance and accountability. The mixed-methods approach of qualitative interviews, case studies, and surveys proved effective in validating the hypothesis, providing empirical and doctrinal evidence to demonstrate that a cohesive and proactive framework is essential for mitigating data governance risks and ensuring robust regulatory compliance in the context of M&A.

6.1 Suggestions

1. Amendment to existing laws –
   A. The Companies Act, 2013
      a. Introduce clauses under Section 230 to mandate data ownership transfer protocols, retention and sharing guidelines for data during mergers and disclosure of data breaches during due diligence. These additions will ensure clarity on the handling of data as an asset during M&A, protecting stakeholders and ensuring seamless regulatory compliance, as highlighted by cases like Yahoo-Verizon.
      b. Introduce a new Section 230A immediately after Section 230, mandating valuation guidelines for data assets in M&A. Specify methodologies based on data sensitivity, compliance costs and monetization potential. Additionally, include mandatory third-party audits for high stakes mergers. It will transparency in data valuation and reduce disputes during integration, drawing parallels with the EU's approach in cases like Facebook-WhatsApp.
   B. The Information Technology Act, 2000 – Expand Section 43A to explicitly include obligations for anonymization of sensitive data during M&A, mandatory adoption of secure data-sharing protocols (e.g., encryption) and breach notification within 72 hours during M&A transactions. This amendment addresses vulnerabilities during due diligence and mitigates risks of financial and reputational damage, as evidenced in the Yahoo-Verizon and Marriott-Starwood cases.
   C. The Competition Act, 2002 - Expand Section 4 to include evaluation of data consolidation as a non-price factor contributing to market dominance, this would prevent anti-competitive practices resulting from unregulated data consolidation, as seen in Google-DoubleClick and Google-Fitbit mergers.
   D. The Digital Personal Data Protection Act, 2023 –
      a. Add a sub-clause under Section 32 clarifying that voluntary undertakings given by an acquired company can be renegotiated or modified post-merger. This is to ensure operational continuity and compliance in scenarios where acquiring companies inherit obligations from the target entity, as highlighted in the paper.

b. Introduce Section 35A mandating companies involved in M&A to submit regulatory impact assessments. These assessments must detail compliance with DPDP Act principles like lawful processing and purpose limitation an address potential cross-border data transfer issues. This will align M&A practices with regulatory requirements and streamline approval processes, reducing ambiguities in compliance.
c. Add a sub-clause in Section 5 requiring anonymization of sensitive data before sharing during M&A due diligence. This is to protect sensitive information during high-risk stages of M&A and prevent breaches, as emphasized in stakeholder responses and past incidents like Marriott-Starwood.

2. Adopt Comprehensive Data Governance Protocols - Companies must implement robust data-sharing protocols using encryption, sandboxing environments, and anonymization during M&A. Blockchain should be used to log immutable records of data exchanges for transparency and accountability. AI-driven tools can assist in automating audits and risk assessments. These measures reduce risks of breaches, ensure lawful processing, and align with global data protection standards.
3. Develop Cross-Border and Compliance Frameworks - Adopt binding corporate rules (BCRs) or standard contractual clauses (SCCs) for cross-border data transfers. Establish compliance teams comprising legal, IT, and cybersecurity experts to monitor adherence to laws like DPDP Act and GDPR. Submit regulatory impact assessments (RIAs) pre-merger to address potential risks and streamline approval. These frameworks provide clarity, mitigate legal conflicts, and ensure smoother multinational operations.
4. Promote Data Ethics and Employee Awareness - Enforce corporate data ethics policies emphasizing user consent, transparency, and accountability. Conduct regular training sessions to educate employees on secure data handling and compliance with data protection laws like the DPDP Act. Ethical governance fosters trust, while training minimizes internal risks and strengthens overall compliance.
5. Utilize Advanced Technology for Data Integration and Security - Leverage AI for identifying risks, ensuring data minimization, and predicting the impact of integrating data systems. Employ blockchain for secure and transparent handling of sensitive information. Establish data valuation practices to ensure accurate integration assessments. Advanced technology enhances precision, supports regulatory compliance, and optimizes the value and security of data assets in M&A.
6. Harmonisation Recommendations - To facilitate harmonised EU-India M&A data governance, India should: (1) amend the DPDP Act establishing explic-

it cross-border transfer mechanisms equivalent to GDPR SCCs/BCRs with presumptively lawful transfer mechanisms approved by the Data Protection Authority, restricting transfers only upon demonstrating compelling public policy reasons; (2) establish an Adequacy Declaration framework whereby jurisdictions meeting specified standards receive recognition, simplifying transfers without transfer-specific contractual mechanisms; (3) incorporate explicit AI governance provisions equivalent to the EU AI Act's classification framework and deployer obligations, addressing regulatory arbitrage risks; (4) codify data ownership and valuation principles in corporate law statutes (Companies Act amendments) establishing standardised valuation methodologies incorporating data sensitivity, compliance costs, and monetisation potential; and (5) establish mechanisms enabling Indian companies to obtain BCR-equivalent status recognised by EU supervisory authorities for multinational intra-group transfers, potentially through bilateral arrangements with EU authorities whereby GDPR-equivalent frameworks receive mutual recognition

6.2 Path Towards Ethical Data Governance

As we stand on the brink of a new era in data protection, it is imperative for legal professionals, policymakers, and corporate leaders to collaborate towards creating a coherent legal framework that effectively addresses the complexities of data management in M&A. The future demands not just adherence to regulations but a commitment to ethical data stewardship that prioritizes privacy and accountability.

As Albert Einstein once said, "In the middle of difficulty lies opportunity." This sentiment resonates profoundly within the realm of corporate transactions today. By embracing the challenges posed by evolving data governance laws, organizations have the opportunity to innovate and lead in responsible data practices, ultimately fostering trust among stakeholders and paving the way for sustainable growth.

REFERENCES

Companies Act. (1956).

Companies Act. (2013).

Competition Act. (2002).

Digital Personal Data Protection Act. (2023). (India).

European Commission. (2017, May 18). Mergers: Commission fines Facebook 110 million euros for providing misleading information about WhatsApp takeover. https://ec.europa.eu/commission/presscorner/detail/en/ip_17_1369

Federal Trade Commission. (2024, October 9). FTC takes action against Marriott and Starwood over multiple data breaches. https://www.ftc.gov/news-events/news/press-releases/2024/10/ftc-takes-action-against-marriott-starwood-over-multiple-data-breaches

Gandhi, A., & Nagpal, N. (2024, August 16). Transfer of data in M&A deals: Best practices. *SS Rana & Co. Advocates*. https://ssrana.in/articles/merger-acquisition-deals-transfer-data/

General Data Protection Regulation. (2018). Regulation (EU) 2016/679 of the European Parliament and of the Council of 27 April 2016, OJ L 119, 4.5.2016, p. 1–88.

Google/DoubleClick. (2008). Case COMP/M.4731, Commission decision C 927 (European Commission).

Google/Fitbit. (2020). Case M.9660, Commission decision C 9105 (European Commission)

Information Technology Act. (2000). (India).

Justice K.S. Puttaswamy v. Union of India, (2019) 1 SCC 1 (India).

Malone, D., & Turner, J. (2010). The merger of AOL and Time Warner: A case study. *Journal of the International Academy for Case Studies*, *16*(7).

Mandayam, N. (2024, November 18). India restricts WhatsApp sharing data with other Meta entities, imposes 25.4 million dollar fine. *Reuters*.

Marriott International/Starwood Hotels & Resorts Worldwide. (2016). Case M.7902, Commission decision C 4097 (European Commission).

Regulation (EU) 2023/2854 (2023). of the European Parliament and of the Council of 13 December 2023 on harmonised rules on fair access to and use of data (Data Act), OJ L 363, 22.12.2023, p. 1–115.

Regulation (EU) 2024/1689 (2024). of the European Parliament and of the Council of 13 June 2024 laying down harmonised rules on artificial intelligence (AI Act), OJ L 188, 12.7.2024, p. 1–120.

Saraswathy, B. (2019). The Flipkart–Walmart deal: A look into competition and other related issues. *Antitrust Bulletin*, *64*(1), 136–147. DOI: 10.1177/0003603X18823619

Schrems, M. (2020). Facebook Ireland Limited v. Maximilian Schrems (Schrems II), Case C-311/18, ECLI:EU:C:2020:559 (Court of Justice of the European Union).

Securities and Exchange Commission v. Yahoo, SEC Release No. 33-10485 (2018).

Srikrishna Committee. (2018). *A free and fair digital economy: Protecting privacy, empowering Indians*. Government of India.

Sundaram, A. (2004). Mergers and acquisitions and corporate governance. In *Advances in mergers & acquisitions*. DOI: 10.1016/S1479-361X(04)03009-1

Chapter 4
MSME Financial Standards as a Governance Framework for Trustworthy Artificial Intelligence in Accounting

Sinta Ramaiyanti
http://orcid.org/0000-0001-6060-5413
Riau University, Indonesia

Vera Oktari
http://orcid.org/0000-0002-2212-6355
Riau University, Indonesia

Mayla Khoiriyah
http://orcid.org/0000-0002-9849-7291
Riau University, Indonesia

Lila Anggraini
Riau University, Indonesia

Nurrahma Dewi
Riau University, Indonesia

Ulfa Afifah
http://orcid.org/0000-0001-5473-6329
Riau University, Indonesia

ABSTRACT

Artificial intelligence is transforming accounting practice, taking over tasks from bookkeeping to forecasting with a speed that once seemed impossible. Yet efficiency alone does not resolve enduring worries about fairness, transparency, and accountability. International frameworks such as the OECD AI Principles and the EU AI Act set high-level aspirations, but they are often too abstract for the realities of micro, small, and medium-sized enterprises (MSMEs), especially in emerging economies.

DOI: 10.4018/979-8-3373-6761-3.ch004

This chapter argues that the simplified standards already familiar to MSMEs—rooted in prudence, reliability, comparability, and transparency—can be reinterpreted as a practical governance pathway for AI. By aligning these commitments with fairness, explainability, and auditability, sector-specific rules offer a means to anchor trust in digital tools. At the same time, the chapter emphasizes that standards alone cannot suffice, and that hybrid models integrating legal, ethical, and sociotechnical safeguards will be essential.

1. INTRODUCTION

Accordingly, this chapter conceptualizes governance not at the level of algorithmic systems themselves but at the level of AI-enabled accounting outputs as they enter standardized financial representations. Over the past decade, artificial intelligence (AI) has evolved from a peripheral technological innovation to a central infrastructural component of contemporary accounting systems. Advances in machine learning, natural language processing, and large-scale data analytics have enabled the automation of bookkeeping, continuous transaction monitoring, and the deployment of predictive models that inform financial decision-making (Kokina & Davenport, 2017; Sutton et al., 2016). Accounting functions traditionally grounded in professional judgment and rule-based procedures are increasingly mediated by algorithmic systems, reshaping how financial information is produced, validated, and interpreted within organizations.

This transformation has profound implications for the governance of accounting information. Accounting has historically served as a foundational institution of economic trust, providing standardized representations of organizational performance that enable coordination among managers, investors, creditors, regulators, and other stakeholders. The credibility of accounting information rests on principles such as transparency, consistency, auditability, and accountability, institutionalized through accounting standards and professional oversight mechanisms (Bhimani et al., 2019). As AI systems become embedded in accounting processes, these foundational principles are increasingly mediated by algorithmic logic, raising critical questions about how trust is maintained when financial judgments are partially delegated to machines.

Scholars have begun to recognize that AI adoption in accounting is not merely a technical shift but an institutional one. While AI-enabled systems promise efficiency gains, reduced errors, and enhanced analytical capacity, they also introduce new risks tied to opacity, bias, and the diffusion of accountability (Benke & Pelger, 2021; Power, 2021). Algorithmic decision-making systems often rely on complex models whose internal operations are difficult to interpret, challenging the traditional requirement that accounting outputs be explainable and verifiable. In this context, trust in accounting information can no longer be assumed to derive solely from professional expertise or compliance with formal rules; it must also be actively governed in relation to algorithmic processes.

These governance challenges are particularly acute for micro, small, and medium-sized enterprises (MSMEs). MSMEs constitute the vast majority of business entities worldwide and play a critical role in employment generation, innovation, and economic resilience, particularly in developing and emerging economies (OECD, 2019; Asian Development Bank, 2023). Despite their economic significance, MSMEs typically operate with constrained resources, limited institutional capacity, and lower levels of technological governance maturity. As AI-powered accounting tools become increasingly accessible through cloud-based platforms and software-as-a-service models, MSMEs are adopting these technologies without necessarily possessing the expertise or infrastructure required to govern them effectively.

The adoption of AI in MSME accounting contexts presents a paradox. On the one hand, AI-enabled systems offer MSMEs opportunities to professionalize accounting practices, improve compliance, and enhance decision-making. On the other hand, the opacity and complexity of algorithmic systems risk undermining the very trust that accounting standards are designed to foster. Unlike large corporations, MSMEs rarely have dedicated compliance units, internal audit functions, or AI ethics committees to oversee algorithmic decision-making. As a result, AI governance in MSMEs often remains implicit, fragmented, or entirely absent, creating vulnerabilities in the production and interpretation of financial information (Moll & Yigitbasioglu 2019).

In response to these challenges, a growing body of literature on trustworthy AI emphasizes governance frameworks that ensure transparency, accountability, fairness, and human oversight throughout the AI lifecycle (European Commission High-Level Expert Group on AI, 2019; National Institute of Standards and Technology, 2023). However, much of this literature assumes organizational contexts with high governance capacity, advanced technical expertise, and substantial regulatory support. These assumptions limit the applicability of existing AI governance models for MSMEs, where governance solutions must be practical, scalable, and embedded within existing organizational routines rather than imposed as separate regulatory structures.

Accounting standards, particularly those designed for MSMEs, remain an under-explored institutional resource in this context. MSME financial reporting standards are explicitly formulated to address informational asymmetry, limited managerial capacity, and heterogeneous enforcement environments. By prescribing clear rules for recognition, measurement, documentation, and disclosure, these standards translate the abstract principles of transparency and accountability into operational practices that shape everyday accounting behavior (Sian & Roberts, 2009; Devi et al., 2019). In doing so, they function not only as technical reporting guidelines but also as governance mechanisms that structure how trust is produced and maintained in economic exchanges.

Despite this alignment, existing research has largely treated AI governance and accounting standards as separate domains. Studies on AI in accounting have focused on adoption drivers, technological capabilities, and professional transformation, often treating governance issues as secondary or external concerns (Appelbaum et al., 2017; Sutton et al., 2016). Conversely, scholarship on AI governance has emphasized ethical principles, regulatory frameworks, and societal impacts, while engaging only sparingly with sector-specific institutional infrastructures, such as accounting standards (Cath et al., 2018). This separation has led to a fragmented understanding of how AI-enabled accounting systems can be governed in practice, particularly in MSME contexts.

This chapter addresses this gap by arguing that MSME financial standards can serve as an institutional governance framework for trustworthy AI in accounting. Rather than proposing new AI-specific regulations or ethical guidelines, the chapter conceptualizes existing MSME accounting standards as rule-based constraints that shape algorithmic behavior within accounting systems. By embedding AI governance within familiar, enforceable reporting frameworks, this approach offers a pragmatic pathway to align AI-enabled accounting practices with principles of transparency, accountability, and trust, without imposing disproportionate burdens on resource-constrained organizations.

In doing so, the chapter makes three core contributions. First, it reframes AI governance in accounting as an institutional challenge rather than a purely technical or ethical one. Second, it highlights the governance potential of MSME financial standards as mechanisms to constrain algorithmic decision-making and preserve human accountability. Third, it provides a conceptual foundation for integrating AI governance into everyday accounting practice, offering insights relevant to MSMEs, auditors, regulators, and standard setters operating in diverse institutional environments.

By situating trustworthy AI within the institutional logic of accounting standards, this chapter contributes to broader debates about how trust in algorithmic systems can be cultivated through existing governance infrastructures. In the context of MSMEs, where governance capacity is inherently limited, such integration is not merely desirable but necessary to ensure that the adoption of AI in accounting strengthens rather than undermines the foundations of economic trust.

The chapter adopts a conceptual and institutional analysis rather than an empirical testing approach, consistent with the objectives of theory-building in accounting governance research.

2. ARTIFICIAL INTELLIGENCE IN ACCOUNTING AND GOVERNANCE CHALLENGES

2.1 The Evolution of Artificial Intelligence in Accounting Practice

The adoption of artificial intelligence in accounting has progressed through several distinct phases over the past decade. Early applications focused on rule-based automation, such as robotic process automation (RPA) for routine bookkeeping, invoice processing, and reconciliation. These systems were designed to replicate predefined accounting rules, delivering efficiency gains without fundamentally altering decision-making authority (Sutton et al., 2016). As machine learning techniques matured and data availability increased, AI applications in accounting expanded beyond automation into pattern recognition, predictive analytics, and continuous auditing.

Contemporary AI-enabled accounting systems increasingly rely on supervised and unsupervised learning models to classify transactions, detect anomalies, and generate forecasts that inform managerial and financial decisions (Appelbaum et al., 2017; Kokina & Davenport, 2017). These systems do not merely execute accounting rules; they infer patterns from historical data and adapt over time. As a result, accounting outputs are no longer solely the product of explicit professional judgment or standardized procedures but are partially shaped by probabilistic models whose logic may not be fully transparent to users.

This evolution has significant implications for the institutional role of accounting. Traditionally, accounting has functioned as a rule-governed system grounded in codified standards and professional oversight. AI-driven accounting systems, by contrast, introduce data-driven, adaptive, and context-sensitive decision-making. While these capabilities enhance analytical power, they also blur the boundary between calculation and judgment, raising questions about how accountability and trust are maintained when financial representations are produced through algorithmic inference rather than explicit rule application (Power 2021).

2.2 Algorithmic Opacity and the Challenge of Explainability

One of the most widely discussed governance challenges in AI-enabled accounting systems is algorithmic opacity. Many machine learning models, particularly those based on complex architectures such as deep neural networks, operate in ways that are difficult to interpret, even for their designers (Burrell, 2016; Guidotti et al., 2019). In accounting contexts, this opacity conflicts with long-standing professional and regulatory expectations that financial information be explainable, traceable, and verifiable.

Explainability is not merely a technical preference in accounting; it is a foundational requirement for auditability and accountability. Financial statements must be examinable, challengeable, and defendable by preparers, auditors, and regulators. When AI systems generate accounting classifications or estimates without transparent reasoning, it becomes difficult to assess whether outputs comply with applicable standards or reflect acceptable professional judgment. This tension is particularly acute in areas involving estimates, provisions, and risk assessments, where AI outputs may significantly influence reported financial positions (Benke & Pelger 2021).

Scholars have noted that opacity in AI systems can shift accountability away from human actors, creating an "accountability gap" in algorithmic decision-making (Raisch & Krakowski, 2021). In accounting, such gaps undermine the institutional trust that financial reporting is intended to provide. If preparers cannot meaningfully explain how AI-assisted outputs were produced, their ability to assume responsibility for those outputs is weakened, even when formal accountability remains assigned to them under accounting standards.

2.3 Bias, Data Quality, and MSME-Specific Vulnerabilities

Beyond opacity, AI-enabled accounting systems are vulnerable to biases embedded in training data and model design. Machine learning models learn from historical accounting records that may reflect inconsistent practices, reporting errors, or structural biases, particularly in MSME environments where data governance practices are often underdeveloped (Mehrabi et al., 2021; Rai, 2020). When such data are used to train AI systems, biases can be reproduced or amplified in automated classifications and predictions.

For MSMEs, data-related vulnerabilities are particularly pronounced. Unlike large organizations with standardized enterprise systems and dedicated data governance teams, MSMEs often rely on fragmented accounting records, manual data entry, and heterogeneous software solutions. These conditions increase the risk that AI models trained on MSME data will produce unreliable or skewed outputs, potentially distorting financial information rather than improving its quality (Moll & Yigitbasioglu 2019).

Bias in AI-assisted accounting is not limited to social or demographic dimensions; it can also manifest as systematic misclassification of transactions, inconsistent valuation patterns, or disproportionate flagging of certain activities as anomalous. These outcomes challenge the assumption that AI inherently improves objectivity in accounting. Instead, they highlight the need for governance mechanisms that ensure algorithmic outputs remain aligned with standardized accounting principles and professional expectations (Benke & Pelger 2021).

2.4 Accountability and the Redistribution of Responsibility

The diffusion of AI in accounting also reshapes traditional accountability structures. Conventional accounting systems are organized around clearly defined roles and responsibilities, with preparers, managers, and auditors occupying distinct positions in the reporting process. AI-enabled systems, however, distribute decision-making among human and algorithmic actors, complicating attribution when errors or misstatements occur (Raisch & Krakowski 2021).

This redistribution of responsibility raises fundamental governance questions. If an AI system produces an incorrect classification or forecast that materially affects financial statements, responsibility may be diffused among software providers, data sources, system designers, and human users. In MSME contexts, where external oversight is limited and reliance on third-party software providers is common, this diffusion can weaken accountability and undermine stakeholder trust.

Accounting standards traditionally address accountability by assigning ultimate responsibility for financial statements to management. However, the growing autonomy of AI systems challenges the practical enforceability of this principle. Without mechanisms to constrain and document algorithmic decision-making, accountability risks becoming nominal rather than substantive, thereby eroding the institutional foundations of financial reporting (Power 2021).

2.5 Limitations of Existing AI Governance Frameworks in Accounting Contexts

In response to these challenges, a growing body of AI governance literature has articulated principles for trustworthy AI, emphasizing transparency, accountability, fairness, and human oversight (European Commission High-Level Expert Group on AI, 2019; NIST, 2023). Although these frameworks offer valuable normative guidance, they are often abstract and detached from sector-specific operational realities.

Most AI governance frameworks assume organizational environments with high governance capacity, including legal expertise, technical oversight, and formal compliance structures. These assumptions limit their applicability to MSMEs, where governance solutions must be integrated into existing routines rather than implemented as standalone systems (OECD, 2021). As a result, AI governance in MSME accounting contexts remains fragmented, with ethical principles articulated at a high level but only weakly translated into everyday accounting practice.

This gap underscores the need for governance approaches that are institutionally embedded and operationally enforceable. Rather than relying solely on new AI-specific rules, governance mechanisms must leverage existing institutional frameworks that already shape accounting behavior. Accounting standards, particularly those designed for MSMEs, offer a promising yet underutilized foundation for such integration.

2.6 Accounting as an Institutional Technology of Trust

To fully appreciate the governance implications of AI-enabled accounting systems, it is necessary to revisit the institutional role of accounting. Accounting has long been understood not merely as a technical tool for recording transactions but as an institutional technology that produces and stabilizes trust in economic relations. Through standardized representations of organizational activities, accounting enables coordination among actors who lack direct access to underlying economic processes, thereby reducing uncertainty and facilitating collective decision-making (Power, 2021; Bhimani et al 2019).

This trust-producing function of accounting is grounded in its rule-based nature. Accounting standards codify acceptable methods for recognition, measurement, and disclosure, transforming complex economic realities into structured, comparable information. These standards do not eliminate judgment; rather, they channel it within institutionally sanctioned boundaries that make financial representations socially credible. In this sense, accounting standards function as governance devices that discipline organizational behavior by making it visible, comparable, and auditable.

The introduction of AI into accounting systems challenges this institutional logic in subtle yet significant ways. As financial representations are increasingly generated through algorithmic inference rather than explicit rule application, the basis of trust shifts from institutionalized standards to technical systems whose legitimacy may not be widely understood. This shift raises concerns about whether algorithmic accounting outputs can fulfill the same trust-producing role as traditional accounting representations, particularly when the logic underlying those outputs is opaque or probabilistic rather than rule-based (Benke & Pelger 2021).

For MSMEs, this tension is exacerbated by the lack of alternative trust infrastructure. Large corporations often complement accounting with extensive internal controls, audit committees, and governance mechanisms that can absorb some of the opacity introduced by algorithms. MSMEs, by contrast, rely heavily on standardized accounting outputs as primary signals of credibility to external stakeholders. If AI-enabled accounting systems undermine the interpretability or auditability of these outputs, the institutional trust function of accounting is weakened, with potentially significant consequences for access to finance, regulatory compliance, and stakeholder relationships.

2.7 The Problem of Automation Bias and Over-Reliance in Accounting

Another governance challenge associated with AI-enabled accounting systems is automation bias. Automation bias is the tendency of human users to over-rely on algorithmic outputs, even when those outputs are incorrect or insufficiently contextualized (Rai, 2020). In accounting contexts, this risk is particularly salient because AI systems are often perceived as objective, data-driven, and less prone to error than human judgment.

The institutional authority of accounting further intensifies this risk. When AI systems produce accounting classifications or financial analyses that align with standardized formats, users may be less inclined to question their validity. This dynamic can erode professional skepticism, a core principle of accounting and auditing practice, and shift decision-making authority from human actors to algorithmic systems without adequate scrutiny (Power 2021).

For MSMEs, where accounting expertise is often limited and reliance on external software providers is common, automation bias can become entrenched. Managers may accept AI-generated accounting outputs as authoritative simply because they conform to standardized reporting formats, even when underlying assumptions or data inputs are flawed. Without governance mechanisms that require explanation, documentation, and human validation, AI systems risk becoming de facto decision-makers rather than decision-support tools.

2.8 Platformization of Accounting and Governance Externalization

The governance challenges associated with AI in accounting are further complicated by the platformization of accounting technologies. Many AI-enabled accounting tools are delivered through cloud-based platforms from third-party vendors, which centralize algorithmic development and data processing beyond MSMEs' organizational boundaries (Moll & Yigitbasioglu, 2019). While this model lowers adoption barriers, it also externalizes key governance functions related to model design, data handling, and system updates.

This externalization creates power and information asymmetries between MSMEs and technology providers. MSMEs typically have limited visibility into how AI models embedded in accounting platforms operate, how training data are selected, or how system updates may alter accounting outputs over time. These asymmetries undermine traditional accountability mechanisms, which assume that organizations exercising control over accounting systems can also be held responsible for their outputs.

From a governance perspective, platformization raises questions about where responsibility for trustworthy accounting lies. If AI-enabled accounting systems are effectively governed by external vendors, MSMEs' capacity to ensure compliance with accounting standards and ethical expectations is constrained. This dynamic further underscores the need for governance mechanisms that operate at the level of accounting outputs rather than at the level of algorithm design alone.

2.9 Why AI Governance Must Be Embedded in Accounting Institutions

Taken together, the challenges discussed in this section highlight a central insight: AI governance in accounting cannot be effectively addressed through abstract ethical principles or technical solutions alone. Instead, governance must be embedded within the institutional frameworks that already structure accounting practice. Accounting standards represent one such framework, offering rule-based constraints that can be applied to AI-enabled systems regardless of their technical complexity or organizational location.

By focusing governance efforts on accounting outputs rather than algorithmic internals, standards-based approaches align governance with institutional accountability structures already recognized by regulators, auditors, and stakeholders. This alignment is particularly important for MSMEs, where governance capacity is limited and reliance on external technology providers is high. Embedding AI governance within accounting standards thus offers a pragmatic pathway to ensure that AI adoption strengthens rather than undermines the institutional role of accounting as a technology of trust.

3. MSME FINANCIAL STANDARDS AS INSTITUTIONAL GOVERNANCE MECHANISMS

3.1 Accounting Standards as Institutions of Economic Governance

Accounting standards occupy a distinctive position in modern economic systems as institutional mechanisms that govern behavior through standardized representation rather than direct control. Unlike regulatory instruments that prescribe or prohibit specific actions, accounting standards shape how economic activities are translated into formal representations that can be evaluated, compared, and sanctioned (Power, 2021; Bhimani et al., 2019).

From an institutional perspective, accounting standards can be understood as rule-based infrastructures that stabilize expectations in environments of uncertainty and information asymmetry (Scott, 2014). By prescribing what counts as valid financial information, standards create shared interpretive frameworks that enable coordination among actors who lack direct visibility into organizational processes. This coordination is central to accounting's role in facilitating trust-based economic exchange, particularly in market systems where trust cannot be derived from interpersonal relationships alone.

Importantly, the governance capacity of accounting standards does not depend on continuous enforcement or discretionary oversight. Instead, standards embed governance in routine practices by constraining how transactions are recognized, measured, and disclosed. These constraints operate ex ante by limiting acceptable accounting treatments and ex post through auditability and verification (Power, 2021). As a result, accounting standards exemplify a form of indirect governance that relies on institutionalized routines rather than centralized supervision.

3.2 Governance-by-Rules and the Logic of Institutional Constraint

The governance function of accounting standards is best understood through the concept of governance by rules. Governance-by-rules refers to institutional arrangements in which behavior is guided not by ad hoc judgments or discretionary authority but by predefined rules that structure decision-making processes (Scott, 2014). In accounting, these rules specify recognition thresholds, measurement bases, documentation requirements, and disclosure obligations that collectively define the boundaries of acceptable financial representation.

This rule-based logic is particularly effective in contexts where direct monitoring is costly or impractical. Rather than overseeing every transaction or decision, governance-by-rules relies on the disciplining effects of standardized procedures that make behavior visible and comparable. Deviations from these procedures can be detected through audits, peer comparisons, or regulatory review, creating incentives for compliance even without constant oversight. (Power, 2021).

In AI-enabled accounting, governance-by-rules takes on renewed significance. AI systems rely on pattern recognition and probabilistic inference, often optimizing for accuracy or efficiency rather than institutional compliance (Rai, 2020). Without rule-based constraints, algorithmic systems may produce outputs that are statistically plausible yet institutionally inappropriate. Accounting standards provide a mechanism for aligning algorithmic outputs with institutional expectations by defining what constitutes an acceptable accounting outcome, regardless of the underlying model's technical sophistication (Benke & Pelger, 2021).

3.3 MSME Financial Reporting Standards and Institutional Proportionality

Financial reporting standards designed specifically for MSMEs embody the principle of institutional proportionality. Institutional proportionality recognizes that governance mechanisms must be calibrated to the capacity and context of the organizations they govern (Sian & Roberts, 2009). MSME standards, therefore, differ from comprehensive reporting regimes such as full IFRS by prioritizing clarity, simplicity, and enforceability over exhaustive disclosure or complex valuation techniques (Devi et al., 2019).

This proportionality is not a weakness but a deliberate institutional design choice. By reducing optionality and limiting discretionary accounting treatments, MSME standards enhance comparability and reduce the cognitive and compliance burden on smaller firms. These features increase the likelihood that standards will be applied consistently in practice, thereby strengthening governance effectiveness.

In AI-enabled accounting contexts, institutional proportionality is a critical governance asset. MSMEs typically lack the resources to implement standalone AI governance frameworks or to conduct detailed oversight of algorithmic systems (Moll & Yigitbasioglu, 2019). By embedding governance expectations in existing accounting standards, proportionality ensures that AI governance is achieved through mechanisms MSMEs are already required to understand and apply. This integration minimizes governance fragmentation and reduces the risk that AI adoption outpaces institutional capacity. (Benke & Pelger, 2021).

Table 1. Conceptual Mapping of MSME Financial Reporting Standards to Trustworthy AI Governance Requirements

MSME financial reporting standard mechanism	Institutional logic enforced	Canonical trustworthy AI governance dimension	Governance implication for AI-enabled accounting systems
Recognition and measurement criteria	Rule-bounded determination of when and how economic events become accounting numbers	Transparency and explainability	AI outputs must be reproducible against explicit accounting logic, reducing black-box classification
Source-document linkage and audit trail requirements	Traceability between reported figures and underlying transactions	Auditability and traceability	Enables independent verification of AI-assisted postings through documented data pathways
Consistency principle (intra-entity, over time)	Stability of accounting treatment across reporting periods	Reliability and robustness	Flags algorithmic drift when outputs deviate from established accounting practices
Comparability objective (inter-entity)	Standardized reporting basis for stakeholder evaluation	Fairness and outcome consistency	Limits arbitrary variance arising from heterogeneous data sources or model configurations
Disclosure requirements	Accountability to external users of financial information	Accountability and oversight	Requires documentation of AI use, assumptions, and limitations within financial reports
Management responsibility and sign-off	Human accountability for reporting integrity	Human-in-the-loop governance	Preserves managerial responsibility despite algorithmic assistance

3.4 Accounting Standards as Boundary Objects Between Technology and Institutions

Accounting standards also serve as boundary objects that mediate between technological systems and institutional expectations. Boundary objects are artifacts that are flexible enough to be interpreted across different domains yet robust enough to maintain a common identity (Star & Griesemer 1989). In the context of AI-enabled accounting, standards function as boundary objects that translate institutional norms of transparency and accountability into technical requirements that can be implemented within software systems (Benke & Pelger 2021).

For developers of accounting technologies, standards provide explicit specifications that guide system design, validation, and output formatting. For users, standards provide a familiar interpretive framework for evaluating and questioning AI-assisted outputs. For auditors and regulators, standards establish criteria for assessing compliance and accountability. This multi-actor relevance reinforces the institutional authority of accounting standards and amplifies their governance impact (Power, 2021).

When AI systems are embedded in accounting processes governed by MSME standards, boundary object functionality ensures that technological innovation remains aligned with institutional norms. Rather than requiring stakeholders to understand complex algorithmic models, standards enable governance through familiar representational forms. This alignment is particularly important in MSME contexts, where technological opacity could otherwise undermine trust in financial information.

3.5 Institutional Trust, Standardization, and the Mediation of Algorithmic Authority

At a deeper level, the governance role of accounting standards is inseparable from their function in building institutional trust. Institutional trust differs from interpersonal trust in that it is anchored in standardized procedures rather than personal relationships (Giddens, 1990). Accounting standards contribute to institutional trust by ensuring that financial information is produced in accordance with shared rules that are recognized and enforceable across organizational boundaries (Power, 2021).

The introduction of AI into accounting systems creates new forms of authority grounded in technical expertise and data-driven inference. Without institutional mediation, this algorithmic authority risks displacing traditional bases of trust, shifting credibility from standardized procedures to opaque technical systems (Rai, 2020). Accounting standards counterbalance this shift by reasserting the primacy of rule-based representation over algorithmic optimization.

In MSME contexts, where stakeholders rely heavily on standardized financial reports as signals of credibility, the mediation of algorithmic authority is especially important. By embedding AI systems within the constraints of MSME standards, organizations can harness the benefits of automation and analytics while preserving the institutional foundations of trust that underpin economic exchange (Benke & Pelger 2021).

3.6 Accounting Standards as Algorithmic Constraints in AI-Enabled Systems

The incorporation of artificial intelligence into accounting systems fundamentally alters how accounting standards are applied in practice. In traditional accounting processes, standards are applied explicitly through human interpretation and professional judgment. AI-enabled systems, by contrast, operationalize accounting logic implicitly by embedding rules, thresholds, and classification schemas into algorithmic processes that automate or augment accounting tasks (Rai 2020).

From an institutional governance perspective, this shift requires reconceptualizing how standards function. Rather than serving solely as interpretive guides for human actors, accounting standards increasingly operate as algorithmic constraints that delimit the space of permissible outputs from AI systems. These constraints do not govern algorithmic behavior by inspecting internal model architectures but by regulating which outputs are permitted to enter formal accounting representations (Benke & Pelger 2021).

This output-oriented approach to governance is particularly relevant in MSME contexts. MSMEs often rely on third-party accounting platforms and software-as-a-service solutions, which limit their ability to influence model design, training data selection, or system updates (Moll & Yigitbasioglu, 2019). By contrast, governing AI at the level of accounting outputs through standardized recognition, measurement, and disclosure requirements allows MSMEs to exert institutional control over AI-enabled systems without requiring technical expertise.

3.7 Operationalizing Algorithmic Constraint Through Accounting Rules

The constraining function of accounting standards is expressed through several interrelated mechanisms. Recognition and measurement rules define the conditions for recognizing and measuring economic events and for recording those entries. When embedded in AI-enabled systems, these rules constrain algorithmic classification by requiring outputs to conform to predefined accounting categories and valuation bases (Power 2021).

Documentation and audit-trail requirements further reinforce algorithmic constraints by mandating traceability from accounting outputs to underlying transactions. In AI-enabled environments, this traceability requires preserving data inputs, processing steps, and validation checks that support algorithmic outputs. While full transparency into model internals may be neither feasible nor necessary, standards-based documentation ensures that AI-assisted accounting outputs can be examined and challenged within established assurance frameworks (Benke & Pelger 2021).

Consistency and comparability principles also serve as governance mechanisms by limiting algorithmic variability over time and across entities. AI systems are inherently adaptive and may change their behavior as they learn from new data. Without institutional constraints, this adaptability risks producing inconsistent accounting treatments that undermine comparability. Accounting standards counteract this risk by imposing stability requirements that flag deviations and require justification, thereby disciplining algorithmic learning within acceptable institutional bounds. (Power, 2021).

3.8 Auditability as a Cornerstone of Institutional Accountability

Auditability occupies a central role in the governance architecture of accounting and assumes heightened importance in AI-enabled environments. Auditability ensures that financial information can be independently examined, verified, and challenged, thereby sustaining institutional trust in accounting outputs (Power, 2021). In the absence of auditability, accountability becomes nominal, and trust is reduced to reliance on technical authority.

AI-enabled accounting systems challenge traditional audit practices by introducing opacity, complexity, and scale. Automated transaction processing and continuous analytics produce large volumes of output that may be difficult to scrutinize with conventional audit techniques. MSME financial standards mitigate these challenges by embedding auditability requirements into reporting practices, thereby preserving institutional accountability even as accounting processes become increasingly automated (Benke & Pelger 2021).

Documentation requirements play a critical role in this context. By mandating the retention of source documents, explanations, and reconciliation records, standards ensure that AI-assisted outputs remain anchored in verifiable evidence. This anchoring does not require auditors to fully understand algorithmic models; rather, it enables them to assess whether outputs comply with accounting logic defined by the standards and whether appropriate controls are in place (Power, 2021). Auditability is thus preserved at the institutional level, even if technical opacity persists at the algorithmic level.

3.9 Accountability, Human Oversight, and the Preservation of Responsibility

Accountability in accounting is traditionally grounded in assigning responsibility to identifiable human actors, particularly management and the preparers of financial statements. AI-enabled accounting systems complicate this arrangement by distributing decision-making among human and algorithmic actors, raising concerns about the dilution of responsibility and the erosion of professional accountability (Rai 2020).

MSME financial standards address this challenge by preserving human responsibility for compliance and reporting integrity, regardless of the tools used to produce accounting outputs. Management sign-off requirements and professional accountability obligations ensure that AI systems are treated as decision-support tools rather than autonomous authorities. This human-in-the-loop arrangement aligns with widely endorsed principles of trustworthy AI governance and preserves the normative foundations of accounting accountability (Benke & Pelger 2021).

In MSME contexts, where governance structures are often informal and resource-constrained, maintaining human accountability is especially important. Without clear institutional anchors, AI systems risk becoming de facto decision-makers, with human actors deferring to algorithmic outputs because of perceived technical superiority. Accounting standards counteract this tendency by reinforcing the primacy of human judgment and responsibility within standardized reporting frameworks (Power 2021).

3.10 Institutional Scope, Enforcement, and Boundary Conditions

While MSME financial reporting standards have significant potential as institutional governance mechanisms for AI-enabled accounting systems, their effectiveness is neither universal nor unconditional. The governance capacity of standards is shaped by institutional scope, enforcement environments, and jurisdictional variation. Recognizing these conditions is essential to avoid overstating the role of accounting standards and to situate standards-based AI governance within realistic institutional boundaries (Scott, 2014).

A central institutional distinction concerns the difference between MSME-oriented standards and comprehensive reporting regimes, such as full IFRS. Full IFRS frameworks are designed for complex organizations with access to specialized expertise, advanced valuation techniques, and formal governance infrastructures. They often rely on principles-based guidance that presupposes significant professional judgment and interpretive capacity. In contrast, MSME standards emphasize rule clarity, reduced optionality, and proportional disclosure, reflecting the constrained environments in which smaller firms operate (Sian & Roberts, 2009; Devi et al., 2019). From a governance perspective, this distinction is consequential because greater discretion increases the risk of opacity and dilution of accountability when AI systems are involved (Benke & Pelger 2021).

However, the governance effectiveness of MSME standards depends on enforcement and institutional embedding. Standards derive their constraining power not only from their formal content but also from their integration into regulatory, professional, and market institutions. Auditors, tax authorities, lenders, and regulators play a critical role in reinforcing compliance by relying on standardized financial information for evaluation and decision-making. When these institutions are weak or fragmented, the governance capacity of accounting standards may be attenuated, limiting their ability to constrain AI-enabled accounting practices (Scott, 2014).

Jurisdictional variation further shapes the operation of standards-based AI governance. In jurisdictions with strong regulatory enforcement and professional oversight, MSME standards can serve as effective governance mechanisms even without AI-specific regulation. In contrast, in environments with weak enforcement, informal accounting practices, or limited professional capacity, the constraining effects of standards may be uneven. In such contexts, AI-enabled accounting systems may reinforce existing institutional weaknesses rather than mitigate them, particularly when algorithmic tools are adopted without complementary investments in documentation, auditability, and human oversight (Moll & Yigitbasioglu 2019).

Another boundary condition concerns the growing platformization of accounting technologies. Many MSMEs rely on cloud-based accounting platforms developed and maintained by third-party vendors. While MSME standards can constrain the accounting outputs these platforms produce, they do not directly govern upstream decisions about model design, data selection, or system updates. This creates a structural asymmetry in which governance is exercised at the output level rather than at the level of algorithmic development. While output-oriented governance is pragmatic and institutionally feasible for MSMEs, it may be insufficient to address systemic risks associated with platform concentration or opaque vendor practices (Moll & Yigitbasioglu, 2019).

3.11 Synthesis: Institutionalizing Trust Through Standards-Based AI Governance

Taken together, the analysis in Section 3 shows that MSME financial reporting standards provide a robust institutional foundation for governing AI-enabled accounting systems under specific conditions. By constraining algorithmic outputs, preserving auditability, and anchoring accountability in human roles, these standards operationalize trustworthiness through routine accounting practices rather than through abstract ethical commitments. (Power, 2021).

This standards-based approach to AI governance offers several advantages. It leverages existing institutional infrastructure, reduces the need for specialized technical oversight, and aligns governance mechanisms with regulatory and assurance practices already familiar to MSMEs and their stakeholders. However, its effectiveness depends on enforcement environments, jurisdictional contexts, and technological architectures. Recognizing these boundary conditions is essential to developing realistic, context-sensitive approaches to trustworthy AI in accounting. (Benke & Pelger, 2021).

4. CONCEPTUAL FRAMEWORK FOR STANDARDS-BASED AI GOVERNANCE IN MSME ACCOUNTING

4.1 Purpose, Scope, and Conceptual Architecture of the Framework

This section develops a conceptual framework that integrates the analytical arguments from the preceding sections into a coherent model for governing AI-enabled accounting systems in MSMEs. The primary purpose of the framework is to show how governance can be achieved through institutional mechanisms already embedded in accounting practice, rather than through novel regulatory instruments or abstract ethical principles. In this respect, the framework directly addresses long-standing concerns in the AI governance literature about the limited translatability of high-level governance ideals into organizational contexts with constrained resources and limited oversight capacity (Scott, 2014; Power, 2021).

The motivation for developing this framework stems from a structural mismatch between dominant approaches to trustworthy AI and the operational realities of MSMEs. Much of the existing literature on AI governance presumes the availability of specialized technical expertise, internal control systems, and formal governance structures capable of monitoring algorithmic behavior. These assumptions may hold in large organizations but are largely incompatible with MSME environments, where accounting functions are often centralized in small teams and supported by standardized software solutions. As a result, AI governance models that rely on discretionary oversight, continuous monitoring, or model-level transparency risk becoming aspirational rather than operational when applied to MSMEs (Rai 2020).

Against this backdrop, the framework advances an institutional governance perspective that situates AI governance within financial reporting standards. Accounting standards constitute a distinctive form of governance infrastructure: they do not prescribe specific business decisions or regulate technologies directly. Instead, they govern by shaping how economic activities are represented, evaluated, and sanctioned within formal accounting systems. This representational function allows standards to exert governance effects indirectly by constraining the forms of information that can enter institutional decision-making processes (Power, 2021).

The scope of the framework is therefore deliberately circumscribed. Rather than addressing AI governance in general, it focuses on AI-enabled accounting systems used by MSMEs and the institutional mechanisms that produce and maintain trust in accounting information. This focus reflects an understanding of trust not as a psychological attribute or ethical aspiration but as an institutional outcome sustained through standardized procedures, auditability, and accountability. In this sense, the framework aligns with institutional theories that conceptualize trust as emerging from rule-based coordination rather than interpersonal familiarity (Scott, 2014).

Conceptually, the framework is organized around three interdependent layers. The first layer comprises AI-enabled accounting processes, including automated transaction classification, algorithmic bookkeeping, anomaly detection, and predictive analytics. These processes enhance efficiency and analytical capacity but also introduce risks related to opacity, automation bias, and adaptive behavior. The second layer comprises MSME financial reporting standards, which serve as an institutional mediation layer that constrains how AI-generated information is translated into formal accounting representations. The third layer comprises trustworthy accounting outcomes, such as transparency, auditability, accountability, and stakeholder confidence, which emerge when AI-enabled outputs remain aligned with standardized reporting expectations.

These layers are not conceived as sequential stages but as mutually reinforcing components of an institutional system. AI-enabled processes generate information at scale; accounting standards stabilize and discipline this information through rule-based constraints; and trustworthy outcomes arise when accounting outputs remain interpretable and contestable within existing assurance and regulatory frameworks. Governance, in this model, is therefore not an external intervention imposed on AI systems but an endogenous property of institutional alignment between technology and standardized representation.

By framing AI governance in accounting as a problem of institutional design rather than technological control, the framework shifts the analytical focus from algorithmic transparency to representational legitimacy. This shift is particularly consequential for MSMEs, where governance capacity derives less from technical inspection and more from conformity with institutionalized accounting practices recognized by auditors, regulators, lenders, and other stakeholders. The framework thus provides a theoretically grounded and practically viable approach to governing AI-enabled accounting systems in contexts where conventional AI governance mechanisms are unlikely to be effective.

4.2 MSME Financial Reporting Standards as the Core Mediating Governance Layer.

At the center of the conceptual framework is the mediating role of MSME financial reporting standards as institutional governance mechanisms that structure the interaction between AI-enabled accounting processes and organizational decision-making. This mediating role is not incidental; it reflects the historically embedded function of accounting standards as rule-based infrastructures that translate complex economic activity into standardized, institutionally intelligible representations. In

AI-enabled accounting environments, this function acquires renewed significance as algorithmic systems increasingly participate in the production of financial information.

AI-enabled accounting systems operate through data-driven inference, automation, and continuous processing. They classify transactions, generate postings, detect anomalies, and increasingly provide forward-looking assessments. While these capabilities promise efficiency and analytical depth, they also introduce governance risks that are qualitatively different from those associated with traditional accounting automation. These risks include opacity in decision logic, automation bias in human interpretation, adaptive behavior that may undermine consistency, and the displacement of professional judgment by algorithmic outputs (Benke & Pelger, 2021; Rai, 2020). Without institutional mediation, such risks threaten the interpretability and contestability of accounting information.

MSME financial reporting standards mediate these risks by imposing rule-based constraints on how AI-generated information is admitted into formal accounting representations. Recognition rules determine which economic events may be recorded as accounting entries; measurement rules define permissible valuation bases; documentation and disclosure requirements ensure traceability; and consistency principles discipline variation across time and reporting entities. Through these mechanisms, standards do not govern AI systems directly; rather, they govern the translation of algorithmic outputs into institutionally valid accounting information (Power, 2021).

This output-oriented governance logic is central to the framework. Rather than attempting to regulate algorithmic internals such as model architecture, training data, or parameter optimization, the framework locates governance at the level of accounting outputs that enter financial statements and managerial reports. This distinction is analytically important. Governing algorithmic internals presupposes technical expertise, access to proprietary systems, and continuous oversight capabilities that are typically unavailable to MSMEs. Governing outputs, by contrast, aligns with existing institutional obligations that MSMEs already face in preparing, presenting, and defending financial information to external stakeholders. (Moll & Yigitbasioglu, 2019).

By constraining outputs rather than processes, MSME standards serve as institutional filters that stabilize accounting representations despite technological change. AI systems may update, learn, or be replaced, but the standards used to evaluate their outputs remain relatively stable. This stability anchors governance in institutional continuity rather than technological volatility, preserving comparability and interpretability across reporting periods. In this sense, standards-based governance counteracts the tendency of adaptive AI systems to produce idiosyncratic or non-comparable outputs that, while statistically plausible, may be institutionally inappropriate.

The mediating function of MSME standards also preserves the separation between technological authority and accounting accountability. AI systems may contribute to the production of accounting information, but they do not acquire institutional authority over financial representation. Authority remains vested in standardized rules and in the human actors responsible for their application. This separation is critical in preventing the reallocation of accountability from accountable professionals to opaque technical systems, a risk frequently identified in discussions of algorithmic governance (Rai, 2020).

Moreover, the mediation provided by MSME standards is not merely restrictive; it is generative of trust. By ensuring that AI-assisted accounting outputs conform to standardized reporting expectations, these standards render those outputs intelligible within existing assurance, regulatory, and contractual frameworks. Auditors can evaluate compliance without interrogating algorithms; regulators can enforce reporting requirements without developing AI-specific expertise; and lenders and investors can rely on standardized financial statements as credible signals of organizational performance. In this framework, trust is institutionalized through conformity with shared rules rather than delegated to technological claims of accuracy or objectivity (Power, 2021).

Figure 1 visualizes this mediating role by positioning MSME financial reporting standards between AI-enabled accounting processes and decision-relevant outcomes. The figure underscores that governance effectiveness arises from alignment between algorithmic outputs and standardized representations, not from algorithmic transparency alone. In MSME contexts, where governance capacity is derived from institutional compliance rather than technical oversight, this mediating function serves as the core mechanism for achieving trustworthy AI-enabled accounting.

4.3 Trustworthy Accounting Outcomes and Institutional Alignment (Expanded)

The final component of the conceptual framework concerns the production of trustworthy accounting outcomes. In AI-enabled accounting, trustworthiness cannot be reduced to technical accuracy, predictive performance, or computational sophistication. Instead, trust is an institutional achievement grounded in standardized procedures that render accounting information intelligible, contestable, and enforceable across organizational boundaries (Power, 2021). This distinction is central to understanding why governance through financial reporting standards remains indispensable even as accounting processes become increasingly automated.

From an institutional perspective, trust in accounting information depends on the stability of representational forms rather than on the transparency of underlying processes. Stakeholders rarely observe how accounting numbers are produced;

instead, they rely on the assumption that those numbers conform to recognized standards and can be audited if necessary. AI-enabled accounting systems complicate this arrangement by introducing new forms of epistemic authority grounded in data-driven inference and technical expertise. Without institutional mediation, such authority risks displacing standardized representation as the basis for trust, shifting credibility from rule-based procedures to opaque algorithmic systems (Rai 2020).

By embedding AI-enabled accounting systems within MSME financial reporting standards, the framework reasserts the primacy of institutionalized representation over algorithmic optimization. Trustworthy outcomes are achieved not by exposing model internals or maximizing technical explainability, but by ensuring that accounting outputs remain consistent with standardized reporting rules that are socially recognized and institutionally enforceable. In this model, trust is produced through conformity with shared rules rather than through claims of objectivity, neutrality, or technological superiority.

The framework also highlights the temporal dimension of trust. Accounting information acquires meaning over time through consistency, comparability, and the ability to trace change across reporting periods. AI systems, by contrast, are inherently adaptive and may alter their behavior as they learn from new data. While such adaptability is valuable for analytical purposes, it poses risks to longitudinal interpretability if left unconstrained. By disciplining algorithmic adaptation through standards-based consistency requirements, the framework ensures that AI-enabled accounting contributes to temporal stability rather than undermining it (Power, 2021).

Institutional alignment across stakeholders further reinforces trustworthiness. Auditors, regulators, lenders, and other users of financial information operate within institutional environments structured around standardized accounting representations. When AI-assisted outputs conform to MSME standards, they remain intelligible within these environments and can be evaluated using existing assurance and enforcement mechanisms. This alignment reduces the need for stakeholders to develop AI-specific expertise and preserves the institutional division of labor that underpins modern accounting systems.

Human accountability is a final and essential element of trustworthy outcomes. Accounting standards anchor responsibility in identifiable human actors, typically management and preparers of financial statements. AI-enabled accounting systems challenge this arrangement by introducing distributed agency among human and algorithmic actors. The framework addresses this challenge by preserving human responsibility for accounting outputs and positioning AI systems as decision-support tools rather than autonomous authorities. This human-in-the-loop configuration not only aligns with widely endorsed principles of trustworthy AI but also safeguards the normative foundations of accounting accountability (Benke & Pelger, 2021).

Taken together, the framework demonstrates that trustworthy AI in MSME accounting is not achieved through technological control alone or through abstract ethical commitments detached from practice. Rather, trust is institutionalized through the alignment of AI-enabled processes with standardized accounting rules that structure representation, accountability, and auditability. By situating AI governance within financial reporting standards, the framework offers a conceptually robust and practically viable approach to governing AI-enabled accounting systems in organizational contexts where conventional AI governance mechanisms are unlikely to be effective.

5. IMPLICATIONS OF STANDARDS-BASED AI GOVERNANCE FOR MSMES

5.1 Implications for MSME Accounting Practice and Organizational Governance

The standards-based AI governance framework developed in this chapter has significant implications for MSME accounting practice and internal organizational governance. Rather than treating artificial intelligence as a transformative authority that redefines accounting decision-making, the framework reorients AI as an institutionally constrained decision-support mechanism embedded within established accounting routines. This repositioning aligns with institutional perspectives that emphasize governance through rule-based coordination rather than discretionary technological control (Power, 2021).

First, the framework clarifies AI's role within MSME accounting workflows. AI-enabled systems increasingly assist with transaction classification, bookkeeping automation, reconciliation, and anomaly detection. Without institutional constraints, such systems may be treated as quasi-authoritative sources of accounting truth, particularly in small organizations where accounting expertise is limited and automation is perceived as neutral or objective. By embedding AI use within financial reporting standards, the framework reinforces the principle that accounting validity derives from conformity with standardized rules rather than from algorithmic output alone. This orientation directly mitigates the risk of automation bias, a persistent governance challenge in algorithmic decision-support environments (Rai 2020).

This shift has significant implications for managerial responsibility. MSME managers often rely heavily on automated accounting outputs due to time constraints and resource limitations. The framework reasserts management's accountability for financial representations by emphasizing that responsibility for compliance and reporting integrity cannot be delegated to AI systems. Even when accounting processes are automated, managers remain institutionally responsible for ensuring that outputs conform to applicable standards. This reaffirmation aligns with foundational principles of accountability in accounting governance, where authority is anchored in identifiable human actors rather than in technical systems (Power, 2021).

The framework also shapes how MSMEs structure internal accounting controls. Internal control arrangements in MSMEs are often informal, relying on trust, familiarity, and manual oversight rather than formalized procedures. AI-enabled accounting introduces scale and speed that can overwhelm such informal mechanisms. By anchoring governance in accounting standards, the framework provides MSMEs with a stable, rule-based reference point for evaluating AI-assisted outputs. Recognition rules, documentation requirements, and consistency principles serve as practical control mechanisms that can be applied even in the absence of sophisticated internal audit infrastructures.

Another implication concerns organizational learning and capability development. By embedding AI governance within familiar accounting standards, the framework reduces cognitive and organizational barriers to AI adoption. MSMEs need not develop specialized AI governance expertise; instead, they leverage existing knowledge of accounting rules to interpret, validate, and challenge AI-assisted outputs. Over time, this integration supports incremental learning and institutional capacity-building, enabling MSMEs to adopt advanced technologies without undermining governance or accountability.

Finally, the framework shapes how MSMEs engage with external stakeholders, including auditors, tax authorities, and financial institutions. MSMEs are typically evaluated using standardized financial statements rather than the sophistication of their internal systems. When AI-enabled accounting outputs conform to financial reporting standards, they remain intelligible and credible within existing institutional evaluation processes. This continuity reduces the risk that AI adoption will introduce uncertainty or mistrust in external relationships and reinforces the role of accounting standards as a shared governance language across organizational boundaries (Scott, 2014).

Together, these implications suggest that standards-based AI governance reshapes MSME accounting practice not by adding new governance layers but by reactivating the latent governance capacity of existing accounting standards. By constraining AI-enabled accounting within rule-based institutional frameworks, MSMEs can adopt advanced technologies while preserving accountability, interpretability, and trust in financial information. This approach offers a pragmatic pathway for aligning technological innovation with organizational governance in contexts where resources, expertise, and formal oversight structures are inherently limited.

For MSMEs, the framework can be operationalized through routine governance questions embedded in everyday accounting practice, such as whether AI-assisted classifications can be reproduced under standard recognition and measurement rules, whether automated outputs are supported by auditable documentation, and whether management retains the capacity to review and override algorithmic suggestions when inconsistencies arise. Rather than functioning as a standalone assessment tool, these questions are intended to be integrated into existing accounting workflows, reinforcing institutional accountability without introducing additional compliance layers. In this way, standards-based AI governance becomes actionable through familiar accounting routines rather than abstract ethical evaluation.

5.2 Implications for Auditors, Regulators, and Technology Providers

The standards-based AI governance framework developed in this chapter has distinct implications for key institutional actors beyond MSMEs, particularly auditors, regulators, and accounting technology providers. These actors play critical roles in sustaining the credibility, enforceability, and scalability of accounting systems, and their interactions with AI-enabled accounting practices shape the broader governance environment in which MSMEs operate. By situating AI governance within financial reporting standards, the framework reframes the responsibilities and expectations of these actors, reducing governance complexity while preserving institutional accountability.

For auditors, the framework clarifies the basis for evaluating AI-enabled accounting outputs. Auditing has historically relied on standardized accounting representations, documentation, and traceability rather than direct observation of organizational processes. AI-enabled accounting challenges traditional audit approaches by introducing opacity and automation at scale. However, the framework shows that auditability need not depend on technical inspection of algorithms. Instead, audit assurance can be maintained by assessing whether AI-assisted outputs conform to established financial reporting standards, are supported by adequate documentation, and exhibit consistency across reporting periods. This standards-centered approach preserves the relevance of existing audit methodologies and limits the need for auditors to rely exclusively on specialized AI expertise, thereby maintaining the institutional division of labor between accounting assurance and technological development.

For regulators, the framework offers an alternative to expansive AI-specific regulation for governing AI in accounting. Regulatory responses to AI often emphasize ex ante controls, transparency mandates, or sector-wide ethical principles that can be difficult to enforce in practice, particularly among MSMEs. By contrast, standards-based governance uses existing, enforceable regulatory instruments, such as financial reporting requirements, audit obligations, and sanctions for misrepresentation. Regulators can therefore indirectly govern AI-enabled accounting practices by reinforcing compliance with MSME financial reporting standards, reducing the need for parallel AI governance regimes that risk fragmentation or regulatory overload.

The framework also has implications for accounting technology providers, including developers of cloud-based accounting platforms and AI-enabled bookkeeping tools. These providers increasingly mediate accounting practice by embedding classification logic, default settings, and automated decision rules into software used by MSMEs. The standards-based framework signals that technological innovation must remain aligned with institutional accounting requirements rather than optimizing solely for efficiency or predictive accuracy. In practical terms, this means technology providers should design systems that facilitate compliance with financial reporting standards, support documentation and audit trails, and allow human users to exercise judgment and override automated outputs when necessary. While the framework does not directly regulate technology providers, it establishes institutional expectations that shape market demand for standards-aligned accounting technologies.

Importantly, the framework preserves institutional stability across these actor groups. Auditors continue to assess compliance rather than algorithms; regulators enforce reporting standards rather than technical design choices; and technology providers innovate within the constraints of standardized representation. This stability reduces coordination costs and mitigates the risk that AI adoption will disrupt established accountability relationships. By anchoring governance in accounting standards, the framework aligns technological change with institutional continuity, facilitating incremental adaptation rather than disruptive overhaul.

At the same time, the framework highlights the interdependence of these actors in sustaining trustworthy AI-enabled accounting. Auditors rely on documentation produced by technology platforms; regulators depend on audit outcomes to enforce compliance; and technology providers incorporate regulatory and audit expectations into system design. Standards-based AI governance thus operates as a coordinating mechanism that aligns incentives and responsibilities across institutional boundaries, reinforcing trust without centralizing control or expanding discretionary oversight.

Table 2. Institutional Implications of Standards-Based AI Governance for Key Stakeholder

Institutional actor	Traditional governance role	Shift introduced by standards-based AI governance	Elements that remain institutionally stable
Auditors	Verify compliance with accounting standards through documentation and testing	Focus remains on output compliance and auditability rather than on inspecting AI models	Audit methodologies, assurance principles, reliance on standardized representations
Regulators	Enforce financial reporting requirements and sanction misrepresentation	Indirect governance of AI-enabled accounting through strengthened standards enforcement	Legal authority, reporting obligations, enforcement mechanisms
Technology providers	Supply accounting software and automation tools	Increased responsibility for designing systems aligned with accounting standards and audit requirements	Innovation autonomy, competitive differentiation, technological development processes
MSMEs	Prepare and present financial statements	Greater clarity that AI outputs must be validated against accounting standards.	Managerial responsibility, compliance obligations, use of standardized reporting
External stakeholders (e.g., lenders)	Rely on financial statements for evaluation	Continued reliance on standardized outputs despite increased automation	Evaluation criteria, contractual reliance on accounting information

5.3 Boundary Conditions, Risks, and Non-Applicability

While the standards-based AI governance framework advanced in this chapter offers a pragmatic, institutionally grounded approach to governing AI-enabled accounting in MSMEs, its effectiveness is neither universal nor unconditional. Recognizing the boundary conditions under which the framework operates is essential to avoid overstatement and to situate its contribution within realistic institutional contexts. Governance capacity, in this model, emerges from the interaction among standards, enforcement environments, and organizational practices rather than from standards alone.

A primary boundary condition concerns the strength of institutional enforcement. Financial reporting standards derive their governance effectiveness not only from their formal content but also from their integration into regulatory, professional, and market-based enforcement mechanisms. In environments where compliance monitoring is weak, audit practices are informal, or sanctions for misrepresentation are rarely applied, the constraining power of standards may be attenuated. Under such conditions, embedding AI-enabled accounting within standards may have limited impact on actual practice, as algorithmic outputs may enter financial representations without meaningful institutional scrutiny.

A related risk arises from the persistence of informal accounting practices among MSMEs. In many contexts, financial reporting is treated as a procedural obligation rather than an institutionalized governance mechanism. When accounting standards are applied superficially or retroactively, their capacity to constrain AI-enabled processes is significantly reduced. In such cases, AI systems may reinforce existing informality by automating nonstandardized practices, thereby amplifying rather than mitigating governance deficiencies. The framework assumes a minimum level of standards adoption and internalization that may not be present across all MSME environments.

The framework also faces limitations in contexts characterized by high platform dependence. Many MSMEs rely on cloud-based accounting systems provided by third-party vendors, which embed proprietary algorithms, default settings, and automated decision rules beyond the direct control of users. While standards-based governance can constrain the outputs produced by these systems, it does not directly address upstream decisions related to model design, data selection, or system updates. This creates a structural asymmetry in which governance is exercised primarily at the level of representation rather than at the level of technological production. In highly concentrated platform ecosystems, this asymmetry may limit the effectiveness of standards-based constraints, particularly if vendor practices are opaque or weakly aligned with accounting standards.

Another boundary condition concerns the scope of applicability across different reporting regimes. The framework is most effective in environments governed by rule-oriented MSME standards that emphasize clarity, reduced optionality, and enforceability. In contrast, highly principles-based reporting regimes that rely extensively on professional judgment may introduce greater discretion into the translation of AI outputs into accounting representations. While such regimes offer flexibility, they may also increase the risk of opacity and accountability dilution when AI systems are involved. The governance advantages identified in this chapter therefore cannot be assumed to generalize uniformly across all accounting frameworks.

Finally, the framework does not claim to replace AI-specific regulatory or ethical initiatives. Instead, it serves as a complementary layer of governance focused on a specific institutional locus: the production and representation of accounting information. Risks related to data protection, cybersecurity, discrimination, or broader societal impacts of AI fall outside the immediate scope of financial reporting standards and require additional regulatory or organizational interventions. Treating accounting standards as a comprehensive solution to AI governance would therefore misrepresent their institutional role and exceed their functional capacity.

Taken together, these boundary conditions underscore the importance of contextual sensitivity in applying standards-based AI governance. The framework is most effective when accounting standards are meaningfully enforced, internalized in organizational practice, and embedded within broader institutional ecosystems that support accountability and auditability. When these conditions are absent, the governance capacity of standards may be limited, and additional mechanisms may be required. By explicitly acknowledging these limits, the framework avoids over-claiming and reinforces its role as a realistic, context-aware approach to governing AI-enabled accounting in MSMEs.

6. LIMITATIONS AND DIRECTIONS FOR FUTURE RESEARCH

6.1 Institutional and Contextual Limitations

While the standards-based AI governance framework developed in this chapter offers a conceptually robust and practically grounded approach to governing AI-enabled accounting in MSMEs, its applicability is constrained by institutional and contextual factors. These limitations do not undermine the framework's internal coherence; rather, they delineate the environments in which its governance mechanisms are most likely to operate effectively. Acknowledging these boundary conditions is essential to situate this chapter's contribution within the broader literature on institutional governance, accounting regulation, and AI adoption.

A primary limitation concerns variation in the enforcement of financial reporting standards across jurisdictions and institutional settings. Accounting standards derive their governance capacity not solely from their formal prescriptions but from the extent to which they are embedded within enforcement ecosystems comprising regulators, professional bodies, auditors, and market actors. In settings where regulatory oversight is weak, audit practices are informal, or sanctions for non-compliance are inconsistently applied, the constraining effects of standards on accounting behavior may be significantly attenuated (Devi et al., 2019; World Bank, 2020). Under such conditions, embedding AI-enabled accounting systems into MSME financial reporting standards may offer limited governance leverage, as algorithmic outputs can be incorporated into financial representations without meaningful institutional scrutiny.

A related limitation arises from the persistence of informal and hybrid accounting practices among MSMEs, particularly in emerging and developing economies. Empirical studies have shown that many MSMEs apply accounting standards partially, selectively, or retrospectively, often treating financial reporting as a compliance formality rather than as an institutionalized governance mechanism (Sian & Roberts, 2009; Uyar et al., 2020). In such contexts, the governance potential of standards-based AI frameworks depends on a minimum level of internalization of standards within organizational routines. Where this condition is absent, AI-enabled accounting systems risk reinforcing existing informality by automating non-standardized practices, thereby amplifying rather than mitigating governance deficiencies.

Institutional capacity constraints further condition the effectiveness of the proposed framework. MSMEs typically operate with limited accounting expertise, resource constraints, and highly centralized decision-making structures. While the framework is designed to leverage existing accounting standards to accommodate these constraints, its successful implementation still presupposes basic capabilities in documentation, record-keeping, and managerial oversight.

In organizational contexts where these foundational practices are underdeveloped, the ability of standards to function as an effective governance mechanism, whether applied to human or AI-assisted accounting, may be compromised (OECD, 2019).

Jurisdictional diversity in accounting regimes also introduces important contextual limitations. The framework is most compatible with MSME-oriented reporting standards that emphasize rule clarity, reduced optionality, and proportional disclosure requirements. In contrast, highly principles-based accounting regimes, which rely extensively on professional judgment and interpretive flexibility, may offer weaker institutional constraints on AI-enabled accounting outputs. While principles-based approaches provide adaptability, they may also increase discretion and opacity when combined with algorithmic systems, complicating alignment between AI outputs and standardized representations (Benke & Pelger, 2021).

Finally, broader institutional complementarities shape the governance capacity of accounting standards. Financial reporting standards interact with tax systems, credit evaluation practices, and contractual arrangements that rely on standardized accounting information. Where these complementary institutions are fragmented or weakly aligned, the governance effects of standards-based AI integration may be diluted. The framework, therefore, assumes a minimum level of institutional coherence in which accounting standards serve as a shared reference point across regulatory, financial, and professional domains.

Taken together, these institutional and contextual limitations underscore that standards-based AI governance should be understood as a contingent, context-sensitive approach rather than a universally applicable solution. Its effectiveness depends on enforcement strength, organizational practices, jurisdictional design choices, and institutional complementarities that extend beyond the technical properties of AI systems themselves. By explicitly recognizing these conditions, the framework avoids overclaiming and situates its contribution within realistic governance environments, consistent with contemporary institutional analyses of accounting and AI adoption.

6.2 Technological and Organizational Boundaries

Beyond institutional and enforcement-related conditions, the applicability of standards-based AI governance in MSME accounting is further shaped by technological and organizational boundaries. These boundaries stem from how AI systems are designed, deployed, and embedded in organizational processes, as well as from the structural characteristics of MSMEs. Recognizing these constraints is essential to avoid conflating institutional governance mechanisms with technical control over algorithmic systems.

A key technological boundary concerns the growing platformization of accounting technologies. Many MSMEs rely on cloud-based accounting platforms and software-as-a-service solutions that integrate AI capabilities such as automated classification, predictive analytics, and continuous reconciliation. While accounting standards can constrain the outputs of these systems, they do not directly govern upstream decisions about model architecture, training data selection, parameter updates, or system retraining cycles. This separation creates a structural asymmetry in which governance is exercised primarily through representational outputs rather than algorithmic production (Moll & Yigitbasioglu, 2019; Vasarhelyi et al 2020).

This output-oriented mode of governance reflects pragmatic institutional realities rather than conceptual shortcomings. For MSMEs, model-level oversight, such as validating training datasets or auditing algorithmic logic, is typically infeasible given resource and expertise constraints. Standards-based governance, therefore, delineates what counts as an acceptable accounting outcome, irrespective of the internal mechanics that generate it. While this approach preserves auditability and accountability at the institutional level, it cannot fully address risks associated with opaque vendor practices, proprietary algorithms, or platform concentration (Benke & Pelger, 2021).

Organizational boundaries further condition the effectiveness of the framework. MSMEs are characterized by centralized decision-making, limited segregation of duties, and informal governance structures. In such environments, AI-enabled accounting systems may become deeply embedded in daily operations, blurring the distinction between decision support and decision authority. Even when standards-based constraints are formally in place, organizational reliance on automated outputs may result in the de facto delegation of judgment to technological systems. This dynamic highlights a boundary between formal accountability arrangements and lived organizational practices, where human oversight exists in principle but may be weakened in practice (Rai, 2020).

Human–AI interaction dynamics represent an additional boundary condition. The effectiveness of standards-based governance presupposes that human actors remain capable of interpreting, questioning, and overriding AI-assisted accounting outputs.

However, cognitive biases, time pressures, and perceived technical authority may reduce users' willingness or ability to exercise such judgment. While accounting standards provide a normative reference point for validation, they cannot guarantee that users will actively engage with this reference in high-automation environments. This limitation underscores the need to complement governance mechanisms embedded in standards with organizational practices that sustain professional skepticism and accountability (Power, 2021).

A further boundary arises from the evolving nature of AI systems themselves. Machine learning models are adaptive by design, updating their behavior in response to new data and feedback. While accounting standards impose consistency and comparability requirements, they do not inherently regulate the dynamics of algorithmic learning. As a result, tensions may emerge between institutional demands for stability and technological tendencies toward continuous adaptation. Standards-based governance can flag deviations at the output level, but it may not prevent subtle shifts in model behavior that accumulate over time, particularly in continuous-accounting environments (Vasarhelyi et al., 2020).

Finally, the framework is bounded by the scope of accounting standards as governance instruments. Financial reporting standards are designed to govern the representation of economic activity, not the full lifecycle of AI systems. Issues such as data governance, cybersecurity, privacy, and broader ethical considerations extend beyond the remit of accounting standards and require complementary regulatory and organizational responses. The standards-based approach advanced in this chapter should therefore be understood as one layer within a multi-layered governance architecture, addressing a specific institutional locus rather than offering a comprehensive solution to all AI-related risks.

In sum, technological and organizational boundaries define the governance capacity of accounting standards in AI-enabled MSME contexts. These boundaries do not negate the value of standards-based AI governance but clarify its domain of effectiveness. By operating at the level of standardized representation and accountability, the framework offers a feasible, institutionally grounded mechanism for governing AI-assisted accounting, while acknowledging that certain technological and organizational risks lie beyond its immediate reach. This recognition reinforces the need for complementary governance arrangements that align technological innovation with organizational capacity and institutional accountability.

6.3 Directions for Future Research

Future research may also explore the interaction between standards-based accounting governance and emerging AI-specific regulatory frameworks. As jurisdictions introduce AI regulations addressing transparency, accountability, and risk management, an important question concerns how these regimes intersect with existing accounting infrastructures. Analytical work could examine whether accounting standards function as complementary governance layers, points of tension, or sites of regulatory overlap, thereby informing more coherent and proportionate policy design.

The standards-based AI governance framework advanced in this chapter opens several promising avenues for future research at the intersection of accounting, institutional governance, and artificial intelligence. While the present chapter develops a conceptual and analytical foundation, further empirical and comparative work is needed to assess how these governance mechanisms operate across diverse organizational and institutional contexts.

A first direction for future research concerns empirical validation at the organizational level. Qualitative case studies and field-based research could examine how MSMEs implement AI-enabled accounting systems within the constraints of financial reporting standards, and how managers, accountants, and auditors interpret and negotiate these constraints in practice. Such studies would provide insight into whether standards-based governance effectively mitigates automation bias, preserves accountability, and sustains auditability in real-world settings. Longitudinal designs may be particularly valuable for assessing how AI-assisted accounting practices evolve over time and how institutional constraints interact with adaptive algorithmic systems.

A second research direction involves cross-jurisdictional and comparative analysis. MSME financial reporting standards vary significantly across countries in terms of rule specificity, enforcement strength, and institutional embedding. Comparative studies could investigate how these differences shape the governance capacity of accounting standards in AI-enabled environments. Such research would contribute to a more nuanced understanding of how institutional design choices influence the alignment between accounting standards and trustworthy AI principles, particularly in emerging and developing economies.

Another promising avenue is the design and evaluation of standards-aligned accounting technologies. Research informed by design science or by interdisciplinary collaboration between accounting scholars and information systems researchers could examine how AI-enabled accounting platforms operationalize accounting standards across software architectures, interfaces, and validation processes. Such work would bridge institutional theory and technological implementation, offering actionable insights for developers and standard setters alike.

Finally, future research could extend the framework beyond financial reporting to adjacent domains of organizational governance, such as sustainability reporting, integrated reporting, or management accounting. As AI systems increasingly support non-financial measurement and disclosure, examining whether standards-based governance mechanisms can similarly constrain and legitimize algorithmic outputs in these domains would be an important extension of the present analysis.

Collectively, these research directions position the standards-based AI governance framework not as a definitive solution but as a generative platform for further inquiry. By articulating clear institutional mechanisms through which accounting standards can mediate AI adoption, this chapter provides a foundation upon which empirical, comparative, and design-oriented research can build, advancing scholarly understanding of trustworthy AI in accounting and organizational governance.

CONCLUSION

This chapter examined the role of MSME financial reporting standards as institutional governance mechanisms for AI-enabled accounting systems. Rather than treating trustworthy artificial intelligence in accounting as a predominantly technical or ethical design problem, the analysis reframed AI governance as an institutional challenge rooted in the representation, validation, and accountability of financial information. By centering financial reporting standards, the chapter demonstrated how existing accounting infrastructures can mediate the integration of AI into organizational practice without undermining trust, auditability, or responsibility.

The core contribution of this chapter is articulating a standards-based governance logic that constrains algorithmic outputs rather than regulating algorithmic internals. In MSME contexts, where technical oversight capacity is limited and governance structures are often informal, this output-oriented approach offers a pragmatic, institutionally feasible pathway to align AI-enabled accounting with established norms of transparency, consistency, and accountability. By positioning accounting standards as rule-based institutions that shape acceptable representations of economic activity, the chapter highlighted their latent capacity to function as governance instruments in technologically mediated environments.

The analysis further demonstrated that MSME-oriented financial reporting standards offer distinctive governance advantages, particularly through their emphasis on proportionality, reduced discretion, and enforceability. These features enhance their suitability for governing AI-assisted accounting practices, especially compared with highly principles-based regimes that rely heavily on professional judgment. By embedding AI within standardized accounting routines, MSMEs can adopt advanced technologies while preserving the institutional foundations of financial credibility and stakeholder trust.

At the same time, the chapter explicitly acknowledged the institutional, technological, and organizational boundaries that condition the effectiveness of standards-based AI governance. Variations in enforcement strength, informal accounting practices, platform dependency, and human–AI interaction dynamics shape the extent to which accounting standards can, in practice, constrain algorithmic behavior. Recognizing these limitations avoids overclaim and situates the proposed framework within realistic governance environments, reinforcing its analytical credibility.

Taken together, the chapter advances a reframing of trustworthy AI in accounting that emphasizes institutional design over technical control. It suggests that the governance of AI-enabled accounting systems does not necessarily require the proliferation of new regulatory regimes or ethical overlays but can be meaningfully supported through the reactivation and reinterpretation of existing accounting standards. For MSMEs in particular, this approach offers a viable means of integrating AI into accounting practice while maintaining accountability, interpretability, and trust.

By grounding AI governance in the institutional logic of accounting standards, this chapter contributes to ongoing scholarly debates at the intersection of accounting, governance, and digital transformation. It positions financial reporting standards not as passive compliance tools but as active governance infrastructures capable of shaping how algorithmic systems are embedded, evaluated, and trusted within organizational life.

REFERENCES

Appelbaum, D., Kogan, A., Vasarhelyi, M. A., & Yan, Z. (2017). Impact of business analytics and enterprise systems on managerial accounting. *International Journal of Accounting Information Systems, 25*, 29–44. DOI: 10.1016/j.accinf.2017.03.003

Asian Development Bank. (2023). *Asia Small and Medium-Sized Enterprise Monitor 2023: Towards green and resilient MSMEs*. Asian Development Bank.

Benke, K., & Pelger, C. (2021). AFA: A critical perspective on artificial intelligence in accounting. *Accounting, Organizations and Society, 92*, 101243. DOI: 10.1016/j.aos.2021.101243

Bhimani, A., Horngren, C. T., Datar, S. M., & Rajan, M. V. (2019). *Management and cost accounting* (7th ed.). Pearson.

Burrell, J. (2016). How the machine 'thinks': Understanding opacity in machine learning algorithms. *Big Data & Society, 3*(1), 1–12. DOI: 10.1177/2053951715622512

Cath, C., Wachter, S., Mittelstadt, B., Taddeo, M., & Floridi, L. (2018). Artificial intelligence and the 'good society': The US, EU, and UK approach. *Science and Engineering Ethics, 24*, 505–528. DOI: 10.1007/s11948-017-9901-7 PMID: 28353045

Devi, S., Hooper, K., & Davey, H. (2019). Accounting and accountability in microfinance institutions: A systematic literature review. *Journal of Accounting in Emerging Economies, 9*(3), 437–463.

European Commission High-Level Expert Group on Artificial Intelligence. (2019). *Ethics guidelines for trustworthy AI*. European Commission.

Giddens, A. (1990). *The consequences of modernity*. Stanford University Press.

Guidotti, R., Monreale, A., Ruggieri, S., Turini, F., Giannotti, F., & Pedreschi, D. (2019). A survey of methods for explaining black box models. *ACM Computing Surveys, 51*(5), 93. DOI: 10.1145/3236009

Kokina, J., & Davenport, T. H. (2017). The emergence of artificial intelligence: How automation is changing auditing. *Journal of Emerging Technologies in Accounting, 14*(1), 115–122. DOI: 10.2308/jeta-51730

Mehrabi, N., Morstatter, F., Saxena, N., Lerman, K., & Galstyan, A. (2021). A survey on bias and fairness in machine learning. *ACM Computing Surveys, 54*(6), 115. DOI: 10.1145/3457607

Moll, J., & Yigitbasioglu, O. (2019). The role of internet-related technologies in shaping the work of accountants: New directions for accounting research. *The British Accounting Review*, *51*(6), 100833. DOI: 10.1016/j.bar.2019.04.002

National Institute of Standards and Technology. (2023). *Artificial Intelligence Risk Management Framework (AI RMF 1.0)*. U.S. Department of Commerce.

Organisation for Economic Co-operation and Development. (2019). *OECD SME and Entrepreneurship Outlook 2019*. OECD Publishing.

Organisation for Economic Co-operation and Development. (2021). *The digital transformation of SMEs*. OECD Publishing.

Power, M. (2021). The microfoundations of the audit society: Organizations and the logic of the audit trail. *Academy of Management Review*, *46*(3), 489–506. DOI: 10.5465/amr.2018.0151

Rai, A. (2020). Explainable AI: From black box to glass box. *Journal of the Academy of Marketing Science*, *48*(1), 137–141. DOI: 10.1007/s11747-019-00710-5

Raisch, S., & Krakowski, S. (2021). Artificial intelligence and management: The automation–augmentation paradox. *Academy of Management Review*, *46*(1), 192–210. DOI: 10.5465/amr.2018.0072

Scott, W. R. (2014). *Institutions and organizations: Ideas, interests, and identities* (4th ed.). SAGE.

Sian, S., & Roberts, C. (2009). UK small owner-managed businesses: Accounting and financial reporting needs. *Journal of Small Business and Enterprise Development*, *16*(2), 289–305. DOI: 10.1108/14626000910956065

Star, S. L., & Griesemer, J. R. (1989). Institutional ecology, 'translations' and boundary objects: Amateurs and professionals in Berkeley's Museum of Vertebrate Zoology, 1907–39. *Social Studies of Science*, *19*(3), 387–420. DOI: 10.1177/030631289019003001

Sutton, S. G., Holt, M., & Arnold, V. (2016). The reports of my death are greatly exaggerated—Artificial intelligence research in accounting. *International Journal of Accounting Information Systems*, *22*, 60–73. DOI: 10.1016/j.accinf.2016.07.005

Uyar, A., Nimer, K., Kuzey, C., Shahbaz, M., & Schneider, F. (2020). Can e-government initiatives alleviate corruption? The moderating effect of financial development. *Technological Forecasting and Social Change*, *157*, 120055. DOI: 10.1016/j.techfore.2020.120055

Vasarhelyi, M. A., Kogan, A., & Tuttle, B. M. (2020). Big data in accounting: An overview. *Accounting Horizons*, *34*(2), 1–14.

World Bank. (2020). *World Development Report 2020: Trading for development in the age of global value chains*. World Bank.

Chapter 5
Explainable AI (XAI) for Classical ML and LLMs

Brijendra Parasnath Gupta
http://orcid.org/0000-0003-3597-350X
Siddhant College of Engineering, Pune, India

Nazirjon Rajabov
http://orcid.org/0000-0002-8155-5790
Alfraganus University, Tashkent, Uzbekistan

Ergashev Nuriddin Gayratovich
http://orcid.org/0000-0002-8274-6193
Karshi State Technical University, Karshi, Uzbekistan

Gulkhayo Otajonova
Mamun University, Khiva, Uzbekistan

Erkin Kholiyarov
Termez University of Economics and Service, Termez, Uzbekistan

Jumayev Akbar
Tashkent State University of Economics, Uzbekistan

Sultonmakhmud Polvanov
Urgench State University Named After Abu Rayhan Biruni, Uzbekistan

ABSTRACT

Explainable Artificial Intelligence (XAI) constitutes a foundational pillar of responsible AI deployment, addressing the opacity of data-driven decision systems by making their internal logic transparent, auditable, and contestable. This chapter provides a systematic account of explainability and interpretability across the full spectrum of AI models — from classical supervised learning algorithms such as decision trees, support vector machines, and gradient-boosted ensembles to contemporary Large Language Models (LLMs) built on transformer architectures. Beginning with a structured taxonomy of XAI properties — scope, stage, model-dependency, and output type — the chapter critically examines canonical explanation methods including SHAP, LIME, attention visualization, mechanistic circuit analysis, and counterfactual generation.

DOI: 10.4018/979-8-3373-6761-3.ch005

1. INTRODUCTION

The proliferation of machine learning systems across domains as varied as clinical diagnosis, financial credit scoring, criminal justice risk assessment, and autonomous navigation has generated an acute and pressing societal demand: the demand to understand, interrogate, and trust the decisions that these systems make. The term Explainable Artificial Intelligence (XAI) describes a body of research and practice dedicated to rendering AI and machine learning systems interpretable to human stakeholders. While algorithmic performance — measured by predictive accuracy, throughput, or competitive benchmark scores — has historically dominated the AI research agenda, the practical deployment of AI in high-stakes domains has revealed that performance alone is insufficient. A system that cannot be explained cannot be trusted, audited, contested, or safely improved.

The challenge of explainability is not monolithic. It manifests differently depending on the complexity of the underlying model, the nature of the prediction task, the identity and expertise of the intended audience, and the regulatory environment in which the system operates. A clinician demanding to understand why a deep learning model flagged a particular radiological scan as malignant requires a different form of explanation from a software engineer debugging a production recommendation system or a regulator auditing an automated loan approval pipeline. Arrieta et al. (2021) established an influential taxonomy of XAI concepts, distinguishing between transparency — properties inherent to the model — and post-hoc explainability — methods applied after training to extract explanations from an otherwise opaque system. This foundational distinction underpins the conceptual architecture of the present chapter.

Recent years have witnessed a dramatic shift in the AI landscape with the rise of Large Language Models (LLMs) — architecturally complex, billion-parameter transformer systems trained on internet-scale corpora. These systems simultaneously complicate and enrich the XAI landscape. They complicate it because their sheer parametric depth makes traditional feature-attribution methods, developed for classical ML, difficult to scale or apply. They enrich it because LLMs can themselves generate natural language explanations of model behaviour, thereby acting as explanation interfaces for less communicative systems. Mumuni and Mumuni (2025) and Seveso et al. (2024) both survey this dual positioning of LLMs within XAI, while Wu et al. (2024) elaborate ten specific strategies for exploiting LLM explainability in applied contexts.

The societal urgency of XAI extends beyond academic interest. As AI systems become embedded in consequential institutional processes — determining parole eligibility, diagnosing disease, allocating financial credit, informing hiring decisions — the absence of interpretability becomes a matter not only of technical inadequacy but of social and democratic accountability. Citizens affected by automated decisions have a legitimate interest in understanding the basis on which those decisions were made. Without explainability, the appeal and contestation mechanisms essential to procedural justice are effectively disabled. This chapter situates XAI at the intersection of technical methodology, epistemic responsibility, and the evolving regulatory landscape.

This chapter is structured to take the reader systematically through the landscape of XAI for both classical ML and LLMs. Section 2 establishes the definitional and taxonomic foundations. Section 3 surveys XAI methods for classical machine learning models. Section 4 examines XAI for LLMs, covering both mechanistic and post-hoc approaches. Section 5 explores the bidirectional relationship between LLMs and XAI. Section 6 addresses regulatory requirements. Section 7 discusses evaluation frameworks and limitations. Section 8 presents open research challenges, and Section 9 concludes the chapter.

2. CONCEPTUAL FOUNDATIONS AND TAXONOMY OF XAI

2.1 Interpretability Versus Explainability

The terms interpretability and explainability are frequently used interchangeably in both academic literature and industry practice, yet they encode a meaningful conceptual distinction. Interpretability refers to the degree to which humans can consistently predict the behaviour of a model — that is, the extent to which the model's decision logic is directly comprehensible. Explainability, by contrast, refers to the capacity of a model or an auxiliary system to provide post-hoc justifications or rationales for specific decisions, even when the underlying model itself is not structurally transparent. A linear regression model is interpretable: its coefficients directly express the marginal effect of each predictor on the outcome. A deep neural network is not inherently interpretable, but it may be made explainable through the application of auxiliary methods such as SHAP or LIME.

Rudin et al. (2022) draw a sharp and consequential distinction: for high-stakes decisions, they argue that post-hoc explainability of black-box models is insufficient and potentially misleading, advocating instead for the deployment of intrinsically interpretable models such as decision trees, rule lists, and generalised additive models. Their position, supported by extensive empirical and theoretical argumentation, challenges a widely held assumption — namely, that sufficiently powerful post-hoc explanation methods can compensate for structural opacity. This debate remains active and unresolved in the XAI literature, and its resolution has material implications for the design and regulation of AI systems deployed in healthcare, criminal justice, and financial services.

Belle and Papantonis (2021) provide a complementary framing, distinguishing between three levels of interpretability: simulatability (the ability to mentally simulate a model's behaviour), decomposability (the ability to interpret individual model components), and algorithmic transparency (understanding of the full training process). These levels roughly correspond to the cognitive hierarchy of how humans engage with model behaviour, from coarse holistic understanding to detailed mechanistic analysis. Simulatability, the most demanding of these properties, requires that the model be sufficiently simple for a human to trace through its entire computation — a property satisfied by small decision trees and linear models but not by any contemporary deep learning system. Decomposability is more tractable: even in complex neural networks, individual neurons, layers, or attention heads may be interpretable in isolation, even when the integrated system is not.

A further distinction of practical importance is that between global and local interpretability. A globally interpretable model can be understood in its entirety — its decision logic applies uniformly and can be described by a compact set of rules or parameters. A locally interpretable model provides explanations specific to individual predictions, without claiming that these explanations generalise across the input distribution. This distinction maps onto the scope dimension of the XAI taxonomy discussed in Section 2.2 and is particularly salient for complex models whose decision boundaries are highly non-linear and context-dependent.

2.2 Taxonomic Dimensions of XAI Methods

XAI methods can be classified along several orthogonal dimensions, each encoding a distinct property of the explanation. Arrieta et al. (2021) and Holzinger et al. (2022) collectively identify at least four primary axes of classification that structure the landscape of contemporary XAI methods.

The first dimension is scope: explanations may be local or global. Local explanations characterise the behaviour of a model for a specific input instance — answering the question 'Why did the model make this particular prediction?' Global explanations characterise the overall behaviour of a model across its input distribution — answering 'How does this model generally work?' SHAP admits both local (individual Shapley values) and global (summary plots) interpretations, making it one of the most flexible methods in terms of scope.

The second dimension is the stage of explanation: ante-hoc (intrinsic) or post-hoc (extrinsic). Ante-hoc methods are properties of the model architecture itself, such as the decision rules of a decision tree or the regression coefficients of a linear model. Post-hoc methods are applied after training and are independent of the model architecture, making them applicable to arbitrary black-box systems.

The third dimension is model-dependency: model-specific methods are designed to exploit properties of a particular model architecture (e.g., gradient-based attribution methods for neural networks), while model-agnostic methods can be applied to any predictive model by treating it as a black box and querying it with perturbed inputs. LIME and SHAP in its KernelSHAP formulation are canonical model-agnostic methods; integrated gradients and attention-based explanations are model-specific.

The fourth dimension concerns the form of the explanation output. Explanations may take the form of feature importance scores (which predictors most influence the prediction?), saliency maps (which spatial regions of an image drive the prediction?), decision rules (what logical conditions lead to this outcome?), exemplars (which training examples are most relevant to this prediction?), or natural language rationales (what verbal justification can be offered?). Figure 1 synthesises these dimensions into a unified taxonomic map.

Figure 1. XAI Taxonomy: Dimensions of Explainability Methods.

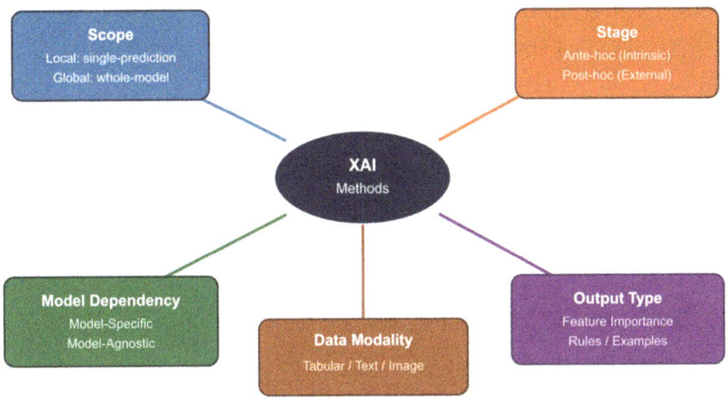

Each dimension offers independent classification axes for XAI methods (Arrieta et al., 2021; Holzinger et al., 2022)

Figure 1 illustrates the five orthogonal classification axes — Scope, Stage, Model Dependency, Output Type, and Data Modality — by which XAI methods are systematically categorised (adapted from Arrieta et al., 2021; Holzinger et al., 2022).

2.3 Audiences and Purposes of Explanation

Explanations are not context-free artefacts; they are communication acts directed at specific audiences with specific needs. Das and Rad (2021) identify at least four distinct stakeholder groups with different explanation requirements. Developers and data scientists require technical explanations that facilitate debugging, error analysis, and iterative model improvement. Domain experts — clinicians, legal professionals, financial analysts — require explanations grounded in domain-relevant concepts that support professional judgment. End users require accessible, actionable explanations that allow them to understand, challenge, and appeal automated decisions. Regulators and auditors require systematic, legally legible justifications that demonstrate compliance with normative requirements such as the GDPR's right to explanation or the EU AI Act's transparency obligations. Matching the form and granularity of explanations to these varied audiences is one of the central design challenges in applied XAI.

The concept of explanation appropriateness — whether an explanation serves its intended communicative function for its intended audience — has received increasing attention in human-computer interaction and cognitive science research. Miller (2019) draws on social science literature to argue that AI explanations should be contrastive (explaining why X rather than Y occurred), selective (highlighting the most important causal factors rather than enumerating all of them), and social (responsive to the interactive context of the explanation request). These findings challenge technically oriented XAI researchers who may optimise for completeness and formal correctness at the expense of communicative effectiveness. The design of explanation

3. EXPLAINABILITY METHODS FOR CLASSICAL MACHINE LEARNING

3.1 Intrinsically Interpretable Models

A category of classical ML models achieves interpretability by design, without requiring any post-hoc explanation apparatus. Decision trees produce explicit, hierarchical rule structures that can be read as logical if-then chains. Linear and logistic regression models express relationships between predictors and outcomes as weighted sums, with coefficient magnitudes and directions providing direct interpretability. Generalised additive models (GAMs) extend linear models by permitting nonlinear predictor-outcome relationships while preserving additive structure, enabling the contribution of each feature to be visualised independently. Rudin et al. (2022) advocate for this class of models in high-stakes domains, arguing that the interpretability of these models is not merely aesthetically desirable but operationally necessary for the safe deployment of AI in consequential settings.

Rule-based systems such as decision rule lists and scorecards occupy a related but distinct niche. Scorecards, used extensively in clinical risk prediction and credit scoring, assign points to feature values and sum them to produce a total risk score. Their transparency is maximal: any stakeholder can manually compute their score and understand exactly which factors contributed to it. The interpretability of these models, however, comes at a cost: they typically exhibit lower predictive accuracy than complex ensemble methods on the same tasks. This accuracy-interpretability trade-off is one of the defining tensions of the XAI field.

Despite this trade-off, the empirical case for intrinsically interpretable models in high-stakes settings is stronger than commonly assumed. Rudin et al. (2022) document multiple cases in clinical risk prediction, recidivism assessment, and credit scoring in which carefully designed interpretable models achieved performance comparable to black-box alternatives. The key insight is that the accuracy gap between interpretable and complex models is often overstated in the literature, particularly when the comparison is made on datasets that are sufficiently large, clean, and well-engineered. The perceived superiority of black-box models frequently reflects inadequate feature engineering or model selection for the interpretable baseline rather than a fundamental performance ceiling.

Optimal decision trees and rule lists — selected using combinatorial optimisation techniques rather than greedy heuristics — represent an important methodological advance in this space. Angelino et al. (2018) developed CORELS (Certifiably Optimal Rule Lists), a branch-and-bound algorithm for finding rule lists that are provably optimal under a regularised objective. Similarly, Rudin and colleagues developed optimal classification trees that guarantee global optimality rather than local-greedy approximations. These methods produce models that are both fully interpretable and demonstrably optimal within a well-defined model class, challenging the assumption that interpretability necessarily requires sacrificing performance.

3.2 SHAP: Shapley Additive Explanations

SHAP (SHapley Additive exPlanations), introduced by Lundberg et al. (2022), grounds feature attribution in cooperative game theory. The Shapley value — imported from economics — assigns to each player in a coalition game its fair share of the coalition's payoff, computed as the marginal contribution of that player averaged over all possible orderings of the coalition. Applied to ML, Shapley values assign to each feature its average marginal contribution to the model's prediction, computed across all possible subsets of features. SHAP is the only method that satisfies all of the following axiomatic properties simultaneously: local accuracy (the explanation is a faithful local linear approximation of the model), missingness (features with no effect receive zero attribution), and consistency (if a model changes such that a feature's marginal contribution increases, its attribution does not decrease).

Lundberg et al. (2022) demonstrate that SHAP unifies several previously disparate explanation methods — including LIME, DeepLIFT, and layer-wise relevance propagation — as special cases of additive feature attribution. For tree-based models such as XGBoost and Random Forest, the TreeSHAP algorithm computes exact Shapley values in polynomial time by exploiting the tree structure, making it scalable to production settings. Salih et al. (2025) provide a comprehensive comparative perspective on SHAP and LIME, situating both methods in the context of biomedical AI applications and evaluating their practical strengths and limitations.

SHAP's global summary plots (beeswarm, bar, and waterfall diagrams) aggregate local Shapley values to reveal population-level feature importance patterns. SHAP dependence plots reveal interaction effects between pairs of features. These tools have made SHAP the de facto standard for feature-attribution explanation in industrial ML pipelines. Limitations include computational cost for KernelSHAP on large models, sensitivity to feature correlation, and the philosophical debate over whether Shapley values constitute causally meaningful attributions.

3.3 LIME: Local Interpretable Model-Agnostic Explanations

LIME (Ribeiro et al., 2016, cited in multiple subsequent works) produces local explanations by fitting a simple, interpretable surrogate model in the neighbourhood of a specific input instance. Given an input x and a complex black-box model f, LIME generates a set of perturbed samples in the neighbourhood of x, obtains predictions for these samples from f, and fits a weighted linear model g to this local dataset, where weights reflect proximity to x. The coefficients of g provide a local linear approximation of f's decision boundary near x.

LIME is model-agnostic and applicable to any black-box classifier or regressor. It works for tabular, text, and image data, making it one of the most versatile explanation methods. For text data, LIME highlights the words whose presence or absence most strongly affects the prediction. For image data, it identifies the superpixel regions most responsible for the model's decision. Salih et al. (2025) and Hassija et al. (2024) note that LIME's key limitation is instability: because the neighbourhood is sampled stochastically, explanations can vary significantly between runs for the same input, undermining their reliability. The choice of kernel bandwidth, number of samples, and neighbourhood definition also substantially affects results.

3.4 Counterfactual Explanations

Counterfactual explanations address the question: 'What is the smallest change to the input that would change the model's decision?' Wachter et al. (2021) introduced the counterfactual explanation framework in the context of GDPR compliance, arguing that counterfactuals provide an operationally adequate and legally tractable form of algorithmic transparency. A counterfactual explanation for a loan rejection might read: 'Your application was rejected; if your annual income were 15% higher, it would have been approved.' This form of explanation is actionable, providing the denied party with a concrete path to recourse.

Guidotti (2022) provides a comprehensive literature review and benchmarking study of counterfactual explanation methods, cataloguing over fifty distinct approaches and evaluating them on dimensions including proximity (how close is the counterfactual to the original?), plausibility (is the counterfactual realistic?), diversity (are multiple distinct counterfactuals available?), and sparsity (how few features need to change?). The computational problem of finding optimal counterfactuals under these competing constraints is generally NP-hard, motivating a range of heuristic, optimisation-based, and generative approaches.

3.5 Additional Methods: Attention, Probing, and Saliency

For classical deep learning models applied to tabular and image data, gradient-based saliency methods such as Integrated Gradients, GradCAM, and SmoothGrad compute attribution scores by examining how the output changes with respect to perturbations or gradients of the input features. Reyes et al. (2022) review the application of these methods to medical imaging, noting that saliency maps in radiology AI can guide clinical trust and highlight potential failure modes, but require careful validation against expert annotations to avoid misleading interpretations.

Dwivedi et al. (2023) provide a comprehensive survey of XAI techniques, covering rule extraction, prototype-based explanations, and concept-based explanations. Concept-based explanations — methods such as TCAV (Testing with Concept Activation Vectors) — assess the degree to which human-defined abstract concepts (such as 'striped texture' or 'asymmetry') are linearly represented in a model's internal representations, providing a conceptual bridge between human reasoning and learned feature representations.

4. EXPLAINABILITY AND INTERPRETABILITY FOR LARGE LANGUAGE MODELS

4.1 The Opacity Challenge in LLMs

Large Language Models present qualitatively distinct challenges for explainability. A transformer-based LLM with hundreds of billions of parameters operates through mechanisms — attention patterns, multi-layer feedforward computations, residual stream accumulation — that are both numerically vast and functionally opaque in ways that differ fundamentally from classical ML. The sheer scale of these models makes direct inspection intractable, and the distributed, high-dimensional nature of their internal representations resists reduction to human-interpretable concepts. Zhao et al. (2024) survey the full landscape of LLM explainability, organising methods by the type of explanation they produce and the level of the model they analyse. Danilevsky et al. (2021) provide an earlier survey of XAI specifically for NLP tasks, establishing the baseline approaches that subsequent LLM-specific work builds upon.

Despite these challenges, the interpretability of LLMs is not merely an academic curiosity but an operational requirement. When an LLM is deployed in a clinical support system, a legal research assistant, or an educational tool, stakeholders need to understand not merely what the model outputs but why, on what basis, and with what degree of confidence. The failure modes of LLMs — hallucination, factual error, sycophancy, harmful generation — are substantially harder to diagnose and correct without interpretability tools that reveal the internal mechanisms producing these outputs. The alignment research community has identified interpretability as one of the key enablers of safe AI: without the ability to verify that a model's internal representations and computations correspond to its stated reasoning, the trustworthiness of that reasoning cannot be assured.

The transformer architecture introduces specific interpretability challenges that have no direct analogue in classical ML. The multi-head self-attention mechanism allows each token's representation to be influenced by every other token in the context, creating complex, context-dependent information routing that is difficult to characterise using local attribution methods. The residual stream architecture — in which each transformer block adds its contribution to a running residual — means that information is accumulated non-linearly across layers, making it difficult to attribute specific behaviours to specific components. The superposition hypothesis (Elhage et al., 2022) suggests that many features are encoded as overlapping, non-orthogonal directions in activation space, meaning that individual neurons do not correspond to human-interpretable concepts in the straightforward way that simplified accounts of neural networks often assume.

4.2 Attention Mechanisms as Explanations

Attention mechanisms were initially proposed as an explanation of how transformer models weight different parts of the input when producing outputs. The intuition is straightforward: if an attention head assigns high weight to a particular token when generating a specific output, this weight can be interpreted as evidence that the model finds that token relevant. Ferrando et al. (2024) provide a detailed technical primer on transformer internal mechanisms, covering the roles of attention heads, feedforward networks, layer normalisation, and the residual stream in shaping model behaviour.

However, the interpretive value of attention weights is contested. Multiple studies have demonstrated that high attention weight does not necessarily indicate causal relevance — attention can be high for tokens that contribute minimally to the output, and causally critical tokens may not receive proportionally high attention in the final layer. Räuker et al. (2023) survey the broader literature on interpreting deep neural networks, noting that attention visualisation must be supplemented with causal analysis to produce reliable interpretations. Despite these caveats, attention visualisation remains a widely used and heuristically valuable tool for initial model exploration.

4.3 Mechanistic Interpretability

Mechanistic interpretability represents the most ambitious and technically demanding approach to LLM explainability: it seeks to reverse-engineer the algorithms that transformer models implement, identifying specific circuits, components, and computations responsible for particular model behaviours. Olsson et al. (2022) made a foundational contribution to this programme by identifying induction heads — two-layer attention circuits that enable in-context learning by detecting and extending patterns — as a key mechanism underlying the remarkable few-shot learning capabilities of transformer models.

Meng et al. (2022) advanced this agenda by developing ROME (Rank-One Model Editing), a method for localising factual associations in GPT models to specific layers and attention heads, and then directly editing these associations to modify specific model behaviours. Their finding that factual knowledge is concentrated in the middle layers of transformer models (specifically in the feedforward networks of those layers) provided concrete mechanistic insight into how LLMs store and retrieve factual information. Hase et al. (2023) subsequently challenged this claim, demonstrating surprising discrepancies between causal localisation (identifying where information is stored) and successful knowledge editing (actually modifying that information), raising important questions about the relationship between mechanistic analysis and model modification.

Räuker et al. (2023) systematically review methods for interpreting deep neural networks' internal structures, covering probing classifiers (linear models trained to predict labels from intermediate representations), activation patching (surgical interventions on activations to test causal hypotheses), concept erasure, and sparse autoencoder analysis. The emerging programme of mechanistic interpretability, championed by researchers at Anthropic and elsewhere, aims to produce not merely heuristic explanations but verified accounts of the algorithms implemented by specific model components.

4.4 Post-hoc Methods Applied to LLMs

Classical post-hoc XAI methods — SHAP, LIME, integrated gradients — can in principle be applied to LLMs by treating the model as a black box and attributing token-level influence scores. Hsieh et al. (2024) provide a comprehensive guide to XAI covering both classical models and LLMs, evaluating the applicability and limitations of attribution methods across this range. The primary challenges in applying these methods to LLMs are computational: KernelSHAP requires a large number of forward passes through the model; for a 70B parameter LLM, even a modest number of perturbations can be prohibitively expensive.

Kroeger et al. (2024) conduct an empirical investigation of whether LLMs themselves can function as post-hoc explainers — that is, whether asking an LLM to explain another model's behaviour produces faithful explanations. Their findings are sobering: LLMs often produce plausible-sounding but unfaithful explanations, confabulating reasoning that does not reflect the actual computational processes driving model outputs. This finding underscores the need for rigorous evaluation metrics that distinguish genuine mechanistic faithfulness from superficial verbal plausibility.

Figure 2. Explainability Stack for Large Language Models.

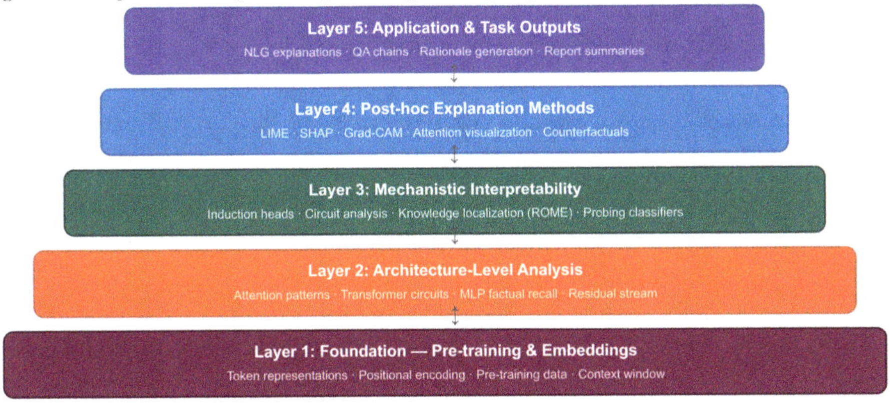

Explainability operates at multiple levels. Lower layers address internal model structure; higher layers address human-interpretable outputs. (Zhao et al., 2024; Ferrando et al., 2024; Räuker et al., 2023)

Figure 2 illustrates the five levels at which LLM interpretability can be examined, from foundation-level pre-training and embeddings through mechanistic circuit analysis to application-layer natural language explanations (adapted from Zhao et al., 2024; Ferrando et al., 2024; Räuker et al., 2023).

5. THE DUAL ROLE OF LLMS IN THE XAI ECOSYSTEM

5.1 LLMs as Subjects of Explanation

In their first role, LLMs are the objects of explanation — complex, opaque systems whose internal workings need to be made interpretable. This is the role addressed in Section 4. As subjects of explanation, LLMs pose challenges of scale, architecture, and distributed representation that exceed those of classical ML, but are addressed by a rapidly growing body of mechanistic interpretability, attention analysis, and probing research.

5.2 LLMs as Explanation Generators

In their second and increasingly prominent role, LLMs function as explanation generators — AI systems that produce natural language explanations of other AI systems' decisions or their own reasoning processes. Wu et al. (2024) systematically elaborated ten distinct strategies for exploiting this capacity, including chain-of-thought explanation prompting, explanation generation for structured prediction tasks, and LLM-mediated translation of technical XAI outputs (such as SHAP values) into accessible natural language. These strategies have practical value: for non-technical users who cannot interpret a feature attribution score, an LLM-generated narrative explanation may provide more actionable understanding.

Seveso et al. (2024) provide a structured survey of the bidirectional relationship between XAI and LLMs, identifying five main interaction patterns: XAI for LLMs (explaining how LLMs work), LLMs for XAI (using LLMs to generate or improve explanations), XAI of LLM-generated content (explaining why an LLM produced a specific output), LLMs as XAI agents (LLMs that proactively explain), and interactive XAI through LLMs (dialogue-based explanation systems). Zytek et al. (2024) extend this analysis by identifying future research directions, including grounding LLM-generated explanations in verifiable evidence, combining LLM explanations with formal XAI methods, and developing robust evaluation protocols for narrative explanations.

The explanation-generation capacity of LLMs raises important epistemological concerns, however. An LLM-generated explanation may be fluent, internally consistent, and superficially plausible while being factually incorrect about the computational processes it purports to describe. Kroeger et al. (2024) demonstrate empirically that LLMs acting as post-hoc explainers frequently produce explanations that do not accurately reflect model behaviour, a finding that emphasises the distinction between verbal plausibility and mechanistic faithfulness. Rigorous evaluation frameworks that hold LLM-generated explanations to the same standards as formal XAI methods are therefore essential.

5.3 XAI 2.0 and Interdisciplinary Frontiers

Longo et al. (2024) articulate a manifesto for what they term XAI 2.0, arguing that the field must expand beyond its historical technical focus to embrace interdisciplinary perspectives from cognitive science, philosophy of mind, social science, and law. Their manifesto identifies eleven open challenges: causal XAI, counterfactual reasoning at scale, user-centred evaluation, legal compliance, social context sensitivity, adversarial robustness of explanations, evaluation metrics, quantum XAI, multimodal explanations, continual learning explainability, and affective computing. This expansive research agenda reflects growing recognition that explainability is fundamentally a sociotechnical problem — one that cannot be solved by technical methods alone but requires deep engagement with the human and institutional contexts in which AI systems are deployed.

6. REGULATORY REQUIREMENTS AND THE ROLE OF XAI

6.1 The EU AI Act and Transparency Obligations

The European Union AI Act, which entered into force in 2024, establishes a risk-based regulatory framework for AI systems, with transparency and explainability requirements calibrated to the risk level of specific applications. For high-risk AI systems — including those used in biometric identification, critical infrastructure, employment, education, law enforcement, migration, and the administration of justice — the Act mandates that providers ensure sufficient transparency to enable deployers and affected persons to interpret the system's output. Panigutti et al. (2023) provide a detailed analysis of the role of XAI in the context of the AI Act, mapping the Act's transparency requirements to existing XAI methods and identifying significant gaps where current methods do not fully satisfy regulatory demands.

The AI Act's requirements are technically non-prescriptive: they specify outcomes (sufficient interpretability for affected persons) rather than specific technical methods. This creates both opportunity and challenge for XAI research. The opportunity is that diverse methods — feature attribution, natural language explanations, counterfactuals, model documentation — can all potentially satisfy the requirements, provided they are appropriately validated and contextualised. The challenge is that the Act's language is deliberately vague, and the operationalisation of 'sufficient interpretability' remains contested both legally and technically.

The Act also introduces general-purpose AI (GPAI) model provisions that apply specifically to LLMs and other foundation models above certain capability thresholds. Providers of GPAI models with systemic risk are required to conduct adversarial testing, report serious incidents, and ensure adequate cybersecurity protections. The transparency requirements for GPAI models include publication of model architecture, training data, and testing procedures — obligations that the XAI community must help operationalise through the development of standardised model documentation practices. The Model Cards and Datasheets for Datasets frameworks, developed in the research community, provide a starting point for this documentation standardisation.

6.2 GDPR and the Right to Explanation

Article 22 of the GDPR establishes a right not to be subject to solely automated decisions with significant effects, and Recital 71 specifies a right to obtain an explanation of the decision and to challenge it. Wachter et al. (2021) analysed the legal and technical implications of this right, arguing that counterfactual explanations provide an operationally sound basis for compliance: they do not require disclosure of proprietary model details, they are actionable, and they describe the decision boundary in a form that is both interpretable to non-experts and legally contestable. This analysis has been highly influential in both legal and technical communities, though subsequent scholarship has raised questions about whether counterfactuals fully satisfy the GDPR's explanation requirements in all contexts.

In the healthcare domain, Rajpurkar et al. (2022) highlight the particular salience of explainability for clinical AI applications, where explanations must satisfy not only regulatory requirements but also professional clinical standards, patient autonomy rights, and medical ethics norms. The intersection of XAI, medical regulation, and clinical practice represents one of the most active and consequential frontiers of applied XAI research.

Beyond healthcare, sector-specific regulatory developments are emerging across financial services, criminal justice, and hiring. The Equal Credit Opportunity Act in the United States already requires creditors to provide specific reasons for adverse actions, creating a de facto right to explanation that predates modern XAI. The emerging regulatory environment for algorithmic hiring tools — including proposed legislation in several US states and municipalities requiring bias audits and explanation capabilities — adds further momentum to the regulatory demand for XAI. The XAI community's capacity to provide technically sound, legally legible, and practically deployable explanation solutions will determine whether these regulatory demands are met substantively or merely formally.

7. EVALUATION FRAMEWORKS AND LIMITATIONS OF XAI

7.1 Evaluation Metrics and Benchmarks

The evaluation of explanation quality is itself a deeply challenging problem. Unlike model performance, which can be measured objectively against held-out data, explanation quality is multidimensional and partly subjective. Agarwal et al. (2022) developed OpenXAI, a comprehensive benchmark for evaluating feature attribution explanations, providing standardised datasets, model-explanation pairs, and evaluation metrics. Their framework identifies six core evaluation dimensions: faithfulness (does the explanation accurately reflect the model's computation?), stability (does the explanation change minimally for similar inputs?), robustness (is the explanation resistant to adversarial manipulation?), completeness (does the explanation account for the full prediction?), sparsity (is the explanation concise?), and human-grounded evaluation (do human users find the explanation useful and comprehensible?).

Faithfulness is arguably the most fundamental of these criteria. An explanation that is easy to understand but does not accurately describe the model's actual computation may be worse than no explanation at all, as it creates false confidence in a potentially flawed system. Longo et al. (2024) identify evaluation methodology as one of the most significant open challenges in XAI, noting that ground-truth benchmarks for explanation quality are rare, human evaluation is expensive and subject to cognitive biases, and automated proxy metrics often correlate poorly with human judgments of quality.

7.2 Known Limitations and Failure Modes

XAI methods are not merely imperfect but can be systematically misleading. Agarwal et al. (2022) and Das and Rad (2021) both document failure modes including instability (LIME explanations vary between runs), inconsistency (SHAP and LIME produce different feature rankings for the same model and instance), sensitivity to hyperparameter choices, and vulnerability to adversarial manipulation (explanations can be gamed to appear benign while the underlying model behaves discriminatorily). Hassija et al. (2024) review these limitations comprehensively, concluding that no existing XAI method is both theoretically grounded and practically reliable across all settings.

For LLMs specifically, the gap between explanation and reality is particularly concerning. Mechanistic interpretability provides the most rigorous approach to faithful explanation but remains limited to relatively small models and specific circuits. Post-hoc methods applied to LLMs face prohibitive computational costs and the confabulation problem identified by Kroeger et al. (2024). Natural language explanation generation by LLMs is fluent but unreliable. This trilemma — between rigour, scalability, and accessibility — defines the central technical challenge of LLM explainability.

Table 1. Comparison of Major XAI Methods Across Key Evaluation Dimensions

Method	Scope	Model Dependency	Faithfulness	Scalability to LLMs	Key Reference
SHAP	Local + Global	Agnostic / Tree-specific	High (TreeSHAP)	Limited (KernelSHAP cost)	Lundberg et al., 2022; Salih et al., 2025
LIME	Local	Model-Agnostic	Moderate (unstable)	Moderate	Salih et al., 2025; Hassija et al., 2024
Counterfactuals	Local	Model-Agnostic	High (action-grounded)	Limited (NP-hard search)	Wachter et al., 2021; Guidotti, 2022
Attention Visualisation	Local + Global	Transformer-specific	Low (causal contested)	High	Ferrando et al., 2024; Räuker et al., 2023
Mechanistic Interp.	Local + Global	Model-Specific	Very High	Very Limited (scale)	Olsson et al., 2022; Meng et al., 2022
LLM-Generated NL Explanation	Local	Agnostic (via prompting)	Low (confabulation risk)	High	Kroeger et al., 2024; Zytek et al., 2024
Decision Trees / Rules	Global (intrinsic)	Model-Specific (intrinsic)	Perfect (ante-hoc)	N/A (classical only)	Rudin et al., 2022; Belle & Papantonis, 2021

Figure 3. Comparative evaluation of seven canonical XAI methods across four quality dimensions.

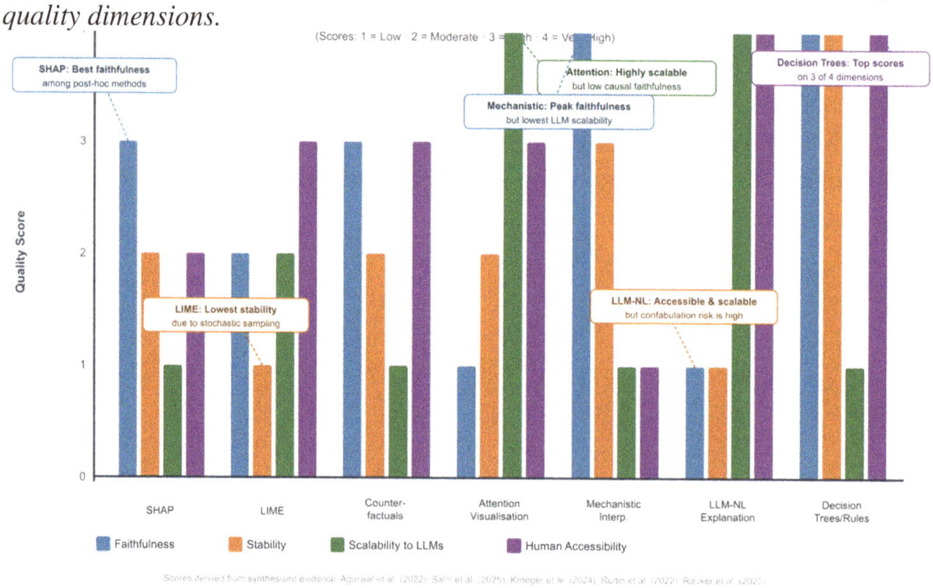

Figure 3 illustrates the Mechanistic Interpretability achieves peak faithfulness but near-zero LLM scalability; LLM-generated natural language explanations maximise accessibility and scalability but carry elevated confabulation risk; Decision Trees/ Rules score highly on three of four dimensions. Placement: Section 7 (Evaluation Frameworks and Limitations). Scores synthesised from Agarwal et al. (2022), Salih et al. (2025), Kroeger et al. (2024), Rudin et al. (2022), and Räuker et al. (2023).

8. OPEN CHALLENGES AND FUTURE RESEARCH DIRECTIONS

8.1 Causal Explainability

One of the most persistent and consequential gaps in current XAI methodology is the treatment of causality. The majority of XAI methods — including SHAP, LIME, and most attention-based methods — produce associational rather than causal explanations. They identify which features co-vary with the model's predictions, not which features causally determine them. This distinction matters enormously in practice: an explanation that highlights race or gender as a top predictive feature in a credit-scoring model may accurately describe the statistical association the model has learned but provides no guidance on whether this association is legitimate or discriminatory. Longo et al. (2024) identify causal XAI as a foundational open challenge, calling for the integration of causal discovery and inference methods into XAI pipelines.

The integration of causal reasoning into LLM explainability is particularly underdeveloped. Mechanistic interpretability methods such as activation patching operationalise a form of causal analysis, but are limited in scope and scale. Formalising causal accounts of LLM behaviour — potentially using structural causal models, counterfactual inference, or do-calculus frameworks — represents a major open research programme.

8.2 Human-Centred and Context-Sensitive XAI

The development of XAI methods has historically been driven by technical rather than human-centred considerations: researchers optimise for properties such as faithfulness, stability, and computational efficiency without systematically evaluating whether the resulting explanations are actually useful to, understood by, or trusted by the humans who will use them. Das and Rad (2021) call for a more systematically human-centred approach to XAI research, integrating methods from HCI, cognitive science, and behavioural economics to understand how people process, understand, and are affected by AI explanations.

Context sensitivity is a related and underexplored dimension. The optimal form of an explanation depends heavily on the cognitive background, professional expertise, and decision-making context of the user. A fixed explanation format cannot optimally serve both a domain expert making high-stakes decisions and a lay user receiving a recommendation. Adaptive explanation systems that dynamically modulate explanation form, granularity, and vocabulary based on user context and feedback represent an important frontier for both research and deployment.

8.3 Evaluation, Benchmarking, and Standards

The absence of widely accepted evaluation standards for XAI methods is a significant impediment to scientific progress and practical deployment. The field currently lacks agreed benchmark datasets specifically designed for explanation evaluation, standardised metrics for faithfulness and human-grounded quality, and community-wide norms for reporting explanation quality alongside model performance. Agarwal et al. (2022) made an important step toward addressing this gap with OpenXAI, but the benchmark covers only tabular classification tasks and a limited set of explanation methods.

For LLMs, the evaluation challenge is even more acute. Benchmarks for mechanistic interpretability findings, methods for verifying the accuracy of LLM-generated explanations, and human evaluation protocols for narrative explanations are all nascent areas. The development of a shared evaluation infrastructure — analogous to GLUE or SuperGLUE for NLP performance benchmarking — for XAI methods across model types and explanation modalities would substantially accelerate the field.

8.4 Multimodal and Domain-Specific XAI

Increasingly, AI systems operate in multimodal settings — processing and integrating text, images, audio, and structured data simultaneously. Classical XAI methods were developed primarily for unimodal settings and face significant challenges when applied to multimodal architectures. Attributing a prediction to components of different modalities requires new formalisations and evaluation protocols. LLMs with vision capabilities (vision-language models) present particularly complex explainability challenges, as explanations must integrate across textual and visual representations.

Domain-specific XAI remains an active area of specialised development. In healthcare, Rajpurkar et al. (2022) and Reyes et al. (2022) highlight the need for explanations that are clinically meaningful, validated against expert judgment, and aligned with regulatory requirements. In drug discovery and chemoinformatics, Rodríguez-Pérez and Bajorath (2022) demonstrate that interpretable ML models — particularly those using SHAP-based feature analysis — can reveal chemically meaningful structure-activity relationships that accelerate molecular design. These domain-specific applications reveal that generic XAI methods must be adapted, validated, and contextualised to serve specialised professional communities effectively.

8.5 Adversarial Robustness and Gaming of Explanations

A distinctive and troubling vulnerability of XAI systems is their susceptibility to adversarial manipulation. Research has demonstrated that it is possible to train models that produce benign-looking explanations while internally implementing discriminatory or harmful decision rules — a phenomenon sometimes called 'Potemkin explainability.' This possibility has significant implications for regulatory compliance: if explanation outputs can be decoupled from actual model behaviour, compliance demonstrations based on XAI outputs become unreliable. Developing explanation methods that are provably robust to adversarial gaming, and evaluation frameworks that can detect explanation-reality mismatches, are important open challenges for both the research community and regulatory bodies.

9. CONCLUSION

This chapter has traced the landscape of explainability and interpretability in AI across the full spectrum from classical machine learning to large language models. The central argument is that explainability is not a monolithic property but a multidimensional family of requirements — technical, epistemic, legal, and social — whose appropriate operationalisation depends on the model architecture, the application domain, the regulatory context, and the identity and needs of the human stakeholder.

For classical ML, a mature ecosystem of explainability methods — SHAP, LIME, counterfactuals, decision trees, rule-based models — provides a range of tools from intrinsically interpretable models that sacrifice complexity for transparency to post-hoc methods that approximate the behaviour of complex black-box systems. Each method involves trade-offs across dimensions of faithfulness, stability, computational cost, and accessibility. Rudin et al. (2022) remind us that for high-stakes decisions, the trade-off between accuracy and interpretability is not always acceptable: the deployment of opaque models in consequential settings should be justified by demonstrably superior performance that intrinsically interpretable models cannot match.

For large language models, the explainability challenge is both more urgent and more complex. Mechanistic interpretability offers the most rigorous path to genuine understanding but remains limited in scale and scope. Post-hoc methods face computational and faithfulness limitations. LLM-generated natural language explanations offer accessibility but carry significant confabulation risks. Addressing these challenges will require sustained research investment and genuine interdisciplinary collaboration across AI, cognitive science, philosophy, law, and the social sciences.

The regulatory landscape — centred on the EU AI Act and GDPR — provides an increasingly concrete and demanding framework of transparency obligations. The XAI community's response to these obligations will shape not only academic research priorities but the practical deployment of AI in health, finance, law, and public administration. The aspiration articulated in Longo et al.'s (2024) XAI 2.0 manifesto — to develop explainability as a genuinely interdisciplinary, human-centred, and causally grounded scientific programme — represents the appropriate ambition for the field as AI systems become more deeply embedded in the fabric of human society. Transparency and trust are not optional features of responsible AI ecosystems; they are foundational requirements without which the legitimate deployment of AI at scale cannot be sustained.

Looking ahead, the most promising avenues for progress in XAI are those that combine technical rigour with human-centred design, that ground associational explanations in causal frameworks, that develop evaluation standards robust enough to resist adversarial gaming, and that engage seriously with the institutional and regulatory contexts in which explanations must function. Transparency and trust are not optional features of responsible AI ecosystems; they are foundational requirements without which the legitimate deployment of AI at scale cannot be sustained. Meeting these requirements will demand not only technical ingenuity but genuine engagement with the full complexity of the sociotechnical systems in which AI is deployed.

REFERENCES

Agarwal, C., Krishna, S., Saxena, E., Pawelczyk, M., Johnson, N., Puri, I., Zitnik, M., & Lakkaraju, H. (2022). OpenXAI: Towards a transparent evaluation of model explanations. *Advances in Neural Information Processing Systems*, *35*, 15346–15361. DOI: 10.52202/068431-1148

Arrieta, A. B., Díaz-Rodríguez, N., Del Ser, J., Bennetot, A., Tabik, S., Barbado, A., García, S., Gil-López, S., Molina, D., Benjamins, R., Chatila, R., & Herrera, F. (2021). Explainable Artificial Intelligence (XAI): Concepts, taxonomies, opportunities and challenges toward responsible AI. *Information Fusion*, *58*, 82–115. DOI: 10.1016/j.inffus.2019.12.012

Belle, V., & Papantonis, I. (2021). Principles and practice of explainable machine learning. *Frontiers in Big Data*, *4*, 688969. DOI: 10.3389/fdata.2021.688969 PMID: 34278297

Danilevsky, M., Qian, K., Aharonov, R., Katsis, Y., Kawas, B., & Sen, P. (2021). A survey of the state of Explainable AI for natural language processing. arXiv preprint arXiv:2010.00711.

Das, A., & Rad, P. (2021). Opportunities and challenges in Explainable Artificial Intelligence (XAI): A survey. arXiv preprint arXiv:2006.11371.

Dwivedi, R., Dave, D., Naik, H., Singhal, S., Omer, R., Patel, P., Qian, B., Wen, Z., Shah, T., Morgan, G., & Ranjan, R. (2023). Explainable AI (XAI): Core ideas, techniques and solutions. *ACM Computing Surveys*, *55*(9), 194. DOI: 10.1145/3561048

Ferrando, J., Sarti, A., Barez, F., & Costa-jussa, M. R. (2024). A primer on the inner workings of transformer-based language models. arXiv preprint arXiv:2405.00208.

Guidotti, R. (2022). Counterfactual explanations and how to find them: Literature review and benchmarking. *Data Mining and Knowledge Discovery*, *38*(5), 2770–2824. DOI: 10.1007/s10618-022-00831-6

Hase, P., Bansal, M., Kim, B., & Ghandeharioun, A. (2023). Does localization inform editing? Surprising differences in causality-based localization vs. knowledge editing in language models. *Advances in Neural Information Processing Systems*, *36*, 73429–73451. DOI: 10.48550/arXiv.2301.04213

Hassija, V., Chamola, V., Mahapatra, A., Singal, A., Goel, D., Huang, K., Scardapane, S., Spinelli, I., Mahmud, M., & Hussain, A. (2024). Interpreting black-box models: A review on Explainable Artificial Intelligence. *Cognitive Computation*, *16*(1), 45–74. DOI: 10.1007/s12559-023-10179-8

Holzinger, A., Saranti, A., Molnar, C., Biecek, P., & Samek, W. (2022). Explainable AI methods—A brief overview. In A. Holzinger, R. Goebel, R. Fong, T. Moon, K.-R. Müller, & W. Samek (Eds.), *AI—Beyond Explainable AI (*LNCS 13200, pp. 13–38). Springer. DOI: 10.1007/978-3-031-04083-2_2

Hsieh, W.-C., Chen, C.-C., Wu, M.-H., & Li, J.-H. (2024). A comprehensive guide to Explainable AI: From classical models to LLMs. arXiv preprint arXiv:2412.00800.

Kroeger, N., Ley, D., Krishna, S., Agrawal, C., & Lakkaraju, H. (2024). Are large language models post hoc explainers? arXiv preprint arXiv:2310.05797.

Longo, L., Brcic, M., Cabitza, F., Choi, J., Confalonieri, R., Del Ser, J., Guidotti, R., Hayashi, Y., Herrera, F., Holzinger, A., Jiang, R., Khosravi, H., Lecue, F., Malgieri, G., Páez, A., Samek, W., Schneider, J., Speith, T., & Stumpf, S. (2024). Explainable Artificial Intelligence (XAI) 2.0: A manifesto of open challenges and interdisciplinary research directions. *Information Fusion*, *106*, 102301. DOI: 10.1016/j.inffus.2024.102301

Lundberg, S. M., Erion, G., Chen, H., DeGrave, A., Prutkin, J. M., Nair, B., Katz, R., Himmelfarb, J., Bansal, N., & Lee, S.-I. (2022). From local explanations to global understanding with Explainable AI for trees. *Nature Machine Intelligence*, *2*(1), 56–67. DOI: 10.1038/s42256-019-0138-9 PMID: 32607472

Meng, K., Bau, D., Andonian, A., & Belinkov, Y. (2022). Locating and editing factual associations in GPT. *Advances in Neural Information Processing Systems*, *35*, 17359–17372. DOI: 10.48550/arXiv.2202.05262

Mumuni, A., & Mumuni, F. (2025). Explainable artificial intelligence (XAI): From inherent explainability to large language models. arXiv preprint arXiv:2501.09967.

Olsson, C., Elhage, N., Nanda, N., Joseph, N., DasSarma, N., Henighan, T., Mann, B., Askell, A., Bai, Y., Chen, A., Conerly, T., Drain, D., Ganguli, D., Hatfield-Dodds, Z., Hernandez, D., Johnston, S., Jones, A., Kernion, J., Lovitt, L., & Olah, C. (2022). In-context learning and induction heads. Transformer Circuits Thread. arXiv.2209.11895

Panigutti, C., Hamon, R., Hupont, I., Fernandez Llorca, D., Fano Yela, D., Junklewitz, H., Scalzo, S., Mazzini, G., Sanchez, I., Soler Garrido, J., & Gomez, E. (2023). The role of explainable AI in the context of the AI Act. In *Proceedings of the 2023 ACM Conference on Fairness, Accountability, and Transparency (FAccT '23)* (pp. 1139–1150). ACM. DOI: 10.1145/3593013.3594069

Rajpurkar, P., Chen, E., Banerjee, O., & Topol, E. J. (2022). AI in health and medicine. [PubMed]. *Nature Medicine*, *28*(1), 31–38. DOI: 10.1038/s41591-021-01614-0 PMID: 35058619

Räuker, T., Ho, A., Casper, S., & Hadfield-Menell, D. (2023). Toward transparent AI: A survey on interpreting the inner structures of deep neural networks. In *2023 IEEE Conference on Secure and Trustworthy Machine Learning (SaTML)* (pp. 464–483). IEEE. DOI: 10.1109/SaTML54575.2023.00039

Reyes, M., Meier, R., Pereira, S., Silva, C. A., Dahlweid, F.-M., Tengg-Kobligk, H. V., Summers, R. M., & Wiest, R. (2022). On the interpretability of artificial intelligence in radiology: Challenges and opportunities. *Radiology. Artificial Intelligence*, *2*(3), e190043. DOI: 10.1148/ryai.2020190043 PMID: 32510054

Rodríguez-Pérez, R., & Bajorath, J. (2022). Evolution of support vector machine and regression modeling in chemoinformatics and drug discovery. *Journal of Computer-Aided Molecular Design*, *36*(5), 355–362. DOI: 10.1007/s10822-022-00442-9 PMID: 35304657

Rudin, C., Chen, C., Chen, Z., Huang, H., Semenova, L., & Zhong, C. (2022). Interpretable machine learning: Fundamental principles and 10 grand challenges. *Statistics Surveys, 16*, 1–85. DOI: 10.1214/21-SS133

Salih, A., Boscolo Galazzo, I., Raisi-Estabragh, Z., Lekadir, K., Menegaz, G., & Petersen, S. E. (2025). A perspective on Explainable Artificial Intelligence methods: SHAP and LIME. *Advanced Intelligent Systems*, *7*(1), e202400304. DOI: 10.1002/aisy.202400304

Seveso, A., Cambria, E., Malandri, L., Mercoroi, F., & Nobani, N. (2024). XAI meets LLMs: A survey of the relation between Explainable AI and Large Language Models. arXiv preprint arXiv:2407.15248.

Wachter, S., Mittelstadt, B., & Russell, C. (2021). Counterfactual explanations without opening the black box: Automated decisions and the GDPR. *SSRN*, *31*(2), 841–887. DOI: 10.2139/ssrn.3063289

Wu, X., Deng, Z., Luo, J., Li, S., Tang, R., Ma, Y., Jiang, T., Zhao, S., & Liu, N. (2024). Usable XAI: 10 strategies towards exploiting explainability in the LLM era. arXiv preprint arXiv:2403.08946.

Zhao, H., Yang, F., Liu, N., Deng, H., Cai, H., Wang, S., Yin, D., Du, M., & Chen, H. (2024). Explainability for large language models: A survey. *ACM Transactions on Intelligent Systems and Technology*, *15*(2), 20. DOI: 10.1145/3639372

Zytek, A., Pidò, S., & Veeramachaneni, K. (2024). LLMs for XAI: Future directions for explaining explanations. arXiv preprint arXiv:2405.06064.

KEY TERMS AND DEFINITIONS

Attention Mechanism: An attention mechanism is a deep learning technique that allows models to focus on the most relevant parts of input data while processing information. Commonly used in natural language processing, it improves performance by assigning different weights to different input elements.

Counterfactual Explanation: Counterfactual explanations describe how minimal changes to input features could alter a model's prediction. They answer "what-if" questions, helping users understand decision boundaries by showing specific alternative scenarios that would lead to different outcomes.

Explainable Artificial Intelligence (XAI): Explainable Artificial Intelligence (XAI) refers to methods and techniques that make the decisions and outputs of AI systems understandable to humans. It aims to improve transparency, trust, accountability, and fairness by showing how models reach conclusions rather than operating as "black boxes."

Interpretability: Interpretability is the degree to which a human can understand the internal workings, logic, or decision-making process of a machine learning model. Highly interpretable models allow users to see how inputs influence outputs, helping build trust, detect bias, and support informed decision-making.

LIME (Local Interpretable Model-Agnostic Explanations): LIME is a method that explains individual predictions by approximating complex models with simpler, interpretable models locally. It perturbs input data, observes changes in predictions, and identifies which features most influenced the model's decision for a specific instance.

SHAP (Shapley Additive Explanations): SHAP is an explainability technique based on game theory that assigns importance values to each feature in a model's prediction. It shows how much each input contributes positively or negatively to the final output, offering consistent, detailed, and locally accurate explanations.

Chapter 6

Transparent-by-Design AI:

Explainability, Evaluation, and Continuous Monitoring for Classical ML and LLM Ecosystems

C. V. Suresh Babu
http://orcid.org/0000-0002-8474-2882
Hindustan Institute of Technology and Science, India

S. Nanda Kumar
http://orcid.org/0009-0008-0070-6763
Hindustan Institute of Technology and Science, India

S. Abhishek
Hindustan Institute of Technology and Science, India

S. Sivasridharun
http://orcid.org/0009-0002-6084-0151
Hindustan Institute of Technology and Science, India

ABSTRACT

This chapter per the authors aims to advance transparency and trust in data and AI ecosystems by examining explainability, evaluation, and continuous monitoring for classical machine learning models and large language models. The target groups include researchers, AI practitioners, policymakers, and governance professionals seeking operational and regulatory guidance. The chapter adopts a lifecycle-based analytical approach, synthesizing recent literature, governance frameworks, and practical transparency artifacts such as model cards, evaluation metrics, and

DOI: 10.4018/979-8-3373-6761-3.ch006

monitoring pipelines. The findings highlight that transparency-by-design, coupled with robust evaluation and post-deployment monitoring, significantly improves accountability, risk mitigation, and stakeholder trust. The chapter concludes that integrating technical, human-centered, and governance perspectives is essential for deploying trustworthy and sustainable AI systems at scale.

1. INTRODUCTION

1.1 Background: Transparency as a Pillar of Trust

Transparency is a core element of trust. Stakeholders have the same expectations of algorithmic systems: that they will be able to understand how and why they are being used to make significant decisions. Trust is relational: stakeholders will require confidence that algorithms are being used ethically, that all decisions made using these algorithms can be examined, and that there are mechanisms to correct any harm done by the algorithms when they fail (Rai et al., 2025).

The presence or absence of justified trust has a direct correlation with the degree of asymmetry between information held by developers and that held by users. In many cases, developers have detailed knowledge of the architecture of the systems being used to develop algorithms, while users only have partial understanding. This results in an imbalance of authority between developers and users, with users bearing the burden of harm resulting from algorithmic failure. In recent years, there have been many examples in the real world in which the consequences of algorithmic failure (due to a lack of transparency) have been severe. Healthcare algorithms have demonstrated significant deterioration in performance for individuals who have historically been underrepresented. Financial algorithms have been shown to perpetuate systemic discrimination against qualified applicants by providing loan applications for only the most qualified applicants. Eligibility determination processes in public systems have used opaque criteria (Koene, 2019), and have produced inequitable outcomes. Transparency allows organizations to serve a variety of critical functions: providing insight into specific decisions, promoting accountability through traceability, supporting fair evaluation; optimizing outcomes. If an organization lacks transparency, the organization is either unable to perform its functions or will not be held accountable to stakeholders.

1.2 Why XAI Matters for Classical ML and LLMs

Explainable AI encompasses technologies, practices, and governance enabling comprehension of AI decision processes. The accuracy-interpretability trade-off reveals that complex models yield superior accuracy at the expense of user insight into contributing factors, yet interpretable methods can approximate performance while enhancing transparency (Wiratsin et al., 2025). Organizations thus often retrofit post-hoc interpretability onto non-transparent classical ML in high-risk contexts without altering core methods (Ortigossa et al., 2024).

Classical explainability illuminates feature weights, visualizations, and surrogates, elucidating predictor impacts on predictions. Limitations emerge with nonlinearities and correlations, complicating reliable insights.

LLM interpretability diverges fundamentally from classical ML due to transformers' distributed, billion-parameter processing across layers, rendering intuitive human resolution infeasible. Unique failures like confident hallucinations demand methods addressing retrofitting, architectural constraints, failure modes, safety risks, and trust calibration for stakeholders to assess outcomes judiciously.

1.3 Problem Landscape: Opaqueness, Bias, Risk & Stakeholder Concerns

Complex ML algorithms, particularly deep neural networks (DNNs), pose interpretation challenges due to their "black box" nature, hindering oversight and trust (Wiratsin et al., 2025). Algorithmic bias persists as training data mirrors historical inequities, yielding discriminatory outcomes in healthcare (poor minority performance), finance, and public decisions like credit or sentencing (Sides et al., 2025). Regulations like the EU AI Act mandate transparency, fairness, and recourse for high-risk systems.

XAI methods yield mixed results. Classical post-hoc tools (SHAP, LIME, rule extraction) are model-agnostic but flawed: SHAP assumes feature independence, LIME diverges locally from global behavior, and both exhibit instability to input perturbations (Linardatos et al., 2020; Roberts et al., 2022). LLM interpretability pivots to mechanistic reverse-engineering of transformers, promising insights into hallucinations and bias, yet struggles scaling beyond billion-parameter models to trillion-scale combinatorial complexity.

Evaluation gaps persist: XAI metrics lack standardization, hyperparameter sensitivity hampers reproducibility, and image/tabular frameworks fail LLMs. In healthcare, opacity erodes clinician trust—decision logic must align with judgment—and stakeholders (clinicians, regulators, patients) hold divergent transparency expectations (Rai et al., 2025).

1.4 Objectives and Scope

This chapter embeds transparency as a fundamental principle across all AI lifecycle phases, differing from existing XAI surveys that review techniques in isolation or within narrow domains. Rather than cataloging explanation methods, it provides an end-to-end view of operational transparency, integrating technical, organizational, and governance dimensions of accountability.

The framework includes four integrated objectives. First, it proposes a unified conceptual model positioning Explainability, Evaluation, and Monitoring as interdependent pillars for AI trustworthiness, where design-phase transparency propagates through evaluation and monitoring to enable systemic accountability. This advances prior work by viewing transparency as an emergent property of holistic lifecycle practices, beyond isolated technical interventions.

Second, it compares interpretability techniques across classical ML and LLMs by type (intrinsic vs. post-hoc), synthesizing trade-offs and limitations such as SHAP, LIME, and mechanistic interpretability. Classical ML analysis evaluates post-hoc stability, fidelity, and feature interactions; LLMs integrate diverse methods (attention visualization, influence functions, mechanistic circuitry, counterfactuals), noting strengths, scalability challenges, and context-dependent reliability.

Third, it advances practical governance through model cards, datasheets, audit trails, and risk registers, bridging literature gaps with actionable strategies for implementation.

Fourth, it integrates technical, governance, and human-centered views to foster trustworthy AI, highlighting trade-offs and tailored strategies. Unlike purely technical XAI surveys, it emphasizes sociotechnical factors—stakeholder needs, governance, and human values—positioning explanations as social mechanisms that elevate transparency to genuine accountability.

1.5 Structure of the Chapter

The following Sections develop arguments in favour of designing systems that are transparent by design. Section 2 provides definitions of fundamental concepts that differentiate between transparency, interpretability, and explainability, and also includes the author's intrinsic versus post-hoc taxonomies as well as lifecycle perspectives. Section 3 describes traditional machine learning (ML) explainability methods (i.e., interpretable models and post-hoc techniques), along with their shortcomings when it comes to interpreting complex, non-linear interactions. Section 4 discusses how these issues relate to LLMs and the interpretability of these models, discussing attention, influence functions, and hallucination risk. Section 5 provides examples of what positions and documents would include in order to translate the technical concepts into organizational documentation and artifacts. Section 6 consolidates the evaluation frameworks used to evaluate transparency and trustworthiness. Section 7 discusses how developers should monitor for post-deployment drift detection, monitoring, and human-in-loop governance over time. Section 8 situates transparency in governance, policy, and ethical considerations in the use of AI. Section 9 focuses on case studies of healthcare, financial services, education, and public administration. Section 10 discusses both the technical limitations associated with the study and the resulting areas of emerging research. Finally, the final Section summarizes and presents a unified vision of trustworthy AI and its foundations of fairness, accountability and agency for humans.

2. FOUNDATIONS OF MODEL TRANSPARENCY AND INTERPRETABILITY

2.1 Defining Transparency, Interpretability, and Explainability

Precision in terminology is essential for productive AI comprehensibility discussions. Transparency, Interpretability, and Explainability—often conflated—denote distinct facets of AI understanding. Interpretable Machine Learning extracts meaningful model insights on data relationships and learned patterns, with relevance varying by audience and context (Murdoch et al., 2019).

Transparency signifies availability of an AI system's internal state and functionality, encompassing architecture, representations, training documentation, data sources, procedures, and decisions—independent of human comprehension. Interpretability addresses cognitive grasp of outputs (Linardatos et al., 2020), expressing decision processes via comprehensible forms (math, rules, visuals, domain language), influenced by audience expertise and biases; data scientists' explanations may fail clinicians.

Explainability enables AI to justify instance-specific decisions, building trust via targeted insight (Gilpin et al., 2018). Unlike system-wide interpretability/transparency, it answers "why this outcome now?" for non-technical users. Examples illustrate: neural networks offer technical transparency but poor interpretability/explainability; decision trees excel via simple paths; high-feature linear regression overwhelms cognition despite transparency.

2.2 Classical ML vs. LLMs: Differences in Opacity

Machine Learning (ML) Systems have a variety of Opacities. Traditional ML Models fall into a continuum of being understandable; linear and tree-based models are the most transparent (due to visualizations of how the model makes decisions and articulated decision logic); complexity decreases as the model becomes more complex (neural networks, etc) creating a trade-off of accuracy vs interpretability.

Research indicates that the trade-off is not as absolute as previously believed. When humans evaluate whether a model's explanation is adequate to explain the model's performance, there are no significant differences in the performance of humans completing tasks with either an interpretable or a non-interpretable model; therefore, post-hoc explanations can fill the gap left by the lack of inherent interpretability (Bell et al., 2022).

The potential for large language models (LLMs) to create distinct challenges from classical ML is due to their reliance on transformer architecture, which distributes decision-making across billions of parameters across numerous layers. The process by which an LLM generates its next token prediction is also completely opaque; while interpretable models rely on the ability to identify features as having importance, LLMs generate decisions through representations of ideas in multiple dimensions; therefore, human intuition cannot relate to the process of LLM decision-making (Gilpin et al., 2018). Furthermore, unlike classical ML, LLMs develop unique failure modes (i.e., hallucination and the generation of factual inaccuracies that are stylistically correct) and require unique interpretation strategies than classical ML.

2.3 Taxonomy of Interpretability: Intrinsic vs. Post-hoc

Different architectures enabling direct interpretation, unlike post-hoc methods, form a taxonomical framework impacting trustworthiness, computational cost, and deployability. The Predictive, Descriptive, and Relevant (PDR) framework by Murdoch et al. (2019) evaluates interpretations: predictive accuracy assesses unseen data fidelity, descriptive accuracy measures decision-making alignment, and relevancy gauges audience-specific insights in problem contexts.

Intrinsic interpretability uses transparent models without external explanations. Linear models exemplify this, with coefficients denoting feature contributions, predictions as weighted sums, and uncertainty via statistics. Decision trees offer universal interpretability through rule-based paths; rule-based systems and Bayesian networks provide it architecturally. Advantages include stakeholder trust via domain-knowledge verification, avoiding post-facto approximations (Linardatos et al., 2020). Performance trade-offs exist but are less severe than assumed; analyses across datasets show non-monotonic interpretability-accuracy links, with interpretable models outperforming opaque ones contextually (Atrey et al., 2025).

Post-hoc methods apply after training to opaque models. Model-agnostic techniques treat models as black boxes, probing input-output relations. LIME perturbs features, fitting surrogate models to observe output changes. SHAP uses Shapley values for feature contributions to predictions. Permutation Importance evaluates performance drops from feature shuffling. These offer model-independent flexibility and non-invasiveness, though fidelity varies with unrelated inputs; robust metrics now account for distribution shifts, improving prior alignments.

2.4 Key Properties of Trustworthy Explanations

Stakeholder service quality differs widely between high-quality and lower-quality explanations. Fidelity refers to how closely the representation of the model's means to reach a decision is to that of the model. Faithful explanations capture the actual output of a model whereas post-hoc explanations may provide false guidance. A multi-faceted approach to measuring explanation quality is used to compare explanation types on correct, consistent, and confidence factors. "Robustness and Stability" provide assurance that providing a variety of explanation types produces similar levels of trust from users. The research shows that greater robustness increases the users' level of trust in an explanation, making both high-fidelity and low-fidelity explanations equal in building users' trust when compared with explanations that do not provide fidelity (Wang et al. 2023). Users may have difficulty determining the reliability of high-fidelity explanations as opposed to low-fidelity explanations (Wang et al. 2023).

Comprehensibility measures how an audience understands an explanation based on their technical skills and experience in that field. Clinicians understand explanations framed using clinical concepts better than those using machine learning terminology.

Actionability measures the extent to which a user can take meaningful action, including making a better decision or identifying an error and providing an appropriate intervention based on an explanation. Counterfactual explanations allow users to change an input to generate an alternative output, while attribution-based explanations only provide the importance of a feature in producing the output, demonstrating greater actionability compared with attribution-based explanations.

2.5 Transparency Across the AI Lifecycle

To achieve transparency, embedding across the entire AI lifecycle must be done by a systematic approach; not just one point in time. HASC provides a complete model of accountability; through the implementation of a system card, the integrator identifies and manages system-context risk (Sidhpurwala, et al. 2025), as well as incorporates security and safety throughout the lifecycle. This changes organisations from reactive transparency to proactive transparency.

Figure 1. Transparency Lifecycle Architecture

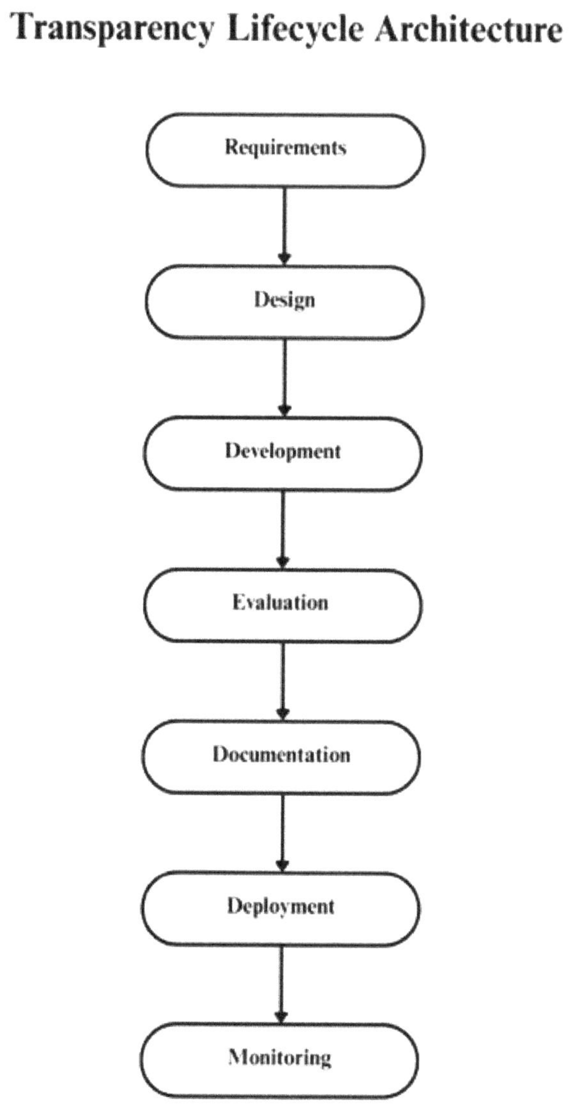

3. EXPLAINABILITY IN CLASSICAL MACHINE LEARNING

3.1 Inherently Interpretable Models

Classical machine learning models vary in interpretability, from highly interpretable to opaque. Linear regression, decision trees, and rule-based systems offer inherent interpretability without post-hoc explanations due to their structures. Basic linear and logistic regression embody intrinsic interpretability. Predictions arise from weighted linear combinations, where each coefficient quantifies an independent variable's contribution per unit increase (e.g., a 0.5 coefficient indicates a 0.5 rise in predicted value per unit variable increase). T-statistics gauge variable importance by dividing coefficients by standard errors; larger absolute values signal greater influence. The coefficient of determination measures the proportion of outcome variance explained by independents. Decision trees deliver interpretability via hierarchical rules: internal nodes test features, branches show outcomes, and leaves yield predictions. CART builds trees by selecting impurity-minimizing splits; interpretation traces root-to-leaf paths detailing feature tests for predictions. Rule-based systems and Bayesian networks achieve interpretability through explicit logic. Rule-based systems use if-then rules mirroring human reasoning in natural language. Bayesian networks depict conditional independencies graphically—edges for dependencies, absences for independencies—facilitating domain expertise integration and human-aligned reasoning.

3.2 Post-Hoc XAI Techniques for Classical ML

The use of complex models for accurate predictions by practitioners results in loss of inherent interpretability. Post-hoc methods of explanation provide some degree of interpretability and understanding by applying analyses following training, but not altering the model. These post-hoc explanation techniques offer useful insights into classical ML models that utilize complex methodologies.

3.2.1 Feature Importance Methods

Permutation feature importance quantifies performance degradation when the feature values are permuted. Larger decreases in performance suggest higher importance because the model relies greatly on the permuted feature. However, this approach is sensitive to feature correlations; with highly correlated features, permuting one feature may not decrease the performance if compensating correlated features are present, likely underestimating its importance.

CVPFI overcomes these two limitations Kaneko, 2023. It estimates the importance with multiple folds and thus provides much more stable feature rankings. By focusing one's analysis on features that lie on Pareto fronts-those for which CVPFI is large and feature similarity is low-accurate interpretation is possible even in high-dimensional problems.

SHAP uses game-theoretic Shapley values to quantify marginal feature contributions. The most important advantages of SHAP are its theoretical rigor; it also obeys the desirable local accuracy, missingness, and consistency properties, allowing both local and global explanations. However, computing SHAP exactly is exponentially expensive, approximations are required, and the method relies on features being independent, a requirement that is often violated by correlated data.

The results from various feature ranking approaches often conflict with each other (Roberts et al., 2022). Confidence increases with multiple methods agreeing on a consistent outcome, while disagreements point to complex interactions among features or unreliability specific to a method.

3.2.2 Partial Dependence and ICE Plots

Partial dependence plots display marginal dependencies between features and predictions by averaging over the values of other features. In the case of Partial Dependence (PD) plots, while the resulting curve may highlight linear, non-linear, monotonic or other complexities in the relationship between features and a target variable; PD plots assume independence of the features involved and may therefore create unrealistic data points through averaging across combinations if two features are correlated.

Individual Conditional Expectation (ICE) plots solve this limitation of PD plots by presenting each variable's effect on predictions individually instead of through aggregation. Since each curve represents how predictions change with respect to only one variable, an ICE plot can illustrate the heterogeneity across individual prediction variables, including both positive and negative associations for different cases. A Centered Individual Conditional Expectation (cICE) plot aids in interpreting these data by subtracting the baseline from each curve, making differences in predicted values more easily visible (Goldstein et al. 2013; Elshawi et al. 2019).

3.2.3 Surrogate Models

Surrogate approaches employ simpler, interpretable models to approximate the behavior of complex systems. Rule extraction is a representative example: from intricate models, practitioners extract interpretable rules. Evaluations across the rule-extraction methods C4.5Rule-PANE, REFNE, RxREN, RxNCM, and TREPAN assessed fidelity, hit rate, and rule complexity. The quality of these methods balances between fidelity and parsimony.

LIME works by adding perturbations to the inputs of a given instance and fits a simple linear model to approximate the complex model's behavior locally. It identifies features that influence the given prediction without modifying the original model. However, the quality of the explanation depends on the adequacy of the local neighborhood; poor local approximations lead to unfaithful explanations. LIME assumes feature independence, and its performance suffers with correlated features. Moreover, since LIME only offers local explanations, global understanding over multiple explanations is labor-intensive and requires manual work.

3.3 Handling Uncertainty and Bias in ML Explanations

Explanations are inherently uncertain. Estimates of feature importance are different for different data samples; explanation methods make assumptions that are often violated; and explanations are interpreted differently by different stakeholders. It follows then that robust theory development requires researchers to communicate uncertainty clearly and transparently in their findings, and also articulate possible sources of bias influencing the result. A typical example of such uncertainty communication is the Confidence Intervals reporting for FI estimates. Since the estimates of FI are the result of some stochastic process, sampling variability cannot be avoided completely. By way of example, an estimate for FI=0.25 along with wide confidence intervals conveys a larger uncertainty on the actual value of FI than the same estimate but coupled with narrow confidence intervals. It is also required that uncertainty regarding individual predictions be quantified. Should clinicians treat disease-risk predictions of 75% and 95% identically? Conformal prediction produces prediction intervals with guaranteed coverage properties. Unlike methods predicated on Gaussian assumptions or Bayesian frameworks, conformal prediction yields statistically valid regions that are widely applicable. It splits data into training, calibration, and test sets, computes nonconformity scores, and defines probability thresholds determining the intervals. Importantly, conformal prediction enforces error-rate constraints: at 95% confidence, 95% of the prediction regions contain the true values (Ajirak et al., 2025).

Classically, machine learning systems propagate and amplify biases in the training data. The underrepresentation of some populations or historic discrimination represented in the training data makes models inherit such biases. Explanations of biased models may feature features that seem to drive decisions but are actually a replica of discriminatory patterns. In real-world practice, auditing explanations for bias is necessary by checking predictions and feature importance across demographic subgroups and identifying disparities. Investigate if such disparities reflect real causal logic or biased training data.

3.4 Limitations of Traditional ML XAI in Complex Real-World Settings

Despite notable progress in post-hoc explainability methods for classical machine learning, significant limitations remain that undermine their reliability and practical application. Most methods assume feature independence, an assumption frequently violated by correlated features in real-world data. This leads to unstable importance measures, where rankings shift inconsistently based on proxy feature presence, eroding trust in explanations. Different methods often yield contradictory results on the same data. Practitioners note discrepancies between LIME and SHAP, or between permutation-based and gradient-based scores, signaling either complex model behavior or inherent method unreliability.

Verifying explanation faithfulness is challenging. Fidelity checks—such as concealing unimportant features to assess performance drops—are incomplete, risking stakeholders' incorrect mental models from unfaithful explanations. Classical explainability also struggles with complex feature interactions and nonlinearities (Goldstein et al., 2013). High-order interactions resist simple explanations; partial dependence plots (PDPs) and individual conditional expectation (ICE) plots assume independent features, while additive importance misrepresents interaction-dependent logic. High-dimensional settings (hundreds to thousands of features) intensify issues: SHAP computation becomes prohibitive, PDP/ICE visualization exceeds cognitive limits, and key drivers are hard to identify. Techniques for low-dimensional tabular data fail to scale effectively.

Key takeaways: While SHAP and LIME provide mature feature-importance tools, they falter with correlated features, high-order nonlinearities, and high dimensionality. Practitioners must verify fidelity and stability; no method excels universally (Linardatos et al., 2020).

4. EXPLAINABILITY IN LARGE LANGUAGE MODELS (LLMS)

4.1 Challenges of Interpretability in Transformer Architectures

Transformer-based LLMs raise interpretability challenges that are qualitatively different from those posed by classical machine learning. Whereas the decision-making process of a linear model or a decision tree is at least in principle transparent, transformers scatter decision-making over billions of parameters across many layers, with interactions that resist easy intuition. Self-attention mechanisms facilitate long-range token dependencies but at the cost of opaqueness: attention weights inform about patterns of focus without providing any information regarding why the model is attending to something or what it may "know" about the attended tokens. Several attention heads process diverse aspects in parallel: one about syntactic dependencies, another about semantic similarities. Their functionality when combined, however, remains obscure. Attention visualization typically operates over a single layer, and intuition about the interaction across more than ninety-six layers is beyond the reach of human comprehension.

Components relying on multi-layer perceptrons constitute large portions of the parameter count and remain almost entirely opaque in their role as learned knowledge repositories. Internal representations in each of the layers live in high-dimensional spaces in which all human intuition about relationships between numerical, semantic, and conceptual quantities breaks down. Transformer architectures embed input tokens into continuous representations, propagate those through attention and MLP operations across many blocks, and map the final representations to a probability distribution over vocabulary. Interaction among all layers and all parameters yields next-token prediction.

Table 1. Classical ML vs. LLMs – Interpretability Landscape

Dimension	Classical ML	LLMs
Opacity source	Model complexity	Distributed layers
Decision logic	Feature importance	Token interaction
Key failure mode	Bias, drift	Hallucinations
Explanation method	LIME, SHAP	Attention, influence
Evaluation metric	Fidelity	Hallucination rate
Stakeholder need	Feature ranking	Confidence signal

4.2 Explaining LLM Behavior: Methods and Constraints

4.2.1 Attention Visualizations

Attention visualization techniques identify which input tokens receive elevated attention weights from each position. Visualizations often reveal discernible patterns, such as task-relevant word concentration in text classification or question–passage attention flow in reading comprehension, and intuitive explanations may be provided by showing that the model pays attention to specific words that would give the predicted outcome.

Nevertheless, fundamental limitations remain. Attention weights capture focus, not causality: tokens with high attention might correlate with decisions without being causal factors. High attention could reflect learned heuristics rather than robust decisions, which means possibly models rely on spurious correlations that visualizations highlight. Visualizations show only one layer; to get a complete picture, integration over many layers is necessary, which is not cognitively possible. If multi-head attention exists, several patterns exist concurrently; single visualizations cannot represent this complexity. Empirical work has demonstrated that attention visualizations can be misleading and may draw attention to tokens which appear important but are not causally relevant to the outcome.

4.2.2 Influence Functions

The influence functions indicate which training instances have the greatest influence on particular predictions by essentially answering the question, "Which training examples does this model rely upon for this prediction?" They quantify the change in model parameters and predictions in response to the removal or alteration of training examples.

For LLMs, the potential value rests in knowing the knowledge bases these models draw upon; finding the training texts that shape outputs gives one relevant insights. Practical limitations do exist, however. Exact computation of influence requires second-order optimization and Hessian matrices, which is prohibitively computationally expensive for models with billions of parameters; resorting to approximations introduces error. For LLMs that are trained on trillions of tokens, influential instance identification faces data access challenges: original training data is often unavailable due to privacy concerns or the infeasibility of scanning extremely large datasets. Even when influence functions identify training instances, the resulting explanations offer only indirect insight, leaving users to reason about why certain instances affected specific predictions (Aamir et al., 2023).

4.2.3 Counterfactual Reasoning

Counterfactual explanations describe input changes that would lead to alternative outputs: for instance, "Removing 'not' from your query would change the response." This framing is in accordance with human causal reasoning. Work using structural causal models provides theoretical underpinnings and shows that LLMs can generate fluent counterfactuals for analogy tasks and natural language processing tasks (Suresh Babu, C. V., Kowsika, S., et. al. (2023). However, these counterfactuals generated by LLMs have a number of different issues: namely, logical inconsistency, entity-relation mismatch, where changes lead to semantically incoherent scenarios. The major causes are reversed entity order and mismatches of the structure of entity-relations (Li et al., 2023).

Generative models, including VAEs, GANs, and diffusion models, allow for counterfactuals of meaningful scenarios to complex problems by finding latent encodings and using conditional generative generation to obtain counterfactual variants that reside within data manifolds (Kirilenko et al., 2024). The integration of multimodal LLMs with the generation of counterfactuals allows for enhanced comprehension by reasoning on the kind of proposed changes.

4.3 LLM-Specific Risks: Hallucinations, Uncertainty, Bias

4.3.1 Hallucinations

Hallucinations are prominent failures particular to LLMs: the confident generation of factually incorrect information, embedded in stylistic fluency such that false content is undistinguishable from correct content. The underlying reasons are multifaceted: (1) inaccuracies and biases in training data can lead to the perpetuation of out-of-date information, since models learn patterns without any robust mechanism to verify them; (2) uncertainty in predictions can yield responses that are confident but wrong, as models "fill gaps" with plausible-sounding yet incorrect information. Autoregressive generation introduces intrinsic dependencies whereby early errors cascade to later tokens, conditioning future outputs on the wrong information and thereby amplifying hallucination. Several such detection methods exist; however, many limitations remain. For intrinsic mechanisms, attention kernel maps, hidden activations, and output prediction probabilities all enable detection without additional computational cost. Detection by computing the computation of attention scores through eigen-decomposition is efficient and results in significant speedups of around 45× to 450×. Analyses of hidden states show a consistent pattern in how representations are changed when the model is hallucinating compared to honest outputs. Black-box approaches-typically semantic consistency, reference-based fact-checking, or retrieval-based verification-are generally less reliable.

The mitigation strategies include retrieval-augmented generation that augments prompts with relevant external knowledge and reduces hallucination rates significantly, fine-tuning on factual data, prompt engineering that evokes cautious responses, and ensemble methods. Still, a number of limitations remain: retrieval systems may fail to find relevant information, and models can also ignore the retrieved data.

4.3.2 Representational Bias

Large language models encode biases in the training data on a variety of dimensions, including gender, race, culture, and ideology (Gallegos et al., 2023). These biases make themselves manifest as stereotypical model descriptions of professions, the use of gender-associated language patterns, and the expression of political orientations consistent with the composition of the training data. A thorough evaluation requires systematic testing of outputs across demographic groups, professions, cultural contexts, and perspectives. The bias evaluation taxonomy includes metrics at the embedding level-learned representations-the probability level-token distributions-and generated-text level-actual outputs. Counterfactual testing-changing the demographics of references and observing changes to outputs-reveals inappropriate sensitivities to demographics (Gallegos et al., 2023).

4.4 Safety Alignment and LLM Evaluation

Alignment with safety is a procedure where LLMs are taught to decline requests that could be harmful and craft responses that meet laid-down criteria on safety. The main basis for this approach is RLHF, whereby humans give ratings to the models for safety; the models are optimized for maximum safety and minimum harm. Such a framework raises interpretability challenges: why does a model approve one harmful request but reject related variations? What internal criteria govern these assessments of safety?

Safety alignment is implemented by representations and safety-sensitive mechanisms learned throughout the model. The identification of these mechanisms allows the practitioner to detect any fine-tuning data that could degrade alignment. However, alignment remains fragile: fine-tuning unrelated to safety can erode alignment; adversarial prompts can jailbreak models that are otherwise aligned; and safety can sometimes conflict with usefulness.

A full safety evaluation includes testing on various abusive usage scenarios: the actual behavior of a model is considered under adversarial conditions, rather than just toxicity metrics. Mitigation strategies to reduce social bias span multiple stages: pre-processing-augmenting training data, in-training-modifying objectives, intra-processing-adjusting the behavior at inference time, and post-processing-filtering of outputs-each presenting associated trade-offs (Gallegos et al., 2023).

4.5 Human-Centered Explainability for LLMs

Utility of explanation hinges upon capability to enable decisions by stakeholders. For LLMs, this means human-centered explainability that tailors itself to a variety of stakeholder groups. End-users rarely need mechanistic explanations; instead, they need signals of reliability versus uncertainty, clear caveats as to limitations-e.g., "training data through April 2024", alternative interpretations, and transparency as to bias. Domain experts-such as clinicians validating LLMderived clinical summaries, attorneys reviewing legal analyses, and scientists using research assistanceneed explanations tailored to their domain. Clinicians, for example, need models that clearly separate chart-derived information from model-generated inferences. Attorneys need to know if analyses are based on real case law or overgeneralization. For clinical applications, calibration reflective of stakeholder input, verification by synthetic data, structured audits, and ongoing monitoring suited to dynamic environments are required beyond general fairness principles to include detailed implementation guidance (Templin et al., 2025).

Applications of LLMs entailing strong regulation or independent auditing require comprehensive, systematic documentation of the training methodologies; the criteria guiding the inclusion of data; the performance characteristics; limitations already identified; and failure modes. This kind of documentation forms a basis for independent assessments of appropriateness for LLM deployment in particular application contexts.

Key Takeaways: Interpretability for LLMs requires methods fundamentally different from the ones used in classical machine learning. Attention visualizations do not establish causality; influence functions suffer from scalability issues; hallucinations require their own detection methods. The needs of the stakeholders also vary: from confidence signals by end users to explanations consonant with domain knowledge by domain experts (Gilpin et al., 2018).

5. TRANSPARENCY ARTIFACTS AND DOCUMENTATION STANDARDS

5.1 Model Cards, System Cards & Fact Sheets

Model cards provide structured documentation templates for machine learning models, capturing essential details on development, assessment, and deployment. Key elements include: (1) model specifics such as developer name, date, version, type, and algorithms; (2) use context covering primary applications, excluded uses, and target users; (3) contextual factors influencing performance in specific settings; and (4) metrics with disaggregated evaluations across demographic axes, evaluation methods, and conditions. They address bias and fairness by assessing performance variations (e.g., accuracy, false positive rates) along dimensions like race, gender, geography, and intersections, while disclosing training data characteristics including sources, collection methods, preprocessing, and limitations.

System cards extend model cards to encompass entire AI systems, not just individual models. They employ a system accountability benchmark with 56 criteria in a 4x4 matrix: rows for components (data, model, code, system) and columns for lifecycle stages (development, assessment, mitigation, assurance). This facilitates systematic auditing of accountability across components and stages, recording fulfillment, gaps, and resolutions (Gursoy & Kakadiaris, 2022).

This distinction underscores that models operate within broader systems involving data flows, processing, human oversight, and policies. While model cards focus on model-specific elements, system cards emphasize integration and governance. Examples of fair models failing due to absent oversight, distant impacts, or undetected drift highlight the necessity for system-level accountability (Sidhpurwala et al., 2025).

Implications for practitioners: Those implementing ML/LLM solutions should view documentation as a necessity of operations rather than a compliance task. Model cards and system cards help to make informed deployment choices. Breakdown information about performance helps to understand risks of fairness. Understanding the method of evaluation used helps to understand the limits of robustness. Awareness of limitations helps to understand usage limits. Incorporating documentation into MLOps pipelines helps to minimize effort and ensures that documentation is up-to-date. For practitioners, documentation enables accountability to stakeholders. Clinicians reviewing diagnostic models understand the logic behind the decisions; auditors assessing systems verify the adequacy of governance processes; and end users understand limitations in the system.

5.2 Datasheets for Datasets and Metadata Requirements

Documentation of datasets fundamentally forms the future behavior of machine learning systems; datasets have traditionally attained less documentation attention than models, though they are critical. Datasheets for datasets introduce structured frameworks for documentation (Gebru et al., 2018).

Datasheets include: motivation (the reason for creation, the problem being solved, and who funded it); composition (number of instances, number of features, completeness, gaps); collection process (subject recruitment, subject compensation, subject consent, annotator instructions, quality control); pre-processing/cleaning (transformations from raw data to released form, instance removal, outlier handling, treatment of missing values); uses and recommendations (intended uses, inappropriate uses with example scenarios); and limitations and ethical considerations (time frame, location, demographic breakdown, and privacy considerations).

Metadata standards allow the structured description and the discovery of datasets and models. They include administrative information about a metadata catalog, such as creator and date of publication, technical information, including schema and format, and quality indicators, such as completeness. Practically every different platform uses a different schema: DataCite focuses on identification and citation; Zenodo extends DataCite with additional descriptors; and Kaggle captures information about the execution environment. Metadata harmonization seeks to ensure consistency across different platforms, a problem that has long existed because of the complexity of the schema and the semantic depth involved. However, standardized metadata promotes interoperability, and increased homogeneity of metadata improves the ease of data discovery and reuse.

Implications for policymakers and regulators: Documentation standards offer specific ways for regulatory compliance. Instead of requiring black-box algorithmic audits, the regulator could demand documentation such as model cards, system cards, and datasheets and assess these for completeness, accuracy, and recognition of limitations. The NIST AI Risk Management Framework and the growing EU AI Act increasingly specify documentation requirements. Policymakers should standardize documentation requirements across industries to facilitate consistent accountability that addresses domain-specific variability. Documentation requirements should be accompanied by audit access: regulators must check actual system behavior against documented assertions and examine discrepancies. For policymakers, documentation enables governance that moves from adversarial testing to collaborative accountability: organizations that keep current and complete documentation show governance maturity; auditable documentation enables evidence-based governance rather than assumption-based governance.

5.3 Data Provenance, Lineage, and Traceability

Governance demands tracking the origin and evolution of data through organizations. Data provenance records the data's origin, transformations, and current location, while data lineage traces its path from input through processing to final output. Traceability enables reconstructing this lineage to answer questions like "How did we reach this conclusion?". These concepts underpin accountability. If model decisions err, can faults trace to training data? If bias emerges, can sources—data, models, or processing—be identified? For privacy, can outputs link to specific individuals' data? Without provenance and lineage documentation, auditing AI systems and addressing failures becomes impossible.

Provenance documentation details data origins from sources like sensors, transactions, surveys, administrative systems, or public datasets. Context matters: sensor data differs from surveys; transactions reflect markets, surveys capture preferences;

administrative data embodies processes. Essential content covers collection methods, covered populations, identified gaps, sampling strategies, and quality assurance.

Lineage documentation maps data transformations in processing pipelines. Raw data undergoes cleaning, combination, feature engineering, scaling, and normalization before model input. Each step alters characteristics—dropping records, creating/removing features, composing engineered ones—necessitating explanation of final dataset content and any information loss.

5.4 Logging, Audit Trails, and Reproducibility Records

Operational systems require the implementation of extensive logging, which enables post-incident analysis and identification of impending issues. Logging captures system events such as inputs, processing performed, and outputs produced. Audit trails preserve information against modification and hence are usable for forensic analysis.

Minimum logging should capture: system inputs-provided data or requests, model inferences-generated predictions or outputs, system actions-decisions made and incorporated feedback, and performance metrics-accuracy, confidence. The logs should include timestamps so that temporal behavior can be reconstructed. Contextual information should include the versions of the models in use, active versions of dependencies, and current system parameters. Audit trails produce stakeholder-examinable records that support comprehension of system behavior and interpretation of decisions. In high-stake applications such as health care or finance, audit trails can be legally necessary: clinicians rely on diagnostic system information, and patients may understand and appeal decisions. Audit trails must be complete but understandable-provide sufficient detail to allow expert review yet be interpretable to the relevant audience.

Reproducibility records document the generation of results in a way that facilitates independent verification or reproduction. These include code versions, data versions, parameter settings, random seeds, and software dependencies needed. Complete reproducibility records should allow independent parties to rerun analyses and get the same result, maintaining scientific integrity and debugging when unexpected results occur.

5.5 Integrating Documentation into MLOps/LLMOps Pipelines

Documentation standards prove effective only when consistently followed. Integrating documentation into MLOps and LLMOps pipelines ensures creation, updating, and maintenance of transparency artifacts across the machine learning lifecycle—from data preparation to monitoring (Mitchell et al., 2018). Model card processes embed developer templates within workflows, yielding accurate records of practices; automated extraction of metrics, parameters, and architectures minimizes manual effort. Data governance logs provenance and lineage centrally, capturing transformations for full reconstruction, while model training records datasets, timestamps, and parameters.

Audit logging must embed from system inception via infrastructure automating inputs/outputs, decisions, and metrics, ensuring coverage without developer reliance. Governance mandates creation, review, auditing, and updates: Responsible AI boards assess cards pre-deployment for risks and limitations, evolving documentation with production insights. For researchers, MLOps integration evaluates transparency innovations—XAI, monitoring, provenance—requiring complete lifecycle documentation to prove organizational impact (Mitchell et al., 2018).

6. EVALUATION FRAMEWORKS FOR TRANSPARENT AND TRUSTWORTHY AI

6.1 Evaluation Principles: Fairness, Safety, Reliability, Explainability

A thorough assessment of artificial intelligence systems should go beyond accuracy and include fairness, safety, reliability, and explainability. Fairness assessment involves the analysis of fair treatment, the potential for the perpetuation of fairness, and the expectations of stakeholders for fair treatment. Safety evaluation involves the operation of a system without harm, the rejection of inappropriate requests, and graceful degradation when operating outside the boundaries of competence. Reliability involves performance, the availability of recovery strategies following an error, and performance under changing conditions. Explainability evaluation assesses whether explanations accurately reflect model behavior, are stable and reproducible, can be understood by intended audiences, and support appropriate human judgment.

These dimensions are interconnected and interact in many meaningful ways, producing various trade-offs. Models tuned for accuracy may be biased; those regularized by fairness objectives can suffer loss of accuracy for the majority population; and design tuned for explainability can incur performance costs. Every model evaluation should consider these dimensions together, logging the analytic choices taken and describing resultant performance profiles. This is how stakeholders can gain insight into suitability while considering strengths and limitations.

6.2 Metrics for XAI Quality Assessment

A number of complementary metrics is required when trying to evaluate explainability methods; no single metric captures all the dimensions of explanation quality. Different approaches target aspects: functional metrics evaluate against formal definitions, application-grounded evaluation involves domain experts, human-grounded metrics measure non-expert understandability.

6.2.1 Fidelity Metrics

Fidelity measures the representation of true-decision-making accurately. A faithful explanation captures actual model behavior and not perceived behavior. The deletion method provides a practical fidelity assessment: features identified as important are progressively deleted from inputs, recording changes in prediction confidence. Important deleted features should reduce confidence substantially; the deletion of unimportant features should maintain stability. This is quantified by dAUC, or Deletion Area Under the Curve, where higher scores represent the important-ranked features influencing predictions.

Complementary insertion methods start with the feature removal and progressively insert important-identified features while recording confidence changes. The confidence should raise rapidly for the important feature insertions and keep low for unimportant insertions. Insertion Area Under the Curve or iAUC quantifies that. A fidelity assessment for both methods is whether removing or adding important features produces expected behavior changes (Skliarov & Singh, 2025).

6.2.2 Explainability-User Fit Metrics

Beyond mere faithfulness, explanations must deliver insight and support informed decision-making. The Meta-predictor framework assesses how effectively explanations enable users to build accurate mental models by having them predict model behavior on unseen data. User performance in these predictions objectively measures whether explanations convey the true decision rationale.

This approach mitigates flaws in prior methods. Trust surveys like "Do you trust the model?" suffer from confirmation bias, where users affirm sufficiency without genuine comprehension. In contrast, prediction accuracy on new instances provides concrete evidence of conveyed understanding. The Utility-K score quantifies improvement over a no-explanation baseline, confirming if explanations enhance comprehension significantly.

Human-centered evaluation must account for comprehension variations across demographics and expertise levels. Identical explanations elicit different understanding: clinicians grasp clinically framed ones better than machine learning terminology, while financial analysts prefer investment-logic over statistical framings. Domain experts benefit from technical details overwhelming to lay audiences, who require simplified summaries omitting expert-essential nuances. Thus, explanation design demands audience-tailored communication, validated via user studies with diverse stakeholder groups mirroring real populations. High fidelity alone fails transparency's core goal—enabling understanding—without demonstrated audience comprehension.

6.2.3 Stability and Robustness Metrics

Stability metrics evaluate explanation consistency under perturbations: identity metrics confirm identical inputs produce matching explanations (instability arises from run-to-run variations), while separability metrics ensure distinct inputs yield unique explanations, avoiding concealment of underlying mechanics (Agrawal et al., 2025). Computational efficiency is vital for real-world use; prolonged calculations may deliver accurate explanations but prove impractical for time-sensitive applications.

Explanations introduce risks like overconfidence from misleading trustworthiness signals or verbose details fostering false comprehension amid complex boundaries, eroding skepticism in high-stakes contexts—countered by confidence reporting, constraint documentation, uncertainty expression, and calibration training (Agrawal et al., 2025). Adversaries exploit them for manipulation, reverse-engineering boundaries for attacks (e.g., fraud via feature importance in credit detection or misdiagnoses in healthcare), prompting coarsened public explanations with full auditor access (Skliarov & Singh, 2025). Explanation gaming occurs when explainability optimization amplifies spurious correlations or palatable rankings, prioritizing performative over true accountability; governance demands audits, method rationales, alternatives, and limitation documentation to enforce fidelity (Agrawal et al., 2025).

6.3 Testing for Bias, Drift, and Adversarial Vulnerabilities

Fairness assessment requires systematic testing across demographic groups for performance consistency and equity. Disparate Impact (DI) measures differences in positive-prediction rates between groups, with a value of 1.0 indicating equality and elevated values signaling disproportionate positives for one group (Li et al., 2023). Equalized Odds (EOD) evaluates true positive rate disparities, where 0 denotes equivalent sensitivity and larger magnitudes reveal detection rate differences. These metrics embody distinct fairness notions, often mutually incompatible—a model may achieve equal opportunity yet exhibit disparate impact. Evaluations must transparently specify adopted fairness definitions and rationales, reporting group-specific metrics rather than aggregates. For example, 95% overall accuracy might conceal subgroup variances like 98% in one group and 85% in another (Dang et al., 2024). Bias mitigation identifies sources via pre-processing (data resampling or sensitive attribute removal), in-processing (algorithmic fairness constraints), or post-processing (output adjustments), each entailing unique performance-fairness trade-offs.

Drift detection monitors performance stability. Concept drift alters feature-target relationships, as when house-price models falter from stable to volatile markets. Data drift shifts input distributions, like evolving applicant demographics in credit scoring. Performance drift marks rising errors in prior accurate models. Detection relies on tracking predictions against outcomes, baseline comparisons, and retraining triggers upon degradation. Adversarial vulnerability testing gauges robustness to deliberate perturbations. Adversarial examples—perceptually similar yet misdirecting inputs—probe model fragility. Generating such perturbations assesses accuracy retention, critical in security-sensitive applications where attackers could engineer failures.

6.4 Third-Party Audits and Regulatory Evaluations

Independent auditing provides external validation that systems meet documented standards and purported claims. Third-party auditors review documentation (model cards, system cards, datasheets), assess evaluation procedures and results, test governance structures, and perform independent testing. Auditors assess the truthfulness and completeness of documentation, the extent of testing, the sufficiency of known-risk management, and the suitability of governance.

But more and more, regulatory reviews require documentation of governance frameworks and the ability to demonstrate governance. The NIST AI Risk Management Framework provides structured guidance on how to do so: Govern-establish policy and oversight; Map-identify system-specific risks; Measure-assess sufficiency of mitigations; Manage-implement interventions and monitor effectiveness. And regulators like the FDA are increasingly requiring proof that an AI system is safe and functions as intended, using model cards to make sure performance is transparently documented across demographic and condition variables (Gilpin et al., 2018).

6.5 Benchmarking Explainability for ML and LLM Systems

The process of benchmarking systematically contrasts multiple explanation methods by applying uniform metrics across a wide range of datasets and model architectures. Comprehensive frameworks go beyond single metrics to assess fidelity-whether or not the explanations reflect the model behavior, stability-consistency across measures, identity-if identical inputs produce identical explanations, separability-distinct inputs result in distinct explanations, and computational efficiency-resource requirements.

The results of benchmarking show that no method is leading for all the metrics and tasks: some methods achieve high fidelity and low stability; some methods are fast but unstable. Results help practitioners choose methods according to contextual needs and constraints: it may be desired to take one method when computational efficiency is the priority or another if stability and reproducibility are more important.

Benchmarking exercises need to use diverse datasets and model classes for generalizability. Evaluations on a single dataset or with a single model may produce misleading results. Findings such as method A outperforming method B on one health dataset may also not generalize into other datasets or domains outside of medicine. Multi-domain, multi-architecture, and data-characteristic evaluation should be done with any comprehensive benchmarking exercise to explain when and why methods do and fail (Skliarov & Singh, 2025).

Key takeaways: A comprehensive assessment requires the consideration of fidelity, stability, useralignment and efficiency metrics all at once. No metric is enough on its own; it becomes the responsibility of the practitioner to select appropriate combinations for the context. Benchmarking has exposed the existence of trade-offs-which differ across tasks and datasets (Agrawal et al., 2025).

7. CONTINUOUS MONITORING OF DEPLOYED ML/LLM SYSTEMS

7.1 Monitoring Objectives: Drift, Bias, Performance, Safety

Deployed ML and LLM systems may subsequently drift away from their pre-deployment evaluation characteristics as environments, populations, and patterns of use change. Ongoing monitoring then becomes the primary means of detecting and responding to such shifts. Monitoring takes place along four interrelated dimensions:

- **Performance:** Does predictive quality remain stable over time?
- **Drift:** Have input distributions or data–label relationships changed?
- **Bias:** Are fairness properties stable across different demographic groups?
- **Safety:** Does the system continue to avoid harmful or undesirable behaviors, including emergent behavior in LLMs?

Deployment environments often differ from development settings: models trained on historical data encounter new populations, changing social conditions or adversarial inputs. Without monitoring, degradation in either performance or fairness can remain undetected. Thus, active monitoring makes lifecycle transparency practical and supports the validity of explanations and fairness assessments under evolving conditions (Linardatos et al., 2020; Li et al., 2023).

7.2 Real-Time Model Behavior Tracking

Real-time behavioral tracking logs input, outputs, and contextual metadata as predictions are made. This can include feature values, model scores, and final decisions in traditional machine learning. For large language models, the logs may include prompts, generated outputs, and metadata such as decoding parameters and confidence-related indicators when available.

Raw logs need to be converted into semantic monitoring signals. Performance monitoring uses outcome labels as they arrive to estimate time-varying metrics, such as rollingwindow accuracy, AUROC, calibration, and error rates by segment. Drift monitoring compares current input distributions to training distributions using summary statistics and divergence measures, sending alerts if the measured deviations exceed pre-set thresholds. These monitoring pipelines must be interfaced with data infrastructure and operational workflows so that computation, visualization, and alerting of metrics are automated and reproducible (Mitchell et al., 2018; Sidhpurwala et al., 2025).

7.3 Monitoring LLM Hallucinations and Toxicity

For LLMs, monitoring has to explicitly address the problems of hallucinations and harmful content. Hallucinations are confidently stated but factually incorrect outputs that undermine reliability and can cause real-world harm when users treat responses as authoritative. Recent surveys of LLM hallucinations indicate that such errors are often systematic, arising from gaps in training data, weak grounding, and miscalibrated confidence rather than pure randomness.

Monitoring hallucinations may involve:

- User feedback flags signaling incorrect or invalid responses.
- Fully automated fact-checking against curated knowledge bases within constrained domains
- Heuristics or calibration-based thresholds that identify low-reliability outputs.

Toxicity and harmful content monitoring detects hate speech, harassment, and unsafe advice, measuring toxicity rates across demographics to spot disproportionate harms to marginalized groups (Gallegos et al., 2023). Pipelines use toxicity classifiers and lexical filters to flag issues, despite detector biases, with feedback loops refining safety via iterative labeling (Gallegos et al., 2023; Sajjadi et al., 2025).

LLM outputs are highly sensitive to prompt wording, context, and formulation. Semantically identical queries with varied phrasing yield divergent responses, enabling adversarial exploits that bypass filters or expose biases—e.g., "describe scientific procedures for" evading "dangerous instructions" blocks (Sajjadi et al., 2025). Monitoring must flag prompt patterns triggering problematic outputs, tracking metadata like length, complexity, intent, and linguistics.

Output comparisons for equivalent semantics reveal sensitivities requiring fixes via prompt engineering, filter adjustments, or redesigns. Transparency documentation logs these patterns for reliability assessment, with institutions sharing adversarial prompt databases to enhance resilience.

7.4 Alerts, Feedback Loops, and Human-in-the-Loop Governance

Monitoring effectiveness hinges on thresholds and alerts aligned with application risks. For metrics like performance decay, drift, fairness disparities, hallucination rates, and toxicity, high-stakes domains (e.g., clinical or credit systems) demand low degradation tolerances, unlike low-stakes recommendation services.

Human-in-the-loop governance converts alerts into action, avoiding noise. Structures define responsibilities for triaging, suspending operations, retraining, mitigation, and updating risk documentation. Human review remains vital for ambiguous cases, root-cause analysis, and documenting new behaviors or limitations.

Human-centered frameworks emphasize explanations supporting decision-making, not mere artifacts. Monitoring verifies if explanations stay comprehensible for overrides amid evolving data or workflows (Agrawal et al., 2025). Augmented LLM systems integrating tools (search APIs, calculators, retrievers) complicate oversight: LLM failures differ from tool integration issues. RAG relies on retrieval quality—poor retrieval yields subpar outputs despite sound LLM reasoning. Function-calling creates error cascades in sequences.

Disaggregated monitoring tracks LLM outputs, tool invocations, tool quality, and end-to-end performance separately. It analyzes tool information usage (incorporation vs. ignoring), flagging integration failures. Tool availability and latency monitoring distinguishes them from core LLM issues. Documentation details tool dependencies, failure modes, and contingency strategies for stakeholders.

7.5 Integrating Monitoring into MLOps/LLMOps

Monitoring forms an integral building block of MLOps and LLMOps pipelines, encompassing automated data collection, metric computation, dashboard generation, and alerting within deployment environments. Model and dataset versioning ensures monitoring signals link precisely to specific versions and snapshots, enabling accurate problem diagnosis (Mitchell et al., 2018; Sidhpurwala et al., 2025).

In traditional machine learning, monitoring configurations—covering performance, drift, and fairness—must integrate with deployment workflows, automatically pairing each deployed model with its dedicated monitors. In the case of systems that use large language models (LLMs), the monitoring process should also consider:

Base models compared to fine-tuned variants:

- Changes in the prompts, tools, or retrieval components within a RAG system.
- Safety-related components, such as filters or classifiers that can degrade over time.

Monitoring outcomes should feed back into transparency artifacts. When new risks, failure modes, or domain shifts are discovered, model cards, system cards, and datasheets can be updated to ensure that external stakeholders see a correct and up-to-date view of system behavior.

7.6 Adaptive Re-Training and Model Lifecycle Management

Continuous monitoring is inherently supportive of adaptive retraining and system management. Ongoing performance degradation, drift, or fairness issues may require retraining or model replacement. However, simple retraining on new data can pose the risk of amplifying biases or overfitting to a particular environment. Work on fairness in related domains like healthcare has shown that retraining needs to be accompanied by explicit, disaggregated fairness analysis.

Lifecycle management prescribes decisions regarding:

- Deployment of new model versions.
- Reversion to earlier versions.
- Shadow mode operation of models to be evaluated comparatively.
- Complete retirement of models.

Decisions should be documented on system cards, along with the rationale, evidence from monitoring, and expected impact. New releases should be assessed before release, in proportion to initial releases but informed by focused tests developed from results gained by production monitoring. In high-risk situations, parallel or shadow releases enable assessment with actual traffic with no risk to end users (Agrawal et al. 2025; Sidhpurwala et al. 2025). In the lifecycle, continuous monitoring, full documentation, and governance create a feedback loop that sustains transparency and trustworthiness over time, making transparency as a design principle an ongoing trait rather than a single design goal.

8. GOVERNANCE, POLICY, AND ETHICAL CONSIDERATIONS

8.1 Stakeholder Roles and Accountability Structures

Explainable AI integration demands defined stakeholder roles and accountability mechanisms. Modern governance complicates single-point accountability amid AI's growing complexity, sparking debates on blame allocation—developers, organizations, regulators, or users—in system failures (Lim & Lim, 2025). Risk management literature highlights five key features: balancing innovation-safety, adaptability across contexts, stakeholder inclusion, governance transparency, and long-term risk focus (Hohma et al., 2023).

Distributed responsibility frameworks address single-point limitations by recognizing hybrid accountability among developers, users, and regulators (Lim & Lim, 2025). They enable pre-deployment algorithm impact assessments for potential harms and collective regulation. Wieringa outlines five algorithmic accountability components: identifying responsible parties, specifying forums, defining stakeholder relationships, setting fulfillment criteria, and outlining consequences ((Suresh Babu, C. V., Sudhir Manoharan et al, 2024)). Together, these form a practical architecture translating ideals into defined accountability structures.

8.2 Alignment of XAI With Legal and Regulatory Standards

Explainable AI (XAI) has shifted from optional to essential. The EU AI Act categorizes systems by risk, mandating high-risk ones in healthcare, employment, and public administration to maintain detailed records, perform impact assessments, and deliver comprehensible explanations to affected parties. Prohibited activities like large-scale social scoring and untargeted biometric surveillance compel designs prioritizing human oversight and contestability over pure automation.

Complementary frameworks like NIST's AI Risk Management Framework and ISO/IEC 42001 embed explainability in governance. NIST's Govern–Map–Measure–Manage cycle demands defining explanation needs, validating fidelity/stability, and continuously tracking explanation risks. ISO/IEC 42001 standardizes transparent, accountable AI processes organization-wide. In finance, these forces have normalized feature attribution, model cards, and subgroup fairness reports, as regulators demand auditable, explainable models over black boxes.

Real Failures Driving Trends

1. **Healthcare LLM (2024)**: Hallucinated fake study → contraindicated chemo. No monitoring. **EU AI Act**: High-risk, needs human oversight.
2. **Credit Drift (2023)**: Post-pandemic model denied young professionals. No drift detection. **Result**: $2.3M fine, mandated audits.
3. **Policy Chatbot (2025)**: Hallucinated regulations via adversarial prompts. **NIST**: Requires continuous monitoring.

Trend: Static explainability → continuous governance with regulatory enforcement.

Table 2. Transparency Tools Mapped to AI Risks and Lifecycle Stages

Transparency Tool	Primary Risk Addressed	Lifecycle Stage	Regulatory Alignment
Model Cards	Bias, Performance Drift	Design, Deployment	NIST Measure, EU AI Act Documentation
Datasheets	Data Quality, Fairness	Pre-Deployment	ISO/IEC 42001 Data Governance
System Cards	Integration Failures	Post-Deployment	NIST Manage, EU AI Act Monitoring
Risk Registers	Safety, Hallucinations	All Stages	NIST Map, ISO/IEC 42001 Risk Management
Audit Trails	Accountability Gaps	Runtime	EU AI Act High-Risk Logging
Explanation Logs	Over-trust, Fidelity	Inference	NIST Govern, EU AI Act Explainability

8.3 Risk Registers, Safety Evaluations, Incident Reporting

Effective AI risk management demands systematic risk register documentation, capturing risk items, nature, mitigations, and responsibilities at organizational-unit levels for visibility and traceability. Minimum contents include unique identifiers, risk descriptions, likelihood–impact ratings, owners, and specified mitigation actions (Hohma et al., 2023).

LLM-supported risk register management offers potential alongside limitations. AI accelerates risk identification/evaluation, aids duplicate consolidation, description standardization, and uncovers undocumented risks—enhancing coverage and accuracy under human oversight. However, AI hallucinations (e.g., fabricating risks/ mitigations) necessitate mandatory human review to validate changes, preserving accuracy and commitment to mitigations (Hohma et al., 2023).

In healthcare, AI-driven approaches bolster patient safety via machine learning and NLP for classifying incidents like delayed medications, fall risks, and near-misses. While AI strengthens systematic risk detection and reporting, it heightens explainability demands: systems must justify flagging certain incidents as high-risk (Suresh Babu, C. V., Kowsika, S., et. al. (2023).

8.4 Ethical Challenges: Consent, Transparency Fatigue, Over-Trust

Informed consent in algorithmic decision-making challenges traditional static disclosure models, which fail against AI's secondary, contextual, and unforeseeable data uses. Instead, consent functions as an ongoing trust assurance, with organizations committing to sustained transparency and responsiveness where pre-deployment information remains incomplete; dynamic systems thus link consent to continuous monitoring (Grote & Berens, 2020). Healthcare exemplifies the stakes: non-transparent recommendations deprive patients of meaningful consent by omitting confidence metrics on diagnoses or treatments, prompting key questions about essential algorithmic details needed to protect epistemic autonomy and dignity (Suresh Babu, C. V., Sudhir Manoharan et al, 2024).

Transparency fatigue emerges when user needs are ignored in disclosures, as context-free technical explanations fail to build trust—users often dismiss irrelevant accuracy metrics, confuse confidence scores, and resent verbose details (Afroogh et al., 2024). Over-trust risks undue reliance despite errors or bias framed as "objective risks," with information overload fostering flawed mental models (Zerilli et al., 2022). Governance should trigger bias audits and mitigation from disparate impact explanations used diagnostically, countering compliance theater where stale documentation misleads stakeholders; policies must enforce monitoring-linked updates, responsibility for inaccuracies, and actionable artifacts over symbolic ones.

8.5 Sociotechnical Perspectives on Trust and Human Factors

Trust emerges from interactions among human, contextual, and technological factors, rather than transparency alone. It reflects users' willingness to accept AI recommendations, share tasks, disclose information, and provide support, particularly when novel decisions arise from training data. Thus, accuracy, reliability, transparency, and explainability prove essential (Afroogh et al., 2024).

Human factors like personality traits shape trust disposition—open individuals trust AI more than cautious ones, often overriding external conditions. Contextual elements include decision stakes, domain familiarity, and organizational norms; technological ones encompass algorithmic reliability, data quality, mathematical suitability, and decision-process transparency. Matching observable processes to users' expectations boosts trustworthiness, akin to clinicians citing studies. Perceived trustworthiness hinges on system relevance, availability, user detection, and utilization, grounded in five principles: beneficence, non-maleficence, autonomy, justice, and explicability. Tensions, such as AI's lack of empathy viewed as bias-free or overly detached, demand governance decisions tailored to deployment contexts. Sociotechnical views emphasize integrating organizational governance, stakeholder engagement, and legal accountability to embed diverse perspectives in design and deployment.

9. CASE STUDIES AND REAL-WORLD APPLICATIONS

9.1 Healthcare: Transparent Diagnostic Systems

Systematic reviews of AI integration in clinical decision support systems (CDSSs) demonstrate improved diagnostic accuracy and risk stratification, yet opacity has impeded adoption. A meta-analysis of 62 studies (2018–2025) across radiology, oncology, neurology, and critical care found that CDSSs with high predictive accuracy and explanation fidelity ($\geq$0.85) increased clinician trust by 12–18 percentage points compared to those without quantified explanations.

Explainability's clinical value extends beyond trust to informed consent, enabling patients and professionals to grasp decision rationales; shared decision-making, requiring clinically interpretable outputs; and contestability via auditing and dispute resolution. It confirms reliance on clinically relevant factors, detects errors/biases, and supports patient communication of AI-informed decisions. Amid debates, some question explainability's necessity for CDSS quality or trust (Hildt, 2025), revealing a context-dependent dynamic: novices benefit from detailed counterfactuals, experts from concise, framework-aligned ones. Opaque models with hundreds of features persist, indicating explainability aids but does not mandate adoption.

9.2 Finance: Explainable Credit Risk Models

Credit risk evaluation mandates explainability due to regulatory demands. AI systems risk perpetuating discrimination against marginalized groups via biased training data, poor contextual interpretation, and flawed post-hoc tools like SHAP and LIME, which fail to ensure accountability and fairness (Shah, 2025). Mixed-methods studies highlight these weaknesses as key drivers of discriminatory outcomes (Shah, 2025).

Finance regulators enforce explicability: the Office of the Comptroller of the Currency requires rigorous model documentation and validation, while the European Banking Authority deems transparency essential for AI use. Non-compliance invites reputational harm, litigation, and penalties. Ye and Chen's (2025) five-dimensional framework evaluates: (i) consistency for similar cases; (ii) complexity for non-technical comprehension; (iii) local situational explanations; (iv) global model behavior; and (v) fidelity to true decisions. Organizations blending ML accuracy with XAI thus achieve compliant, transparent credit risk management.

9.3 Education: Interpretation of Learning Analytics

Learning analytics systematically analyzes data to inform educational practice, transforming raw inputs into actionable insights. Studies in higher education demonstrate its promise in predicting student outcomes and targeting interventions for at-risk learners. A sequential mixed-methods study of 922 biostatistics students combined LMS logs with interviews, identifying engagement metrics like time-on-task and participation as strong success predictors for early risk detection. Thematic analysis revealed six themes—behavioral engagement differences, assessment, emotional struggle, self-efficacy, knowledge/skill development, and structured support—indicating low performers benefit from guidance and repeated exposure.

Interpretability proves crucial in learning analytics, converting quantitative patterns into meaningful interventions. While analytics forecast performance from engagement data, educators require explanations of success behaviors and intervention impacts. AI-driven EFL tools exemplify personalized real-time feedback for engagement and curriculum adaptation (Almutairi et al., 2025), yet demand educator competencies in interpretation and data literacy for effective translation to instruction. Privacy and ethics necessitate informed consent, pedagogical focus over data optimization (Sander, 2016), and transparency in collection and decision impacts. Learning analytics maximizes potential through reflective practice, enabling dynamic adjustments.

9.4 Public Sector: Algorithmic Governance

AI revolutionizes government decision-making, enhancing evidence-informed processes via algorithms that predict infrastructure needs, detect fraud, and target vulnerable populations. A review of 43 studies confirms AI automates routine administrative tasks like benefit eligibility, freeing decision-makers for complex issues and improving overall efficiency, though it raises accountability concerns (Alon-Barkat et al., 2025).

Algorithmic discrimination poses serious risks in public services. Responsibility attributions hold organizations equally accountable for AI versus human discrimination, but citizens assign greater blame to in-house algorithms than outsourced ones, creating accountability gaps that shield external providers (Alon-Barkat et al., 2025). Transparent algorithmic governance addresses this through four pillars: (1) pre-implementation impact assessments; (2) robust oversight frameworks; (3) disclosure of AI use, inspectable code, and independent audits; and (4) enforcement via human review, contestability, and redress. These ensure improved decision quality while preserving democratic legitimacy (Alon-Barkat et al., 2025).

9.5 Industry: Monitoring LLM-Based Systems

Production LLM systems introduce unique monitoring challenges, particularly at integration points with databases and APIs. Feasibility evaluation demands rigorous testing for response quality in real-world scenarios, while ongoing monitoring optimizes performance via real-time latency/error detection (including hallucinations), drift tracking through feedback, scalability planning, compliance, and cost control.

Monitoring blends automated (for generic development tasks) and custom metrics (for production use cases), such as sentiment for user satisfaction, embedding-based relevance, and first-attempt resolution. Organizations set Service-Level Objectives (SLOs) mandating query resolution rates within time windows, triggering threshold-based alerts and remediation filters for problematic outputs. Enterprise tools like PagerDuty and Slack integrate with incident response; end-to-end versioning prevents regressions. Implementation hurdles include comprehensive technical/business metric coverage, surge alerts for cost/latency, and synthetic data testing. Properly executed, these enable service stability, proactive drift detection, and data-driven infrastructure optimization.

10. CHALLENGES, OPEN QUESTIONS, AND RESEARCH OPPORTUNITIES

10.1 Technical Limitations of Current XAI Techniques

Despite advances in explainable AI, fundamental technical challenges limit LIME and SHAP reliability. LIME suffers fidelity issues—linear surrogates inadequately capture local model behaviors, perturbation sampling yields unrepresentative data, and simplistic surrogates fail complex dynamics. Stability proves more severe: minor input changes, varying perturbations/samplings, or reruns drastically alter explanations, yielding inconsistent results that undermine trust. Knab et al. attribute this to hyperparameters (sampling, neighborhood, surrogate choice) introducing exploitable variability.

SHAP offers game-theoretic advantages with global/local explanations and guarantees, yet exhibits data-dependent performance. Bias-variance analyses reveal LIME excels in dense regions, SHAP in sparse ones (Roberts et al., 2022); SHAP's completeness reduces sparse bias but inflates dense variance. No method dominates universally—domain-specific evaluation remains essential (Roberts et al., 2022).

Both grapple with feature dependencies, assuming independence despite real correlations that spawn unrealistic scenarios. Collinearity destabilizes rankings: removing one correlated feature lets others compensate, spawning spurious importance attributions.

10.2 Gaps in Evaluation and Monitoring Infrastructure

XAI quantification remains fragmented and manipulable, lacking standardized, reliable metrics that hinder comparisons and reproducibility. Hyperparameter dependencies and baselines (e.g., Integrated Gradients choices or faithfulness perturbation orders) enable result manipulation. This governance gap prevents explainability from ensuring accountability, fostering arbitrary, gamed compliance.

Current metrics inadequately address modern systems like LLMs and multimodal architectures. Image/tabular-focused algorithms fail autoregressive generation and billion-parameter scales; few techniques handle cross-modal dependencies, creating critical gaps as multimodal adoption surges (Seth & Sankarapu, 2025). Robust evaluation lags, impairing interpretability. Governance requires monitoring explanation quality, drift, and integration for proactive responses. Yet most organizations lack mature mechanisms; inference-generated explanations rarely log faithfulness changes amid model/data evolution.

10.3 Trade-Offs: Performance vs. Transparency vs. Privacy

Accuracy-interpretability trade-offs spark debate, though practice often accepts performance drops for interpretability. Composite interpretability scores reveal non-monotonic correlations: while accuracy typically rises with reduced interpretability, interpretable models sometimes outperform opaque ones contextually (Atrey et al., 2025).

Privacy-explainability tensions emerge prominently. Differential privacy's noise addition combats membership inference but sharply degrades interpretability (Saifullah et al., 2024); perturbation-based XAI resists this better than gradient methods, while federated learning preserves local heterogeneity to enhance it.

Security risks intensify with explainability: detailed explanations expose model vulnerabilities, aiding attackers in crafting boundary-probing inputs. Security-sensitive applications thus curtail explanation granularity to thwart reconnaissance, balancing the trade-off deliberately.

10.4 Future Directions for LLM Explainability

Large language models present distinct explainability challenges, with mechanistic interpretability—reverse-engineering transformer circuits—emerging as a promising yet arduous frontier. Unlike correlational methods pinpointing influential inputs, it pursues causal insights into internal subgraphs driving behaviors, decomposing tasks into human-comprehensible sub-problems. Recent advances uncover interpretable circuits: induction heads enabling in-context learning, subfunction attributions, and concept-selective neurons. These successes span million- to billion-parameter models, but trillion-parameter frontier systems introduce combinatorial complexity, where neurons contribute to thousands of distributed representations, hindering scalability.

Mechanistic interpretability yields practical benefits despite hurdles. Circuit identification facilitates knowledge editing—targeting fact-storing neurons to correct misinformation without retraining—reducing hallucinations and enhancing safety. It also elucidates generalization, training dynamics, and failures from adversarial or out-of-distribution inputs.

10.5 Research Frontiers: Federated XAI and Synthetic Data Governance

Federated learning with explainability prioritizes privacy-preserving interpretability, enabling distributed model training without centralizing sensitive data. Empirical studies on blockchain-optimized XAI in federated incremental learning demonstrate collaborative training—crucial for healthcare, where hospitals share medical models sans patient data exposure—while blockchain audit trails ensure tamper-proof transparency in development and decisions (Lopez-Ramos et al., 2024). Tensions arise, however: local node explanations fail to generalize globally, and blockchain adds governance complexity. Ongoing research scales mechanistic interpretability federally, stabilizes distributed explanations, and crafts privacy-safe local insights.

Synthetic data governance tackles bias and fairness but introduces ethical hurdles. GAN-generated datasets boost fairness—e.g., elevating COMPAS recidivism parity from 0.72 to 0.89 sans accuracy loss (Fabuyi, 2024)—yet embed creator biases, risking underrepresented group homogeneity or variation shortfalls (Shanley et al., 2024). Differential privacy enhances safeguards but amplifies sociodemographic biases (Susser et al., 2024). Governance must counter incentives undervaluing real data work, prioritizing community engagement for diverse real-world representation over synthetic proxies, ensuring benefits without entrenching inequities (Shanley et al., 2024).

11. CONCLUSION

11.1 Summary of Key Contributions

This dissertation provides an integrative analysis of transparency, explainability, and trustworthiness across the AI lifecycle, advocating frameworks that blend technical methods, governance, ethics, and human-centered evaluation. It argues that transparency demands integration from problem formulation through deployment monitoring, beyond isolated post-hoc fixes.

Section 2 delineates transparency (information access), interpretability (human comprehension), and explainability (decision rationale communication), stressing technical details alone insufficient for stakeholder accountability (Linardatos et al., 2020). Section 3 covers classical ML: interpretable models (linear, trees, rules) versus black-box ones (ensembles, neural nets), with post-hoc tools like LIME and SHAP aiding despite fidelity/stability issues. Section 4 addresses LLM challenges—transformer scale limiting attention methods, mechanistic interpretability's scalability hurdles, and failures like hallucinations.

Sections 5–8 operationalize transparency via model/system cards, datasheets, risk registers, and governance for multi-stakeholder accountability aligned with EU AI Act/NIST, mitigating consent, fatigue, and over-trust issues (Afroogh et al., 2024; Lim & Lim, 2025).

Section 9 applies to domains: clinical CDSS for trust/consent; finance's regulatory explainability (consistency, complexity, local/global/fidelity) (Ye & Chen, 2025; Shah, 2025); education's analytics for interventions (Almutairi et al., 2025);

public sector's anti-discrimination governance (Alon-Barkat et al., 2025); enterprise LLMs' production monitoring.

Section 10 confronts challenges: LIME/SHAP instabilities, feature dependencies (Knab et al., 2025; Roberts et al., 2022); non-monotonic accuracy trade-offs, privacy tensions (Atrey et al., 2025; Saifullah et al., 2024); emerging federated/synthetic data governance (Lopez-Ramos et al., 2024; Shanley et al., 2024).

11.2 Toward Transparency-by-Design AI Ecosystems

Findings indicate that transparency by design will become standard for major AI systems, necessitating paradigm shifts in technology, organizations, policy, and culture.

Technically, research must prioritize inherently interpretable architectures over post-hoc methods, including hybrids blending deep learning capacity with understandable logic (Atrey et al., 2025). Mechanistic interpretability requires scaling to frontier models via automated circuit discovery, while federated XAI must advance privacy-preserving explanations for healthcare and finance (Bhardwaj & Sumangali, 2025; Lopez-Ramos et al., 2024).

Organizationally, embed explainability and monitoring from design inception: automate model cards/datasheets via MLOps, let risk registers shape architecture, enforce pre-deployment governance, and integrate continuous monitoring with explanation logging, drift detection, and alerts. Culturally, position transparency as a developer advantage—facilitating debugging, regulatory compliance, reputation management, and rapid issue response—rather than a burden, boosting adoption. Policy must harmonize outcome-focused standards without stifling innovation, building on EU AI Act, NIST, and national risk-based frameworks that escalate transparency for high-risk uses (Lund et al., 2025; Radanliev, 2025).

11.3 The Future of Explainable and Trustworthy ML/LLM Systems

The future of AI transparency hinges on interrelated advances. Mechanistic interpretability will illuminate frontier model computations, enabling causal interventions like hallucination correction and bias removal without retraining, shifting from correlational to principled explanations. Human-AI collaboration evolves toward adaptive, personalized explanations based on expertise, task stakes, and interaction data, evaluated via objective metrics like decision quality gains rather than subjective trust (Afroogh et al., 2024). Governance stabilizes through institutionalized ethics boards, third-party certifications, international standards for documentation/audits, and mandatory incident reporting akin to data protection regimes.

Emerging domains and refined regulation further shape progress. Synthetic data governance enhances bias mitigation with demographic fidelity when real data is scarce (Fabuyi, 2024); federated XAI supports privacy-safe collaboration, especially in healthcare (Bhardwaj & Sumangali, 2025; Lopez-Ramos et al., 2024); privacy techniques like differential privacy resolve transparency trade-offs (Saifullah et al., 2024). Domain-specific policies escalate: healthcare differentiates diagnostic vs. research tools; finance mandates auditability; public sectors emphasize contestability and human oversight. Ultimately, transparency's maturity reveals its sociotechnical essence—demanding robust governance over perverse incentives to avoid compliance theater. Powerful, understandable, accountable AI is essential for human flourishing across high-stakes contexts, ensuring stakeholders comprehend impacts, organizations resolve issues swiftly, and society augments capabilities without unaccountable power concentration.

REFERENCES

Aamir, A., Tamosiunaite, M., & Wörgötter, F. (2023). Interpreting the decisions of CNNs via influence functions. *Frontiers in Computational Neuroscience*, *17*, 1172883. DOI: 10.3389/fncom.2023.1172883 PMID: 37564901

Afroogh, S., Akbari, A., Malone, E., Kargar, M., & Alambeigi, H. (2024). Trust in AI: Progress, Challenges, and Future Directions. *ArXiv*. https://arxiv.org/abs/2403.14680

Agrawal, K., El Shawi, R., & Ahmed, N. (2025). Explainable artificial intelligence-Eval: A framework for comparative evaluation of explanation methods in healthcare. *Digital Health*, *11*, 20552076251368045. DOI: 10.1177/20552076251368045 PMID: 41036433

Ajirak, M., Ravishankar, A., & Djuric, P. M. (2025). Uncertainty Quantification in Probabilistic Machine Learning Models: Theory, Methods, and Insights. *ArXiv*. https://arxiv.org/abs/2509.05877 DOI: 10.23919/EUSIPCO63237.2025.11226403

Almutairi, M., Alamry, A., Rahman, G., & Mudhsh, B. A. (2025). The role of AI-powered learning analytics in enhancing EFL curriculum design and learning outcomes in higher education. *International Journal of Innovative Research and Scientific Studies*, *8*(7), 477–487. DOI: 10.53894/ijirss.v8i7.10480

Alon-Barkat, S., Busuioc, M., Schwoerer, K., & Weißmüller, K. (2025). Algorithmic Discrimination in Public Service Provision: Understanding Citizens' Attribution of Responsibility for Human vs Algorithmic Discriminatory Outcomes. *Journal of Public Administration: Research and Theory*, *35*(4), 469–488. Advance online publication. DOI: 10.1093/jopart/muaf024

Atrey, P., Brundage, M. P., Wu, M., & Dutta, S. (2025). Demystifying the Accuracy-Interpretability Trade-Off: A Case Study of Inferring Ratings from Reviews. *ArXiv*. https://arxiv.org/abs/2503.07914

Bell, A., Solano-Kamaiko, I., Nov, O., & Stoyanovich, J. (2022). It's just not that simple: An empirical study of the accuracy–explainability trade-off in machine learning for public policy. In *Proceedings of the 2022 ACM Conference on Fairness, Accountability, and Transparency (FAccT '22)* (pp. 248–266). Association for Computing Machinery. DOI: 10.1145/3531146.3533090

Bhardwaj, T., & Sumangali, K. (2025). A federated incremental blockchain framework with privacy preserving XAI optimization for securing healthcare data. *Scientific Reports*, *15*(1), 38001. DOI: 10.1038/s41598-025-21852-3 PMID: 41168334

Dang, V. N., Cascarano, A., Mulder, R. H., Cecil, C., Zuluaga, M. A., Hernández-González, J., & Lekadir, K. (2024). Fairness and bias correction in machine learning for depression prediction across four study populations. *Scientific Reports*, *14*(1), 7848. DOI: 10.1038/s41598-024-58427-7 PMID: 38570587

Elshawi, R., Al-Mallah, M. H., & Sakr, S. (2019). On the interpretability of machine learning-based model for predicting hypertension. *BMC Medical Informatics and Decision Making*, *19*(1), 146. DOI: 10.1186/s12911-019-0874-0 PMID: 31357998

Fabuyi, J. (2024). Leveraging synthetic data as a tool to combat bias in artificial intelligence (AI) model training. *Journal of Engineering Research and Reports*, *26*(12), 24–46. DOI: 10.9734/jerr/2024/v26i121337

Gallegos, I. O., Rossi, R. A., Barrow, J., Tanjim, M. M., Kim, S., Dernoncourt, F., Yu, T., Zhang, R., & Ahmed, N. K. (2023). Bias and Fairness in Large Language Models: A Survey. *ArXiv*. https://arxiv.org/abs/2309.00770

Gebru, T., Morgenstern, J., Vecchione, B., Vaughan, J. W., Wallach, H., Daumé, H.III, & Crawford, K. (2018). Datasheets for Datasets. *ArXiv*. https://arxiv.org/abs/1803.09010

Gilpin, L. H., Bau, D., Yuan, B. Z., Bajwa, A., Specter, M., & Kagal, L. (2018). Explaining Explanations: An Overview of Interpretability of Machine Learning. *ArXiv*. https://arxiv.org/abs/1806.00069 DOI: 10.1109/DSAA.2018.00018

Goldstein, A., Kapelner, A., Bleich, J., & Pitkin, E. (2013). Peeking Inside the Black Box: Visualizing Statistical Learning with Plots of Individual Conditional Expectation. *ArXiv*. https://arxiv.org/abs/1309.6392

Grote, T., & Berens, P. (2020). On the ethics of algorithmic decision-making in healthcare. *Journal of Medical Ethics*, *46*(3), 205–211. DOI: 10.1136/medethics-2019-105586 PMID: 31748206

Gursoy, F., & Kakadiaris, I. A. (2022). System Cards for AI-Based Decision-Making for Public Policy. *ArXiv*. https://arxiv.org/abs/2203.04754

Hildt, E. (2025). What is the role of explainability in medical artificial intelligence? A case-based approach. *Bioengineering (Basel, Switzerland)*, *12*(4), 375. DOI: 10.3390/bioengineering12040375 PMID: 40281735

Hohma, E., Boch, A., Trauth, R., & Lütge, C. (2023). Investigating accountability for artificial intelligence through risk governance: A workshop-based exploratory study. *Frontiers in Psychology*, *14*, 1073686. DOI: 10.3389/fpsyg.2023.1073686 PMID: 36760454

Kaneko, H. (2023). Interpretation of Machine Learning Models for Data Sets with Many Features Using Feature Importance. *ACS Omega*, *8*(25), 23218–23225. DOI: 10.1021/acsomega.3c03722 PMID: 37396269

Kirilenko, D., Barbiero, P., Gjoreski, M., Luštrek, M., & Langheinrich, M. (2024). Generative models for counterfactual explanations. *CEUR Workshop Proceedings*, *3841*, 1–15.

Knab, P., Marton, S., Schlegel, U., & Bartelt, C. (2025). Which LIME should I trust? Concepts, Challenges, and Solutions. *ArXiv*. https://arxiv.org/abs/2503.24365

Koene, A. (2019). A governance framework for algorithmic accountability and transparency. DOI: 10.2861/59990

Li, F., Wu, P., Ong, H. H., Peterson, J. F., Wei, W. Q., & Zhao, J. (2023). Evaluating and mitigating bias in machine learning models for cardiovascular disease prediction. *Journal of Biomedical Informatics*, *138*, 104294. DOI: 10.1016/j.jbi.2023.104294 PMID: 36706849

Li, Y., Xu, M., Miao, X., Zhou, S., & Qian, T. (2023). *Prompting large language models for counterfactual generation: An empirical study* (arXiv:2305.14791). *arXiv*. https://arxiv.org/abs/2305.14791

Lim, E. C. N., & Lim, C. E. D. (2025). Polycentric AI Governance: A Multi-Stakeholder Approach to Distributed Responsibility and Ethical Technology Management. *International Journal of Advanced AI Applications*, *1*(4), 77–97.

Linardatos, P., Papastefanopoulos, V., & Kotsiantis, S. (2020). Explainable AI: A Review of Machine Learning Interpretability Methods. *Entropy (Basel, Switzerland)*, *23*(1), 18. DOI: 10.3390/e23010018 PMID: 33375658

Lopez-Ramos, L., Leiser, F., Rastogi, A., Hicks, S., Strümke, I., Madai, V., Budig, T., Sunyaev, A., & Hilbert, A. (2024). *Interplay between federated learning and explainable artificial intelligence: A scoping review* (arXiv:2411.05874). *arXiv*. *L* arXiv.2411.05874DOI: 10.48550

Lund, B., Orhan, Z., Mannuru, N. R., Bevara, R. V. K., Porter, B., Vinaih, M. K., & Bhaskara, P. (2025). Standards, frameworks, and legislation for artificial intelligence (AI) transparency. *AI and Ethics*, *5*(4), 3639–3655. Advance online publication. DOI: 10.1007/s43681-025-00661-4

Mitchell, M., Wu, S., Zaldivar, A., Barnes, P., Vasserman, L., Hutchinson, B., Spitzer, E., Raji, I. D., & Gebru, T. (2018). *Model Cards for Model Reporting*. ArXiv., DOI: 10.1145/3287560.3287596

Murdoch, W. J., Singh, C., Kumbier, K., & Yu, B. (2019). *Interpretable machine learning: Definitions, methods, and applications*. ArXiv., DOI: 10.1073/pnas.1900654116

Ortigossa, E., Gonçalves, T., & Nonato, L. (2024). EXplainable Artificial Intelligence (XAI)–From Theory to Methods and Applications. *IEEE Access : Practical Innovations, Open Solutions*, *12*, 80799–80846. DOI: 10.1109/ACCESS.2024.3409843

Radanliev, P. (2025). AI Ethics: Integrating Transparency, Fairness, and Privacy in AI Development. *Applied Artificial Intelligence*, *39*(1), 2463722. Advance online publication. DOI: 10.1080/08839514.2025.2463722

Rai, A., Hurley, M. E., Herrington, J., Storch, E. A., Zampella, C. J., Parrish-Morris, J., Sonig, A., Lázaro-Muñoz, G., & Kostick-Quenet, K. (2025). Stakeholder Criteria for Trust in Artificial Intelligence-Based Computer Perception Tools in Health Care: Qualitative Interview Study. *Journal of Medical Internet Research*, *27*, e78757. DOI: 10.2196/78757 PMID: 41385782

Roberts, C. V., Elahi, E., & Chandrashekar, A. (2022). On the Bias-Variance Characteristics of LIME and SHAP in High Sparsity Movie Recommendation Explanation Tasks. *ArXiv*. https://arxiv.org/abs/2206.04784

Saifullah, S., Mercier, D., Lucieri, A., Dengel, A., & Ahmed, S. (2024). The privacy-explainability trade-off: Unraveling the impacts of differential privacy and federated learning on attribution methods. *Frontiers in Artificial Intelligence*, *7*, 1236947. DOI: 10.3389/frai.2024.1236947 PMID: 39021435

Sajjadi, M., Kara, B., Eyupoglu, C., & Karakuş, O. (2025). A survey on hallucination in large language models: Definitions, detection, and mitigation (Preprint). *Preprints*. DOI: 10.20944/preprints202510.0540.v1

Sander, P. (2016). *Using learning analytics to predict academic outcomes of students*. University of Oregon Scholars Bank.

Seth, P., & Sankarapu, V. K. (2025). *Bridging the gap in XAI: Why reliable metrics matter for explainability and compliance* (arXiv:2502.04695). *arXiv*. https://arxiv.org/abs/2502.04695

Shah, I. H. (2025, July 22). Investigating the risks of algorithmic bias and explainability failures in credit risk models. *SSRN*. DOI: 10.2139/ssrn.5361937

Shanley, D., Hogenboom, J., Lysen, F., Wee, L., Lobo Gomes, A., Dekker, A., & Meacham, D. (2024). Getting real about synthetic data ethics: Are AI ethics principles a good starting point for synthetic data ethics? *EMBO Reports*, *25*(5), 2152–2155. DOI: 10.1038/s44319-024-00101-0 PMID: 38388694

Sides, T., Kbaier, D., Farrell, T., & Third, A. (2025). Bridging trust gaps: Stakeholder perspectives on AI adoption in the United Kingdom NHS primary care. *Digital Health*, *11*, 20552076251386706. DOI: 10.1177/20552076251386706 PMID: 41323094

Sidhpurwala, H., Fox, E., Mollett, G., Gabarda, F. C., & Zhukov, R. (2025). Blueprints of Trust: AI System Cards for End to End Transparency and Governance. *ArXiv*. https://arxiv.org/abs/2509.20394

Skliarov, M., Shawi, R. E., Dhaoui, C., & Ahmed, N. (2025). A comparative evaluation of explainability techniques for image data. *Scientific Reports*, *15*(1), 41898. DOI: 10.1038/s41598-025-25839-y PMID: 41290895

Suresh Babu, C. V. Sudhir Manoharan., L., G. K., & V., S. K. (2024). Application of Support Vector Machine Algorithm in Automated Lending Protocols for Decentralized Finance Platforms. In L. Vardari & I. Qabrati (Eds.), Decentralized Finance and Tokenization in FinTech (pp. 1-20). IGI Global. DOI: 10.4018/979-8-3693-3346-4.ch001

Suresh Babu, C. V., Kowsika, S., Sai Tejaswi, M., Janarakshani, T. R., & Mercysha Princy, S. (2023). Framework for Detection of Cyberbullying in Text Data Using Natural Language Processing and Machine Learning. In Chitadze, N. (Ed.), *Cyber Security Policies and Strategies of the World's Leading States* (pp. 69–85). IGI Global., DOI: 10.4018/978-1-6684-8846-1.ch005

Susser, D., Schiff, D. S., Gerke, S., Cabrera, L. Y., Cohen, I. G., Doerr, M., Harrod, J., Kostick-Quenet, K., McNealy, J., Meyer, M. N., Price, W. N.II, & Wagner, J. K. (2024). Synthetic health data: Real ethical promise and peril. *The Hastings Center Report*, *54*(5), 8–13. DOI: 10.1002/hast.4911 PMID: 39487776

Templin, T., Fort, S., Padmanabham, P., Seshadri, P., Rimal, R., Oliva, J., Hassmiller Lich, K., Sylvia, S., & Sinnott-Armstrong, N. (2025). Framework for bias evaluation in large language models in healthcare settings. *NPJ Digital Medicine*, *8*(1), 414. DOI: 10.1038/s41746-025-01786-w PMID: 40624264

Wang, B., Zhou, J., Li, Y., & Chen, F. (2023, November). Impact of fidelity and robustness of machine learning explanations on user trust. In Australasian Joint Conference on Artificial Intelligence (pp. 209-220). Singapore: Springer Nature Singapore.

Wiratsin, I., Rahman, R., & Hanafusa, H. (2025). Effectiveness of explainable artificial intelligence (XAI) in improving human trust in machine learning models: A systematic literature review. *IEEE Access : Practical Innovations, Open Solutions*, *55*(3), 1–15. DOI: 10.1109/ACCESS.2025.3575022

Ye, R., & Chen, J. (2025). *Unlocking the black box: A five-dimensional framework for evaluating explainable AI in credit risk* (arXiv:2511.04980). *arXiv*. https://arxiv.org/abs/2511.04980

Zerilli, J., Bhatt, U., & Weller, A. (2022). How transparency modulates trust in artificial intelligence. *Patterns (New York, N.Y.)*, *3*(4), 100455. DOI: 10.1016/j.patter.2022.100455 PMID: 35465233

Chapter 7
Human-in-the-Loop and Participatory Approaches to Trustworthy AI

Otmane Azeroual
http://orcid.org/0000-0002-5225-389X
University of Hagen, Germany

ABSTRACT

This chapter examines Human-in-the-Loop (HITL) and participatory approaches for trustworthy AI, emphasizing human oversight, stakeholder engagement, and ethical alignment across the AI lifecycle. It discusses implementation challenges, best practices, and case studies, highlighting iterative feedback loops that enhance accuracy, transparency, and legitimacy. Future directions focus on scalable HITL, inclusive governance, interdisciplinary collaboration, and adaptive policies to ensure socially responsible AI.

INTRODUCTION

As artificial intelligence (AI) systems increasingly permeate high-stakes domains such as healthcare, finance, public administration, and criminal justice, concerns regarding their transparency, accountability, and ethical alignment have intensified. While advances in machine learning and automation have enabled unprecedented efficiency and predictive power, they have also exposed significant risks related to algorithmic bias, opacity, loss of human agency, and diminished public trust. In response to these challenges, the concepts of *Human-in-the-Loop* (HITL) and participatory approaches have emerged as central paradigms for the development of trustworthy AI systems. These approaches emphasize the continued involvement

DOI: 10.4018/979-8-3373-6761-3.ch007

of human judgment and stakeholder participation throughout the AI lifecycle, from design and training to deployment and governance.

HITL systems are designed to integrate human oversight, intervention, or decision-making into automated processes, particularly in contexts where errors may carry substantial social, ethical, or legal consequences. Rather than viewing automation as a replacement for human cognition, HITL frameworks conceptualize AI as a decision-support technology that augments human capabilities while preserving accountability and contextual reasoning (Amershi et al., 2014; Shneiderman, 2020). Research has shown that fully autonomous systems often struggle with edge cases, value-laden judgments, and dynamic social environments, reinforcing the need for human involvement to detect errors, correct model behavior, and interpret outputs responsibly (Raji et al., 2020).

Participatory approaches extend the logic of HITL beyond individual operators to include a broader range of stakeholders in AI development and governance. Drawing on traditions from participatory design, science and technology studies, and democratic governance, these approaches advocate for the inclusion of end users, domain experts, civil society actors, and affected communities in shaping AI systems (Wang et al., 2019; Delgado et al., 2023). Such participation is particularly critical in addressing power asymmetries and value conflicts embedded in data collection, model objectives, and deployment contexts. Scholars argue that without meaningful participation, AI systems risk reinforcing existing social inequalities and marginalizing vulnerable groups whose perspectives are often underrepresented in technical design processes (Costanza-Chock, 2020).

The growing emphasis on trustworthy AI—reflected in international policy frameworks such as the EU's Ethics Guidelines for Trustworthy AI and the OECD AI Principles—has further elevated the importance of HITL and participatory governance mechanisms. Trustworthy AI is commonly defined through principles including human agency and oversight, transparency, fairness, robustness, and accountability (Ai, 2019; OECD, 2019). HITL mechanisms operationalize these principles by ensuring that humans remain responsible for critical decisions, while participatory approaches enhance legitimacy and social acceptance by aligning AI systems with societal values and expectations.

This chapter is organized to provide a systematic exploration of HITL and participatory approaches to trustworthy AI. It begins by establishing the foundational principles of HITL AI, emphasizing the integration of human judgment into problem definition, data curation, model development, deployment, and monitoring. The discussion then expands to participatory approaches, highlighting stakeholder engagement methodologies that operationalize fairness, accountability, and societal alignment across AI lifecycle stages. Subsequent sections address implementation challenges, evidence-based best practices, and real-world case studies across domains such as healthcare, finance, public administration, autonomous systems, and education. The final section considers future directions and policy implications, focusing on scalability, adaptive regulation, ethical foresight, interdisciplinary collaboration, and global governance strategies.

The relevance of this chapter extends to AI researchers, practitioners, policymakers, regulators, and interdisciplinary stakeholders involved in AI deployment, as well as educators and organizational leaders seeking to align AI systems with ethical and societal standards. By providing a comprehensive synthesis of theoretical foundations, practical implementation, empirical evidence, and forward-looking strategies, the chapter equips readers with conceptual frameworks and operational insights necessary for designing AI systems that are both technically performant and socially legitimate.

The chapter advances the understanding that HITL and participatory AI are not merely technical solutions but constitute socio-technical governance processes essential for sustainable AI development. Future research should continue to explore scalable HITL architectures, inclusive participatory methodologies, and adaptive regulatory mechanisms that can dynamically respond to evolving societal needs, ethical concerns, and technological advancements. By foregrounding human agency and multi-stakeholder engagement, this work provides a roadmap for developing AI systems capable of delivering equitable, accountable, and socially aligned outcomes across complex and high-stakes domains.

FOUNDATIONS OF HUMAN-IN-THE-LOOP (HITL) AI

HITL AI represents an emerging paradigm in AI research and practice, emphasizing continuous human involvement throughout the AI lifecycle to ensure trustworthy, ethical, and contextually relevant outcomes (Amershi et al., 2014; Zheng et al., 2024). Unlike fully automated systems, HITL approaches recognize that human judgment, domain expertise, and ethical reasoning remain essential components in designing, deploying, and monitoring AI applications, particularly in high-stakes domains such as healthcare, finance, and autonomous systems. The HITL paradigm challenges the conventional notion that AI systems can function independently without human oversight, highlighting the risks of opaque, biased, or socially misaligned decision-making when human perspectives are excluded (Rahwan, 2018).

The foundational principle of HITL AI is the integration of human expertise into iterative model development. This begins with problem definition and value-setting, where humans identify goals, constraints, and ethical considerations that guide the AI's learning objectives (Amershi et al., 2014). This stage ensures that AI models are aligned with organizational or societal priorities, integrating considerations such as fairness, accountability, and transparency. Human input at this stage also informs data collection strategies, emphasizing the need for representative, high-quality datasets that reflect the diversity of real-world contexts and mitigate algorithmic bias (Mehrabi et al., 2021).

During data and model development, HITL AI combines automated learning with human annotation, correction, and evaluation. Humans may label datasets, curate features, or intervene to correct model outputs in real time, creating a feedback loop that improves both model accuracy and contextual reliability (Zheng et al., 2024). Interactive learning techniques, such as active learning, are frequently employed, allowing AI systems to query humans on uncertain or ambiguous cases. This collaboration enhances interpretability and facilitates the detection of errors that purely automated processes might overlook (Hong et al., 2020).

Deployment and decision-making in HITL AI maintains human oversight over critical decisions, particularly in applications with significant ethical, legal, or social implications. For instance, in medical diagnostics, clinicians review algorithmic recommendations before treatment decisions, ensuring patient safety and maintaining trust in the system. Similarly, in financial services, human auditors evaluate AI-generated credit or investment recommendations, preventing potentially harmful outcomes arising from algorithmic biases or untested assumptions (Doshi-Velez & Kim, 2017). HITL approaches thus embed accountability into the operational phase, providing mechanisms for human judgment to guide, override, or interpret machine recommendations.

A central aspect of HITL AI is continuous monitoring, feedback, and auditing, which establishes a dynamic learning loop between humans and AI systems (Rahwan, 2018). This phase ensures that AI models remain robust under changing environmental conditions and evolving data distributions. Humans evaluate performance metrics, ethical compliance, and societal impacts, offering corrective feedback that iteratively refines the model. Such monitoring mitigates risks of automation-induced harm, including bias reinforcement, unanticipated failures, or loss of public trust. It also supports transparency and explainability, crucial components of trustworthy AI, as humans document decision rationales and interpret model behavior for stakeholders (Arrieta et al., 2020).

The overarching objective of HITL AI is to produce trustworthy AI outcomes, characterized by fairness, accountability, transparency, safety, and alignment with human values. Figure 1 illustrates this lifecycle, depicting the interplay between human and AI agents across problem definition, model development, deployment, and monitoring. The cyclic feedback from monitoring to model refinement underscores the iterative nature of HITL AI, highlighting its capacity to adapt to new data, emerging ethical concerns, and evolving societal requirements. By incorporating humans at multiple touchpoints, HITL AI fosters systems that are not only technically robust but also socially responsible and aligned with ethical norms (Rahwan, 2018; Zheng et al., 2024).

HITL approaches have demonstrated empirical benefits in several domains. In healthcare, human-AI collaboration has been shown to improve diagnostic accuracy, reduce false positives, and enhance clinician confidence in AI-assisted recommendations (Esteva et al., 2019). In autonomous systems, HITL frameworks allow human operators to intervene during critical decision-making, reducing accidents and improving system reliability (Bostrom & Yudkowsky, 2014). Moreover, in natural language processing and content moderation, HITL methodologies enable human reviewers to correct algorithmic misclassifications, ensuring ethical standards are maintained in user-facing AI services (Amershi et al., 2014).

Despite these advantages, HITL AI also presents challenges. Integrating humans effectively requires careful interface design, cognitive load management, and well-defined decision protocols to prevent human errors or fatigue from undermining AI performance (Zheng et al., 2024). Furthermore, balancing human oversight with automation efficiency remains a critical research question, particularly in large-scale, high-frequency decision contexts. Future research must explore scalable HITL architectures, formal methods for integrating human feedback, and governance structures that ensure accountability without excessive operational burden (Rahwan, 2018).

In summary, Foundations of HITL AI highlight the inseparability of human judgment and machine intelligence in producing trustworthy, effective, and ethically aligned AI systems. By embedding humans in problem definition, data curation, model development, decision-making, and monitoring, HITL AI establishes iterative, adaptive feedback loops that enhance technical performance while safeguarding societal and ethical values. Figure 1 provides a visual representation of this lifecycle, illustrating the continuous interplay between humans and AI agents in achieving responsible AI outcomes.

Figure 1. HITL AI Lifecycle.

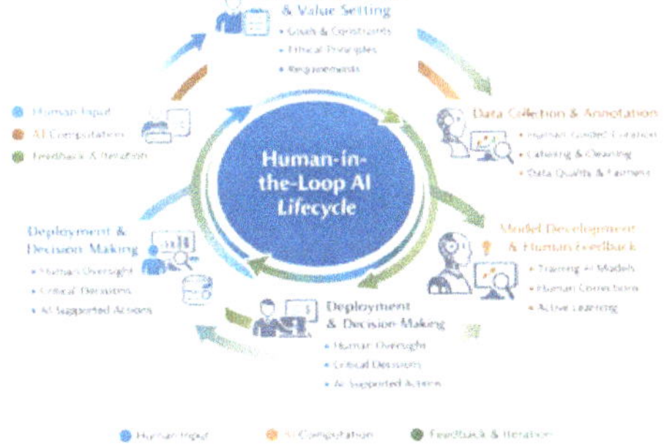

While HITL AI establishes the critical role of individual human judgment in shaping algorithmic outputs and ensuring ethical alignment, the scope of human involvement can be extended beyond direct operators. Effective AI governance requires integrating broader societal perspectives to capture diverse values, contextual knowledge, and normative priorities. Participatory approaches build on the foundational principles of HITL by structuring multi-stakeholder engagement, ensuring that AI systems reflect not only technical accuracy but also societal legitimacy. Thus, the transition from individual human oversight to inclusive stakeholder participation provides a framework for embedding fairness, accountability, and transparency throughout the AI lifecycle.

PARTICIPATORY APPROACHES AND STAKEHOLDER ENGAGEMENT

The integration of participatory approaches and stakeholder engagement into AI development has emerged as a critical strategy for achieving trustworthy, ethical, and socially aligned AI systems. HITL methodologies provide foundational mechanisms for embedding human judgment into AI processes, yet broader participatory approaches extend beyond direct model interaction to include the structured involvement of diverse stakeholders across the entire AI lifecycle. This perspective recognizes that AI systems are socio-technical constructs whose design, deployment, and societal effects are profoundly shaped by human values, institutional norms, and collective decision-making processes (Fjeld et al., 2020). Participatory AI emphasizes that legitimacy, accountability, and societal trust cannot be secured solely through technical performance metrics; instead, they require deliberate mechanisms for stakeholder input, deliberation, and governance throughout development and deployment phases.

Stakeholder engagement encompasses the systematic identification, inclusion, and empowerment of actors who are directly affected by or have influence over AI technologies. Key stakeholders include end-users, domain experts, civil society organizations, regulatory authorities, marginalized communities, and interdisciplinary researchers (Mello Rose, 2022). Participatory design methodologies encourage early and continuous involvement of these groups, facilitating co-creation processes that make AI systems responsive to contextual needs, ethical considerations, and cultural norms. This alignment supports principles of responsible AI—fairness, transparency, explainability, and accountability—by ensuring that technical and normative dimensions of AI design reflect the priorities of those impacted by the technology (Jobin et al., 2019). Integrating stakeholder feedback at multiple stages, from problem formulation and data annotation to model evaluation and deployment, reduces the likelihood of systemic bias, ethical oversights, and unintended societal harms.

Empirical evidence indicates that participatory engagement enhances both technical performance and societal acceptance of AI systems. For example, involving domain experts and affected communities in data labeling improves annotation quality and reduces biases, while collaborative evaluation procedures reveal limitations that automated testing alone may not identify (Binns, 2018). Participatory governance frameworks enhance transparency and accountability by documenting decision-making processes, creating auditability, and establishing mechanisms for external oversight. These practices intersect with the growing focus on explainable AI (XAI), as transparency alone is insufficient if system behavior fails to reflect social expectations or respond to stakeholder concerns (Doshi-Velez & Kim, 2017).

Figure 2. Implementation Frameworks for Participatory AI: Methods, Stakeholders, and Governance Mechanisms.

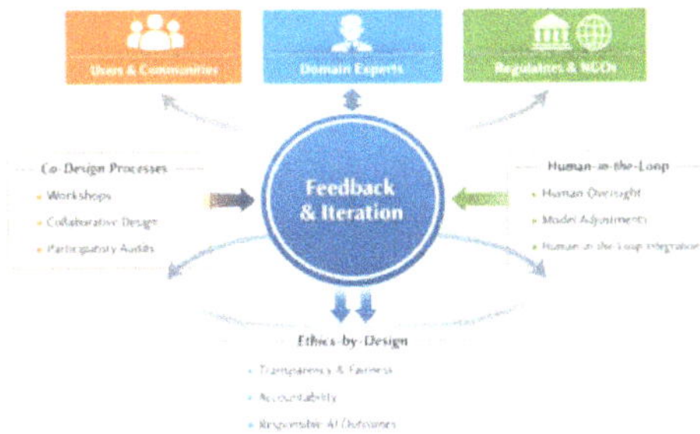

To visualize the interplay of stakeholders, participatory methods, and HITL integration, Figure 1 illustrates the core components of participatory AI governance. The infographic highlights how iterative feedback loops connect end-users, technical experts, regulatory authorities, and civil society across AI lifecycle stages, embedding ethics-by-design principles and supporting multi-level decision-making. This representation underscores the dynamic relationships and mutual dependencies that sustain socially aligned AI systems, emphasizing the role of structured participation in operationalizing fairness, accountability, and transparency from the outset.

Participatory approaches also influence policy and regulatory landscapes. Multi-stakeholder engagement enables policymakers to develop context-sensitive regulations, standards, and ethical guidelines informed by practical constraints and societal priorities (Floridi et al., 2018). Regulatory sandboxes operationalize participatory principles by incorporating feedback from industry, civil society, and technical experts, allowing iterative testing of AI systems in controlled environments while monitoring ethical compliance (Moraes, 2025). Such mechanisms illustrate how participatory governance can complement adaptive, risk-based regulation, bridging normative expectations with operational feasibility. Furthermore, participatory processes facilitate harmonization of divergent perspectives, which is particularly relevant in global AI ecosystems characterized by cultural, geographic, and socioeconomic heterogeneity.

Challenges persist in implementing participatory frameworks effectively. Power asymmetries may privilege corporate or governmental actors over marginalized groups, risking tokenistic engagement (Eubanks, 2018). Effective participation requires resources for sustained engagement, capacity-building, and methodological rigor to translate qualitative stakeholder input into quantitative model adjustments. Without addressing these challenges, participation risks reproducing existing inequities, undermining legitimacy, and limiting public trust in AI systems.

Practical implementations of participatory approaches include co-design workshops, citizen panels, multi-stakeholder advisory boards, participatory auditing, and collaborative model evaluation. Digital platforms facilitate scalable engagement, enabling broader participation while ensuring transparency regarding how stakeholder input informs AI design and deployment (Zhang, 2024). Across these initiatives, a common theme emerges: participatory approaches shift AI governance from top-down, expert-driven processes toward inclusive, iterative, and context-sensitive practices, aligning technological functionality with societal expectations.

Embedding participatory insights reinforces ethics-by-design principles. By integrating stakeholder perspectives into model design, data curation, and deployment strategies, organizations operationalize fairness, accountability, and transparency at the outset, rather than retrofitting ethical considerations post hoc (Arrieta et al., 2020). This approach enhances both technical reliability and social legitimacy, promoting wider societal acceptance and sustainable innovation. As AI systems expand into critical sectors such as healthcare, finance, education, and governance, participatory engagement becomes essential for aligning technological development with societal values, equity, and long-term trust.

Looking forward, the continued integration of participatory approaches into institutional frameworks, regulatory practices, and technical standards will be vital for socially responsible AI. Research and practice must focus on scalable engagement methods, equitable inclusion of underrepresented stakeholders, and systematic operationalization of diverse perspectives within AI lifecycle processes. By emphasizing iterative, transparent, and context-sensitive participation, AI development can achieve a dynamic balance between innovation and societal alignment, ensuring that human values remain central as systems grow in complexity and scope.

While participatory approaches offer robust mechanisms for incorporating societal perspectives into AI development, operationalizing these methodologies presents significant challenges. Translating stakeholder input into actionable model adjustments, managing human cognitive load, and integrating diverse perspectives without compromising system performance require careful technical and organizational strategies. Understanding the complexities and potential pitfalls of both HITL and participatory implementation sets the stage for identifying evidence-based best practices. This transition highlights the need to examine implementation challenges systematically to ensure that theoretical frameworks translate into practical, ethically aligned, and socially legitimate AI systems.

IMPLEMENTATION CHALLENGES AND BEST PRACTICES

The implementation of HITL and participatory approaches in AI represents a crucial step toward achieving trustworthy, ethical, and socially aligned systems. While these frameworks promise enhanced accountability, transparency, and ethical alignment, operationalizing them across diverse domains remains a highly complex task. HITL and participatory approaches require continuous human involvement throughout the AI lifecycle, encompassing problem definition, data collection, model development, deployment, and monitoring. Integrating human judgment and stakeholder input at these multiple stages is not straightforward; it demands careful consideration of cognitive, technical, organizational, and regulatory dimensions.

One of the primary challenges is managing human cognitive load. HITL AI systems often place significant demands on human operators, who must interpret model outputs, correct errors, and make high-stakes decisions in real time. Cognitive overload, fatigue, or misinterpretation of AI recommendations can reduce the effectiveness of human intervention, leading to suboptimal or even harmful outcomes. Designing user interfaces that provide clear, contextualized information and adaptive alerts is therefore essential. Dynamic task allocation, which determines the balance between automated and human-led decisions based on system confidence and contextual risk, has been shown to mitigate errors while maintaining efficiency. The design of these interaction points requires interdisciplinary collaboration, combining insights from human factors, cognitive psychology, and machine learning to ensure that the human-AI collaboration is effective and sustainable.

Another major challenge lies in translating qualitative human feedback into quantitative model improvements. Human input is often diverse, subjective, and context-dependent, creating methodological difficulties for integration into algorithmic learning processes. Approaches such as active learning, reinforcement learning with human feedback (RLHF), and hybrid models combining rule-based constraints with machine learning techniques provide mechanisms to operationalize human judgment at scale. Iterative testing and validation protocols are essential to ensure that human interventions lead to measurable improvements in model accuracy, fairness, and reliability. The aggregation of diverse feedback also requires robust methods to reconcile conflicting perspectives, ensuring that the system remains consistent and ethically aligned across multiple operational contexts.

Organizational and cultural factors further complicate implementation. Successful HITL and participatory AI deployment depends not only on technical design but also on organizational readiness and culture. Resistance may arise from stakeholders perceiving AI as a threat to professional expertise, disruptions to established workflows, or skepticism regarding system reliability. Addressing these concerns necessitates structured engagement strategies, including co-design workshops, interdisciplinary meetings, and continuous educational programs to foster understanding and trust. Incentivizing transparency and ethical conduct through formal governance structures can reinforce the adoption of participatory practices, aligning operational processes with the principles of responsible AI.

Data quality, representativeness, and bias mitigation are also central to the successful implementation of HITL and participatory AI. Inadequate or unrepresentative datasets can propagate bias and reinforce systemic inequities, undermining the ethical and technical goals of AI systems. Participatory annotation methods, which involve diverse stakeholders in labeling, reviewing, and validating data, have been demonstrated to improve both data quality and social alignment. These processes enable AI systems to capture context-specific nuances and address edge cases that automated pipelines may overlook. Iterative refinement, cross-validation, and rigorous quality control mechanisms are essential to reconcile variability in human annotations and ensure reliability. By integrating human insight into data curation and model evaluation, HITL frameworks can reduce unintended harms and enhance system robustness.

Ethical, legal, and regulatory considerations represent another layer of complexity. HITL and participatory AI operate at the intersection of technical capability and societal norms, necessitating compliance with data protection laws, anti-discrimination regulations, and sector-specific ethical guidelines. Divergent regulatory landscapes, particularly in multinational contexts, pose significant challenges. Participatory governance frameworks provide mechanisms to embed ethical and legal considerations into operational processes, aligning model behavior with societal expectations. Transparent documentation of human interventions, audit trails, and formal decision protocols enhance accountability and enable external review, supporting both regulatory compliance and public trust.

Empirical studies underscore the tangible benefits of these frameworks. In healthcare, HITL systems combining clinician oversight with algorithmic recommendations have been shown to improve diagnostic accuracy, reduce false positives, and increase clinician confidence. In financial and administrative domains, human review of AI-generated decisions prevents potentially harmful outcomes arising from biased or incomplete algorithmic inferences. The iterative feedback loops established by HITL frameworks create a dynamic system capable of adapting to emerging challenges, evolving data distributions, and shifting ethical priorities. By continuously refining models through human judgment and participatory engagement, organizations can operationalize both technical performance and social legitimacy.

Addressing these challenges requires a set of integrated best practices. Co-design and iterative stakeholder engagement ensure that AI systems reflect diverse perspectives and are aligned with contextual realities. Scalable feedback mechanisms enable human judgment to inform algorithmic learning without imposing unsustainable operational burdens. Transparent documentation of decisions, human interventions, and ethical evaluations ensures accountability and facilitates regulatory compliance. Organizational strategies that cultivate a culture of collaboration, continuous learning, and ethical responsibility support the effective adoption of HITL and participatory approaches. High-quality, representative datasets curated through participatory processes reduce bias, enhance fairness, and improve overall system reliability.

Figure 3 illustrates the multidimensional nature of HITL implementation, highlighting the interplay between human factors, technical integration, and organizational and regulatory contexts. It contrasts common implementation challenges with evidence-based best practices, showing how iterative feedback loops, stakeholder engagement, and structured governance mechanisms enable the operationalization of trustworthy, ethical, and socially aligned AI systems. The figure emphasizes the dynamic interdependencies among cognitive load management, feedback integration, data quality, and organizational alignment, providing a comprehensive visual framework for understanding the complex landscape of HITL and participatory AI deployment.

Figure 3. Implementation Challenges and Best Practices in HITL AI.

By systematically addressing cognitive, technical, organizational, and regulatory challenges, organizations can establish HITL and participatory systems that are both operationally effective and socially responsible. Integrating human judgment at multiple touchpoints ensures that AI systems remain contextually relevant, ethically aligned, and robust against both technical errors and societal risks. Participatory engagement facilitates broader stakeholder alignment, legitimizing AI interventions and promoting public trust. Collectively, these strategies underscore that HITL and participatory AI are not merely technical innovations but socio-technical processes requiring iterative, inclusive, and adaptive governance. As AI continues to permeate critical sectors, the development and dissemination of best practices for implementation will remain a cornerstone of achieving trustworthy, accountable, and human-centered AI.

Having established the key challenges and best practices in deploying HITL and participatory AI, it becomes essential to examine how these frameworks operate in real-world contexts. Case studies provide empirical insights into the effectiveness, scalability, and sector-specific adaptations of human-centered AI. They illustrate how cognitive, organizational, and technical strategies are applied across healthcare, finance, public administration, autonomous systems, content moderation, and education. By linking theoretical considerations to tangible applications, these examples demonstrate the concrete benefits of human involvement and stakeholder engagement, bridging the gap between methodological design and practical outcomes.

In summary, the examination of implementation challenges and best practices highlights that HITL and participatory AI are not merely technical adjustments but fundamental socio-technical processes. Successfully operationalizing these frameworks requires the careful balancing of human cognitive capacities, technical integration, organizational readiness, and regulatory compliance. Lessons from existing implementations underscore the importance of iterative feedback loops, transparent documentation, and inclusive stakeholder engagement in ensuring both system robustness and social legitimacy. Critically, these insights demonstrate that human involvement must be systematically embedded across the AI lifecycle—from problem definition and data curation to deployment and ongoing monitoring—to achieve outcomes that are accurate, fair, and ethically aligned. By framing these considerations collectively, the chapter establishes a clear foundation for examining real-world applications and for guiding future research, governance, and policy initiatives that seek to advance trustworthy, human-centered AI.

CASE STUDIES AND APPLICATIONS

HITL AI and participatory approaches have emerged as crucial strategies for developing trustworthy, ethical, and contextually aligned AI systems. Their significance becomes especially evident in real-world applications where AI decisions carry substantial social, economic, or ethical consequences. These case studies demonstrate how HITL and participatory methodologies enhance both the technical performance and societal acceptance of AI systems by integrating human judgment, domain expertise, and stakeholder perspectives throughout the AI lifecycle.

In medical diagnostics, HITL AI has demonstrated profound benefits. AI-driven image analysis systems assist radiologists in detecting tumors, lesions, and other pathological conditions, improving diagnostic accuracy and efficiency. In breast cancer screening, for instance, HITL mechanisms present algorithmically flagged findings to radiologists, who review, validate, or amend these outputs. Evidence indicates that this human-AI collaboration significantly increases both sensitivity and specificity while reducing false positives, contributing to enhanced patient safety (Esteva et al., 2019; Chen et al., 2024). Participatory elements in these systems include the engagement of clinicians, nursing staff, patient advocacy groups, and institutional ethics boards. Their involvement ensures that AI applications are not only technically robust but also aligned with ethical standards, patient expectations, and clinical priorities.

The financial sector provides another illustrative context. AI models in credit assessment, risk analysis, and fraud detection process vast amounts of transactional and behavioral data. HITL frameworks integrate financial experts into decision-making, particularly for edge cases or ambiguous signals. Trinh & Zhang (2024) found that combining algorithmic predictions with human judgment improves credit decision accuracy and reduces discriminatory biases. Participatory approaches further broaden the perspective by including regulators, consumer representatives, and ethical oversight bodies. This collaborative governance ensures that AI systems adhere to fairness, transparency, and accountability requirements while remaining operationally effective.

In the public sector, HITL and participatory approaches have been implemented in areas such as urban planning, social services, and resource allocation. For example, AI-driven traffic management systems use predictive models to optimize traffic flow, while human traffic engineers validate algorithmic recommendations, incorporate contextual knowledge, and adjust for unforeseen events. Participatory components include public consultations, citizen advisory boards, and multi-stakeholder committees that ensure AI-driven policy or infrastructure decisions align with social needs, public interests, and ethical norms (Mishra, 2024). Such frameworks exemplify how combining human oversight with stakeholder engagement enhances transparency, legitimacy, and societal trust in AI-driven governance.

HITL mechanisms also play a critical role in content moderation and natural language processing. Social media platforms utilize AI to flag harmful content such as hate speech, misinformation, or inappropriate materials. Human reviewers are integrated into the decision loop to validate, correct, or contextualize algorithmic outputs. This collaboration improves the accuracy of content moderation, reduces algorithmic bias, and ensures that decisions reflect societal norms and ethical considerations (Binns, 2018). Participatory practices involve including community representatives, ethicists, linguists, and technical experts to define moderation policies, providing a multi-layered governance structure that aligns automated moderation with human values.

In autonomous mobility, HITL frameworks allow human operators to intervene during complex traffic situations or ethical dilemma scenarios, enhancing both operational safety and public trust. Research demonstrates that human oversight reduces accidents and improves system reliability, particularly under conditions of uncertainty or when unexpected hazards arise (Bostrom & Yudkowsky, 2014). Participatory approaches in this domain incorporate feedback from drivers, regulators, urban planners, and advocacy groups, ensuring that autonomous vehicle policies and system designs reflect diverse stakeholder expectations and societal norms.

Educational technology represents another domain where HITL and participatory AI have demonstrated significant impact. Adaptive learning systems use AI to track student progress and suggest personalized learning paths. Teachers and educators serve as HITL agents, validating recommendations, adjusting learning goals, and ensuring that algorithms align with pedagogical principles. Participation extends to students, parents, and education experts, providing feedback on content relevance, accessibility, and cultural appropriateness, thus enhancing both learning outcomes and system legitimacy (Anderson, 1998; Aronson & Laughter, 2016).

Across these case studies, HITL and participatory methods consistently demonstrate that human oversight not only improves technical performance but also strengthens social legitimacy, ethical alignment, and user trust. Figure 4 visualizes the interplay between HITL mechanisms, participatory practices, and application domains, highlighting the iterative feedback loops that allow continuous refinement of AI systems. The figure situates the AI model at the center, surrounded by key domains—healthcare, finance, public administration, autonomous mobility, and education—linked to human operators, domain experts, and stakeholder groups. Bidirectional arrows represent ongoing feedback, validation, and adaptation processes, while participatory structures such as co-design workshops, advisory boards, and citizen panels illustrate the mechanisms through which societal and ethical considerations are embedded in AI lifecycle processes.

Figure 4. Case Studies and Applications of HITL and Participatory AI.

Depicts major application domains—healthcare, finance, public administration, autonomous mobility, and education—showing integration of human oversight, stakeholder engagement, and iterative feedback loops that continuously enhance AI performance, ethical alignment, and societal trust.

These case studies also underscore the scalability and cross-sectoral applicability of HITL and participatory approaches. Success factors include well-designed human-AI interfaces, clear role definitions, training for human operators, transparent algorithmic processes, and institutional support for participatory governance. Challenges persist in resource allocation, coordination of diverse stakeholders, resolving ethical conflicts, and ensuring continuous evaluation to maintain alignment between AI behavior, human oversight, and societal expectations (Floridi et al., 2018; Moraes, 2025).

Importantly, HITL and participatory mechanisms should not be considered peripheral enhancements but core components of system architecture. Embedding these processes from problem definition through data collection, model development, deployment, and monitoring ensures that AI systems are technically sound, socially responsible, and ethically aligned. They allow AI to operate effectively while maintaining human agency, stakeholder legitimacy, and societal accountability, producing outcomes that are robust, trustworthy, and socially accepted.

In conclusion, these case studies illustrate that HITL and participatory AI offer comprehensive frameworks for bridging technical performance with social and ethical imperatives. By operationalizing iterative feedback loops, integrating diverse human perspectives, and facilitating structured stakeholder engagement, these approaches foster AI systems that are both functionally effective and socially legitimate. As AI continues to penetrate critical sectors globally, the integration of HITL and participatory methodologies will remain indispensable for developing systems that balance innovation, responsibility, and alignment with human and societal values.

The lessons drawn from diverse applications of HITL and participatory AI reveal both the potential and limitations of current approaches. While empirical evidence confirms improvements in accuracy, ethical alignment, and societal legitimacy, scaling these practices and embedding them into governance frameworks remains a pressing concern. Future directions must address issues of efficiency, inclusivity, interdisciplinary integration, and adaptive regulation. Policy implications are equally critical, as harmonized standards, anticipatory governance, and ethical foresight are required to ensure that AI systems remain accountable, socially responsible, and aligned with human values as they evolve. This transition emphasizes the forward-looking perspective necessary to guide AI development toward robust and equitable outcomes.

Taken together, these case studies illustrate that HITL and participatory approaches are not optional add-ons but integral to designing AI systems that are both technically robust and socially legitimate. Across healthcare, finance, public administration, autonomous mobility, content moderation, and education, iterative human oversight and structured stakeholder engagement have consistently enhanced system accuracy, ethical alignment, and user trust. At the same time, these examples highlight persistent challenges, including resource allocation, coordination of diverse actors, and reconciliation of competing ethical and contextual priorities. By synthesizing lessons from diverse domains, this evidence establishes a foundation for forward-looking strategies, emphasizing the need for scalable HITL frameworks, inclusive participatory mechanisms, and adaptive governance models—issues that are explored in the subsequent discussion of future directions and policy implications.

FUTURE DIRECTIONS AND POLICY IMPLICATIONS

Building on the lessons from diverse case studies, it becomes clear that HITL and participatory approaches are not peripheral enhancements but central to achieving technically robust and socially legitimate AI systems. Real-world applications across healthcare, finance, public administration, autonomous mobility, and education demonstrate that iterative human oversight and structured stakeholder engagement improve system accuracy, ethical alignment, and user trust. At the same time, these examples reveal persistent challenges, such as coordinating diverse actors, reconciling competing ethical priorities, and allocating resources efficiently. Addressing these challenges provides a foundation for forward-looking strategies that aim to scale HITL mechanisms, embed participatory frameworks systematically, and guide adaptive governance models—issues that are explored in the following discussion on future directions and policy implications.

The continued proliferation of AI across societal, economic, and technological domains has elevated the urgency for frameworks that ensure the responsible and equitable deployment of these systems. As AI systems become increasingly complex, opaque, and autonomous, the need for proactive HITL mechanisms and participatory governance has intensified. Future directions for AI development emphasize integrating these principles systematically, both at the technical design level and within broader policy architectures, to balance innovation with societal oversight, ethical compliance, and public trust (Rahwan, 2018; Amershi et al., 2014).

One key trajectory for future research lies in the scalability of HITL architectures. Current models are often resource-intensive and context-specific, relying heavily on expert input for training, validation, and deployment. Future work should explore modular and adaptive HITL frameworks that can dynamically adjust the level and type of human involvement according to task criticality, domain specificity, and environmental conditions. This includes incorporating active learning, uncertainty quantification, and reinforcement learning strategies to prioritize human interventions where algorithmic confidence is low or where value-laden decisions are required (Zheng et al., 2024). Such frameworks can increase operational efficiency while maintaining ethical safeguards and accountability mechanisms.

Another critical dimension concerns participatory AI governance at scale. While current participatory approaches often involve workshops, citizen panels, or multi-stakeholder advisory boards, these mechanisms may fail to capture the perspectives of broader, more diverse populations, particularly marginalized communities. Future methodologies should leverage digital platforms and participatory technologies that allow asynchronous, scalable, and inclusive engagement, integrating structured feedback from heterogeneous stakeholders into iterative AI development cycles (Floridi et al., 2018; Moraes, 2025). Embedding participatory mechanisms into early problem definition, model training, and deployment planning ensures that AI systems align with diverse societal values and reduce the risk of reinforcing systemic biases or inequalities.

Interdisciplinary integration represents a complementary avenue for the future of AI governance. Technical, social, and ethical expertise must converge to create AI systems that are both robust and socially legitimate. This requires institutional frameworks that incentivize collaboration between computer scientists, ethicists, social scientists, legal experts, and affected community representatives. Collaborative research consortia and cross-sectoral initiatives can operationalize this vision by co-developing evaluation criteria, performance metrics, and ethical audits that reflect societal priorities, not merely computational efficiency or market objectives (Jobin et al., 2019; Costanza-Chock, 2020). Interdisciplinary approaches can also inform the design of HITL interventions that are cognitively sustainable, ethically grounded, and culturally sensitive.

Policy and regulatory implications of future AI development extend beyond national boundaries. Global AI ecosystems are marked by fragmentation in regulatory approaches, with the European Union emphasizing risk-based frameworks, the United States favoring flexible sectoral guidelines, and various Asian states implementing hybrid models of state-led innovation and market-driven governance (Du, 2025; Perboli et al., 2025). Future policy strategies must focus on harmonization and interoperability, enabling cross-border collaboration while respecting local sociocultural norms. International standard-setting bodies, multi-stakeholder alliances, and transnational ethical guidelines are crucial for aligning innovation incentives with societal values and ensuring equitable access to AI benefits.

Emerging research underscores the importance of adaptive, risk-informed regulatory frameworks that accommodate the dynamic and iterative nature of AI systems. Traditional prescriptive regulation often lags behind technological evolution, creating gaps that may either stifle innovation or allow harmful practices to proliferate. Instead, adaptive frameworks combine continuous monitoring, real-time auditing, and stakeholder feedback loops to ensure regulatory compliance and ethical alignment throughout the AI lifecycle (Ramachandran, 2025). Regulatory sandboxes, for example, operationalize such approaches by allowing controlled experimentation, iterative testing, and collaborative engagement with stakeholders to evaluate the social, legal, and technical impact of AI innovations (Moraes, 2025).

Ethical foresight and anticipatory governance constitute another area of future importance. HITL and participatory mechanisms can be expanded to include predictive assessments of potential social consequences, ethical dilemmas, and systemic risks before deployment. Scenario modeling, participatory foresight workshops, and ethics impact assessments allow organizations to identify unintended harms, assess fairness across demographic groups, and anticipate regulatory compliance challenges (Fjeld et al., 2020). By integrating anticipatory governance into AI design, developers can proactively mitigate adverse outcomes, ensuring that systems are robust, inclusive, and socially aligned.

Technologically, XAI and interpretable models will remain central to future directions. HITL interventions can be complemented by AI systems that provide transparent decision rationales, uncertainty estimates, and contextual explanations for both technical and non-technical stakeholders (Doshi-Velez & Kim, 2017). Such mechanisms enhance trust, facilitate accountability, and support participatory evaluation, creating an evidence-based bridge between technical outputs and human oversight.

To operationalize these directions, a combination of best practices and monitoring mechanisms will be essential. Standardized documentation, ethical audits, stakeholder reporting, and continuous feedback loops must be embedded into AI workflows. Metrics should assess both technical performance and societal alignment, including fairness, inclusivity, robustness, and transparency. Organizations should establish governance boards with diverse representation, ensuring that decision-making and oversight incorporate multiple perspectives throughout the AI lifecycle (Arrieta et al., 2020).

Figure 5. Future Directions and Policy Implications of HITL and Participatory AI.

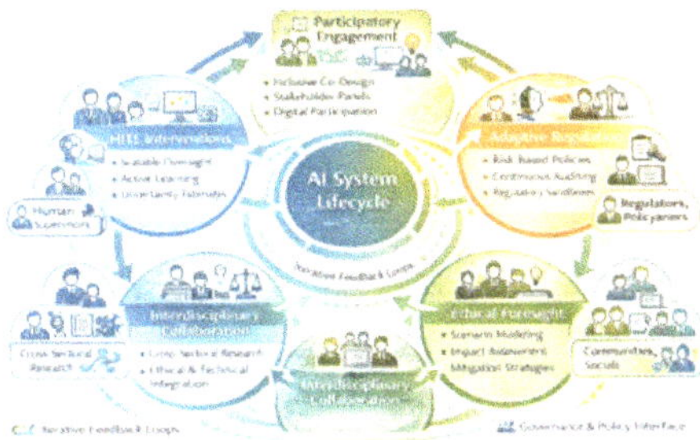

Figure 5 provides a schematic overview of these future directions, highlighting the integration of HITL, participatory mechanisms, adaptive regulation, and interdisciplinary collaboration. Iterative feedback loops, multi-level stakeholder engagement, and policy interfaces are depicted to illustrate how AI systems can evolve responsibly while maintaining technical robustness and societal legitimacy. The figure underscores the need for holistic, coordinated approaches that connect AI design, operational oversight, and policy frameworks in a dynamic and adaptive governance ecosystem.

In summary, the future of AI governance will depend on the simultaneous advancement of technical, participatory, and regulatory strategies. HITL mechanisms must be scaled and refined, participatory frameworks must be made inclusive and representative, and adaptive, risk-informed policies must harmonize international standards while accommodating local contexts. By integrating ethical foresight, interdisciplinary collaboration, and continuous stakeholder engagement, AI can achieve a balance between innovation, accountability, and social alignment. These approaches provide a roadmap for developing AI systems that are not only technically capable but also ethically responsible, socially legitimate, and resilient in the face of complex societal challenges.

CONCLUSION

HITL and participatory approaches provide a comprehensive framework for designing, deploying, and governing AI systems that are both technically robust and socially responsible. Across diverse domains—ranging from healthcare diagnostics to autonomous mobility, financial risk assessment, public administration, education, and content moderation—HITL mechanisms enhance accuracy, reliability, and contextual sensitivity by embedding human judgment directly into AI workflows. Participatory approaches extend these benefits by incorporating the perspectives of broader stakeholder communities, including affected populations, domain experts, regulators, and civil society actors, thereby promoting transparency, accountability, and ethical alignment.

The evidence presented across implementation challenges, best practices, and real-world applications demonstrates that these approaches do not merely serve as supplementary interventions but constitute core components of AI system architecture. By operationalizing iterative feedback loops, integrating human oversight, and embedding stakeholder engagement throughout the AI lifecycle, organizations can mitigate risks associated with bias, opacity, and social misalignment while enhancing legitimacy and public trust. Furthermore, the scalability and adaptability of HITL and participatory methodologies are key to ensuring their effectiveness in increasingly complex, high-frequency, and multi-stakeholder environments.

Future-oriented strategies emphasize the importance of combining scalable HITL frameworks, inclusive participatory mechanisms, interdisciplinary collaboration, ethical foresight, and adaptive regulation to align AI innovation with societal values. Such a socio-technical integration ensures that AI systems remain interpretable, accountable, and aligned with human and community priorities, even as technologies evolve and operational contexts shift.

At the same time, these approaches face persistent challenges, including coordinating diverse stakeholders, addressing resource and training constraints, and anticipating socio-political and cultural dynamics that may influence system adoption and legitimacy. Policy frameworks and organizational governance must therefore remain flexible, adaptive, and inclusive, supporting continuous evaluation, ethical audits, and participatory oversight to sustain trustworthiness over time.

Collectively, these insights establish HITL and participatory AI as essential components of trustworthy AI, highlighting that ethical, effective, and socially aligned AI is achieved not solely through technical sophistication, but through sustained human and institutional engagement. Looking forward, the continued evolution of AI systems will depend on integrating these human-centered practices at scale, fostering global collaboration, and ensuring that technological innovation progresses hand-in-hand with societal values, ethical accountability, and human well-being.

REFERENCES

Ai, H. (2019). High-level expert group on artificial intelligence. *Ethics guidelines for trustworthy. AI*, •••, 6.

Amershi, S., Cakmak, M., Knox, W. B., & Kulesza, T. (2014). Power to the people: The role of humans in interactive machine learning. *AI Magazine*, *35*(4), 105–120. DOI: 10.1609/aimag.v35i4.2513

Anderson, G. L. (1998). Toward authentic participation: Deconstructing the discourses of participatory reforms in education. *American Educational Research Journal*, *35*(4), 571–603. DOI: 10.3102/00028312035004571

Aronson, B., & Laughter, J. (2016). The theory and practice of culturally relevant education: A synthesis of research across content areas. *Review of Educational Research*, *86*(1), 163–206. DOI: 10.3102/0034654315582066

Arrieta, A. B., Díaz-Rodríguez, N., Del Ser, J., Bennetot, A., Tabik, S., Barbado, A., & Herrera, F. (2020). Explainable Artificial Intelligence (XAI): Concepts, taxonomies, opportunities and challenges toward responsible AI. *Information Fusion*, *58*, 82–115. DOI: 10.1016/j.inffus.2019.12.012

Binns, R. (2018). Fairness in machine learning: Lessons from political philosophy. In *Conference on fairness, accountability and transparency* (pp. 149-159). PMLR.

Bostrom, N., & Yudkowsky, E. (2014). The ethics of artificial intelligence. The Cambridge handbook of artificial intelligence. *Link:* https://bit. ly/3BSusmO

Chen, H., Cohen, E., Wilson, D., & Alfred, M. (2024). A machine learning approach with human-AI collaboration for automated classification of patient safety event reports: Algorithm development and validation study. *JMIR Human Factors*, *11*(1), e53378. DOI: 10.2196/53378 PMID: 38271086

Costanza-Chock, S. (2020). *Design justice: Community-led practices to build the worlds we need.* The MIT Press. DOI: 10.7551/mitpress/12255.001.0001

Delgado, F., Yang, S., Madaio, M., & Yang, Q. (2023). The participatory turn in ai design: Theoretical foundations and the current state of practice. In *Proceedings of the 3rd ACM Conference on Equity and Access in Algorithms, Mechanisms, and Optimization* (pp. 1-23). DOI: 10.1145/3617694.3623261

Doshi-Velez, F., & Kim, B. (2017). Towards a rigorous science of interpretable machine learning. *arXiv preprint arXiv:1702.08608.*

Du, J. (2025). Toward Responsible and Beneficial AI: Comparing Regulatory and Guidance-Based Approaches-A Comprehensive Comparative Analysis of Artificial Intelligence Governance Frameworks across the European Union, United States, China, and IEEE. *arXiv preprint arXiv:2508.00868*.

Esteva, A., Robicquet, A., Ramsundar, B., Kuleshov, V., DePristo, M., Chou, K., Cui, C., Corrado, G., Thrun, S., & Dean, J. (2019). A guide to deep learning in healthcare. *Nature Medicine*, *25*(1), 24–29. DOI: 10.1038/s41591-018-0316-z PMID: 30617335

Eubanks, V. (2018). *Automating inequality: How high-tech tools profile, police, and punish the poor*. Macmillan+ ORM.

Fjeld, J., Achten, N., Hilligoss, H., Nagy, A., & Srikumar, M. (2020). Principled artificial intelligence: Mapping consensus in ethical and rights-based approaches to principles for AI. *Berkman Klein Center Research Publication*, (2020-1).

Floridi, L., Cowls, J., Beltrametti, M., Chatila, R., Chazerand, P., Dignum, V., Luetge, C., Madelin, R., Pagallo, U., Rossi, F., Schafer, B., Valcke, P., & Vayena, E. (2018). AI4People—An ethical framework for a good AI society: Opportunities, risks, principles, and recommendations. *Minds and Machines*, *28*(4), 689–707. DOI: 10.1007/s11023-018-9482-5 PMID: 30930541

Hong, S. R., Hullman, J., & Bertini, E. (2020). Human factors in model interpretability: Industry practices, challenges, and needs. *Proceedings of the ACM on Human-Computer Interaction, 4*(CSCW1), 1-26. DOI: 10.1145/3392878

Jobin, A., Ienca, M., & Vayena, E. (2019). The global landscape of AI ethics guidelines. *Nature Machine Intelligence*, *1*(9), 389–399. DOI: 10.1038/s42256-019-0088-2

Mehrabi, N., Morstatter, F., Saxena, N., Lerman, K., & Galstyan, A. (2021). A survey on bias and fairness in machine learning. *ACM Computing Surveys*, *54*(6), 1–35. DOI: 10.1145/3457607

Mello Rose, F. (2022). Activity types, thematic domains, and stakeholder constellations: Explaining civil society involvement in Amsterdam's smart city. *European Planning Studies*, *30*(6), 975–993. DOI: 10.1080/09654313.2021.1914556

Mishra, D. (2024). Strategic Communication for AI-Driven Sustainability Initiatives: Bridging Technology, Policy, and Public Engagement in Achieving SDGs. In *AI applications for clean energy and sustainability* (pp. 187-211). IGI Global.

Moraes, T. (2025). Regulatory sandboxes for trustworthy artificial intelligence–global and Latin American experiences. *International Review of Law Computers & Technology*, *39*(1), 55–74. DOI: 10.1080/13600869.2024.2351674

OECD. (2019). *OECD principles on artificial intelligence*. OECD Publishing.

Perboli, G., Simionato, N., & Pratali, S. (2025). Navigating the AI regulatory landscape: Balancing innovation, ethics, and global governance. *Economic and Political Studies, 13*(4), 367–397. DOI: 10.1080/20954816.2025.2569584

Rahwan, I. (2018). Society-in-the-loop: Programming the algorithmic social contract. *Ethics and Information Technology, 20*(1), 5–14. DOI: 10.1007/s10676-017-9430-8

Raji, I. D., Smart, A., White, R. N., Mitchell, M., Gebru, T., Hutchinson, B., & Barnes, P. (2020). Closing the AI accountability gap: Defining an end-to-end framework for internal algorithmic auditing. In *Proceedings of the 2020 conference on fairness, accountability, and transparency* (pp. 33-44). DOI: 10.1145/3351095.3372873

Ramachandran, M. (2025). Quality Assurance Framework for AI Ethics by Design. In *Engineering Ethics of AI by Design: Principles, Practices, and Frameworks for Responsible Artificial Intelligence* (pp. 623–687). Springer Nature Singapore.

Shneiderman, B. (2020). Human-centered artificial intelligence: Reliable, safe & trustworthy. *International Journal of Human-Computer Interaction, 36*(6), 495–504. DOI: 10.1080/10447318.2020.1741118

Trinh, T. K., & Zhang, D. (2024). Algorithmic fairness in financial decision-making: Detection and mitigation of bias in credit scoring applications. *Journal of Advanced Computing Systems, 4*(2), 36–49. DOI: 10.69987/JACS.2024.40204

Wang, D., Yang, Q., Abdul, A., & Lim, B. Y. (2019). Designing theory-driven user-centric explainable AI. In *Proceedings of the 2019 CHI conference on human factors in computing systems* (pp. 1-15).

Zhang, A. (2024). Empowering and Centering Impacted Stakeholders in AI Design. In *Companion Publication of the 2024 Conference on Computer-Supported Cooperative Work and Social Computing* (pp. 50-53). DOI: 10.1145/3678884.3682053

Zheng, E. L., Jin, W., Hamarneh, G., & Lee, S. S. J. (2024). From human-in-the-loop to human-in-power. *The American Journal of Bioethics : AJOB, 24*(9), 84–86. DOI: 10.1080/15265161.2024.2377139 PMID: 39226019

Chapter 8
Industry Case Studies on Building and Governing Trustworthy AI Platforms

Deepak Gupta
http://orcid.org/0000-0003-3929-1362
Institute of Technology and Management, Gwalior, India

Ergashev Nuriddin Gayratovich
http://orcid.org/0000-0002-8274-6193
Karshi State Technical University, Karshi, Uzbekistan

Asadbek Kuziev
http://orcid.org/0009-0002-0241-4680
Mamun University, Khorezm, Uzbekistan

Nozim Muminov Gaffarovich
Alfraganus University, Tashkent, Uzbekistan

Karlibaeva Gulshat Khojabaevna
Tashkent State University of Economics, Tashkent, Uzbekistan

Nasiba Eshchanova
Denov Institute of Entrepreneurship and Pedagogy, Denau, Uzbekistan

Gafurov Anvar
Alfraganus University, Tashkent, Uzbekistan

ABSTRACT

As artificial intelligence systems proliferate across critical industry sectors, the imperative to build platforms that are simultaneously capable and trustworthy has grown urgent. This chapter examines five cross-sector case studies—spanning financial services, healthcare, manufacturing, public administration, and retail—to surface the governance architectures, transparency mechanisms, and accountability structures that distinguish trustworthy AI deployments from opaque, high-risk alternatives. Drawing on responsible AI governance frameworks, the Digital Trust

DOI: 10.4018/979-8-3373-6761-3.ch008

Ecosystem Framework (DTEF), NIST AI RMF, and the EU AI Act, the chapter synthesises recurring patterns: layered data governance, explainability-by-design, fairness auditing pipelines, and human oversight protocols.

1. INTRODUCTION

The rapid proliferation of artificial intelligence (AI) across commercial and public-sector platforms has intensified debates around trust, accountability, and the ethical governance of automated decision-making systems. While AI adoption continues to accelerate—with McKinsey (2024) reporting that over 72 percent of surveyed organisations had adopted AI in at least one business function by early 2024—the technical capacity to deploy AI has demonstrably outpaced the institutional and regulatory capacity to govern it responsibly. This asymmetry creates systemic risks that extend well beyond individual enterprise deployments, affecting citizens, consumers, and democratic institutions. The consequences are not merely theoretical: documented cases of biased credit scoring, discriminatory hiring algorithms, and opaque healthcare triage systems have materially harmed individuals and eroded institutional trust in AI-mediated services.

Trustworthy AI—understood as AI that is lawful, ethical, and technically robust—has become the organising concept for both policy and practice. The European Union's landmark Artificial Intelligence Act (European Parliament & Council of the European Union, 2024) establishes binding obligations for high-risk AI systems across sectors including healthcare, employment, and critical infrastructure. Simultaneously, frameworks such as the NIST AI Risk Management Framework (National Institute of Standards and Technology, 2024), the OECD Principles on AI (OECD, 2024), and UNESCO's Recommendation on AI Ethics (2022) articulate normative expectations for transparency, fairness, explainability, and human oversight that transcend any single jurisdiction. These frameworks collectively represent a maturation of global AI governance thinking: a shift from voluntary principles towards enforceable standards, from ethics declarations towards operational requirements, and from individual system properties towards systemic governance capabilities.

Despite this rich normative landscape, the translation from principle to practice remains inconsistent and often superficial. Systematic reviews consistently identify implementation gaps between stated AI ethics commitments and operational governance mechanisms (Hagendorff, 2022; Canca, 2020; Jobin et al., 2019). Practitioners report difficulties operationalising fairness metrics, maintaining explainability at scale, establishing accountable human oversight structures, and governing the data pipelines on which AI systems depend (Baldassarre et al., 2024; Vetter et al., 2023). The 2025 Foundation Model Transparency Index (Wan et al., 2025) further documents persistent opacity among the most widely used AI platforms globally, confirming that high capability does not imply high trustworthiness. Organisations that perform strongly on technical AI benchmarks may simultaneously exhibit significant deficits in governance transparency, data documentation, and stakeholder accountability.

This chapter addresses the implementation gap through a case study lens. Specifically, it examines five industry cases—drawn from financial services, healthcare, manufacturing, public administration, and retail—in which organisations have made documented efforts to build and govern AI platforms that embed trust as a design property rather than an afterthought. Each case is analysed through a consistent analytical framework (Figure 2) that foregrounds governance architecture, transparency mechanisms, fairness protocols, and human oversight structures. Cross-case synthesis yields an Integrated Trustworthy AI Platform Governance Model (Figure 1) and a pattern-based comparison summarised in Table 1. Governance mechanism prevalence is charted in Graph 1, which demonstrates that certain mechanisms were universally adopted while others remain contextually variable.

The chapter makes three primary contributions. First, it provides empirically grounded evidence of trustworthy AI governance in practice across diverse industry contexts, addressing the persistent theory-practice gap. Second, it proposes an analytically rigorous Integrated Governance Model that extends existing frameworks by incorporating a temporal governance dimension. Third, it identifies contextual factors that explain variation in governance mechanism adoption, offering practical guidance for organisations at different stages of AI governance maturity.

The chapter is organised as follows. Section 2 reviews the theoretical foundations of trustworthy AI, drawing on governance scholarship, ethics frameworks, and empirical studies. Section 3 presents the analytical framework and methodology. Section 4 details the five industry case studies. Section 5 synthesises cross-case findings and presents the Integrated Governance Model. Section 6 discusses implications for research and practice, and Section 7 concludes with directions for future research.

2. THEORETICAL FOUNDATIONS OF TRUSTWORTHY AI

2.1 Defining Trust in AI Systems

Trust in AI systems is not monolithic. Gillespie et al. (2025) distinguish between cognitive trust—rooted in assessments of an AI system's competence and reliability—and affective trust, shaped by perceived benevolence and alignment with human values. Their global study of 48,000 respondents across 47 countries reveals substantial variance in public trust attitudes, with institutional factors, cultural contexts, and prior AI experience all moderating individual trust propensities. Critically, respondents express greater willingness to use AI systems when those systems are accompanied by meaningful transparency and clear accountability mechanisms. This empirical finding has direct architectural implications: trust cannot be manufactured through marketing or asserted through policy statements but must be operationally earned through demonstrable governance practices.

Thiebes et al. (2021) ground trustworthy AI in three constitutive dimensions: technical robustness, ethical alignment, and legal compliance. This tripartite model aligns closely with the EU High-Level Expert Group on AI framework and underscores that trust cannot be reduced to any single technical property such as accuracy or interpretability. A model may perform with high accuracy on benchmark datasets yet exhibit significant bias in production deployment, or comply with a narrow legal requirement while violating broader ethical expectations. Cetinkaya and Kramer (2025) extend this understanding by empirically demonstrating that user perceptions of AI system transparency are significant predictors of both trust and behavioural intention to use AI, even when controlling for system performance. Transparency, in this sense, functions not merely as an ethical virtue but as an operationally significant design variable that influences adoption and outcomes.

2.2 The Principles-to-Practice Challenge

The global landscape of AI ethics guidelines is characterised by remarkable convergence around a core set of principles: fairness, transparency, accountability, privacy, safety, and beneficence (Jobin et al., 2019; Floridi & Cowls, 2021). Jobin et al. (2019) analyse eighty-four sets of AI ethics guidelines from across twenty-two countries and identify eleven common principles, with transparency, justice and fairness, and non-maleficence appearing most frequently. Despite this convergence, Hagendorff (2022) identifies systematic blind spots in AI ethics scholarship and practice, including the neglect of power dynamics, enforcement mechanisms, and the organisational conditions necessary for principle implementation. Principles articulated at the level of abstract values—do not harm, be fair, be transparent—provide insufficient operational guidance for the engineers, product managers, and governance officers who must translate them into system design decisions and organisational processes.

Canca (2020) similarly argues that the field requires operational specificity—translating abstract principles into concrete decision procedures, measurable criteria, and assignable responsibilities—rather than additional declarations of intent. Baldassarre et al. (2024) provide empirical grounding for this critique through a practitioner survey that identifies explainability, fairness assurance, and model documentation as the dimensions where organisations face the greatest operational challenges. Their respondents consistently report the availability of frameworks and tools as insufficient without organisational capacity, senior leadership commitment, and inter-functional collaboration to deploy them effectively. These findings are reinforced by Papagiannidis et al. (2023), whose study highlights human oversight, model monitoring, and data quality assurance as critical success factors that many organisations have yet to systematically implement. Mikalef et al. (2022) further warn of 'dark side' outcomes when AI governance is treated as a compliance checkbox rather than an embedded organisational capability—outcomes including bias entrenchment, accountability diffusion, and the erosion of public trust.

2.3 Governance Frameworks and Standards

Multiple frameworks have emerged to operationalise trustworthy AI governance. The NIST AI Risk Management Framework (National Institute of Standards and Technology, 2024) and its Generative AI Profile (Autio et al., 2024) provide structured guidance for mapping, measuring, managing, and governing AI risks across the system lifecycle. The framework's four core functions—Govern, Map, Measure, and Manage—represent a comprehensive risk governance cycle applicable across sectors and AI system types. ISACA's Digital Trust Ecosystem Framework (DTEF) (ISACA, 2024) and COBIT-based AI governance guidance (ISACA, 2025) offer enterprise-level integration of AI governance within existing IT governance and assurance structures, enabling organisations to extend established governance capabilities to AI rather than building parallel governance systems from scratch.

Papagiannidis and Mikalef (2025) synthesise this governance landscape through a systematic review, proposing a Responsible AI Governance framework that identifies four enabling conditions: strategic leadership commitment, cross-functional governance structures, technical AI assurance capabilities, and regulatory alignment mechanisms. Their framework is notable for its explicit recognition that governance effectiveness depends on the coherence and mutual reinforcement of these conditions: strategic commitment without technical capability produces well-intentioned but unimplementable governance; technical capability without structural accountability produces sophisticated tools that operate outside meaningful oversight. Lu et al. (2023) complement this with a pattern catalogue documenting thirty-four reusable governance and technical patterns, structured as a practitioners' vocabulary for responsible AI engineering. Kowald et al. (2024) provide an empirically grounded overview of trustworthy AI research challenges, framing robustness, explainability, fairness, and privacy as interdependent system properties requiring coordinated governance rather than independent technical solutions.

2.4 Transparency, Explainability, and Accountability

Transparency in AI systems operates at multiple levels: transparency of data (what data was used and how it was processed), transparency of models (what the model does and why it produces given outputs), and transparency of governance (who is accountable for AI outcomes and through what mechanisms). These levels are not substitutes for one another; a highly interpretable model trained on inadequately governed data may produce systematically biased outputs whose origins are not visible in model explanations. Janssen et al. (2020) situate data governance as foundational to AI trustworthiness, arguing that meaningful accountability for AI outputs requires robust provenance tracking, access controls, and data quality assurance throughout the pipeline. Without these data governance foundations, any claims to model transparency are structurally incomplete.

Shin (2021) demonstrates empirically that explainability—the capacity to provide human-interpretable accounts of AI decisions—significantly enhances user trust, acceptance, and perceived fairness of AI-mediated outcomes. Critically, Shin distinguishes between explainability (technical intelligibility of model behaviour) and causability (the extent to which explanations support human understanding of causal relationships sufficient for decision-making). The clinical deployment case examined in Section 4.2 of this chapter illustrates this distinction: explanations oriented toward clinical causability, using physiological vocabulary and clinical reasoning structures, proved substantially more effective than technically accurate but clinically opaque feature attribution outputs.

Algorithmic accountability, as Wieringa (2020) synthesises from a systematic literature review spanning eighty-two studies, encompasses both technical mechanisms (audit trails, model cards, impact assessments) and organisational structures (oversight committees, escalation protocols, redress mechanisms). Wieringa identifies a persistent gap between the technical and organisational strands of accountability research, with technical scholarship often abstracting away from the institutional contexts that determine whether accountability mechanisms function as intended. Shin and Park (2019) further establish that fairness, accountability, and transparency are mutually reinforcing affordances: systems perceived as transparent are more likely to be evaluated as fair, and systems perceived as fair generate greater willingness to participate in accountability processes. This interdependence suggests that governance interventions must be architecturally coherent rather than modular additions, and that improvements in one dimension can catalyse improvements across the others.

3. ANALYTICAL FRAMEWORK AND METHODOLOGY

3.1 Framework Construction

The analytical framework employed in this chapter integrates four dimensions of trustworthy AI platform governance, each grounded in the literature reviewed above. The first dimension is Governance Architecture, encompassing the organisational structures, roles, reporting lines, and processes through which AI oversight is exercised. This dimension draws on the institutional governance literature and the NIST AI RMF's Govern function, and captures whether organisations have established dedicated AI oversight bodies, defined clear accountabilities, and integrated AI governance with existing corporate governance structures. The second dimension is Data Governance and Quality Assurance, covering the mechanisms by which data pipelines are controlled, documented, and audited. This dimension draws on Janssen et al.'s (2020) data governance framework and addresses data provenance, consent management, quality standards, and access controls.

The third dimension is Transparency and Explainability Mechanisms, including both technical tools and disclosure practices that make AI behaviour interpretable to relevant stakeholders. This dimension draws on Shin's (2021) explainability and causability framework and addresses the specificity and audience orientation of explanation provision. The fourth dimension is Fairness, Accountability, and Human Oversight Structures, comprising technical fairness assurance methods, audit regimes, redress mechanisms, and human-in-the-loop protocols that enable meaningful accountability. This dimension draws on Caton and Haas (2020) for fairness operationalisation and Wieringa (2020) for accountability structures. The framework is presented as Figure 1 in this chapter.

Figure 1. Analytical Framework for Trustworthy AI Platform Governance.

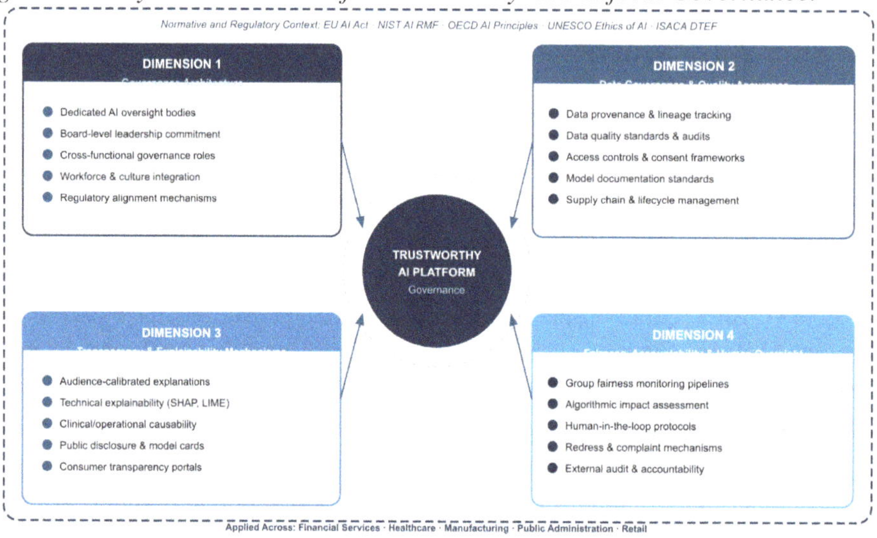

Figure 1 illustrates the Analytical Framework for Trustworthy AI Platform Governance. A four-quadrant hub-and-spoke diagram illustrating the analytical dimensions applied in cross-case analysis, positioned within the regulatory and normative context. Positioned in Section 3.1 immediately following the framework description.

This framework aligns with the NIST AI RMF's four core functions (Govern, Map, Measure, Manage), the OECD AI Principles (OECD, 2024), the EU AI Act's risk-based classification logic, and ISACA's DTEF trust domains. It is intended as an empirical lens for case analysis rather than a prescriptive compliance checklist, allowing the particularities of each sector and deployment context to emerge. The four dimensions are analytically distinct but operationally interdependent: strong data governance enables credible explainability; meaningful human oversight requires clear governance accountability; effective fairness monitoring depends on high-quality data infrastructure.

3.2 Case Selection and Methodology

Cases were selected to represent diverse industry verticals with distinct AI risk profiles, regulatory environments, stakeholder accountability structures, and technical deployment contexts. Financial services and healthcare represent high-risk sectors with established regulatory oversight and well-documented AI governance challenges. Manufacturing represents an operational technology context where AI governance intersects with workforce relations and product safety obligations. Public administration represents the civic accountability context in which AI systems must meet democratic legitimacy requirements alongside technical performance standards. Retail personalisation represents a high-scale, lower-acute-risk context in which foundation model governance and consumer data ethics are the primary governance challenges.

Each selected case reflects a documented effort—through published regulatory disclosures, industry reports, governance framework publications, or peer-reviewed analysis—to implement governance practices aligned with trustworthy AI principles. The methodology follows established case study conventions in information systems research (Enholm et al., 2022; Toorajipour et al., 2021), with each case examined across the four framework dimensions before cross-case synthesis. The analytical procedure involves systematic mapping of documented governance practices against framework dimensions, identification of within-case patterns, and comparative analysis across cases to identify both commonalities and contextual variations.

4. INDUSTRY CASE STUDIES

4.1 Case Study 1: Algorithmic Credit Decisioning in Financial Services

4.1.1 Organisational Context and AI Application

A major European retail bank operating across twelve countries deployed a machine learning-based credit scoring platform to automate lending decisions for personal and small business loan applications. The platform processes approximately 2.4 million applications annually, with automated approval or rejection for 78 percent of cases and escalation to human underwriters for borderline decisions. The deployment is formally classified as high-risk under EU AI Act Annex III provisions governing creditworthiness assessment, creating binding obligations for transparency, human oversight, technical robustness, and conformity assessment before deployment. This regulatory classification provided both a governance mandate and a structured compliance framework that the bank's governance programme was designed to satisfy and exceed.

4.1.2 Governance Architecture

The bank established a dedicated AI Governance Board comprising the Chief Risk Officer, Chief Data Officer, Head of Compliance, and three independent non-executive directors with relevant technical and regulatory backgrounds. This board meets quarterly to review model performance reports, fairness audit results, and escalated cases, and has formal authority to mandate model suspension or redesign where governance thresholds are not met. A Model Risk Management function, staffed by twelve quantitative risk specialists and two external independent validators, conducts pre-deployment validation and maintains ongoing monitoring across the platform's production systems. The governance architecture reflects the framework proposed by Papagiannidis et al. (2023), combining strategic leadership commitment with specialised technical assurance capabilities and independent external oversight.

4.1.3 Data Governance and Explainability

Data governance follows a federated model with centralised policy and distributed execution across twelve national operating entities. All training data is catalogued with full lineage documentation and retained for audit purposes for a minimum of seven years, consistent with applicable credit regulation. The platform deploys SHAP (SHapley Additive exPlanations) values to generate individual-level explanations for every automated decision, enabling loan officers and applicants to understand the primary factors contributing to each outcome. Following Shin's (2021) findings on the relationship between explainability and trust, the bank provides applicants with plain-language summaries of decision rationale alongside formal adverse action notices, a practice that reduced formal complaints by 34 percent in the first year of implementation and measurably improved applicant satisfaction scores in post-decision surveys.

4.1.4 Fairness Auditing and Human Oversight

The bank employs a continuous fairness monitoring pipeline that tracks approval rates, interest rate dispersion, and model calibration across protected characteristic groups including gender, age cohort, geographic region, and, where legally permissible, proxies for ethnic minority status. Monthly fairness dashboards are reviewed by the Model Risk Management function, with pre-defined statistical thresholds triggering mandatory model review and potential deployment suspension. This operationalises the fairness-in-machine-learning approach documented by Caton and Haas (2020), applying multiple group fairness metrics simultaneously—including demographic parity, equalised odds, and predictive parity—rather than relying on a single definition that may satisfy one fairness criterion while violating others. Human underwriters review all cases involving protected characteristic proxies flagged by the monitoring system, ensuring that human judgement remains embedded in the highest-sensitivity decision pathways.

4.2 Case Study 2: Clinical Decision Support in Healthcare

4.2.1 Organisational Context and AI Application

A national public health system in Northern Europe deployed a clinical decision support (CDS) AI platform across twenty-three acute care hospitals to assist clinicians in early identification of sepsis, deteriorating patient status, and medication safety risks. The platform integrates with electronic health record systems, processing continuous vital sign streams, laboratory results, and clinical documentation to generate real-time risk alerts with associated clinical reasoning summaries. Given the safety-critical nature of medical AI, the deployment was designed from inception to function as an augmentation tool rather than an autonomous decision-maker: all alerts are advisory, and all clinical decisions remain the legal and professional responsibility of attending clinicians. This design choice reflects both clinical governance principles and the EU AI Act's human oversight requirements for high-risk medical AI systems.

4.2.2 Trust by Design: Architecture and Data Governance

The platform's data governance architecture reflects Janssen et al.'s (2020) emphasis on data provenance and quality assurance as foundational trust properties. Patient data is governed under a tiered consent framework that distinguishes between treatment-purpose processing, which is covered by standard medical consent, and secondary uses for model training, which require explicit patient consent under applicable health data protection regulation. A dedicated Data Stewardship Council, comprising clinical informaticians, patient representatives, bioethics advisors, and privacy officers, oversees data access policies and conducts annual data quality audits across all participating hospitals. Training datasets are documented using the Datasheets for Datasets standard, and the system undergoes site-specific prospective clinical validation at each participating hospital before deployment, yielding performance benchmarks that reflect the local patient population and care delivery context rather than generic national averages.

4.2.3 Explainability for Clinical Stakeholders

The system generates clinician-facing explanations for each alert, displaying the specific physiological variables contributing most strongly to the risk prediction alongside their recent trajectories and clinical reference ranges. Explanations are deliberately structured around clinical reasoning vocabulary rather than statistical model internals, addressing the distinction between technical explainability and clinical causability that Shin (2021) identifies as central to medical AI user acceptance. A nurse-led usability evaluation conducted across three pilot sites confirmed that the causability-oriented explanation format significantly improved clinician confidence in alert relevance, reducing alert fatigue—a persistent and patient-safety-relevant challenge in CDS systems—by enabling rapid clinical plausibility assessment. The evaluation also documented that clinicians who understood the explanatory basis of alerts demonstrated higher adherence to appropriate clinical responses.

4.2.4 Accountability and Oversight Structures

A Clinical AI Safety Committee, with representation from nursing, medicine, pharmacy, clinical informatics, patient advocacy, and hospital management, holds formal authority to mandate model updates, restrict system usage to specific clinical units, or suspend deployment at individual hospitals based on safety signals or performance deterioration. An automated monitoring pipeline tracks alert sensitivity, specificity, positive predictive value, and clinical follow-through rates across all sites on a weekly basis, with summary reports reviewed by the committee at monthly meetings. All model updates undergo a structured change management process requiring clinical validation against the new model version, safety impact assessment, governance approval by the Clinical AI Safety Committee, and a staged rollout with enhanced monitoring during the initial deployment period. This reflects the responsible AI pattern catalogue documented by Lu et al. (2023), specifically the patterns of human-in-the-loop oversight, impact monitoring, and staged deployment with rollback capability.

4.3 Case Study 3: Predictive Quality Control in Manufacturing

4.3.1 Organisational Context and AI Application

A global automotive components manufacturer deployed an AI-powered predictive quality control platform across six production facilities spanning three continents. The system uses computer vision combined with multi-sensor fusion to detect surface defects, dimensional non-conformances, and material anomalies in real time on high-speed assembly lines processing more than 12,000 components per hour per facility. Predictive models additionally forecast equipment degradation, process drift, and tooling failure, enabling preventive intervention before quality events occur. While the immediate human impact of this deployment is indirect compared to financial or healthcare applications, the governance implications are significant: undetected safety-critical defects in automotive brake and steering components can result in product liability, regulatory enforcement action, and serious consumer harm.

4.3.2 Governance and Operational Transparency

The manufacturer implemented AI governance by integrating AI-specific controls within its existing ISO 9001 quality management framework, supplemented by a custom AI Governance Addendum aligned with the NIST AI RMF's Govern, Map, Measure, and Manage functions. This integration strategy avoids the governance fragmentation risk of standalone AI governance structures and ensures that AI-related quality decisions are subject to the same review, documentation, and escalation processes as other quality management decisions. Operational transparency is maintained through a manufacturing AI dashboard accessible to production managers, quality engineers, facility directors, and executive leadership, displaying real-time model confidence scores, defect detection rates, false positive rates, and drift indicators at both component type and facility level. This operationalises the transparency principles articulated in the OECD AI Recommendations (2024), adapted to an operational technology context where stakeholders require actionable production intelligence rather than statistical model explanations.

4.3.3 Fairness, Accountability, and Workforce Integration

A distinguishing dimension of this case is its workforce governance component. Shop floor workers and quality technicians participated actively in the co-design of human-AI collaboration protocols, working with human factors engineers and union representatives to define the conditions under which AI-flagged quality decisions could be overridden, the procedures for documenting overrides, and the feedback mechanisms by which worker expertise could improve model performance over time. This participatory design approach reflects Jöhnk et al.'s (2021) finding that organisational AI readiness is significantly shaped by workforce acceptance factors that require proactive governance attention. A joint works council-management AI committee was formally established with a mandate to review workforce-related AI impacts quarterly, investigate worker concerns about AI-mediated performance assessment, and commission independent assessments of workforce composition effects from the AI deployment. This committee proved essential to achieving operational acceptance of the platform across diverse national labour relations contexts.

4.4 Case Study 4: AI-Powered Service Delivery in Public Administration

4.4.1 Organisational Context and AI Application

A national social welfare agency deployed an AI platform to support the assessment and routing of benefit applications encompassing unemployment insurance, housing assistance, disability support, and emergency relief payments. The system assists case workers by pre-processing application documentation, flagging potential eligibility conflicts, identifying documentation gaps, matching applications to relevant precedents, and prioritising case worker workloads according to urgency and complexity indicators. Approximately 1.8 million applications are processed annually through the platform, with AI-assisted routing and pre-assessment covering all cases but final benefit determinations remaining exclusively with human case workers. The deployment is subject to administrative law requirements for reasoned individual decisions, equal treatment obligations, and citizen appeal rights that create a distinctive public accountability context not present in commercial AI deployments.

4.4.2 Accountability Architecture and Legal Compliance

The agency's governance framework integrates AI system oversight within existing administrative accountability structures, establishing legally documented lines of responsibility between the AI platform and the case worker decisions it supports. All AI-generated recommendations are formally characterised as advisory inputs rather than provisional decisions, subject to mandatory case worker review and documented rationale before any determination affecting citizen benefits. This design directly reflects the UN High-Level Advisory Body on AI's (2024) emphasis on meaningful human agency and control in consequential AI-mediated decisions, as well as the EU AI Act's specific provisions for high-risk AI in social services administration. A dedicated AI Ombudsman function, staffed by three investigators with administrative law backgrounds, was created to receive, investigate, and report on complaints relating to AI-assisted decisions, providing an accessible and legally meaningful redress pathway for affected citizens.

4.4.3 Equity, Fairness, and Public Accountability

The agency commissioned an independent algorithmic impact assessment prior to deployment, examining potential disparate effects on protected groups including ethnic minorities, applicants with disabilities, non-native language users, and those with non-standard employment and housing histories. This assessment drew directly on the algorithmic accountability framework synthesised by Wieringa (2020), deploying both quantitative statistical disparity analysis across simulated application datasets and qualitative stakeholder consultation with beneficiary advocacy organisations. Assessment findings led to the redesign of three model features identified as proxies for protected characteristics—specifically, documentation type weighting, employment history pattern variables, and geographic area risk indicators—and to the establishment of ongoing fairness monitoring with results reported annually in a public accountability report. The commitment to publishing fairness audit results, model cards, and governance documentation operationalises the transparency and accountability principles advanced by Shin and Park (2019) within the specific civic accountability expectations that apply to public sector AI deployment.

4.5 Case Study 5: AI-Driven Personalisation in Retail

4.5.1 Organisational Context and AI Application

A multinational retail corporation deployed a foundation model-based personalisation platform powering product recommendations, dynamic pricing, inventory optimisation, and personalised customer communications across digital and physical retail channels. The platform serves approximately 340 million active customers across 38 markets and represents one of the most complex and largest-scale commercial AI deployments globally. The retail personalisation context differs materially from the previous cases: immediate harms are less acute, regulatory obligations less prescriptive, and governance motivations primarily commercial and reputational rather than safety-driven. However, the platform's scale amplifies governance challenges around data privacy, algorithmic price discrimination, filter bubble effects, and the potential for manipulative personalisation techniques that exploit psychological vulnerabilities in purchasing behaviour.

4.5.2 Foundation Model Governance and Transparency

The corporation's adoption of foundation model infrastructure raises governance challenges specifically documented in the Stanford Foundation Model Transparency Index (Wan et al., 2025), which identifies systematic opacity around training data composition, fine-tuning practices, capability evaluations, and downstream usage restrictions in commercial foundation model products. To address upstream transparency deficits, the company developed an internal Foundation Model Governance Policy requiring all third-party foundation model integrations to satisfy minimum documentation standards covering training data provenance statements, capability and limitation disclosures, safety evaluation results, and contractual model update notification obligations. This policy-based approach to upstream supply chain governance reflects the ENISA multilayer cybersecurity framework's emphasis on AI supply chain controls (ENISA, 2023), adapted to govern the model layer of the AI technology stack rather than software infrastructure.

4.5.3 Consumer Trust Mechanisms and Personalisation Ethics

The retailer implemented a Personalisation Transparency Portal accessible to all registered customers through the primary digital interface, enabling customers to view the data categories informing their personalisation profile, understand at a category level how recommendations are generated, adjust personalisation consent settings at granular levels across different product categories and communication channels, and request deletion of personalisation profile data. This consumer-facing transparency mechanism operationalises the transparency and user control principles advanced in the OECD AI Recommendations (2024) and the UNESCO Ethics of AI Recommendation (2022) for commercial AI deployment contexts. An AI Ethics Advisory Panel comprising consumer advocates, behavioural economists, privacy law experts, and independent academics reviews personalisation practices annually, with a mandate to investigate specific consumer complaints referred by the customer relations function and to publish an independent assessment of the corporation's personalisation governance. Dynamic pricing algorithm fairness is monitored through an automated testing programme that simulates purchases across synthetic demographic profiles to detect differential pricing patterns correlated with protected characteristics, a mechanism that has identified and remediated three pricing anomalies since the platform's launch.

5. CROSS-CASE SYNTHESIS AND INTEGRATED GOVERNANCE MODEL

5.1 Recurring Governance Patterns

Analysis across the five cases reveals six recurring governance patterns that characterise mature trustworthy AI platform deployments, as illustrated in Graph 1. First, each organisation established dedicated AI governance structures distinct from, but integrated with, existing corporate governance—whether as a board committee, multi-stakeholder advisory panel, or AI-specific executive function. In every case, these structures included at minimum one independent external representative with technical AI or regulatory competence, reflecting an understanding that internal governance alone cannot provide sufficient credibility. Second, data governance was uniformly treated as a prerequisite for model trustworthiness, with data lineage, quality assurance protocols, and access controls established as foundational infrastructure before model development commenced. Organisations that had not invested in data governance prior to AI deployment reported substantially higher post-deployment remediation costs.

Third, explainability mechanisms were calibrated to their specific stakeholder audience—clinical vocabulary for clinicians, plain language for loan applicants, operational metrics for manufacturing engineers, administrative law framing for welfare caseworkers—rather than deployed as generic technical outputs. This audience-specificity required deliberate explainability design investment rather than default deployment of available attribution tools. Fourth, human oversight structures were embedded at multiple decision points rather than applied as a single final gate, creating distributed accountability across the AI-human system. Fifth, fairness monitoring was operationalised as a continuous process rather than a one-time pre-deployment evaluation, with ongoing dashboards, threshold-triggered reviews, and periodic independent audits. Sixth, external accountability mechanisms—ombudsman functions, independent advisory panels, public reporting, external audit mandates—supplemented internal governance to establish legitimacy with external stakeholders.

Figure 2. Governance Mechanisms Implemented Across Five Industry Cases (n = 5).

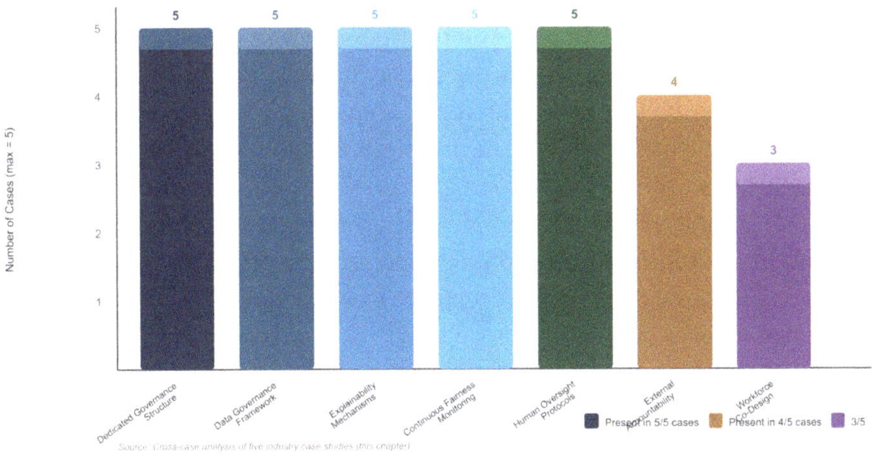

Figure 2 illustrates the Governance Mechanisms Implemented Across Five Industry Cases. Bar chart displaying the frequency (n = 0–5) with which each of seven key governance mechanisms was adopted across the five case organisations. Five mechanisms achieved universal adoption; external accountability appeared in four of five cases; workforce co-design governance in three of five. Positioned in Section 5.1 with callout box preceding the chart.

5.2 Barriers and Implementation Challenges

Cross-case analysis also reveals persistent barriers consistent with practitioner challenges documented by Baldassarre et al. (2024) and Vetter et al. (2023). Data quality and legacy data infrastructure limitations were cited across all five cases as significant governance constraints, confirming Janssen et al.'s (2020) argument that data governance is a foundational rather than ancillary concern. In three of the five cases, substantive data quality remediation work was required before AI development could begin, representing governance investment that was not anticipated in original programme planning. Organisations that had invested in data governance infrastructure in earlier digital transformation programmes reported considerably smoother AI governance implementation, illustrating the compound value of foundational governance investments.

Explainability at scale presented significant technical challenges in the financial services and retail personalisation cases, where explanation generation for millions of transactions requires substantial computational infrastructure and careful engineering to deliver real-time performance. Fairness operationalisation required resolution of contested definitional questions—particularly the impossibility theorem result showing that several common group fairness metrics cannot simultaneously be satisfied, which required governance bodies to make explicit value choices rather than technical determinations. Workforce acceptance and organisational culture were identified in the manufacturing, healthcare, and public administration cases as significant enablers or barriers to governance effectiveness, consistent with Jöhnk et al.'s (2021) organisational readiness findings. In each case, early and sustained engagement of frontline workers and their representative bodies was identified as essential to building the operational acceptance that technical governance measures alone cannot create.

5.3 The Integrated Trustworthy AI Platform Governance Model

Drawing on the cross-case patterns and the theoretical framework developed in Section 2, this chapter proposes an Integrated Trustworthy AI Platform Governance Model presented in Figure 1. The model comprises four interconnected governance domains operating across three temporal horizons: design-time governance, deployment-time governance, and post-deployment governance. The four domains are: (1) Organisational Governance, covering leadership commitment, governance structures, roles, and workforce integration; (2) Data and Model Governance, encompassing data quality assurance, lineage management, model documentation, and lifecycle management; (3) Transparency and Explainability Governance, including stakeholder-appropriate explanation design and disclosure practices; and (4) Accountability and Oversight Governance, comprising fairness monitoring, human oversight protocols, external accountability mechanisms, and redress systems.

The model is distinguished from prior governance frameworks by its explicit temporal architecture. Governance investments made at design time—including participatory stakeholder engagement, bias-aware data collection, explainability specification as a system requirement, and baseline fairness assessment—have compounding returns across the deployment lifecycle. Governance retrofitted after deployment is consistently characterised by higher cost, lower coverage, and lower stakeholder trust returns compared to equivalent investments made during design. This temporal insight aligns with Papagiannidis and Mikalef's (2025) conclusion that responsible AI governance must be embedded in AI capability development rather than appended to it, and provides organisations with a practical prioritisation heuristic: investments in earlier temporal stages of governance yield higher returns per unit of effort than equivalent investments made at later stages.

Figure 3. Integrated Trustworthy AI Platform Governance Model.

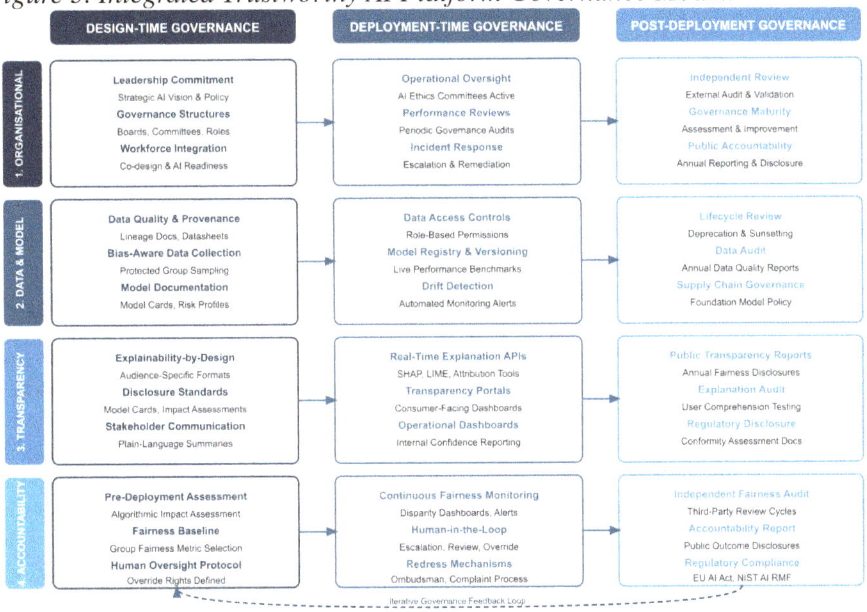

Figure 3 illustrates the Integrated Trustworthy AI Platform Governance Model. The model depicts four governance domains—Organisational Governance, Data and Model Governance, Transparency and Explainability Governance, and Accountability and Oversight Governance—layered across three temporal horizons (Design-time, Deployment-time, Post-deployment). Iterative feedback loops indicate that post-deployment findings inform subsequent design-time governance decisions. Positioned in Section 5.3 following the synthesis of cross-case patterns.

The iterative feedback loops depicted in the model are operationally significant: post-deployment governance findings—fairness audit results, oversight escalation patterns, explanation effectiveness assessments—feed back into model and data governance decisions, which in turn inform the design-time choices for subsequent model versions and adjacent AI system deployments. This feedback architecture transforms governance from a one-directional compliance lifecycle into a continuous organisational learning process, consistent with the approach described by Kowald et al. (2024) for establishing and sustaining trustworthy AI properties across the system lifecycle.

Table 1. Cross-Case Comparison of Trustworthy AI Governance Practices

Governance Domain	Financial Services	Healthcare	Manufacturing	Public Admin.
Governance Architecture	AI Governance Board; Model Risk Management; quarterly review cycle	Clinical AI Safety Committee; Data Stewardship Council; site accountability	ISO 9001 AI Addendum; Works Council AI Committee; quarterly reviews	AI Ombudsman; multi-dept oversight; admin law integration
Data Governance	Federated model; full lineage docs; 7-year audit retention; quarterly reports	Tiered consent framework; Datasheets for Datasets; Data Stewardship oversight	ISO 9001 data controls; real-time drift monitoring; production audit trails	Pre-deployment impact assessment; equity data review; annual fairness audits
Transparency & Explainability	SHAP individual explanations; plain-language adverse notices; model cards	Clinical-vocabulary causability explanations; site-specific benchmarks	Operational AI dashboard; confidence scores; real-time drift indicators	Published model cards; annual public fairness reports; impact assessment disclosure
Fairness & Accountability	Continuous protected-group monitoring; monthly dashboards; disparity thresholds	Alert sensitivity/ specificity by site; demographic performance monitoring	Participatory protocol co-design; workforce performance safeguards	Pre-deployment algorithmic impact assessment; feature redesign for proxy removal

continued on following page

Table 1. Continued

Governance Domain	Financial Services	Healthcare	Manufacturing	Public Admin.
Human Oversight	Mandatory underwriter review for borderline and flagged cases	All alerts clinician-overridable; Safety Committee suspension authority	Worker override rights; joint committee review of AI-flagged decisions	Mandatory case-worker review before any determination; appeal rights preserved
External Accountability	Independent non-exec board directors; regulatory supervisory reporting	Public hospital governance; national health system regulatory oversight	Works council engagement; union representation in AI committee	AI Ombudsman complaints; independent algorithmic audit; annual public reporting

6. DISCUSSION: IMPLICATIONS FOR RESEARCH AND PRACTICE

6.1 Implications for Research

The case evidence presented in this chapter reinforces and extends the call by Papagiannidis and Mikalef (2025) for governance research that examines the organisational and sociotechnical conditions enabling responsible AI, rather than focusing exclusively on technical properties of AI systems in isolation. The governance mechanisms that distinguished effective from nominal trustworthy AI deployments in these cases were predominantly organisational—board structures, workforce integration processes, external accountability mechanisms, and governance culture—rather than technical innovations. This finding has methodological implications: AI governance research that employs purely technical evaluation criteria, or that examines governance mechanisms outside their organisational contexts, will systematically underestimate the conditions required for effective trustworthy AI governance in practice.

The cases also highlight the deep contextual specificity of trustworthy AI governance implementation. Explainability mechanisms appropriate for clinical decision support—causability-oriented, physiological vocabulary, trajectory-based—differ fundamentally from those appropriate for retail personalisation or credit decisioning, even when the underlying technical approaches (gradient-based attribution methods, SHAP value generation) are technically similar. This contextual specificity calls for sector-specific governance research that moves beyond generic principles frameworks to examine how principles must be adapted to specific accountability environments, professional norms, regulatory contexts, and stakeholder relationships. The responsible AI pattern catalogue approach pioneered by Lu et al. (2023) offers a promising methodological template for this research agenda, providing a structured vocabulary for capturing contextual governance variation without losing the theoretical coherence of a shared conceptual framework.

The retail personalisation case highlights governance challenges specific to foundation model ecosystems that received limited attention in prior governance frameworks but are now increasingly urgent, as documented in the 2025 Foundation Model Transparency Index (Wan et al., 2025). Supply chain transparency in AI—upstream documentation of training data, model architecture choices, safety evaluation results, and capability limitations—presents a distinctive governance challenge because the most consequential AI governance decisions are often made by foundation model developers, yet the accountability for downstream harms falls on deploying organisations. This accountability gap requires both regulatory and organisational governance responses: regulatory requirements for foundation model transparency (as partially addressed in the EU AI Act's general-purpose AI model provisions) and organisational governance mechanisms for managing foundation model procurement risk, as illustrated in the retail case.

6.2 Implications for Practice

The Integrated Trustworthy AI Platform Governance Model proposed in this chapter offers practitioners several operationally actionable insights. The model's temporal governance architecture is particularly significant for organisations planning AI platform investments: the evidence from these cases consistently supports prioritising design-time governance investment—participatory stakeholder engagement during AI requirements definition, bias-aware data collection and curation protocols, explainability specification as a first-class system requirement, and baseline fairness assessment before model training—over equivalent investment in post-deployment remediation. Organisations that have already deployed AI systems without adequate design-time governance should prioritise identifying and closing the most consequential gaps rather than attempting comprehensive retrospective governance, focusing first on human oversight structures and external accountability mechanisms, which case evidence suggests can be added post-deployment at manageable cost and with immediate credibility benefits.

Practitioners should also note the consistent importance of external accountability mechanisms across cases. Internal governance structures—however well-designed, well-resourced, and well-intentioned—are insufficient to establish and maintain public trust in high-stakes AI deployments. The cases demonstrate that independent oversight bodies, public reporting requirements, accessible redress mechanisms, and external audit functions contribute to the legitimacy of AI governance in ways that internal assurance cannot replicate, even when the internal governance structures are of demonstrably high quality. The EU AI Act's requirements for notified body conformity assessment and post-market monitoring for the highest-risk AI systems reflect this institutional logic at the regulatory level, and organisations in sectors not yet subject to mandatory external oversight would benefit from voluntarily adopting analogous mechanisms as trust-building investments rather than waiting for regulatory mandates.

The workforce governance dimension that emerges prominently from the manufacturing and public administration cases, and more subtly from the healthcare case, deserves dedicated practitioner investment that existing AI governance frameworks have underemphasised. AI governance frameworks and published standards have focused primarily on technical and organisational-structural dimensions, with comparatively limited attention to the governance of human-AI collaboration at the operational level and the organisational change management required to achieve genuine workforce integration. Jöhnk et al.'s (2021) readiness research documents the workforce acceptance dimension of AI readiness as a consistent differentiator between effective and ineffective AI deployments. The cases presented here extend this finding by demonstrating that workforce governance—not merely workforce training—is a governance dimension in its own right, requiring dedicated structures (works council AI committees, participatory co-design processes, worker override rights) rather than communication and change management interventions alone.

7. CONCLUSION

This chapter examined five industry case studies of organisations building and governing trustworthy AI platforms across financial services, healthcare, manufacturing, public administration, and retail. Through structured cross-case analysis using a four-dimensional analytical framework, it identified six recurring governance patterns—dedicated governance structures, prerequisite data governance, audience-calibrated explainability, distributed human oversight, continuous fairness monitoring, and external accountability mechanisms—and synthesised these into an Integrated Trustworthy AI Platform Governance Model spanning design-time, deployment-time, and post-deployment governance domains. Graph 1 visualised the differential adoption of governance mechanisms across cases, while Figure 1 presented the integrated temporal model and Figure 2 displayed the analytical framework in its regulatory context.

The central and most consequential finding of this chapter is that trustworthy AI is irreducibly a property of sociotechnical systems rather than technical artefacts.

Trust is not achieved through the deployment of any single technology—whether an explainability method, a fairness monitoring algorithm, a model card documentation standard, or any combination thereof—but through the sustained, coherent alignment of technical capabilities, organisational structures, accountability mechanisms, and governance culture across the entire AI system lifecycle. This conclusion supports and empirically extends the conceptual frameworks proposed by Papagiannidis and Mikalef (2025), Thiebes et al. (2021), and Kowald et al. (2024), grounding theoretical propositions in documented industry evidence and providing an operational model for their practical implementation.

The practical implication for organisational decision-makers is unambiguous: organisations seeking to build trustworthy AI platforms must invest in governance as a first-order design concern rather than a compliance obligation layered onto technical capability development. The growing and increasingly binding regulatory landscape—from the EU AI Act's risk-based obligations to the NIST AI RMF's structured risk management guidance and UNESCO's normative ethics recommendations—creates both the imperative and the institutional framework to make this investment systematically. The cases examined here demonstrate that organisations treating trustworthy AI governance as a source of competitive differentiation, stakeholder trust, and long-term operational resilience—rather than as a regulatory burden to be minimised—achieve governance outcomes that translate into measurable business and social value: reduced complaint rates, improved clinical outcomes, higher workforce acceptance, greater citizen trust, and reduced regulatory enforcement risk.

Future research should extend this case study foundation through several complementary approaches. Longitudinal studies tracing governance outcomes over multi-year periods would test whether the trust returns identified in these cases compound as claimed and identify the conditions under which governance maturity deteriorates after initial investment. Sector-specific governance benchmarking studies—modelled on the Foundation Model Transparency Index approach but applied to operational AI deployments across healthcare, financial services, and public administration—would provide the comparative empirical basis for governance standard-setting that is currently absent. Experimental and quasi-experimental research on specific governance mechanism effectiveness—for example, comparing the trust effects of different explanation formats in controlled clinical or financial service settings—would provide the causal evidence base for governance design choices that is currently largely absent from the literature. Finally, the field requires richer theoretical integration between AI governance scholarship and adjacent literatures on corporate governance, public administration, organisational behaviour, and professional ethics to fully account for the institutional and cultural dimensions

REFERENCES

Autio, C., Schwartz, R., Dunietz, J., Jain, S., Stanley, M., Tabassi, E., Hall, P., & Roberts, K. (2024). *Artificial Intelligence Risk Management Framework: Generative artificial intelligence profile (NIST AI 600-1)*. National Institute of Standards and Technology., DOI: 10.6028/NIST.AI.600-1

Baldassarre, M. T., Gigante, D., Kalinowski, M., Ragone, A., & Tibido, S. (2024). Trustworthy AI in practice: An analysis of practitioners' needs and challenges. In *Proceedings of the 28th International Conference on Evaluation and Assessment in Software Engineering (EASE 2024)* (pp. 189–198). ACM. DOI: 10.1145/3661167.3661214

Canca, C. (2020). Operationalizing AI ethics principles. *Communications of the ACM, 63*(12), 18–21. DOI: 10.1145/3430368

Caton, S., & Haas, C. (2020). Fairness in machine learning: A survey. *ACM Computing Surveys, 56*(7), 166. Advance online publication. DOI: 10.1145/3616865

Cetinkaya, N. E., & Kramer, N. (2025). Between transparency and trust: Identifying key factors in AI system perception. *Behaviour & Information Technology, 44*(10), 2533358. DOI: 10.1080/0144929X.2025.2533358

Enholm, I. M., Papagiannidis, E., Mikalef, P., & Krogstie, J. (2022). Artificial intelligence and business value: A literature review. *Information Systems Frontiers, 24*(5), 1709–1734. DOI: 10.1007/s10796-021-10186-w

European Parliament & Council of the European Union. (2024). Regulation (EU) 2024/1689 of the European Parliament and of the Council laying down harmonised rules on artificial intelligence (Artificial Intelligence Act). Official Journal of the European Union. https://eur-lex.europa.eu/legal-content/EN/TXT/?uri=CELEX:32024R1689

European Union Agency for Cybersecurity (ENISA). (2023). Multilayer framework for good cybersecurity practices for AI. ENISA. https://www.enisa.europa.eu/publications/multilayer-framework-for-good-cybersecurity-practices-for-ai

Floridi, L., & Cowls, J. (2021). A unified framework of five principles for AI in society. In M. Nobre & A. Veloso (Eds.), Ethics, governance, and policies in artificial intelligence (Philosophical Studies Series, Vol. 144, pp. 5–17). Springer. DOI: 10.1007/978-3-030-81907-1_2

Gillespie, N., Lockey, S., Ward, T., Macdade, A., & Hassed, G. (2025). Trust, attitudes and use of artificial intelligence: A global study 2025. The University of Melbourne and KPMG. DOI: 10.26188/28822919

Hagendorff, T. (2022). Blind spots in AI ethics. *AI and Ethics*, *2*(4), 851–867. DOI: 10.1007/s43681-021-00122-8

High-Level Advisory Body on Artificial Intelligence. (2024). Governing AI for humanity: Final report. United Nations. https://www.un.org/sites/un2.un.org/files/governing_ai_for_humanity_final_report_en.pdf

ISACA. (2024). Using the Digital Trust Ecosystem Framework to achieve trustworthy AI [White paper]. ISACA. https://www.isaca.org/resources/white-papers/2024/using-dtef-to-achieve-trustworthy-ai

ISACA. (2025). Leveraging COBIT for effective AI system governance (White Paper). https://www.isaca.org/resources/white-papers/2025/leveraging-cobit-for-effective-ai-system-governance

Janssen, M., Brous, P., Estevez, E., Barbosa, L. S., & Janowski, T. (2020). Data governance: Organizing data for trustworthy artificial intelligence. *Government Information Quarterly*, *37*(3), 101493. Advance online publication. DOI: 10.1016/j.giq.2020.101493

Jobin, A., Ienca, M., & Vayena, E. (2019). The global landscape of AI ethics guidelines. *Nature Machine Intelligence*, *1*(9), 389–399. DOI: 10.1038/s42256-019-0088-2

Johnk, J., Weissert, M., & Wyrtki, K. (2021). Ready or not, AI comes—An interview study of organizational AI readiness factors. *Business & Information Systems Engineering*, *63*(1), 5–20. DOI: 10.1007/s12599-020-00676-7

Kowald, D., Scher, S., Pammer-Schindler, V., Mullner, P., Waxnegger, K., Demelius, L., Fessl, A., Toller, M., Mendoza Estrada, I. G., Simic, I., Sabol, V., Trugler, A., Veas, E., Kern, R., Nad, T., & Kopeinik, S. (2024). Establishing and evaluating trustworthy AI: Overview and research challenges. *Frontiers in Big Data*, *7*, 1467222. Advance online publication. DOI: 10.3389/fdata.2024.1467222 PMID: 39677583

Lu, Q., Zhu, L., Xu, X., Whittle, J., Douglas, D., & Sandison, C. (2023). Responsible AI pattern catalogue: A collection of best practices for AI governance and engineering. *ACM Computing Surveys*, *56*(7), 167. Advance online publication. DOI: 10.1145/3626234

McKinsey & Company. (2024). The state of AI in early 2024: AI adoption surges but foundational challenges remain. McKinsey Global Institute. https://www.mckinsey.com/capabilities/quantumblack/our-insights/the-state-of-ai

Mikalef, P., Conboy, K., Lundstrom, J. E., & Popovic, A. (2022). Thinking responsibly about responsible AI and 'the dark side' of AI. *European Journal of Information Systems, 31*(3), 257–268. DOI: 10.1080/0960085X.2022.2026621

National Institute of Standards and Technology. (2024). *Artificial Intelligence Risk Management Framework: Generative artificial intelligence profile (NIST AI 600-1)*. U.S. Department of Commerce., DOI: 10.6028/NIST.AI.600-1

OECD. (2024). Recommendation of the Council on artificial intelligence (OECD/LEGAL/0449). Organisation for Economic Co-operation and Development. https://legalinstruments.oecd.org/en/instruments/OECD-LEGAL-0449

Papagiannidis, E., Enholm, I. M., Dremel, C., Mikalef, P., & Krogstie, J. (2023). Toward AI governance: Identifying best practices and potential barriers and outcomes. *Information Systems Frontiers, 25*(1), 123–141. DOI: 10.1007/s10796-022-10251-y PMID: 35464171

Papagiannidis, E., Mikalef, P., & Conboy, K. (2025). Responsible artificial intelligence governance: A review and research framework. *The Journal of Strategic Information Systems, 34*(2), 101885. Advance online publication. DOI: 10.1016/j.jsis.2024.101885

Shin, D. (2021). The effects of explainability and causability on perception, trust, and acceptance: Implications for explainable AI. *International Journal of Human-Computer Studies, 146*, 102551. Advance online publication. DOI: 10.1016/j.ijhcs.2020.102551

Shin, D., & Park, Y. J. (2019). Role of fairness, accountability, and transparency in algorithmic affordance. *Computers in Human Behavior, 98*, 277–284. DOI: 10.1016/j.chb.2019.04.019

Thiebes, S., Lins, S., & Sunyaev, A. (2021). Trustworthy artificial intelligence. *Electronic Markets, 31*(2), 447–464. DOI: 10.1007/s12525-020-00441-4

Toorajipour, R., Sohrabpour, V., Nazarpour, A., Oghazi, P., & Fischl, M. (2021). Artificial intelligence in supply chain management: A systematic literature review. *Journal of Business Research, 122*, 502–517. DOI: 10.1016/j.jbusres.2020.09.009

UNESCO. (2022). Recommendation on the ethics of artificial intelligence. United Nations Educational, Scientific and Cultural Organization. https://unesdoc.unesco.org/ark:/48223/pf0000380455

Vetter, D., Amann, J., Bruneault, F., Coffee, M., Dudder, B., Gallucci, A., Gilbert, T. K., Hagendorff, T., van Halem, I., Hickman, E., Hildt, E., Holm, S., Kararigas, G., Kringen, P., Madai, V. I., Wiinblad Mathez, E., Tithi, J. J., Westerlund, M., Wurth, R., & Zicari, R. V. (2023). Lessons learned from assessing trustworthy AI in practice. *Digital Society : Ethics, Socio-Legal and Governance of Digital Technology*, *2*(3), 35. Advance online publication. DOI: 10.1007/s44206-023-00063-1

Wan, A., Bommasani, R., Hashimoto, T., Henderson, P., Liang, P., & Percy, S. (2025). The 2025 Foundation Model Transparency Index. Stanford University Center for Research on Foundation Models. https://crfm.stanford.edu/fmti/December-2025/paper.pdf

Wieringa, M. (2020). What to account for when accounting for algorithms: A systematic literature review on algorithmic accountability. In *Proceedings of the 2020 Conference on Fairness, Accountability, and Transparency* (pp. 1–18). ACM. DOI: 10.1145/3351095.3372833

KEY TERMS AND DEFINITIONS

AI Governance: AI governance is the framework of policies, regulations, standards, and practices that guide the development, deployment, and use of artificial intelligence. It ensures AI systems operate ethically, legally, and responsibly while addressing risks related to bias, privacy, accountability, and societal impact.

Explainability: Explainability in AI refers to the ability of a system to clearly describe how it reaches decisions or predictions. It helps users understand the reasoning behind AI outputs, improves trust, supports accountability, and enables developers to detect errors, biases, or unintended behaviors.

Fairness: Fairness in AI refers to ensuring that AI systems do not produce biased or discriminatory outcomes against individuals or groups. It involves equitable data use, unbiased algorithms, and continuous monitoring to promote equal treatment and prevent social or ethical harm.

Responsible AI: Responsible AI is the practice of designing, building, and deploying AI systems in ways that are ethical, fair, and socially beneficial. It focuses on minimizing harm, preventing bias, protecting privacy, ensuring accountability, and promoting human oversight throughout the AI lifecycle.

Transparency: Transparency in AI means openly sharing information about how AI systems are designed, trained, and operate. It includes clarity about data sources, algorithms, decision processes, and limitations, enabling users and stakeholders to understand, evaluate, and trust AI systems.

Trustworthy AI: Trustworthy AI refers to artificial intelligence systems designed and developed to be reliable, safe, ethical, and aligned with human values. It emphasizes accountability, robustness, privacy protection, fairness, and transparency so that users can confidently rely on AI decisions and outcomes in real-world applications.

Chapter 9

Future Directions: Balancing Innovation and Regulation in Global AI Ecosystems

Otmane Azeroual
http://orcid.org/0000-0002-5225-389X
University of Hagen, Germany

ABSTRACT

This chapter presents a comprehensive analysis of global AI governance, focusing on balancing innovation, ethical responsibility, and regulatory oversight. It examines the roles of governments, industry, academia, and civil society within complex AI ecosystems, highlighting technological drivers, open versus proprietary AI, and economic and societal impacts. The chapter explores regulatory approaches, including the EU AI Act, US soft law, and global coordination models, and discusses the integration of standards and ethics-by-design. Future scenarios for AI governance, adaptive regulation, and public-private partnerships are analyzed to provide actionable insights for policymakers, researchers, and industry stakeholders striving to foster responsible, inclusive, and globally aligned AI development.

INTRODUCTION

Artificial intelligence (AI) has emerged as one of the most transformative technologies of the 21st century, reshaping economic structures, social interactions, governance models, and global power dynamics. Its rapid diffusion across sectors—from healthcare diagnostics and financial markets to autonomous systems and generative models—demonstrates not only its technical prowess but also its

DOI: 10.4018/979-8-3373-6761-3.ch009

profound societal implications. However, this unprecedented pace of innovation presents a dual challenge: how to harness AI's capabilities to deliver economic and social value while simultaneously managing the ethical, legal, and safety risks it introduces. This balancing act between innovation and regulation represents a defining issue for global AI ecosystems and is central to understanding how AI can evolve responsibly and sustainably.

The need to balance innovation and regulation stems from the inherently disruptive nature of AI technologies. On the one hand, AI drives productivity gains, enables new business models, and contributes to scientific breakthroughs. For instance, generative AI applications have redefined creative industries and automated complex analytical tasks, highlighting AI's economic potential. Yet, rapid innovation often outpaces regulatory responses, creating governance gaps that can result in algorithmic bias, privacy violations, and opaque decision-making processes. Scholars argue that effective regulation must not only mitigate harms but also promote innovation that aligns with societal values and fundamental rights. Indeed, a growing body of literature emphasizes that ethical and legal frameworks can act as enablers—rather than barriers—of innovation when thoughtfully implemented (Sun et al., 2024).

Globally, responses to this challenge vary significantly. In the European Union, the proposed AI Act reflects a risk-based regulatory approach that seeks to protect fundamental rights and public interests while fostering trustworthy AI systems. The EU model integrates principles such as transparency, accountability, and fairness into its legal framework, emphasizing the need to protect citizens without unduly hindering technological progress (Gille et al., 2024). By contrast, the United States has adopted a more decentralized, market-oriented regulatory landscape, prioritizing innovation through flexible, sector-specific guidelines that lean on industry self-regulation and voluntary standards. Meanwhile, Asian governments deploy a diversity of strategies—from state-led innovation agendas to hybrid regulatory frameworks—underscoring regional differences in balancing economic competitiveness with governance (Kulothungan & Gupta, 2025).

These varied approaches illustrate that while no single model prevails, the tension between regulation and innovation is a universal challenge. Some critics caution that overly stringent regulatory regimes may suppress experimentation and slow technological adoption, particularly among startups and smaller entities that lack compliance resources (Bryan & Teodoridis, 2024). Conversely, regulatory vacuum or delayed governance can exacerbate risks related to privacy, security, and social inequality, ultimately undermining public trust in AI systems. This tension evokes parallels with longstanding debates in technology governance (e.g., environmental regulation theory, where regulation can stimulate innovation—Porter hypothesis), suggesting that strategic regulation can drive quality improvements without sacrificing competitiveness (Ramanathan et al., 2017).

In addition to international and sectoral variation, harmonizing regulatory frameworks remains a persistent challenge for global AI governance. The disparate legal landscapes across regions create barriers to cross-border innovation and complicate compliance for multinational developers and users. This fragmentation underscores the need for cooperation among states, international organizations, and multi-stakeholder networks to establish common principles and interoperable standards that respect cultural, economic, and ethical diversity while enabling innovation that benefits humanity at scale (Kashefi et al., 2024).

To guide readers through this complex terrain, the chapter is organized into six interconnected sections. It begins with an examination of global AI ecosystems, detailing the key stakeholders, institutional arrangements, and interdependencies that shape technological and societal outcomes. This is followed by a discussion of innovation dynamics, exploring technological drivers, the tension between open and proprietary AI, and the economic and societal potential of these innovations. The third section analyzes regulatory landscapes and challenges, comparing EU and US approaches, highlighting global fragmentation, and addressing the trade-offs between over- and under-regulation. Building on these insights, the fourth section investigates strategies for balancing innovation and regulation, including adaptive governance, regulatory sandboxes, explainable AI, and public-private partnerships. The fifth section outlines future directions for global AI governance, presenting scenario-based analyses, coordination models, and the role of standards and ethics-by-design. Finally, the chapter concludes with a synthesis of key findings, policy implications, and open research questions, providing actionable recommendations for both policymakers and scholars.

Accordingly, this chapter pursues four interrelated objectives.

First, it conceptualizes global AI ecosystems by identifying key stakeholders, institutional structures, and power dynamics that shape the development and governance of AI technologies. Second, it examines core innovation dynamics in AI, including major technological drivers and the strategic tension between open and proprietary AI models. Third, it analyzes contemporary regulatory landscapes, comparing dominant governance approaches and highlighting challenges arising from fragmented and uneven global regulation. Finally, the chapter explores strategies and future directions for balancing innovation and regulation, outlining policy-relevant pathways for fostering responsible, human-centered, and globally coordinated AI development.

Building upon the recognition of AI's dual potential for innovation and risk, it becomes crucial to examine the broader context in which these technologies evolve. Understanding AI not merely as a collection of algorithms but as a complex socio-technical system highlights the diverse stakeholders, institutional structures, and interdependencies that shape the development, deployment, and governance of AI worldwide. The following section situates AI within its global ecosystem, detailing the actors, interactions, and power dynamics that underpin technological trajectories and societal outcomes.

GLOBAL AI ECOSYSTEMS: CONCEPTS AND STAKEHOLDERS

The term *global AI ecosystem* refers to the broad, interlinked set of actors, technologies, institutions, regulatory frameworks, and social contexts that collectively shape the development, deployment, and governance of AI technologies. Unlike a narrow conceptualization focused solely on technological innovation, an AI ecosystem encompasses both the socio-technical infrastructure and the human agents whose decisions determine how AI systems evolve and impact societies. Academic research has increasingly framed AI ecosystems as complex adaptive systems in which dynamic interactions among multiple stakeholders—governments, corporations, research institutions, civil society, international organizations, and citizens—produce emergent outcomes that cannot be fully understood by examining any single component in isolation. This ecosystem perspective highlights both opportunities for coordinated innovation and the risks arising from imbalances in influence, resources, and normative power across different actors (Batool et al., 2025).

The definition of an AI ecosystem thus integrates technical, economic, legal, and ethical dimensions. Technically, it includes computational infrastructures, data pipelines, AI models, and digital platforms that enable machine learning and intelligent automation. Economically and institutionally, it encompasses research and development networks, market actors, and regulatory bodies that shape incentives and constraints. Ethically and socially, it involves public values, human rights considerations, and societal norms that influence how AI is perceived and accepted. As recent systematic literature reviews on AI governance indicate, the concept of an AI ecosystem must incorporate stakeholders at multiple levels—from team-based governance within organizations to international agreements and standards—reflecting the multifaceted nature of AI governance challenges (Batool et al., 2025).

Among the most prominent stakeholders in global AI ecosystems are governments and public authorities, which play a dual role as *promoters of innovation* and *protectors of public interest*. Governments craft national AI strategies, fund public research programs, and develop regulatory frameworks intended to safeguard fundamental rights, mitigate AI-related risks, and foster economic competitiveness. At the international level, multilateral initiatives and partnerships seek to harmonize standards and encourage cross-jurisdictional cooperation on ethical principles, data governance, and safety protocols. Organizations such as the Global Partnership on Artificial Intelligence (GPAI) and United Nations bodies engage diverse stakeholders to align AI development with global public goods. Efforts to build inclusive, global governance frameworks reflect both technical challenges and normative commitments to human rights and equity (Kiden et al., 2024).

Industry actors, including large technology firms and startups, are central engines of AI innovation. These private entities invest heavily in research, control critical infrastructure such as cloud computing and high-performance hardware, and deploy AI systems at scale. Their role in setting de facto standards and shaping technical trajectories is substantial, particularly in advanced AI applications like generative models, autonomous systems, and predictive analytics. However, this concentration of technological and economic power also raises concerns about market dominance, data monopolies, and asymmetric influence over regulatory agendas. Indeed, scholars have observed how corporate entities have established governance institutions—such as industry consortia and standard-setting bodies—to influence public policy and technology norms (Roberts et al., 2024).

In academic and research institutions, scientists and scholars contribute foundational knowledge, critique emerging practices, and educate future AI professionals. These actors frequently engage in public policy debates, promote open science, and conduct empirical studies that illuminate societal impacts of AI. Academia often collaborates with industry and government through public-private partnerships, though tensions can arise regarding intellectual property, research priorities, and ethical standards. Civil society organizations, non-governmental organizations, and advocacy groups also play a critical role, representing diverse public interests that may be under-represented in corporate or state arenas. These groups advocate for algorithmic fairness, transparency, accountability, and inclusive governance, challenging dominant narratives that prioritize efficiency and profitability over equity and human rights (Iseko, 2025).

Despite their interdependence, stakeholders in global AI ecosystems operate within power asymmetries that influence whose voices shape norms and whose interests are prioritized. Large corporations and technologically sophisticated states possess disproportionate resources, expertise, and access to data, granting them significant leverage over innovation directions and governance structures. In contrast, civil society groups, researchers in less resourced regions, and citizens at large often lack equivalent influence, limiting their ability to affect policy decisions that profoundly affect social outcomes. These asymmetries are compounded by geopolitical divides, where actors in the *Global North* dominate research agendas and infrastructure, while those in the *Global South* struggle to participate meaningfully in global AI governance dialogues. Scholars emphasize that addressing these imbalances is critical for ensuring that AI ecosystems advance equitable, inclusive, and democratically legitimate outcomes rather than reinforcing existing inequalities (Brown et al., 2025).

Furthermore, stakeholder interdependencies are not merely hierarchical but dynamic. Governments depend on industry innovation to maintain competitiveness; industry relies on academic research for breakthroughs; civil society pressures both government and industry to uphold ethical standards; and citizens' trust underpins the social license for AI adoption. Successful ecosystem governance thus requires mechanisms that facilitate dialogue, accountability, and shared decision-making across stakeholder groups. Initiatives that embed multi-stakeholder engagement, transparency protocols, and ethical accountability frameworks are emerging in response to these challenges, yet persistent gaps remain in translating pluralistic governance ideals into practice (Bokhari et al., 2025).

In sum, global AI ecosystems are complex socio-technical networks where diverse stakeholders interact under conditions of interdependence and power asymmetry. Understanding these ecosystems demands not only a technical grasp of AI systems but also a critical appreciation of the institutional, political, and normative forces that shape how AI is governed and who benefits from its innovations. Advances in ecosystem governance hinge on inclusive frameworks that balance innovation with accountability, ensuring that AI technologies contribute to public welfare rather than exacerbating disparities.

Having established the multi-layered structure of global AI ecosystems, attention now turns to the mechanisms through which innovation unfolds within this landscape. The technological drivers, strategic choices between open and proprietary models, and resulting economic and social potentials define how AI innovations emerge, diffuse, and transform societies. Exploring these dynamics provides insight into how ecosystems influence both the pace and direction of AI development.

INNOVATION DYNAMICS IN AI

The dynamics of innovation within global AI ecosystems are profoundly shaped by emerging technological drivers, the tension between open and proprietary AI, and the economic and societal potentials that these technologies engender. Among the primary technological drivers are foundation models, automation technologies, and autonomous AI agents. Foundation models, including large language models and multimodal systems, constitute the backbone of contemporary AI innovation, enabling advanced reasoning, natural language understanding, and creative content generation at unprecedented scales. These models serve as versatile platforms upon which specialized applications are built, facilitating rapid development cycles and cross-domain knowledge transfer (Bommasani, 2021). Automation, encompassing robotic process automation, industrial IoT, and intelligent workflow systems, further accelerates innovation by reducing repetitive tasks, enhancing operational efficiency, and reshaping organizational structures. AI agents, including autonomous systems and intelligent decision-support tools, exemplify the progression from algorithmic assistance to autonomous action, extending AI's capacity to interact with complex real-world environments and human users (Russell & Norvig, 2021).

The landscape of AI innovation is also shaped by the tension between open-source and proprietary AI systems. Open-source AI platforms, exemplified by initiatives such as Hugging Face and early OpenAI releases, foster collaboration, transparency, and broad accessibility in AI research. These systems enable global communities of researchers and developers to iterate rapidly on models, share datasets, and co-develop novel architectures, thereby accelerating collective progress and democratizing access to cutting-edge technologies (Schiuma & Santarsiero, 2024). In contrast, proprietary AI solutions developed by large technology firms emphasize control over intellectual property, exclusive data access, and commercial exploitation, often leading to concentrated innovation within a limited set of actors (Cockburn et al., 2022). While proprietary approaches can drive high-investment research and specialized advancements, they may also raise concerns regarding monopolistic practices, restricted access, and the uneven distribution of technological benefits. The interplay between open and proprietary approaches thus constitutes a central determinant of innovation trajectories, influencing who can participate in AI development and how innovations diffuse across global ecosystems.

From an economic perspective, AI innovation has significant potential to enhance productivity, create new markets, and transform value chains. Automation and intelligent agents reduce labor-intensive tasks, optimize supply chains, and enable predictive decision-making, contributing to efficiency gains and cost reduction across sectors. Simultaneously, AI-driven innovation generates opportunities for novel products and services, including personalized healthcare solutions, adaptive financial tools, and autonomous transportation systems. The societal implications are equally profound: AI can improve access to education, facilitate scientific discovery, and support sustainable development initiatives. However, these innovations also raise critical challenges, including labor displacement, ethical dilemmas, and the amplification of existing inequalities, necessitating governance frameworks that balance innovation with responsible deployment (Brynjolfsson et al., 2018).

The interplay of these factors is visually summarized in Figure 1, which illustrates the core drivers of AI innovation, the dichotomy of open versus proprietary AI, and the resulting economic and societal impacts. The figure highlights the dynamic interactions among technological enablers, governance choices, and innovation outcomes, emphasizing that the pace and direction of AI innovation are contingent upon multi-stakeholder engagement, regulatory design, and global collaboration. Understanding these innovation dynamics is essential for anticipating both the transformative potential of AI and the structural challenges that arise from uneven access, concentration of resources, and governance asymmetries.

Figure 1. Key Drivers of AI Innovation: foundation models, automation, and AI agents interact with open and proprietary AI approaches to generate economic and societal impacts.

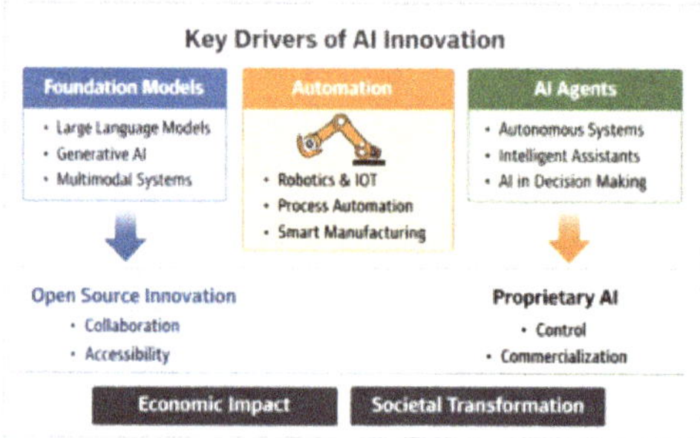

While innovation dynamics determine what is technologically possible, they simultaneously create governance challenges that demand regulatory attention. The acceleration of AI capabilities, coupled with their broad societal impact, necessitates careful analysis of regulatory frameworks, jurisdictional variations, and the global consequences of fragmented governance. The next section examines these regulatory landscapes, highlighting both their achievements and inherent limitations.

REGULATORY LANDSCAPES AND CHALLENGES

The global development of AI presents profound regulatory challenges as policymakers, institutions, and stakeholders attempt to reconcile the dual imperatives of technological innovation and societal risk mitigation. Among existing regulatory frameworks, the European Union's AI Act represents the most advanced and structured approach. Adopted as a proposal in (Act, 2021), the AI Act employs a risk-based regulatory model, categorizing AI applications according to their potential impact on fundamental rights, safety, and societal well-being. High-risk applications, including AI systems used in healthcare diagnostics, critical infrastructure, public administration, and judicial processes, are subject to mandatory transparency, human oversight, and rigorous conformity assessments. Complementing these requirements, the Act introduces regulatory sandboxes to facilitate experimentation under controlled conditions, allowing developers to test AI systems while ensuring compliance with ethical and safety standards. While the EU framework demonstrates a comprehensive attempt to protect citizens and promote trustworthy AI, scholars caution that excessive prescriptiveness may impede innovation, particularly for startups and small and medium-sized enterprises (Veale & Borgesius, 2021). Such overregulation could unintentionally reinforce market concentration, favoring incumbents who can absorb compliance costs.

In contrast, the United States has historically relied on a market-driven governance model, characterized by soft law, voluntary standards, and sector-specific guidelines. Agencies such as the National Institute of Standards and Technology (NIST) provide frameworks for trustworthy AI emphasizing accountability, transparency, and reproducibility without imposing rigid compliance obligations. This approach encourages innovation and rapid adoption, particularly within private-sector research and development, and allows flexibility in adapting to the rapidly evolving AI landscape (Bryson & Winfield, 2017). However, it also risks underregulation, leaving critical gaps in ethical oversight and public protection, and raising concerns about privacy, algorithmic bias, and accountability for high-impact AI systems.

Beyond these major jurisdictions, global AI governance is highly fragmented, with significant disparities in institutional capacity, legal infrastructure, and technological resources. Advanced economies, particularly in North America, Europe, and East Asia, dominate AI research, infrastructure, and investment, while many countries in the Global South face challenges in accessing critical datasets, computational resources, and governance expertise. This fragmentation creates barriers to cross-border deployment, standardization, and the equitable distribution of AI's benefits. International organizations and multi-stakeholder initiatives, including the OECD AI Principles (2019) and the Global Partnership on AI, aim to harmonize norms and promote ethical practices globally, yet adoption remains uneven and enforcement mechanisms are largely voluntary (Floridi et al., 2018). Consequently, regulatory heterogeneity risks creating a "patchwork" of compliance obligations, where multinational developers must navigate conflicting requirements, potentially slowing innovation or incentivizing regulatory arbitrage.

In addition to formal legal instruments, international soft-law frameworks have become influential in shaping both public and private governance practices for trustworthy AI. The OECD AI Principles (2019) constitute one of the earliest and most widely referenced consensus frameworks developed by 42 OECD member and partner countries. These principles emphasize *inclusive growth, sustainable development, human-centered values, transparency, robustness, accountability,* and *governance mechanisms* that enable both innovation and public trust. Specifically, the OECD framework advocates that AI systems should be designed to *respect the rule of law, human rights, democratic values, and diversity*; that there should be *appropriate human oversight*; and that organizations should adopt *risk-management and continuous monitoring* practices to address potential harms. These high-level principles have been explicitly referenced in subsequent national AI strategies (e.g.,

Canada, Japan, EU Member States) and serve as a common normative baseline in multi-stakeholder discussions about responsible AI.

Complementing these value-based principles, the U.S. National Institute of Standards and Technology (NIST) AI Risk Management Framework (AI RMF 1.0) offers a more operational and practice-oriented approach tailored for developers, implementers, and regulators. The NIST AI RMF (2023) identifies core functions — *Govern, Map, Measure, and Manage* — that guide organizations in identifying AI-related risks and implementing mitigation strategies throughout the lifecycle. It foregrounds *contextual risk identification, iterative evaluation, and documentation* of AI systems, providing a structured model for integrating technical, operational, and organizational controls. Unlike binding regulatory requirements, the NIST framework is voluntary, yet it has been widely adopted as a *reference benchmark* in U.S. federal guidance and as the basis for sectoral standards development, particularly in safety-critical and high-assurance domains such as healthcare, transportation, and defense.

Together, the OECD Principles and the NIST AI RMF illustrate two complementary strands in global AI governance: one that articulates normative, human-rights oriented values, and one that provides operational risk management guidance for practitioners. Both frameworks influence a broad range of national policies, corporate governance practices, and international standards efforts (e.g., ISO/IEC JTC 1/SC 42) and help bridge the gap between high-level regulatory ambitions and implementable governance practices.

A central challenge in AI governance is managing the trade-off between overregulation and underregulation. Overregulation may slow technological development, limit experimentation, and create barriers for new entrants, whereas underregulation may expose societies to safety, security, and ethical risks, including bias, discrimination, and erosion of public trust. Striking an effective balance requires adaptive governance frameworks that integrate legal mandates, voluntary standards, and participatory oversight mechanisms. Scholars advocate multi-layered approaches, combining sectoral guidelines, algorithmic auditing, certification mechanisms, and international coordination, to reconcile innovation with accountability (Gasser & Almeida, 2017). Such frameworks should be iterative and flexible, allowing regulators to respond to emerging AI capabilities while mitigating systemic risks.

Moreover, AI regulation intersects with geopolitical and socio-economic considerations. Leading technology firms and high-income states hold disproportionate influence over research agendas, infrastructure, and data access, reinforcing power asymmetries that complicate global governance. Regulatory strategies, therefore, must account not only for technical compliance but also for the ethical, social, and economic consequences of AI deployment. This requires inclusive governance mechanisms that engage a broad spectrum of stakeholders, from public authorities and industry to civil society and marginalized populations, ensuring that AI adoption promotes societal benefit rather than exacerbating inequalities.

Figure 2 visualizes these dynamics, contrasting EU and U.S. regulatory approaches while highlighting global fragmentation, imbalances, and the spectrum of regulatory risk from over- to underregulation. The figure emphasizes that AI governance is not a purely legal challenge but a socio-technical and global one, requiring coordination, transparency, and engagement across multiple levels to ensure both innovation and public trust.

Figure 2. Regulatory Landscapes and Challenges in AI: Comparative overview of EU and U.S. approaches, global imbalances, and regulatory risks, illustrating the tension between innovation and public protection.

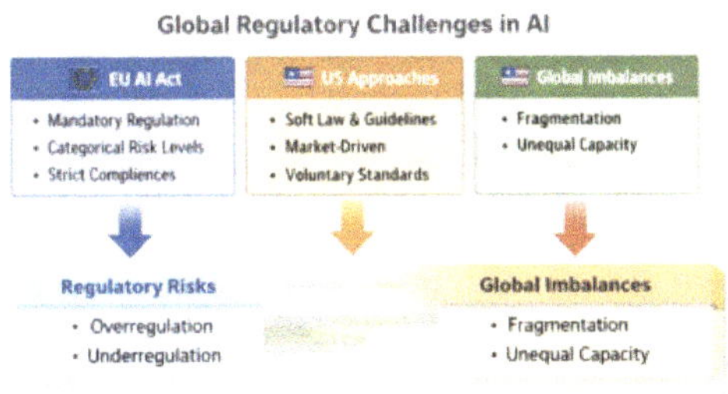

Understanding regulatory approaches alone, however, is insufficient. The critical question is how these frameworks interact with innovation in practice, ensuring that AI systems are both technologically advanced and socially responsible. Achieving this balance requires adaptive governance mechanisms, experimental approaches, and collaborative oversight. The following section explores strategies to harmonize innovation with ethical, legal, and societal safeguards, providing actionable insights for policy and industry alike.

BALANCING INNOVATION AND REGULATION

The rapid advancement of AI presents a fundamental tension between fostering innovation and ensuring responsible, ethical deployment. Striking a balance between these objectives requires regulatory frameworks that are adaptive, risk-aware, and inclusive, enabling innovation to flourish while mitigating potential harms. One of the most promising approaches to achieve this balance is adaptive and risk-based regulation, which tailors requirements to the potential impact of AI systems rather than imposing a one-size-fits-all approach. Such frameworks prioritize oversight on high-risk applications while allowing lower-risk innovations to progress with minimal friction. The European Union's AI Act exemplifies this approach by categorizing AI systems according to risk and imposing differentiated compliance obligations, thereby aligning regulatory intensity with societal stakes (Act, 2021). Adaptive regulation is iterative, allowing policymakers to refine rules in response to emerging technologies, stakeholder feedback, and empirical evidence of AI system impacts, reducing the risk of both overregulation and underregulation (Veale & Borgesius, 2021).

Regulatory sandboxes have emerged as a practical mechanism to operationalize adaptive governance. Sandboxes create controlled environments in which innovators can test AI applications under regulatory supervision, combining experimentation with accountability. By allowing temporary exemptions or modified compliance requirements, sandboxes encourage experimentation and learning, enabling regulators and developers to identify risks, test mitigation strategies, and co-create best practices. Notably, countries such as the United Kingdom and Singapore have successfully implemented AI sandboxes to accelerate innovation in fintech, healthcare, and autonomous systems, demonstrating that such mechanisms can simultaneously promote innovation and safeguard public trust (Moraes, 2025).

Central to balancing innovation and regulation is the development of explainable and trustworthy AI systems. Explainable AI (XAI) ensures that AI-driven decisions are transparent, interpretable, and understandable to humans, which is critical for accountability, user trust, and regulatory compliance. Trustworthy AI extends beyond technical transparency, encompassing fairness, robustness, privacy protection, and alignment with societal values. By embedding these principles into the AI lifecycle—from data collection and model design to deployment and monitoring—developers and regulators can reduce the likelihood of harmful outcomes, improve adoption, and maintain social legitimacy (Arrieta et al., 2020). Explainability and trustworthiness are also essential for regulatory sandboxes and risk-based oversight, as transparent systems facilitate evaluation, monitoring, and certification by both public authorities and independent auditors.

Public–private partnerships (PPPs) represent another critical element in harmonizing innovation and governance. Collaboration between governments, industry, academia, and civil society enables knowledge-sharing, co-development of standards, and alignment of technological capabilities with societal objectives. For example, the Global Partnership on AI (GPAI) and multi-stakeholder AI consortia demonstrate that PPPs can facilitate international coordination, establish ethical norms, and promote cross-border interoperability while leveraging private sector expertise and resources (Floridi et al., 2018). Such partnerships also provide avenues for training and workforce development, ensuring that AI skills and governance competencies are broadly distributed and inclusive, thereby mitigating inequities associated with concentrated technological power.

Figure 3 visualizes how these four pillars interact to balance innovation with regulation. The figure highlights the connections between adaptive and risk-based regulation, regulatory sandboxes, explainable and trustworthy AI, and public–private partnerships, illustrating how their interplay leads to responsible AI outcomes while supporting innovation and societal benefit.

Figure 3. Balancing Innovation and Regulation in AI.

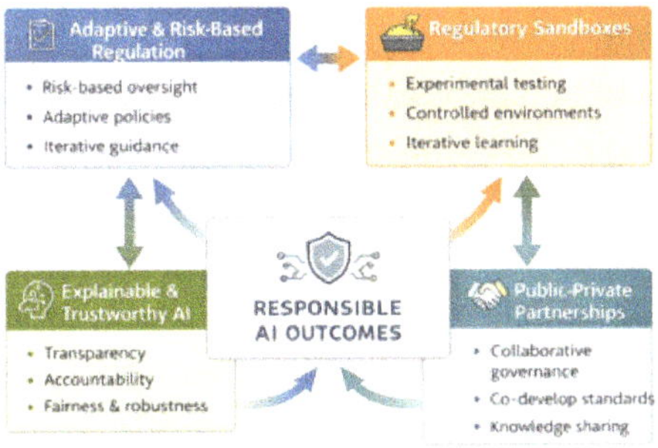

Balancing innovation and regulation also requires a holistic, systems-oriented perspective. Technological, economic, legal, and societal factors are deeply interdependent: innovation thrives under clear yet flexible rules, while governance effectiveness depends on understanding technological possibilities and limitations. Policymakers must therefore adopt multi-layered frameworks combining hard law, soft guidelines, industry standards, ethical codes, and participatory oversight. These frameworks enable iterative learning, stakeholder engagement, and international alignment, creating conditions where AI systems are both innovative and socially responsible (Gasser & Almeida, 2017).

In sum, achieving equilibrium between AI innovation and regulation involves integrating adaptive, risk-based regulatory approaches, sandbox experimentation, explainable and trustworthy AI, and public–private collaboration. Together, these strategies create a regulatory ecosystem that not only mitigates risks but also actively supports technological experimentation, diffusion, and ethical deployment. Such a balanced approach is essential for ensuring that AI delivers societal and economic benefits while maintaining public trust, protecting human rights, and fostering global collaboration in an increasingly complex technological landscape.

With strategies for balancing innovation and regulation clarified, it is essential to look forward and consider how global governance of AI may evolve in the coming years. Multiple scenarios—from optimistic convergence to restrictive or fragmented regimes—illustrate the potential trajectories of AI governance, emphasizing the role of standards, ethics-by-design, and international coordination. The subsequent section outlines these future directions, considering both the opportunities and risks inherent in shaping AI's global trajectory.

FUTURE DIRECTIONS FOR GLOBAL AI GOVERNANCE

The global governance of AI is entering a critical phase, as AI technologies become increasingly pervasive, autonomous, and economically transformative. Effective governance requires navigating complex trade-offs between innovation, ethical responsibility, and equitable access to technological benefits. Looking forward, three broad scenarios can be envisioned for the evolution of global AI governance: optimistic convergence, fragmented governance, and restrictive regulatory regimes. Each scenario presents distinct opportunities and challenges, shaping the strategic decisions of states, corporations, and civil society actors. Figure 4 illustrates how these scenarios interact with global coordination models and the embedding of standards and ethics-by-design to produce responsible AI outcomes.

Figure 4. Future Directions for Global AI Governance: Three scenarios (optimistic convergence, fragmented governance, restrictive regulation), global coordination models, and the role of standards and ethics-by-design in producing responsible AI outcomes.

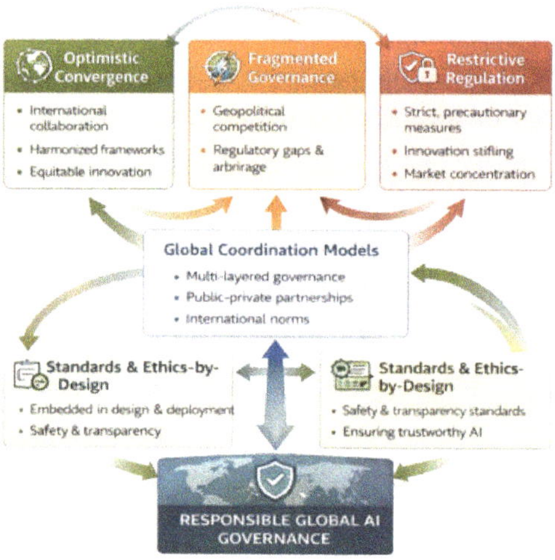

In the optimistic convergence scenario, international cooperation, shared norms, and harmonized regulatory frameworks enable AI to advance global societal and economic objectives while mitigating associated risks. This scenario relies on strong coordination mechanisms through multilateral institutions, such as the OECD, the Global Partnership on AI (GPAI), and the United Nations, which facilitate the co-development of principles for ethical AI, cross-border data sharing, and responsible deployment practices (Floridi et al., 2018). In such a context, high-risk AI applications are regulated proportionally, while lower-risk innovations benefit from flexibility and rapid diffusion. Multi-stakeholder participation—including governments, academia, civil society, and industry—ensures inclusivity, transparency, and legitimacy. In this scenario, standards and ethics-by-design principles are embedded into AI development processes from inception, promoting trustworthy systems that align with societal values and human rights (Jobin et al., 2019). Adoption of international technical standards, certification mechanisms, and interoperable regulatory guidelines facilitates cross-border innovation while preventing regulatory arbitrage and fragmentation. Optimistic convergence maximizes the societal benefits of AI while minimizing risks such as algorithmic bias, privacy breaches, and concentration of technological power.

Conversely, the fragmented governance scenario envisions a world where regulatory approaches diverge significantly between regions, driven by geopolitical competition, differing societal norms, and varying technological capabilities. In this scenario, leading economies develop stringent AI regulations and proprietary technological ecosystems, whereas other jurisdictions implement weaker or inconsistent rules, leading to asymmetries in access, safety, and ethical standards. Fragmentation can produce regulatory arbitrage, where companies relocate high-risk innovation to jurisdictions with minimal oversight, undermining global accountability (Gasser & Almeida, 2017). Additionally, inconsistent technical and ethical standards impede interoperability, data sharing, and collaborative research, while increasing compliance costs for multinational organizations. While fragmented governance allows local adaptation and flexibility, it risks widening global inequalities in AI capabilities and adoption, and may reduce public trust in AI systems due to inconsistent safety and ethical safeguards.

The restrictive regulatory scenario represents a contrasting trajectory, in which governments impose highly prescriptive and precautionary measures to limit AI deployment, motivated by concerns over security, ethical violations, or social disruption. While strict regulation can reduce risks associated with AI failures, bias, and misuse, excessive restrictions may stifle innovation, hinder experimentation, and entrench market dominance by large incumbents who can absorb compliance costs (Veale & Borgesius, 2021). Such regimes may also fragment international markets, impede knowledge diffusion, and slow the adoption of beneficial AI technologies in domains such as healthcare, education, and climate modeling.

Across these scenarios, the development of global coordination models remains central to balancing innovation with accountability. Multi-layered governance approaches, combining national regulations, regional agreements, and international norms, are increasingly advocated. For instance, the European Union's AI Act provides a detailed risk-based legal framework, while the OECD AI Principles and the UNESCO Recommendation on the Ethics of Artificial Intelligence offer aspirational guidance for global adoption (UNESCO, 2022). Public-private partnerships, international consortia, and collaborative research networks play a crucial role in operationalizing these models, enabling the harmonization of technical standards, ethical codes, and certification processes across borders. Cross-sector engagement ensures that both public interest and private-sector expertise are leveraged to develop adaptive, resilient, and equitable governance systems.

A key instrument for achieving harmonization is the implementation of standards and ethics-by-design principles. Standards provide measurable criteria for safety, robustness, transparency, and accountability, while ethics-by-design embeds normative considerations directly into system development. These approaches facilitate risk assessment, auditing, and regulatory compliance, ensuring that AI systems are trustworthy from the outset rather than retrofitted with safeguards post-deployment (Arrieta et al., 2020). Integrating ethics into design processes also enhances explainability, fairness, and societal alignment, building public confidence and supporting regulatory enforcement. International standard-setting organizations, such as ISO/IEC JTC 1/SC 42 for AI, exemplify how harmonized technical and ethical criteria can be disseminated globally to reduce fragmentation and foster interoperability.

Looking forward, the future of global AI governance will likely require hybrid approaches, combining proactive regulation, flexible sandboxes, international coordination, and embedded ethics. Policymakers must anticipate technological developments such as foundation models, autonomous AI agents, and generative systems that operate at scales exceeding previous regulatory experience. Adaptive governance mechanisms, including iterative regulatory review, real-time monitoring, and participatory decision-making, are essential to address emergent risks while preserving opportunities for innovation (Bryson & Winfield, 2017). Success depends on the integration of governance, technical standardization, and ethical design into a cohesive ecosystem capable of responding to evolving challenges and ensuring that AI serves global societal goals.

In conclusion, the future of global AI governance will be shaped by the interplay of regulatory approaches, international cooperation, and embedded ethical design. Optimistic scenarios highlight the benefits of coordinated, inclusive, and standards-based governance, while fragmented or overly restrictive trajectories emphasize the risks of inequity, inefficiency, and stifled innovation. Embedding standards and ethics-by-design within multi-level governance frameworks, coupled with proactive stakeholder engagement and hybrid regulatory models, represents the most promising path for ensuring that AI technologies are developed and deployed responsibly, equitably, and in ways that maximize societal and economic value on a global scale.

Examining future governance scenarios illuminates the interplay between regulatory choices, technological innovation, and societal values. These considerations lead naturally to a broader discussion on the dynamics of AI governance, the implications for stakeholders across sectors and regions, and the lessons that can be drawn for designing adaptive, inclusive, and effective policies. The discussion section synthesizes these insights and reflects on their broader significance.

DISCUSSION

The governance and development of artificial intelligence operate at the intersection of rapid technological innovation, evolving societal values, and increasingly complex regulatory environments. Unlike many conventional technologies, AI systems are characterized by a high degree of autonomy, scalability, and cross-domain transferability, which significantly amplifies both their transformative potential and their associated risks. As a result, the separation of technological advancement from ethical, legal, and social considerations is neither analytically nor practically sustainable. The preceding analyses demonstrate that innovation and governance are deeply interdependent processes, shaped by institutional incentives, market structures, and normative expectations.

A central manifestation of this interdependence can be observed in the tension between open-source collaboration and proprietary innovation models. Open ecosystems promote broad participation, accelerated knowledge diffusion, and collective problem-solving, thereby fostering inclusivity and transparency. In contrast, proprietary systems enable large-scale investment, specialized optimization, and the protection of intellectual property, which are often essential for commercially viable and safety-critical applications. The core governance challenge lies in reconciling these competing dynamics in a manner that aligns private incentives with societal welfare, prevents excessive concentration of power, and avoids regulatory approaches that either stifle creativity or reinforce monopolistic structures.

A second critical insight concerns the pronounced heterogeneity of AI governance across global contexts. Regulatory strategies vary substantially between jurisdictions, reflecting differences in cultural norms, economic priorities, political systems, and institutional capacities. While some regions have adopted comprehensive, risk-based regulatory frameworks with clearly articulated compliance mechanisms, others rely predominantly on soft-law instruments, market-driven self-regulation, or fragmented sector-specific rules. This diversity of approaches introduces significant challenges for both governance effectiveness and international coordination.

Regulatory fragmentation increases the risk of arbitrage, inconsistent enforcement, and uneven levels of protection for individuals and communities affected by AI systems. Moreover, it exacerbates disparities between technologically advanced regions and those with limited regulatory or technical capacity, potentially reinforcing global inequalities in AI development and deployment. Comparative and cross-jurisdictional research is therefore essential to identify conditions under which regulatory diversity can coexist with interoperability, accountability, and shared ethical baselines. Such research can also illuminate systemic vulnerabilities that emerge when governance structures fail to keep pace with transnational AI innovation.

The integration of technical standards and ethics-by-design principles emerges as a foundational element in shaping responsible AI outcomes. Technical standards provide operational benchmarks for safety, robustness, interoperability, and transparency, enabling measurable and enforceable governance practices. Ethics-by-design complements these standards by embedding normative considerations—such as fairness, explainability, accountability, and societal alignment—directly into the design and development phases of AI systems rather than treating them as post hoc constraints.

However, translating high-level ethical principles into actionable technical requirements remains a persistent challenge. This translation requires sustained interdisciplinary collaboration among engineers, ethicists, social scientists, legal scholars, and policymakers. Importantly, the operationalization of ethics-by-design depends not only on technical feasibility but also on social legitimacy and public trust. Participatory approaches to standard-setting, auditing, and evaluation play a critical role in this process by incorporating diverse perspectives and ensuring that governance mechanisms reflect societal values rather than narrowly defined technical or commercial objectives.

Another layer of complexity arises from the dynamic interaction between regulatory interventions and innovation trajectories. Regulatory frameworks that are overly prescriptive or rigid may constrain experimentation, slow knowledge diffusion, and disproportionately advantage large, established actors capable of absorbing compliance costs. Conversely, permissive or underdeveloped regulatory environments can accelerate innovation in the short term but expose societies to significant ethical, social, and economic risks, including discrimination, loss of accountability, and systemic instability.

These tensions underscore the necessity of adaptive and iterative governance models that balance flexibility with protection. Experimental regulatory instruments—such as regulatory sandboxes, phased deployment schemes, and continuous monitoring mechanisms—offer promising pathways for managing uncertainty while enabling innovation. However, empirical evidence on the long-term effectiveness of such approaches remains limited, highlighting an important agenda for future research across sectors and application domains.

The discussion further highlights the importance of multi-level and interdisciplinary perspectives in AI governance. AI is simultaneously a technical artifact, an economic driver, and a socio-political force; its governance therefore demands analytical frameworks that integrate legal, ethical, economic, and societal dimensions. Research methodologies must move beyond siloed approaches and incorporate longitudinal, cross-national, and participatory designs capable of capturing the evolving nature of AI ecosystems.

Key open research questions include the mechanisms through which global norms and standards diffuse across jurisdictions, strategies for aligning private innovation incentives with public interests, and approaches for mitigating systemic risks such as algorithmic bias, labor displacement, and unequal access to technological benefits. Addressing these questions is essential for developing governance models that are both empirically grounded and normatively robust.

CONCLUSION

The preceding analysis provides a holistic perspective on the challenges, opportunities, and complexities inherent in governing artificial intelligence at a global scale. AI is not merely a technological innovation; it is a socio-technical phenomenon with profound ethical, social, economic, and geopolitical implications. Effective governance, therefore, extends beyond risk mitigation and compliance: it requires shaping innovation pathways in ways that maximize societal value, promote inclusivity, and minimize harm. A central insight emerging from this chapter is that AI governance must be multi-dimensional, integrating adaptive regulatory mechanisms, international coordination, ethical embedding, and technical standardization. Each of these dimensions contributes uniquely to fostering trust, ensuring accountability, enabling innovation, and sustaining social legitimacy.

Policy recommendations derived from this analysis emphasize flexibility, proportionality, and inclusivity. Adaptive, risk-based regulations allow differentiated treatment of AI applications according to their potential societal impact, balancing the need for experimentation with safeguards for high-stakes contexts. Complementary tools, such as regulatory sandboxes and iterative monitoring systems, create structured opportunities for learning, evaluation, and refinement of both technology and governance. Multi-stakeholder engagement—including civil society, academia, industry, and international actors—is essential for ensuring that policy design and standard-setting processes reflect diverse perspectives, avoid capture by narrow interests, and reinforce societal legitimacy. Furthermore, embedding ethics-by-design and internationally recognized standards throughout the AI lifecycle strengthens transparency, fairness, and accountability, aligning technical innovation with societal expectations and human rights norms.

Research implications are equally critical. The multi-layered and interdependent nature of global AI ecosystems demands interdisciplinary and cross-sectoral research that examines governance outcomes at local, national, and global levels. Empirical studies should investigate how different regulatory models influence the diffusion of innovation, ethical compliance, market concentration, and social equity. Comparative analyses across jurisdictions can reveal factors that promote convergence toward best practices or, conversely, exacerbate fragmentation and inequality. Longitudinal and multi-sector studies are particularly valuable for assessing long-term consequences of AI on labor markets, economic structures, governance institutions, and societal trust, enabling evidence-based refinement of both policy and technological design.

Another key conclusion concerns the uneven global distribution of AI capabilities and resources. Concentration of technological infrastructure, data, and expertise in high-income countries and leading firms risks reinforcing inequalities, limiting meaningful participation from underrepresented regions, and creating asymmetrical access to AI benefits. To address these disparities, it is crucial to promote open platforms, collaborative standards development, and targeted capacity-building initiatives in less-resourced regions. International cooperation, knowledge sharing, and interoperable governance standards can mitigate fragmentation, foster inclusive innovation ecosystems, and ensure that technological advances contribute equitably to global development objectives.

AI governance should be conceptualized as a continuous, adaptive process rather than a fixed or static endpoint. As AI technologies evolve, governance strategies must adapt in parallel, integrating empirical feedback, stakeholder insights, and ethical considerations. Effective governance therefore relies on the combination of evidence-based policy, proactive regulation, global coordination, and ethics embedded within system design. Pursuing these integrated strategies enables policymakers, researchers, and developers to cultivate AI ecosystems that are both innovative and socially responsible, sustaining public trust while maximizing societal and economic benefits.

Overall, advancing responsible AI at a global level requires deliberate, coordinated, and forward-looking strategies. The convergence of innovation, ethics, regulation, and standards establishes the conditions under which AI can deliver tangible societal and economic benefits while minimizing risks. Research and policy must remain iterative, responsive, and inclusive, recognizing that the rapid pace of technological evolution necessitates continuous reassessment and adaptation. By embracing these approaches, stakeholders can ensure that AI technologies contribute positively to human development, equitable growth, and sustainable global progress, supporting a vision of AI that is not only technologically sophisticated but also ethically grounded and socially beneficial.

REFERENCES

Act, A. I. (2021). Proposal for a regulation of the European Parliament and the Council laying down harmonised rules on Artificial Intelligence (Artificial Intelligence Act) and amending certain Union legislative acts. *EUR-Lex-52021PC0206.*

Arrieta, A. B., Díaz-Rodríguez, N., Del Ser, J., Bennetot, A., Tabik, S., Barbado, A., & Herrera, F. (2020). Explainable Artificial Intelligence (XAI): Concepts, taxonomies, opportunities and challenges toward responsible AI. *Information Fusion, 58*, 82–115. DOI: 10.1016/j.inffus.2019.12.012

Batool, A., Zowghi, D., & Bano, M. (2025). AI governance: A systematic literature review. *AI and Ethics*, •••, 1–15.

Bokhari, S. A. A., Park, S. Y., & Manzoor, S. (2025). Digital government transformation through artificial intelligence: The mediating role of stakeholder trust and participation. *Digital*, *5*(3), 43. DOI: 10.3390/digital5030043

Bommasani, R. (2021). On the opportunities and risks of foundation models. *arXiv preprint arXiv:2108.07258.*

Brown, V., Larasati, R., Kwarteng, J., & Farrell, T. (2025). Understanding AI and power: Situated perspectives from Global North and South practitioners. *AI & Society*, •••, 1–16. DOI: 10.1007/s00146-025-02731-x

Bryan, K. A., & Teodoridis, F. (2024). Balancing market innovation incentives and regulation in AI: Challenges and opportunities. https://www.brookings.edu/articles/balancing-market-innovation-incentives-and-regulation-in-ai-challenges-and-opportunities

Brynjolfsson, E., Rock, D., & Syverson, C. (2018). The productivity J-curve: How intangibles complement general purpose technologies (No. w25148). *National Bureau of Economic Research. doi, 10*, w25148.

Bryson, J., & Winfield, A. (2017). Standardizing ethical design for artificial intelligence and autonomous systems. *Computer, 50*(5), 116–119. DOI: 10.1109/MC.2017.154

Cockburn, I. M., Henderson, R., & Stern, S. (2022). The Impact of Artificial Intelligence on Innovation. In *The Impact of Artificial Intelligence on Innovation: Cockburn, Iain M.| uHenderson, Rebecca M.| uStern, Scott.* [Sl]: *SSRN.*

Floridi, L., Cowls, J., Beltrametti, M., Chatila, R., Chazerand, P., Dignum, V., Luetge, C., Madelin, R., Pagallo, U., Rossi, F., Schafer, B., Valcke, P., & Vayena, E. (2018). AI4People—An ethical framework for a good AI society: Opportunities, risks, principles, and recommendations. *Minds and Machines*, *28*(4), 689–707. DOI: 10.1007/s11023-018-9482-5 PMID: 30930541

Gasser, U., & Almeida, V. A. (2017). A layered model for AI governance. *IEEE Internet Computing*, *21*(6), 58–62. DOI: 10.1109/MIC.2017.4180835

Gille, M., Tropmann-Frick, M., & Schomacker, T. (2024). Balancing public interest, fundamental rights, and innovation: The EU's governance model for non-high-risk AI systems. *Internet Policy Review*, *13*(3). Advance online publication. DOI: 10.14763/2024.3.1797

Iseko, A. (2025). Diversity as Ethical Infrastructure: Reimagining AI Governance for Justice and Accountability. *International Journal of Science. Technology in Society*, *13*(5), 190–204.

Jobin, A., Ienca, M., & Vayena, E. (2019). The global landscape of AI ethics guidelines. *Nature Machine Intelligence*, *1*(9), 389–399. DOI: 10.1038/s42256-019-0088-2

Kashefi, P., Kashefi, Y., & Ghafouri Mirsaraei, A. (2024). Shaping the future of AI: Balancing innovation and ethics in global regulation. *Uniform Law Review*, *29*(3), 524–548. DOI: 10.1093/ulr/unae040

Kiden, S., Stahl, B., Townsend, B., Maple, C., Vincent, C., Sampson, F., . . . Yazdanpanah, V. (2024). Responsible AI governance: a response to UN interim report on governing AI for humanity. *arXiv preprint arXiv:2412.12108*.

Kulothungan, V., & Gupta, D. (2025). Towards adaptive AI governance: Comparative insights from the US, EU, and Asia. In *2025 IEEE 11th Conference on Big Data Security on Cloud (BigDataSecurity)* (pp. 32-38). IEEE.

Moraes, T. (2025). Regulatory sandboxes for trustworthy artificial intelligence–global and Latin American experiences. *International Review of Law Computers & Technology*, *39*(1), 55–74. DOI: 10.1080/13600869.2024.2351674

NIST AI RMF. (2023). Artificial intelligence risk management framework (AI RMF 1.0). *URL:* https://nvlpubs.nist.gov/nistpubs/ai/nist.ai.100-1.pdf

OECD AI Principles. (2019). OECD Recommendation on Artificial Intelligence. OECD. URL: https://www.oecd.org/en/topics/sub-issues/ai-principles.html

Ramanathan, R., He, Q., Black, A., Ghobadian, A., & Gallear, D. (2017). Environmental regulations, innovation and firm performance: A revisit of the Porter hypothesis. *Journal of Cleaner Production*, *155*, 79–92. DOI: 10.1016/j.jclepro.2016.08.116

Roberts, H., Hine, E., Taddeo, M., & Floridi, L. (2024). Global AI governance: Barriers and pathways forward. *International Affairs*, *100*(3), 1275–1286. DOI: 10.1093/ia/iiae073

Russell, S., & Norvig, P. (2021). *Artificial Intelligence* (Global Edition). Pearson Education.

Schiuma, G., & Santarsiero, F. (2024). *Open Innovation Labs*. Springer. DOI: 10.1007/978-3-031-75533-0

Sun, N., Miao, Y., Jiang, H., Ding, M., & Zhang, J. (2024). From principles to practice: A deep dive into AI ethics and regulations. arXiv preprint arXiv:2412.04683.

Unesco. (2022). *Recommendation on the ethics of artificial intelligence*. United Nations Educational, Scientific and Cultural Organization.

Veale, M., & Borgesius, F. Z. (2021). Demystifying the draft EU artificial intelligence act. *arXiv preprint arXiv:2107.03721*. DOI: 10.31235/osf.io/38p5f

Compilation of References

Aamir, A., Tamosiunaite, M., & Wörgötter, F. (2023). Interpreting the decisions of CNNs via influence functions. *Frontiers in Computational Neuroscience*, *17*, 1172883. DOI: 10.3389/fncom.2023.1172883 PMID: 37564901

Act, A. I. (2021). Proposal for a regulation of the European Parliament and the Council laying down harmonised rules on Artificial Intelligence (Artificial Intelligence Act) and amending certain Union legislative acts. *EUR-Lex-52021PC0206.*

Afroogh, S., Akbari, A., Malone, E., Kargar, M., & Alambeigi, H. (2024). Trust in AI: Progress, Challenges, and Future Directions. *ArXiv*. https://arxiv.org/abs/2403.14680

Agarwal, C., Krishna, S., Saxena, E., Pawelczyk, M., Johnson, N., Puri, I., Zitnik, M., & Lakkaraju, H. (2022). OpenXAI: Towards a transparent evaluation of model explanations. *Advances in Neural Information Processing Systems*, *35*, 15346–15361. DOI: 10.52202/068431-1148

Agrawal, K., El Shawi, R., & Ahmed, N. (2025). Explainable artificial intelligence-Eval: A framework for comparative evaluation of explanation methods in healthcare. *Digital Health*, *11*, 20552076251368045. DOI: 10.1177/20552076251368045 PMID: 41036433

Ai, H. (2019). High-level expert group on artificial intelligence. *Ethics guidelines for trustworthy. AI*, •••, 6.

Ajirak, M., Ravishankar, A., & Djuric, P. M. (2025). Uncertainty Quantification in Probabilistic Machine Learning Models: Theory, Methods, and Insights. *ArXiv*. https://arxiv.org/abs/2509.05877 DOI: 10.23919/EUSIPCO63237.2025.11226403

Almutairi, M., Alamry, A., Rahman, G., & Mudhsh, B. A. (2025). The role of AI-powered learning analytics in enhancing EFL curriculum design and learning outcomes in higher education. *International Journal of Innovative Research and Scientific Studies*, *8*(7), 477–487. DOI: 10.53894/ijirss.v8i7.10480

Alon-Barkat, S., Busuioc, M., Schwoerer, K., & Weißmüller, K. (2025). Algorithmic Discrimination in Public Service Provision: Understanding Citizens' Attribution of Responsibility for Human vs Algorithmic Discriminatory Outcomes. *Journal of Public Administration: Research and Theory*, *35*(4), 469–488. Advance online publication. DOI: 10.1093/jopart/muaf024

Amershi, S., Cakmak, M., Knox, W. B., & Kulesza, T. (2014). Power to the people: The role of humans in interactive machine learning. *AI Magazine*, *35*(4), 105–120. DOI: 10.1609/aimag.v35i4.2513

Anderson, G. L. (1998). Toward authentic participation: Deconstructing the discourses of participatory reforms in education. *American Educational Research Journal*, *35*(4), 571–603. DOI: 10.3102/00028312035004571

Annan, N., Beseng, M., Crawford, G., & Kewir, J. K. (2021). Civil society, peacebuilding from below and shrinking civic space: The case of Cameroon's 'Anglophone'conflict. *Conflict Security and Development*, *21*(6), 697–725. DOI: 10.1080/14678802.2021.1997454

Ansell, C., Sørensen, E., Torfing, J., & Trondal, J. (2024). *Robust governance in turbulent times*. Cambridge University Press. DOI: 10.1017/9781009433006

Ansell, C., & Torfing, J. (2022). Introduction to the Handbook on Theories of Governance. In *Handbook on theories of governance* (pp. 1–16). Edward Elgar Publishing., DOI: 10.4337/9781800371972.00007

Appelbaum, D., Kogan, A., Vasarhelyi, M. A., & Yan, Z. (2017). Impact of business analytics and enterprise systems on managerial accounting. *International Journal of Accounting Information Systems*, *25*, 29–44. DOI: 10.1016/j.accinf.2017.03.003

Arnaouti, M. K. C., Cahill, G., Baird, M. D., Mangurat, L., Harris, R., Edme, L. P. P., Joseph, M. N., Worlton, T., & Augustin, S.Jr. (2022). Medical disaster response: A critical analysis of the 2010 Haiti earthquake. *Frontiers in Public Health*, *10*, 995595. DOI: 10.3389/fpubh.2022.995595 PMID: 36388301

Arokun, E. (2025). Complexities of AI trends: Threats to data privacy legal compliance. *Seattle Journal of Technology, Environmental & Innovation Law*, *15*(2), 8. https://digitalcommons.law.seattleu.edu/sjteil/vol15/iss2/8

Aronson, B., & Laughter, J. (2016). The theory and practice of culturally relevant education: A synthesis of research across content areas. *Review of Educational Research*, *86*(1), 163–206. DOI: 10.3102/0034654315582066

Arora, A. (2015). Developing generative AI models that comply with privacy regulations and ethical principles. *International Journal of Research in Electronics and Computer Engineering*, *3*(2), 269–277.

Arrieta, A. B., Díaz-Rodríguez, N., Del Ser, J., Bennetot, A., Tabik, S., Barbado, A., García, S., Gil-López, S., Molina, D., Benjamins, R., Chatila, R., & Herrera, F. (2021). Explainable Artificial Intelligence (XAI): Concepts, taxonomies, opportunities and challenges toward responsible AI. *Information Fusion*, *58*, 82–115. DOI: 10.1016/j.inffus.2019.12.012

Asian Development Bank. (2023). *Asia Small and Medium-Sized Enterprise Monitor 2023: Towards green and resilient MSMEs.* Asian Development Bank.

Atrey, P., Brundage, M. P., Wu, M., & Dutta, S. (2025). Demystifying the Accuracy-Interpretability Trade-Off: A Case Study of Inferring Ratings from Reviews. *ArXiv*. https://arxiv.org/abs/2503.07914

Autio, C., Schwartz, R., Dunietz, J., Jain, S., Stanley, M., Tabassi, E., Hall, P., & Roberts, K. (2024). *Artificial Intelligence Risk Management Framework: Generative artificial intelligence profile (NIST AI 600-1).* National Institute of Standards and Technology., DOI: 10.6028/NIST.AI.600-1

Awwal-Bolanta, O., & Anakanire, O. C. (2024). Artificial intelligence and data Privacy: evaluation of the innovations, legal frameworks and technological protection. In *IIARD – International Institute of Academic Research and Development, Journal of Law and Global Policy* (pp. 36–49). JLGP., DOI: 10.56201/JLGP.v9.no2.2024.pg36.49

Babacan, H. (2025). From crisis to policy action: Tackling climate change through SDG 13. *The International Journal of Community and Social Development, 25166026251351370*(2), 205–221. Advance online publication. DOI: 10.1177/25166026251351370

Baldassarre, M. T., Gigante, D., Kalinowski, M., Ragone, A., & Tibido, S. (2024). Trustworthy AI in practice: An analysis of practitioners' needs and challenges. In *Proceedings of the 28th International Conference on Evaluation and Assessment in Software Engineering (EASE 2024)* (pp. 189–198). ACM. DOI: 10.1145/3661167.3661214

Batool, A., Zowghi, D., & Bano, M. (2025). AI governance: A systematic literature review. *AI and Ethics*, •••, 1–15.

Bell, A., Solano-Kamaiko, I., Nov, O., & Stoyanovich, J. (2022). It's just not that simple: An empirical study of the accuracy–explainability trade-off in machine learning for public policy. In *Proceedings of the 2022 ACM Conference on Fairness, Accountability, and Transparency (FAccT '22)* (pp. 248–266). Association for Computing Machinery. DOI: 10.1145/3531146.3533090

Belle, V., & Papantonis, I. (2021). Principles and practice of explainable machine learning. *Frontiers in Big Data*, *4*, 688969. DOI: 10.3389/fdata.2021.688969 PMID: 34278297

Benke, K., & Pelger, C. (2021). AFA: A critical perspective on artificial intelligence in accounting. *Accounting, Organizations and Society*, *92*, 101243. DOI: 10.1016/j.aos.2021.101243

Bhardwaj, T., & Sumangali, K. (2025). A federated incremental blockchain framework with privacy preserving XAI optimization for securing healthcare data. *Scientific Reports*, *15*(1), 38001. DOI: 10.1038/s41598-025-21852-3 PMID: 41168334

Bhimani, A., Horngren, C. T., Datar, S. M., & Rajan, M. V. (2019). *Management and cost accounting* (7th ed.). Pearson.

Binns, R. (2018). Fairness in machine learning: Lessons from political philosophy. In *Conference on fairness, accountability and transparency* (pp. 149-159). PMLR.

Bokhari, S. A. A., Park, S. Y., & Manzoor, S. (2025). Digital government transformation through artificial intelligence: The mediating role of stakeholder trust and participation. *Digital*, *5*(3), 43. DOI: 10.3390/digital5030043

Bolleyer, N. (2021). Civil society, crisis exposure, and resistance strategies. In *Routledge handbook of illiberalism* (pp. 939–956). Routledge. DOI: 10.4324/9780367260569-68

Bolton, D., Landells, T., & Habib, M. (2023). Collaborating and Competing in Development Agendas: State—Civil Society Tensions in Achieving SDGs. In *The complexities of sustainability* (pp. 77-120).

Bommasani, R. (2021). On the opportunities and risks of foundation models. *arXiv preprint arXiv:2108.07258.*

Bostrom, N., & Yudkowsky, E. (2014). The ethics of artificial intelligence. The Cambridge handbook of artificial intelligence. *Link:* https://bit. ly/3BSusmO

Bravim, J. M., de Carvalho, A. C. V., Segatto, A. P., & Morais-da-Silva, R. L. (2025). Are there key characteristics of social enterprises that foster relationships with government, universities and civil society? *Social Enterprise Journal*, *21*(5), 864–889. Advance online publication. DOI: 10.1108/SEJ-08-2024-0136

Broadhurst, K., & Gray, N. (2022). Understanding resilient places: Multi-level governance in times of crisis. *Local Economy*, *37*(1-2), 84–103. DOI: 10.1177/02690942221100101

Brown, V., Larasati, R., Kwarteng, J., & Farrell, T. (2025). Understanding AI and power: Situated perspectives from Global North and South practitioners. *AI & Society*, •••, 1–16. DOI: 10.1007/s00146-025-02731-x

Bryan, K. A., & Teodoridis, F. (2024). Balancing market innovation incentives and regulation in AI: Challenges and opportunities. https://www.brookings.edu/articles/balancing-market-innovation-incentives-and-regulation-in-ai-challenges-and-opportunities

Brynjolfsson, E., Rock, D., & Syverson, C. (2018). The productivity J-curve: How intangibles complement general purpose technologies (No. w25148). *National Bureau of Economic Research. doi, 10*, w25148.

Bryson, J., & Winfield, A. (2017). Standardizing ethical design for artificial intelligence and autonomous systems. *Computer*, *50*(5), 116–119. DOI: 10.1109/MC.2017.154

Bua, A., & Bussu, S. (Eds.). (2023). *Reclaiming participatory governance: Social movements and the reinvention of democratic innovation*. Taylor & Francis. DOI: 10.4324/9781003218517

Burrell, J. (2016). How the machine 'thinks': Understanding opacity in machine learning algorithms. *Big Data & Society*, *3*(1), 1–12. DOI: 10.1177/2053951715622512

Canca, C. (2020). Operationalizing AI ethics principles. *Communications of the ACM*, *63*(12), 18–21. DOI: 10.1145/3430368

Cath, C., Wachter, S., Mittelstadt, B., Taddeo, M., & Floridi, L. (2018). Artificial intelligence and the 'good society': The US, EU, and UK approach. *Science and Engineering Ethics*, *24*, 505–528. DOI: 10.1007/s11948-017-9901-7 PMID: 28353045

Caton, S., & Haas, C. (2020). Fairness in machine learning: A survey. *ACM Computing Surveys*, *56*(7), 166. Advance online publication. DOI: 10.1145/3616865

Cetinkaya, N. E., & Kramer, N. (2025). Between transparency and trust: Identifying key factors in AI system perception. *Behaviour & Information Technology*, *44*(10), 2533358. DOI: 10.1080/0144929X.2025.2533358

Chaudhry, S. (2022). The assault on civil society: Explaining state crackdown on NGOs. *International Organization*, *76*(3), 549–590. DOI: 10.1017/S0020818321000473

Chen, H., Cohen, E., Wilson, D., & Alfred, M. (2024). A machine learning approach with human-AI collaboration for automated classification of patient safety event reports: Algorithm development and validation study. *JMIR Human Factors*, *11*(1), e53378. DOI: 10.2196/53378 PMID: 38271086

Chen, X. (2023). Understanding the role of Civil Society Organizations (CSOs) in the "central government-local government-society" framework: A case study on public crisis management during the pandemic in China. *International Public Management Journal*, *26*(4), 570–588. DOI: 10.1080/10967494.2022.2115595

Chintoh, N. G. A., Segun-Falade, N. O. D., Odionu, N. C. S., & Ekeh, N. a. H. (2025). Cross-Jurisdictional data Privacy Compliance in the U.S.: Developing a new model for managing AI data across state and federal laws. *3*(2), 537–548. https://doi.org/DOI: 10.51594/gjabr.v3i2.96

Chintoh, N. G. A., Segun-Falade, N. O. D., Odionu, N. C. S., & Ekeh, N. a. H. (2025). Developing a conceptual framework for U.S. data privacy compliance in AI systems: Integrating CCPA and HIPAA Regulations. *International Journal of Frontline Research and Reviews,* *4*(1), 011–019. https://doi.org/DOI: 10.56355/ijfrr.2025.4.1.0034

Cockburn, I. M., Henderson, R., & Stern, S. (2022). The Impact of Artificial Intelligence on Innovation. In *The Impact of Artificial Intelligence on Innovation: Cockburn, Iain M.| uHenderson, Rebecca M.| uStern, Scott.* [Sl]: *SSRN.*

Companies Act. (1956).

Competition Act. (2002).

Cook, A. D. (2021). Humanitarian diplomacy in ASEAN. *Asian Journal of Comparative Politics*, *6*(3), 188–201. DOI: 10.1177/20578911211019247

Costanza-Chock, S. (2020). *Design justice: Community-led practices to build the worlds we need.* The MIT Press. DOI: 10.7551/mitpress/12255.001.0001

Damiyano, D. (2024). Sustainable Social Services Financing for Local Governments. In *Financial Sustainability of Local Governments in Southern Africa* (pp. 198–214). Routledge. DOI: 10.4324/9781003498230-11

Dang, V. N., Cascarano, A., Mulder, R. H., Cecil, C., Zuluaga, M. A., Hernández-González, J., & Lekadir, K. (2024). Fairness and bias correction in machine learning for depression prediction across four study populations. *Scientific Reports*, *14*(1), 7848. DOI: 10.1038/s41598-024-58427-7 PMID: 38570587

Danilevsky, M., Qian, K., Aharonov, R., Katsis, Y., Kawas, B., & Sen, P. (2021). A survey of the state of Explainable AI for natural language processing. arXiv preprint arXiv:2010.00711. https://doi.org//arXiv.2010.00711DOI: 10.48550

Delgado, F., Yang, S., Madaio, M., & Yang, Q. (2023). The participatory turn in ai design: Theoretical foundations and the current state of practice. In *Proceedings of the 3rd ACM Conference on Equity and Access in Algorithms, Mechanisms, and Optimization* (pp. 1-23). DOI: 10.1145/3617694.3623261

Devineni, S. K. (2024). AI in data privacy and security. *International Journal of Artificial Intelligence and Machine Learning*, *3*(1), 35–49. DOI: 10.17605/OSF.IO/WCN8A

Devi, S., Hooper, K., & Davey, H. (2019). Accounting and accountability in microfinance institutions: A systematic literature review. *Journal of Accounting in Emerging Economies*, *9*(3), 437–463.

Dewitte, P. (2025). AI meets the GDPR. In Cambridge University Press eBooks (pp. 133–157). https://doi.org/DOI: 10.1017/9781009367783.010

Digital Personal Data Protection Act. (2023). (India).

Doshi-Velez, F., & Kim, B. (2017). Towards a rigorous science of interpretable machine learning. *arXiv preprint arXiv:1702.08608.*

Du, J. (2025). Toward Responsible and Beneficial AI: Comparing Regulatory and Guidance-Based Approaches-A Comprehensive Comparative Analysis of Artificial Intelligence Governance Frameworks across the European Union, United States, China, and IEEE. *arXiv preprint arXiv:2508.00868.*

Dwivedi, R., Dave, D., Naik, H., Singhal, S., Omer, R., Patel, P., Qian, B., Wen, Z., Shah, T., Morgan, G., & Ranjan, R. (2023). Explainable AI (XAI): Core ideas, techniques and solutions. *ACM Computing Surveys*, *55*(9), 194. DOI: 10.1145/3561048

Elshawi, R., Al-Mallah, M. H., & Sakr, S. (2019). On the interpretability of machine learning-based model for predicting hypertension. *BMC Medical Informatics and Decision Making*, *19*(1), 146. DOI: 10.1186/s12911-019-0874-0 PMID: 31357998

Enholm, I. M., Papagiannidis, E., Mikalef, P., & Krogstie, J. (2022). Artificial intelligence and business value: A literature review. *Information Systems Frontiers*, *24*(5), 1709–1734. DOI: 10.1007/s10796-021-10186-w

Esteva, A., Robicquet, A., Ramsundar, B., Kuleshov, V., DePristo, M., Chou, K., Cui, C., Corrado, G., Thrun, S., & Dean, J. (2019). A guide to deep learning in healthcare. *Nature Medicine*, *25*(1), 24–29. DOI: 10.1038/s41591-018-0316-z PMID: 30617335

Eubanks, V. (2018). *Automating inequality: How high-tech tools profile, police, and punish the poor*. Macmillan+ ORM.

European Commission High-Level Expert Group on Artificial Intelligence. (2019). *Ethics guidelines for trustworthy AI*. European Commission.

European Commission. (2017, May 18). Mergers: Commission fines Facebook 110 million euros for providing misleading information about WhatsApp takeover. https://ec.europa.eu/commission/presscorner/detail/en/ip_17_1369

European Parliament & Council of the European Union. (2024). Regulation (EU) 2024/1689 of the European Parliament and of the Council laying down harmonised rules on artificial intelligence (Artificial Intelligence Act). Official Journal of the European Union. https://eur-lex.europa.eu/legal-content/EN/TXT/?uri=CELEX:32024R1689

European Union Agency for Cybersecurity (ENISA). (2023). Multilayer framework for good cybersecurity practices for AI. ENISA. https://www.enisa.europa.eu/publications/multilayer-framework-for-good-cybersecurity-practices-for-ai

Fabuyi, J. (2024). Leveraging synthetic data as a tool to combat bias in artificial intelligence (AI) model training. *Journal of Engineering Research and Reports*, *26*(12), 24–46. DOI: 10.9734/jerr/2024/v26i121337

Federal Trade Commission. (2024, October 9). FTC takes action against Marriott and Starwood over multiple data breaches. https://www.ftc.gov/news-events/news/press-releases/2024/10/ftc-takes-action-against-marriott-starwood-over-multiple-data-breaches

Fjeld, J., Achten, N., Hilligoss, H., Nagy, A., & Srikumar, M. (2020). Principled artificial intelligence: Mapping consensus in ethical and rights-based approaches to principles for AI. *Berkman Klein Center Research Publication*, (2020-1).

Floridi, L., & Cowls, J. (2021). A unified framework of five principles for AI in society. In M. Nobre & A. Veloso (Eds.), Ethics, governance, and policies in artificial intelligence (Philosophical Studies Series, Vol. 144, pp. 5–17). Springer. DOI: 10.1007/978-3-030-81907-1_2

Floridi, L., Cowls, J., Beltrametti, M., Chatila, R., Chazerand, P., Dignum, V., Luetge, C., Madelin, R., Pagallo, U., Rossi, F., Schafer, B., Valcke, P., & Vayena, E. (2018). AI4People—An ethical framework for a good AI society: Opportunities, risks, principles, and recommendations. *Minds and Machines*, *28*(4), 689–707. DOI: 10.1007/s11023-018-9482-5 PMID: 30930541

Folorunso, A., Adewumi, T. O., Adewa, A., Okonkwo, R., & Olawumi, T. N. Capella University, University of Florida, Ohio University, North Carolina Agricultural and Technical State University, & Ekiti State University. (2024). Impact of AI on cybersecurity and security compliance. *Global Journal of Engineering and Technology Advances, 01–01*, 167–184. https://doi.org/DOI: 10.30574/gjeta.2024.21.1.0193

Gajbhiye, B., Khan, S., & Goel, O. (2024). Regulatory compliance in application security using AI compliance tools. *International Research Journal of Modernization in Engineering Technology and Science*, *6*(8). Advance online publication. DOI: 10.56726/IRJMETS61241

Gallegos, I. O., Rossi, R. A., Barrow, J., Tanjim, M. M., Kim, S., Dernoncourt, F., Yu, T., Zhang, R., & Ahmed, N. K. (2023). Bias and Fairness in Large Language Models: A Survey. *ArXiv*. https://arxiv.org/abs/2309.00770

Gandhi, A., & Nagpal, N. (2024, August 16). Transfer of data in M&A deals: Best practices. *SS Rana & Co. Advocates*. https://ssrana.in/articles/merger-acquisition-deals-transfer-data/

Garcia, S., Carrigan, C., & Wiepking, P. (2023). Global civil society response to the COVID-19 crisis. *Voluntas*, *34*(6), 1310–1321. DOI: 10.1007/s11266-023-00589-5

Gasser, U., & Almeida, V. A. (2017). A layered model for AI governance. *IEEE Internet Computing*, *21*(6), 58–62. DOI: 10.1109/MIC.2017.4180835

Gebru, T., Morgenstern, J., Vecchione, B., Vaughan, J. W., Wallach, H., Daumé, H.III, & Crawford, K. (2018). Datasheets for Datasets. *ArXiv*. https://arxiv.org/abs/1803.09010

General Data Protection Regulation. (2018). Regulation (EU) 2016/679 of the European Parliament and of the Council of 27 April 2016, OJ L 119, 4.5.2016, p. 1–88.

Giddens, A. (1990). *The consequences of modernity*. Stanford University Press.

Gille, M., Tropmann-Frick, M., & Schomacker, T. (2024). Balancing public interest, fundamental rights, and innovation: The EU's governance model for non-high-risk AI systems. *Internet Policy Review*, *13*(3). Advance online publication. DOI: 10.14763/2024.3.1797

Gillespie, N., Lockey, S., Ward, T., Macdade, A., & Hassed, G. (2025). Trust, attitudes and use of artificial intelligence: A global study 2025. The University of Melbourne and KPMG. DOI: 10.26188/28822919

Gilpin, L. H., Bau, D., Yuan, B. Z., Bajwa, A., Specter, M., & Kagal, L. (2018). Explaining Explanations: An Overview of Interpretability of Machine Learning. *ArXiv*. https://arxiv.org/abs/1806.00069 DOI: 10.1109/DSAA.2018.00018

Goldstein, A., Kapelner, A., Bleich, J., & Pitkin, E. (2013). Peeking Inside the Black Box: Visualizing Statistical Learning with Plots of Individual Conditional Expectation. *ArXiv*. https://arxiv.org/abs/1309.6392

Google/DoubleClick. (2008). Case COMP/M.4731, Commission decision C 927 (European Commission).

Google/Fitbit. (2020). Case M.9660, Commission decision C 9105 (European Commission)

Grote, T., & Berens, P. (2020). On the ethics of algorithmic decision-making in healthcare. *Journal of Medical Ethics*, *46*(3), 205–211. DOI: 10.1136/medethics-2019-105586 PMID: 31748206

Guidotti, R. (2022). Counterfactual explanations and how to find them: Literature review and benchmarking. *Data Mining and Knowledge Discovery*, *38*(5), 2770–2824. DOI: 10.1007/s10618-022-00831-6

Guidotti, R., Monreale, A., Ruggieri, S., Turini, F., Giannotti, F., & Pedreschi, D. (2019). A survey of methods for explaining black box models. *ACM Computing Surveys*, *51*(5), 93. DOI: 10.1145/3236009

Gursoy, F., & Kakadiaris, I. A. (2022). System Cards for AI-Based Decision-Making for Public Policy. *ArXiv*. https://arxiv.org/abs/2203.04754

Hagendorff, T. (2022). Blind spots in AI ethics. *AI and Ethics*, *2*(4), 851–867. DOI: 10.1007/s43681-021-00122-8

Hase, P., Bansal, M., Kim, B., & Ghandeharioun, A. (2023). Does localization inform editing? Surprising differences in causality-based localization vs. knowledge editing in language models. *Advances in Neural Information Processing Systems*, *36*, 73429–73451. DOI: 10.48550/arXiv.2301.04213

Hassija, V., Chamola, V., Mahapatra, A., Singal, A., Goel, D., Huang, K., Scardapane, S., Spinelli, I., Mahmud, M., & Hussain, A. (2024). Interpreting black-box models: A review on Explainable Artificial Intelligence. *Cognitive Computation*, *16*(1), 45–74. DOI: 10.1007/s12559-023-10179-8

High-Level Advisory Body on Artificial Intelligence. (2024). Governing AI for humanity: Final report. United Nations. https://www.un.org/sites/un2.un.org/files/governing_ai_for_humanity_final_report_en.pdf

Hildt, E. (2025). What is the role of explainability in medical artificial intelligence? A case-based approach. *Bioengineering (Basel, Switzerland)*, *12*(4), 375. DOI: 10.3390/bioengineering12040375 PMID: 40281735

Hinterleitner, M., Knill, C., & Steinebach, Y. (2024). The growth of policies, rules, and regulations: A review of the literature and research agenda. *Regulation & Governance*, *18*(2), 637–654. DOI: 10.1111/rego.12511

Hohma, E., Boch, A., Trauth, R., & Lütge, C. (2023). Investigating accountability for artificial intelligence through risk governance: A workshop-based exploratory study. *Frontiers in Psychology*, *14*, 1073686. DOI: 10.3389/fpsyg.2023.1073686 PMID: 36760454

Holzinger, A., Saranti, A., Molnar, C., Biecek, P., & Samek, W. (2022). Explainable AI methods—A brief overview. In A. Holzinger, R. Goebel, R. Fong, T. Moon, K.-R. Müller, & W. Samek (Eds.), xxAI—Beyond Explainable AI (LNCS 13200, pp. 13–38). Springer. DOI: 10.1007/978-3-031-04083-2_2

Hong, S. R., Hullman, J., & Bertini, E. (2020). Human factors in model interpretability: Industry practices, challenges, and needs. *Proceedings of the ACM on Human-Computer Interaction, 4*(CSCW1), 1-26. DOI: 10.1145/3392878

Ibones, K. A., Enero, J. V., Jore, J. S., Mamhot, V. I., Matheu, C. M., Pacaldo, H. B. B., & Jardin, R. A. (2024). Enabling role of civil society organizations (CSOs) in local environmental management in the Philippines: A systematic review. *Journal of Civil Society*, *20*(4), 359–379. DOI: 10.1080/17448689.2024.2381826

Ijaiya, H. (2024). Harnessing AI for data privacy: Examining risks, opportunities and strategic future directions. *International Journal of Science and Research Archive*, *13*(2), 2878–2892. DOI: 10.30574/ijsra.2024.13.2.2510

Information Technology Act. (2000). (India).

ISACA. (2024). Using the Digital Trust Ecosystem Framework to achieve trustworthy AI [White paper]. ISACA. https://www.isaca.org/resources/white-papers/2024/using-dtef-to-achieve-trustworthy-ai

ISACA. (2025). Leveraging COBIT for effective AI system governance (White Paper). https://www.isaca.org/resources/white-papers/2025/leveraging-cobit-for-effective-ai-system-governance

Iseko, A. (2025). Diversity as Ethical Infrastructure: Reimagining AI Governance for Justice and Accountability. *International Journal of Science. Technology in Society*, *13*(5), 190–204.

Janssen, M., Brous, P., Estevez, E., Barbosa, L. S., & Janowski, T. (2020). Data governance: Organizing data for trustworthy artificial intelligence. *Government Information Quarterly*, *37*(3), 101493. Advance online publication. DOI: 10.1016/j.giq.2020.101493

Javed, A. (2025). Data Privacy and Security in AI-Driven Customer Platforms: A Cloud Computing Perspective. *European Journal of Computer Science and Information Technology*, *13*(44), 84–95. DOI: 10.37745/ejcsit.2013/vol13n448495

Jobin, A., Ienca, M., & Vayena, E. (2019). The global landscape of AI ethics guidelines. *Nature Machine Intelligence*, *1*(9), 389–399. DOI: 10.1038/s42256-019-0088-2

Johnk, J., Weissert, M., & Wyrtki, K. (2021). Ready or not, AI comes—An interview study of organizational AI readiness factors. *Business & Information Systems Engineering*, *63*(1), 5–20. DOI: 10.1007/s12599-020-00676-7

Justice K.S. Puttaswamy v. Union of India, (2019) 1 SCC 1 (India).

Kakarala, M. K., & Rongali, S. K. (2025). Data privacy and security in AI. *World Journal of Advanced Research and Reviews*, *25*(3), 2517–2523. DOI: 10.30574/wjarr.2025.25.3.0564

Kaneko, H. (2023). Interpretation of Machine Learning Models for Data Sets with Many Features Using Feature Importance. *ACS Omega*, *8*(25), 23218–23225. DOI: 10.1021/acsomega.3c03722 PMID: 37396269

Kashefi, P., Kashefi, Y., & Ghafouri Mirsaraei, A. (2024). Shaping the future of AI: Balancing innovation and ethics in global regulation. *Uniform Law Review*, *29*(3), 524–548. DOI: 10.1093/ulr/unae040

Kiden, S., Stahl, B., Townsend, B., Maple, C., Vincent, C., Sampson, F., . . . Yazdanpanah, V. (2024). Responsible AI governance: a response to UN interim report on governing AI for humanity. *arXiv preprint arXiv:2412.12108*.

Kirilenko, D., Barbiero, P., Gjoreski, M., Luštrek, M., & Langheinrich, M. (2024). Generative models for counterfactual explanations. *CEUR Workshop Proceedings*, *3841*, 1–15.

Knab, P., Marton, S., Schlegel, U., & Bartelt, C. (2025). Which LIME should I trust? Concepts, Challenges, and Solutions. *ArXiv*. https://arxiv.org/abs/2503.24365

Koene, A. (2019). A governance framework for algorithmic accountability and transparency. DOI: 10.2861/59990

Kokina, J., & Davenport, T. H. (2017). The emergence of artificial intelligence: How automation is changing auditing. *Journal of Emerging Technologies in Accounting*, *14*(1), 115–122. DOI: 10.2308/jeta-51730

Kolmodin, S. (2024). Collaboration to support refugees: The importance of local-level relations among civil society organizations. *Journal of Civil Society*, *20*(2), 130–149. DOI: 10.1080/17448689.2024.2319357

Kowald, D., Scher, S., Pammer-Schindler, V., Mullner, P., Waxnegger, K., Demelius, L., Fessl, A., Toller, M., Mendoza Estrada, I. G., Simic, I., Sabol, V., Trugler, A., Veas, E., Kern, R., Nad, T., & Kopeinik, S. (2024). Establishing and evaluating trustworthy AI: Overview and research challenges. *Frontiers in Big Data*, *7*, 1467222. Advance online publication. DOI: 10.3389/fdata.2024.1467222 PMID: 39677583

Krogh, A. H., & Lo, C. (2023). Robust emergency management: The role of institutional trust in organized volunteers. *Public Administration*, *101*(1), 142–157. DOI: 10.1111/padm.12894

Kulothungan, V., & Gupta, D. (2025). Towards adaptive AI governance: Comparative insights from the US, EU, and Asia. In *2025 IEEE 11th Conference on Big Data Security on Cloud (BigDataSecurity)* (pp. 32-38). IEEE.

Kumi, E., & Hayman, R. (2025). Can domestic resource mobilisation by civil society organisations (CSOs) open up civic space in the Global South? *Development in Practice*, *35*(4), 669–687. DOI: 10.1080/09614524.2025.2487791

Lens database (retrieved in 2025). *Scholar search: AI for compliance and data privacy* https://www.lens.org/lens/search/scholar/list?q=ai%20for%20compliance%20and%20data%20privacy

Levine, A. C., Park, A., Adhikari, A., Alejandria, M. C. P., Bradlow, B. H., Lopez-Portillo, M. F., Mutwafy, S., Zumbyte, I., & Heller, P. (2023). The role of civil society organizations (CSOs) in the COVID-19 response across the Global South: A multinational, qualitative study. *PLOS Global Public Health*, *3*(9), e0002341. DOI: 10.1371/journal.pgph.0002341 PMID: 37708149

Li, Y., Xu, M., Miao, X., Zhou, S., & Qian, T. (2023). *Prompting large language models for counterfactual generation: An empirical study* (arXiv:2305.14791). *arXiv*. https://arxiv.org/abs/2305.14791

Li, F., Wu, P., Ong, H. H., Peterson, J. F., Wei, W. Q., & Zhao, J. (2023). Evaluating and mitigating bias in machine learning models for cardiovascular disease prediction. *Journal of Biomedical Informatics*, *138*, 104294. DOI: 10.1016/j.jbi.2023.104294 PMID: 36706849

Lim, E. C. N., & Lim, C. E. D. (2025). Polycentric AI Governance: A Multi-Stakeholder Approach to Distributed Responsibility and Ethical Technology Management. *International Journal of Advanced AI Applications*, *1*(4), 77–97.

Linardatos, P., Papastefanopoulos, V., & Kotsiantis, S. (2020). Explainable AI: A Review of Machine Learning Interpretability Methods. *Entropy (Basel, Switzerland)*, *23*(1), 18. DOI: 10.3390/e23010018 PMID: 33375658

Longo, L., Brcic, M., Cabitza, F., Choi, J., Confalonieri, R., Del Ser, J., Guidotti, R., Hayashi, Y., Herrera, F., Holzinger, A., Jiang, R., Khosravi, H., Lecue, F., Malgieri, G., Páez, A., Samek, W., Schneider, J., Speith, T., & Stumpf, S. (2024). Explainable Artificial Intelligence (XAI) 2.0: A manifesto of open challenges and interdisciplinary research directions. *Information Fusion*, *106*, 102301. DOI: 10.1016/j.inffus.2024.102301

Lore, F., Basile, P., Appice, A., De Gemmis, M., Malerba, D., & Semeraro, G. (2023). An AI framework to support decisions on GDPR compliance. *Journal of Intelligent Information Systems*, *61*(2), 541–568. DOI: 10.1007/s10844-023-00782-4

Lukács, A., & Váradi, S. (2023). GDPR-compliant AI-based automated decision-making in the world of work. In *Elsevier Ltd* (Vol. 50, p. 105848). Computer Law & Security Review. [Journal-article], DOI: 10.1016/j.clsr.2023.105848

Lund, B., Orhan, Z., Mannuru, N. R., Bevara, R. V. K., Porter, B., Vinaih, M. K., & Bhaskara, P. (2025). Standards, frameworks, and legislation for artificial intelligence (AI) transparency. *AI and Ethics*, *5*(4), 3639–3655. Advance online publication. DOI: 10.1007/s43681-025-00661-4

Lundberg, S. M., Erion, G., Chen, H., DeGrave, A., Prutkin, J. M., Nair, B., Katz, R., Himmelfarb, J., Bansal, N., & Lee, S.-I. (2022). From local explanations to global understanding with Explainable AI for trees. *Nature Machine Intelligence*, *2*(1), 56–67. DOI: 10.1038/s42256-019-0138-9 PMID: 32607472

Lu, Q., Zhu, L., Xu, X., Whittle, J., Douglas, D., & Sandison, C. (2023). Responsible AI pattern catalogue: A collection of best practices for AI governance and engineering. *ACM Computing Surveys*, *56*(7), 167. Advance online publication. DOI: 10.1145/3626234

Maddali, R. (2024). AI-powered data security frameworks for regulatory compliance (GDPR, CCPA, HIPAA). *International Journal of Engineering Technology Research & Management*, 1–22. https://doi.org/DOI: 10.5281/zenodo.15072096

Maguluri, K. K. (2024). Advancing Patient Privacy in the Era of Artificial Intelligence: A Deep Learning Approach to Ensuring Compliance with HIPAA and Addressing Ethical Challenges in Healthcare Data Security. https://doi.org/DOI: 10.47059/IJMTLM/V27I5/030

Malone, D., & Turner, J. (2010). The merger of AOL and Time Warner: A case study. *Journal of the International Academy for Case Studies*, *16*(7).

Mandayam, N. (2024, November 18). India restricts WhatsApp sharing data with other Meta entities, imposes 25.4 million dollar fine. *Reuters*.

Marriott International/Starwood Hotels & Resorts Worldwide. (2016). Case M.7902, Commission decision C 4097 (European Commission).

Mbah, N. G. O.Geraldine O Mbah. (2024). Data privacy in the era of AI: Navigating regulatory landscapes for global businesses. *International Journal of Science and Research Archive*, *13*(2), 2040–2058. DOI: 10.30574/ijsra.2024.13.2.2396

McKeague, L. K., & Bies, A. L. (2025). Nonprofits and Interest Groups in Crisis Management. In *Oxford Research Encyclopedia of Politics*. DOI: 10.1093/acrefore/9780190228637.013.1530

McKinsey & Company. (2024). The state of AI in early 2024: AI adoption surges but foundational challenges remain. McKinsey Global Institute. https://www.mckinsey.com/capabilities/quantumblack/our-insights/the-state-of-ai

Mehrabi, N., Morstatter, F., Saxena, N., Lerman, K., & Galstyan, A. (2021). A survey on bias and fairness in machine learning. *ACM Computing Surveys*, *54*(6), 115. DOI: 10.1145/3457607

Mello Rose, F. (2022). Activity types, thematic domains, and stakeholder constellations: Explaining civil society involvement in Amsterdam's smart city. *European Planning Studies*, *30*(6), 975–993. DOI: 10.1080/09654313.2021.1914556

Meng, K., Bau, D., Andonian, A., & Belinkov, Y. (2022). Locating and editing factual associations in GPT. *Advances in Neural Information Processing Systems*, *35*, 17359–17372. DOI: 10.48550/arXiv.2202.05262

Mikalef, P., Conboy, K., Lundstrom, J. E., & Popovic, A. (2022). Thinking responsibly about responsible AI and 'the dark side' of AI. *European Journal of Information Systems*, *31*(3), 257–268. DOI: 10.1080/0960085X.2022.2026621

Mir, G., Durrani, N., Julian, R., Kimei, Y., Mashreky, S., & Doan, T. D. (2024). Social inclusion and sustainable development: Findings from Seven African and Asian contexts. *Sustainability (Basel), 16*(11), 4859. DOI: 10.3390/su16114859

Mirishli, S. (2024). Ethical Implications of AI in Data Collection: Balancing Innovation with Privacy. *ANCIENT LAND, 6*(8), 40–55. DOI: 10.36719/2706-6185/38/40-55

Mishra, D. (2024). Strategic Communication for AI-Driven Sustainability Initiatives: Bridging Technology, Policy, and Public Engagement in Achieving SDGs. In *AI applications for clean energy and sustainability* (pp. 187-211). IGI Global.

Misra, P., & Tiwari, N. Georgia Institute of Technology, & Bansal Institute of Science and Technology. (2022). Impact of machine learning techniques in Privacy compliance. *Turkish Journal of Computer and Mathematics Education*, 746–760. https://www.researchgate.net/publication/365519178

Mitchell, M., Wu, S., Zaldivar, A., Barnes, P., Vasserman, L., Hutchinson, B., Spitzer, E., Raji, I. D., & Gebru, T. (2018). *Model Cards for Model Reporting*. ArXiv., DOI: 10.1145/3287560.3287596

Mizrak, K. C. (2024). Crisis management and risk mitigation: Strategies for effective response and resilience. *Trends, challenges, and practices in contemporary strategic management*, 254-278. DOI: DOI: 10.4018/979-8-3693-1155-4.ch013

Moll, J., & Yigitbasioglu, O. (2019). The role of internet-related technologies in shaping the work of accountants: New directions for accounting research. *The British Accounting Review, 51*(6), 100833. DOI: 10.1016/j.bar.2019.04.002

Moraes, T. (2025). Regulatory sandboxes for trustworthy artificial intelligence–global and Latin American experiences. *International Review of Law Computers & Technology, 39*(1), 55–74. DOI: 10.1080/13600869.2024.2351674

Moya, J., & Goenechea, M. (2022). An approach to the unified conceptualization, definition, and characterization of social resilience. *International Journal of Environmental Research and Public Health, 19*(9), 5746. DOI: 10.3390/ijerph19095746 PMID: 35565141

Moyo, T. M., Tafirenyika, S., Tuboalabo, A., Taiwo, A. E., Bukhari, T. T., & Ajayi, A. E. (2023). Cloud-Based knowledge management systems with AI-Enhanced compliance and data privacy safeguards. *ESIC Market Economics and Business Journal, 4*(2), 67–77. DOI: 10.54660/IJMFD.2023.4.2.67-77

Murdoch, W. J., Singh, C., Kumbier, K., & Yu, B. (2019). *Interpretable machine learning: Definitions, methods, and applications*. ArXiv., DOI: 10.1073/pnas.1900654116

Nair, J. (2024). Reconfiguration and transformation for resilience: Building service organizations towards sustainability. *Journal of Services Marketing*, *38*(4), 404–425. DOI: 10.1108/JSM-04-2023-0144

Nasibov, M. (2021). Civil Society and Pro-Democracy Social Movements: Troubled Relations Within Authoritarian Regimes? *Frontiers in Political Science*, *3*, 708872. DOI: 10.3389/fpos.2021.708872

National Institute of Standards and Technology. (2023). *Artificial Intelligence Risk Management Framework (AI RMF 1.0)*. U.S. Department of Commerce.

NIST AI RMF. (2023). Artificial intelligence risk management framework (AI RMF 1.0). *URL:* https://nvlpubs.nist.gov/nistpubs/ai/nist.ai.100-1.pdf

Njoku, E. T. (2022). Strategic exclusion, co-option and containment: Towards an integrative theory of state-CSOs relations. *Critical Studies on Terrorism*, *15*(4), 917–944. DOI: 10.1080/17539153.2022.2111776

OECD AI Principles. (2019). OECD Recommendation on Artificial Intelligence. OECD. URL: https://www.oecd.org/en/topics/sub-issues/ai-principles.html

OECD. (2019). *OECD principles on artificial intelligence*. OECD Publishing.

OECD. (2024). Recommendation of the Council on artificial intelligence (OECD/LEGAL/0449). Organisation for Economic Co-operation and Development. https://legalinstruments.oecd.org/en/instruments/OECD-LEGAL-0449

Onoja, J. P., Hamza, O., Collins, A., Chibunna, U. B., Eweja, A., & Daraojimba, A. I. (2021). Digital Transformation and Data Governance: Strategies for regulatory compliance and secure AI-Driven business operations. *ESIC Market Economics and Business Journal*, *2*(1), 43–55. DOI: 10.54660/.IJFMR.2021.2.1.43-55

Organisation for Economic Co-operation and Development. (2019). *OECD SME and Entrepreneurship Outlook 2019*. OECD Publishing.

Organisation for Economic Co-operation and Development. (2021). *The digital transformation of SMEs*. OECD Publishing.

Ortigossa, E., Gonçalves, T., & Nonato, L. (2024). EXplainable Artificial Intelligence (XAI)–From Theory to Methods and Applications. *IEEE Access : Practical Innovations, Open Solutions*, *12*, 80799–80846. DOI: 10.1109/ACCESS.2024.3409843

Panigutti, C., Hamon, R., Hupont, I., Fernandez Llorca, D., Fano Yela, D., Junklewitz, H., Scalzo, S., Mazzini, G., Sanchez, I., Soler Garrido, J., & Gomez, E. (2023). The role of explainable AI in the context of the AI Act. In *Proceedings of the 2023 ACM Conference on Fairness, Accountability, and Transparency (FAccT '23)* (pp. 1139–1150). ACM. DOI: 10.1145/3593013.3594069

Papagiannidis, E., Enholm, I. M., Dremel, C., Mikalef, P., & Krogstie, J. (2023). Toward AI governance: Identifying best practices and potential barriers and outcomes. *Information Systems Frontiers*, *25*(1), 123–141. DOI: 10.1007/s10796-022-10251-y PMID: 35464171

Papagiannidis, E., Mikalef, P., & Conboy, K. (2025). Responsible artificial intelligence governance: A review and research framework. *The Journal of Strategic Information Systems*, *34*(2), 101885. Advance online publication. DOI: 10.1016/j.jsis.2024.101885

Perboli, G., Simionato, N., & Pratali, S. (2025). Navigating the AI regulatory landscape: Balancing innovation, ethics, and global governance. *Economic and Political Studies*, *13*(4), 367–397. DOI: 10.1080/20954816.2025.2569584

Pitidis, V., Coaffee, J., & Lima-Silva, F. (2024). Advancing equitable 'resilience imaginaries' in the Global South through dialogical participatory mapping: Experiences from informal communities in Brazil. *Cities (London, England)*, *150*, 105015. DOI: 10.1016/j.cities.2024.105015

Power, M. (2021). The microfoundations of the audit society: Organizations and the logic of the audit trail. *Academy of Management Review*, *46*(3), 489–506. DOI: 10.5465/amr.2018.0151

PubMed. *Scholar search: AI for compliance and data privacy* https://pubmed.ncbi.nlm.nih.gov/?term=ai+for+compliance+and+data+privacy&sort_order=asc

Radanliev, P. (2025). AI Ethics: Integrating Transparency, Fairness, and Privacy in AI Development. *Applied Artificial Intelligence*, *39*(1), 2463722. Advance online publication. DOI: 10.1080/08839514.2025.2463722

Rahwan, I. (2018). Society-in-the-loop: Programming the algorithmic social contract. *Ethics and Information Technology*, *20*(1), 5–14. DOI: 10.1007/s10676-017-9430-8

Rai, A. (2020). Explainable AI: From black box to glass box. *Journal of the Academy of Marketing Science*, *48*(1), 137–141. DOI: 10.1007/s11747-019-00710-5

Rai, A., Hurley, M. E., Herrington, J., Storch, E. A., Zampella, C. J., Parrish-Morris, J., Sonig, A., Lázaro-Muñoz, G., & Kostick-Quenet, K. (2025). Stakeholder Criteria for Trust in Artificial Intelligence-Based Computer Perception Tools in Health Care: Qualitative Interview Study. *Journal of Medical Internet Research*, *27*, e78757. DOI: 10.2196/78757 PMID: 41385782

Raisch, S., & Krakowski, S. (2021). Artificial intelligence and management: The automation–augmentation paradox. *Academy of Management Review*, *46*(1), 192–210. DOI: 10.5465/amr.2018.0072

Raji, I. D., Smart, A., White, R. N., Mitchell, M., Gebru, T., Hutchinson, B., & Barnes, P. (2020). Closing the AI accountability gap: Defining an end-to-end framework for internal algorithmic auditing. In *Proceedings of the 2020 conference on fairness, accountability, and transparency* (pp. 33-44). DOI: 10.1145/3351095.3372873

Rajpurkar, P., Chen, E., Banerjee, O., & Topol, E. J. (2022). AI in health and medicine. *Nature Medicine*, *28*(1), 31–38. DOI: 10.1038/s41591-021-01614-0 PMID: 35058619

Ramachandran, M. (2025). Quality Assurance Framework for AI Ethics by Design. In *Engineering Ethics of AI by Design: Principles, Practices, and Frameworks for Responsible Artificial Intelligence* (pp. 623–687). Springer Nature Singapore.

Ramanathan, R., He, Q., Black, A., Ghobadian, A., & Gallear, D. (2017). Environmental regulations, innovation and firm performance: A revisit of the Porter hypothesis. *Journal of Cleaner Production*, *155*, 79–92. DOI: 10.1016/j.jclepro.2016.08.116

Räuker, T., Ho, A., Casper, S., & Hadfield-Menell, D. (2023). Toward transparent AI: A survey on interpreting the inner structures of deep neural networks. In *2023 IEEE Conference on Secure and Trustworthy Machine Learning (SaTML)* (pp. 464–483). IEEE. DOI: 10.1109/SaTML54575.2023.00039

Regulation (EU) 2023/2854 (2023). of the European Parliament and of the Council of 13 December 2023 on harmonised rules on fair access to and use of data (Data Act), OJ L 363, 22.12.2023, p. 1–115.

Regulation (EU) 2024/1689 (2024). of the European Parliament and of the Council of 13 June 2024 laying down harmonised rules on artificial intelligence (AI Act), OJ L 188, 12.7.2024, p. 1–120.

Reis, O., Okpeke, F., Attipoe, V., & Oluoha, O. M. (2023). A Privacy-First framework for data protection and compliance assurance in digital ecosystems. *Iconic Research and Engineering Journals*, *7*(4), 620–621. https://www.researchgate.net/publication/395415430

Reyes, M., Meier, R., Pereira, S., Silva, C. A., Dahlweid, F.-M., Tengg-Kobligk, H. V., Summers, R. M., & Wiest, R. (2022). On the interpretability of artificial intelligence in radiology: Challenges and opportunities. *Radiology. Artificial Intelligence*, *2*(3), e190043. DOI: 10.1148/ryai.2020190043 PMID: 32510054

Riboldi, M. (2024). The Loci of Power and Connection: A framework for exploring the democratic relationships of civil society organisations. *Interest Groups & Advocacy*, *13*(2), 244–263. DOI: 10.1057/s41309-024-00209-7

Roberts, C. V., Elahi, E., & Chandrashekar, A. (2022). On the Bias-Variance Characteristics of LIME and SHAP in High Sparsity Movie Recommendation Explanation Tasks. *ArXiv*. https://arxiv.org/abs/2206.04784

Roberts, H., Hine, E., Taddeo, M., & Floridi, L. (2024). Global AI governance: Barriers and pathways forward. *International Affairs*, *100*(3), 1275–1286. DOI: 10.1093/ia/iiae073

Rodríguez-Pérez, R., & Bajorath, J. (2022). Evolution of support vector machine and regression modeling in chemoinformatics and drug discovery. *Journal of Computer-Aided Molecular Design*, *36*(5), 355–362. DOI: 10.1007/s10822-022-00442-9 PMID: 35304657

Rudin, C., Chen, C., Chen, Z., Huang, H., Semenova, L., & Zhong, C. (2022). Interpretable machine learning: Fundamental principles and 10 grand challenges. *Statistics Surveys*, *16*(none), 1–85. DOI: 10.1214/21-SS133

Russell, S., & Norvig, P. (2021). *Artificial Intelligence* (Global Edition). Pearson Education.

Saifullah, S., Mercier, D., Lucieri, A., Dengel, A., & Ahmed, S. (2024). The privacy-explainability trade-off: Unraveling the impacts of differential privacy and federated learning on attribution methods. *Frontiers in Artificial Intelligence*, *7*, 1236947. DOI: 10.3389/frai.2024.1236947 PMID: 39021435

Sajjadi, M., Kara, B., Eyupoglu, C., & Karakuş, O. (2025). A survey on hallucination in large language models: Definitions, detection, and mitigation (Preprint). *Preprints*. DOI: 10.20944/preprints202510.0540.v1

Salih, A., Boscolo Galazzo, I., Raisi-Estabragh, Z., Lekadir, K., Menegaz, G., & Petersen, S. E. (2025). A perspective on Explainable Artificial Intelligence methods: SHAP and LIME. *Advanced Intelligent Systems*, *7*(1), e202400304. DOI: 10.1002/aisy.202400304

Salvador, M., & Sancho, D. (2023). Local governments facing turbulence: Robust governance and institutional capacities. *Social Sciences (Basel, Switzerland)*, *12*(8), 462. DOI: 10.3390/socsci12080462

Samant, P. S. (2024). Leveraging ai for enhanced compliance with global data protection regulations in cloud computing environments. *International Research Journal of Modernization in Engineering Technology and Science*. Advance online publication. DOI: 10.56726/IRJMETS53514

Samaratunge, R., & Alam, Q. (2021). Accountability and transparency in emerging countries: Governance, democratic currents and change. *Public Administration and Development*, *41*(4), 147–156. DOI: 10.1002/pad.1963

Sander, P. (2016). *Using learning analytics to predict academic outcomes of students*. University of Oregon Scholars Bank.

Sangaraju, V. V. (2025). AI and Data Privacy in Healthcare: Compliance with HIPAA, GDPR, and emerging regulations. *International Journal of Emerging Trends in Computer Science and Information Technology*, 67–74. https://doi.org/DOI: 10.56472/ICCSAIML25-108

Saraswathy, B. (2019). The Flipkart–Walmart deal: A look into competition and other related issues. *Antitrust Bulletin*, *64*(1), 136–147. DOI: 10.1177/0003603X18823619

Schiuma, G., & Santarsiero, F. (2024). *Open Innovation Labs*. Springer. DOI: 10.1007/978-3-031-75533-0

Schrems, M. (2020). Facebook Ireland Limited v. Maximilian Schrems (Schrems II), Case C-311/18, ECLI:EU:C:2020:559 (Court of Justice of the European Union).

Scott, W. R. (2014). *Institutions and organizations: Ideas, interests, and identities* (4th ed.). SAGE.

Securities and Exchange Commission v. Yahoo, SEC Release No. 33-10485 (2018).

Seth, P., & Sankarapu, V. K. (2025). *Bridging the gap in XAI: Why reliable metrics matter for explainability and compliance* (arXiv:2502.04695). *arXiv*. https://arxiv.org/abs/2502.04695

Shah, I. H. (2025, July 22). Investigating the risks of algorithmic bias and explainability failures in credit risk models. *SSRN*. DOI: 10.2139/ssrn.5361937

Shanley, D., Hogenboom, J., Lysen, F., Wee, L., Lobo Gomes, A., Dekker, A., & Meacham, D. (2024). Getting real about synthetic data ethics: Are AI ethics principles a good starting point for synthetic data ethics? *EMBO Reports*, *25*(5), 2152–2155. DOI: 10.1038/s44319-024-00101-0 PMID: 38388694

Shin, D. (2021). The effects of explainability and causability on perception, trust, and acceptance: Implications for explainable AI. *International Journal of Human-Computer Studies*, *146*, 102551. Advance online publication. DOI: 10.1016/j.ijhcs.2020.102551

Shin, D., & Park, Y. J. (2019). Role of fairness, accountability, and transparency in algorithmic affordance. *Computers in Human Behavior*, *98*, 277–284. DOI: 10.1016/j.chb.2019.04.019

Shneiderman, B. (2020). Human-centered artificial intelligence: Reliable, safe & trustworthy. *International Journal of Human-Computer Interaction*, *36*(6), 495–504. DOI: 10.1080/10447318.2020.1741118

Sian, S., & Roberts, C. (2009). UK small owner-managed businesses: Accounting and financial reporting needs. *Journal of Small Business and Enterprise Development*, *16*(2), 289–305. DOI: 10.1108/14626000910956065

Sides, T., Kbaier, D., Farrell, T., & Third, A. (2025). Bridging trust gaps: Stakeholder perspectives on AI adoption in the United Kingdom NHS primary care. *Digital Health*, *11*, 20552076251386706. DOI: 10.1177/20552076251386706 PMID: 41323094

Sidhpurwala, H., Fox, E., Mollett, G., Gabarda, F. C., & Zhukov, R. (2025). Blueprints of Trust: AI System Cards for End to End Transparency and Governance. *ArXiv*. https://arxiv.org/abs/2509.20394

Skliarov, M., Shawi, R. E., Dhaoui, C., & Ahmed, N. (2025). A comparative evaluation of explainability techniques for image data. *Scientific Reports*, *15*(1), 41898. DOI: 10.1038/s41598-025-25839-y PMID: 41290895

Smidt, H., Johansson, J., & Richter, T. (2025). Civil society under attack: The consequences for horizontal accountability institutions. *Studies in Comparative International Development*, *60*(1), 81–110. DOI: 10.1007/s12116-023-09423-x

Sresth, V., Srivastava, A., & Tiwari, S. (2021). Balancing innovation and security: Advancing data privacy in the age of artificial intelligence and machine learning. *World Journal of Advanced Research and Reviews*, *9*(3), 377–390. DOI: 10.30574/wjarr.2021.9.3.0079

Srikrishna Committee. (2018). *A free and fair digital economy: Protecting privacy, empowering Indians*. Government of India.

Star, S. L., & Griesemer, J. R. (1989). Institutional ecology, 'translations' and boundary objects: Amateurs and professionals in Berkeley's Museum of Vertebrate Zoology, 1907–39. *Social Studies of Science*, *19*(3), 387–420. DOI: 10.1177/030631289019003001

Stupak, I., Mansoor, M., & Smith, C. T. (2021). Conceptual framework for increasing legitimacy and trust of sustainability governance. *Energy, Sustainability and Society, 11*(1), 5. DOI: 10.1186/s13705-021-00280-x PMID: 33758740

Sun, N., Miao, Y., Jiang, H., Ding, M., & Zhang, J. (2024). From principles to practice: A deep dive into AI ethics and regulations. arXiv preprint arXiv:2412.04683.

Sundaram, A. (2004). Mergers and acquisitions and corporate governance. In *Advances in mergers & acquisitions*. DOI: 10.1016/S1479-361X(04)03009-1

Suresh Babu, C. V. Sudhir Manoharan., L., G. K., & V., S. K. (2024). Application of Support Vector Machine Algorithm in Automated Lending Protocols for Decentralized Finance Platforms. In L. Vardari & I. Qabrati (Eds.), Decentralized Finance and Tokenization in FinTech (pp. 1-20). IGI Global. DOI: 10.4018/979-8-3693-3346-4.ch001

Suresh Babu, C. V., Kowsika, S., Sai Tejaswi, M., Janarakshani, T. R., & Mercysha Princy, S. (2023). Framework for Detection of Cyberbullying in Text Data Using Natural Language Processing and Machine Learning. In Chitadze, N. (Ed.), *Cyber Security Policies and Strategies of the World's Leading States* (pp. 69–85). IGI Global., DOI: 10.4018/978-1-6684-8846-1.ch005

Susser, D., Schiff, D. S., Gerke, S., Cabrera, L. Y., Cohen, I. G., Doerr, M., Harrod, J., Kostick-Quenet, K., McNealy, J., Meyer, M. N., Price, W. N.II, & Wagner, J. K. (2024). Synthetic health data: Real ethical promise and peril. *The Hastings Center Report, 54*(5), 8–13. DOI: 10.1002/hast.4911 PMID: 39487776

Sutton, S. G., Holt, M., & Arnold, V. (2016). The reports of my death are greatly exaggerated—Artificial intelligence research in accounting. *International Journal of Accounting Information Systems, 22*, 60–73. DOI: 10.1016/j.accinf.2016.07.005

Syal, R., van Wessel, M., & Sahoo, S. (2021). Collaboration, co-optation or navigation? The role of civil society in disaster governance in India. *Voluntas, 32*(4), 795–808. DOI: 10.1007/s11266-021-00344-8

Talati, N. D. V.Dhruvitkumar V Talati. (2022). Enhancing data security and regulatory compliance in AI-driven cloud ecosystems: Strategies for advanced information governance. *World Journal of Advanced Research and Reviews, 15*(3), 579–594. DOI: 10.30574/wjarr.2022.15.3.0905

Templin, T., Fort, S., Padmanabham, P., Seshadri, P., Rimal, R., Oliva, J., Hassmiller Lich, K., Sylvia, S., & Sinnott-Armstrong, N. (2025). Framework for bias evaluation in large language models in healthcare settings. *NPJ Digital Medicine, 8*(1), 414. DOI: 10.1038/s41746-025-01786-w PMID: 40624264

Thiebes, S., Lins, S., & Sunyaev, A. (2021). Trustworthy artificial intelligence. *Electronic Markets*, *31*(2), 447–464. DOI: 10.1007/s12525-020-00441-4

Toorajipour, R., Sohrabpour, V., Nazarpour, A., Oghazi, P., & Fischl, M. (2021). Artificial intelligence in supply chain management: A systematic literature review. *Journal of Business Research*, *122*, 502–517. DOI: 10.1016/j.jbusres.2020.09.009

Trinh, T. K., & Zhang, D. (2024). Algorithmic fairness in financial decision-making: Detection and mitigation of bias in credit scoring applications. *Journal of Advanced Computing Systems*, *4*(2), 36–49. DOI: 10.69987/JACS.2024.40204

Unesco. (2022). *Recommendation on the ethics of artificial intelligence*. United Nations Educational, Scientific and Cultural Organization.

UNESCO. (2022). Recommendation on the ethics of artificial intelligence. United Nations Educational, Scientific and Cultural Organization. https://unesdoc.unesco.org/ark:/48223/pf0000380455

Utomi, N. E., Osifowokan, N. S., Donkor, N. A., & Yowetu, N. I. A. (2024). Evaluating the Impact of Data Protection Compliance on AI Development and Deployment in the U.S. Health sector. *World Journal of Advanced Research and Reviews*, *24*(2), 1100–1110. DOI: 10.30574/wjarr.2024.24.2.3398

Uyar, A., Nimer, K., Kuzey, C., Shahbaz, M., & Schneider, F. (2020). Can e-government initiatives alleviate corruption? The moderating effect of financial development. *Technological Forecasting and Social Change*, *157*, 120055. DOI: 10.1016/j.techfore.2020.120055

Van Wessel, M., Naz, F., & Sahoo, S. (2021). Complementarities in CSO Collaborations: How working with diversity produces advantages. *Voluntas*, *32*(4), 717–730. DOI: 10.1007/s11266-020-00227-4

Vasarhelyi, M. A., Kogan, A., & Tuttle, B. M. (2020). Big data in accounting: An overview. *Accounting Horizons*, *34*(2), 1–14.

Veale, M., & Borgesius, F. Z. (2021). Demystifying the draft EU artificial intelligence act. *arXiv preprint arXiv:2107.03721*. DOI: 10.31235/osf.io/38p5f

Vetter, D., Amann, J., Bruneault, F., Coffee, M., Dudder, B., Gallucci, A., Gilbert, T. K., Hagendorff, T., van Halem, I., Hickman, E., Hildt, E., Holm, S., Kararigas, G., Kringen, P., Madai, V. I., Wiinblad Mathez, E., Tithi, J. J., Westerlund, M., Wurth, R., & Zicari, R. V. (2023). Lessons learned from assessing trustworthy AI in practice. *Digital Society : Ethics, Socio-Legal and Governance of Digital Technology*, *2*(3), 35. Advance online publication. DOI: 10.1007/s44206-023-00063-1

VOSViewer. (https://www.vosviewer.com/)

Wachter, S., Mittelstadt, B., & Russell, C. (2021). Counterfactual explanations without opening the black box: Automated decisions and the GDPR. *SSRN*, *31*(2), 841–887. DOI: 10.2139/ssrn.3063289

Wan, A., Bommasani, R., Hashimoto, T., Henderson, P., Liang, P., & Percy, S. (2025). The 2025 Foundation Model Transparency Index. Stanford University Center for Research on Foundation Models. https://crfm.stanford.edu/fmti/December-2025/paper.pdf

Wang, B., Zhou, J., Li, Y., & Chen, F. (2023, November). Impact of fidelity and robustness of machine learning explanations on user trust. In Australasian Joint Conference on Artificial Intelligence (pp. 209-220). Singapore: Springer Nature Singapore.

Wang, D., Yang, Q., Abdul, A., & Lim, B. Y. (2019). Designing theory-driven user-centric explainable AI. In *Proceedings of the 2019 CHI conference on human factors in computing systems* (pp. 1-15).

Wieringa, M. (2020). What to account for when accounting for algorithms: A systematic literature review on algorithmic accountability. In *Proceedings of the 2020 Conference on Fairness, Accountability, and Transparency* (pp. 1–18). ACM. DOI: 10.1145/3351095.3372833

Willems, J. (2021). Accountability and transparency: cornerstones of civil society governance. In *Research handbook on nonprofit governance* (pp. 46–70). Edward Elgar Publishing., DOI: 10.4337/9781788114912.00012

Williamson, A. K., Kingston, K. L., & Bennison, L. (2022). Similar or different? Downward accountability across civil society organisational forms. *Voluntas*, *33*(5), 1002–1014. DOI: 10.1007/s11266-021-00441-8

Wiratsin, I., Rahman, R., & Hanafusa, H. (2025). Effectiveness of explainable artificial intelligence (XAI) in improving human trust in machine learning models: A systematic literature review. *IEEE Access : Practical Innovations, Open Solutions*, *55*(3), 1–15. DOI: 10.1109/ACCESS.2025.3575022

Wojczewski, S., Grohma, P., & Kutalek, R. (2023). Risk communication and community engagement with vulnerable groups: Perceptions of social-services CSOs during Covid-19. *International Journal of Disaster Risk Reduction*, *94*, 103817. DOI: 10.1016/j.ijdrr.2023.103817 PMID: 37360248

World Bank. (2020). *World Development Report 2020: Trading for development in the age of global value chains*. World Bank.

Ye, R., & Chen, J. (2025). *Unlocking the black box: A five-dimensional framework for evaluating explainable AI in credit risk* (arXiv:2511.04980). *arXiv*. https://arxiv.org/abs/2511.04980

Zerilli, J., Bhatt, U., & Weller, A. (2022). How transparency modulates trust in artificial intelligence. *Patterns (New York, N.Y.)*, *3*(4), 100455. DOI: 10.1016/j.patter.2022.100455 PMID: 35465233

Zhang, A. (2024). Empowering and Centering Impacted Stakeholders in AI Design. In *Companion Publication of the 2024 Conference on Computer-Supported Cooperative Work and Social Computing* (pp. 50-53). DOI: 10.1145/3678884.3682053

Zhao, H., Yang, F., Liu, N., Deng, H., Cai, H., Wang, S., Yin, D., Du, M., & Chen, H. (2024). Explainability for large language models: A survey. *ACM Transactions on Intelligent Systems and Technology*, *15*(2), 20. DOI: 10.1145/3639372

Zheng, E. L., Jin, W., Hamarneh, G., & Lee, S. S. J. (2024). From human-in-the-loop to human-in-power. *The American Journal of Bioethics : AJOB*, *24*(9), 84–86. DOI: 10.1080/15265161.2024.2377139 PMID: 39226019

About the Contributors

Otmane Azeroual is a world-renowned senior researcher, lecturer, and thought leader in digital transformation, artificial intelligence, and advanced data-driven research infrastructures. His groundbreaking interdisciplinary work at the nexus of computer science, higher education research, innovation management, and industry has set new standards in how data and AI reshape science and society. His research on the design, deployment, and critical evaluation of Current Research Information Systems (CRIS) — combined with cutting-edge AI-powered analytics — is internationally acclaimed and among the most cited in the field. Dr. Azeroual's pioneering contributions drive the evolution of intelligent data ecosystems that empower Open Science, elevate transparency, and revolutionize strategic decision-making in science policy worldwide. Holding a Ph.D. in Engineering Informatics and a robust foundation in business information systems and software engineering, he has authored numerous high-impact publications in top-tier journals and has been a sought-after keynote and plenary speaker at prestigious global conferences. His expertise is recognized by editorial boards and scientific committees internationally, where he shapes the future agenda of research data science. Bridging academia and private industry, Dr. Azeroual uniquely fuses rigorous theoretical insight with practical innovation. His leadership in both sectors fuels transformative digital strategies and sustainable technological solutions. As an inspiring educator, he equips emerging researchers and professionals with cutting-edge knowledge in AI, data science, research analytics, and project management — preparing them to excel in complex, dynamic environments. Passionate about harnessing AI for evidence-based governance, Dr. Azeroual actively collaborates across disciplines to build resilient, transparent, and data-driven research infrastructures that set global benchmarks. His visionary work not only advances scientific understanding but also catalyzes paradigm shifts that benefit institutions, governments, and society at large.

***

Ulfa Afifah earned a Master of Accounting degree from Gadjah Mada University in 2018. Since 2019, the author has been serving as a full-time faculty member in the Department of Accounting, Faculty of Economics and Business, University of Riau. The author's teaching responsibilities encompass a range of subjects within Management Accounting, Taxation, and Auditing, including Cost Accounting, Management Accounting, Business and Professional Ethics, Corporate Budgeting, Leadership and Ethics, Value Added Tax and Luxury Goods Sales Tax, and Audit Practice. In addition, the author is actively involved in several community services that focus on the utilization and development of financial technology in Small and Medium Enterprises.

Susanta Das is a seasoned educator with a proven record of teaching and mentoring diverse students, working at multiple institutions, and providing service to the various initiatives of organizations. He received his Ph.D. and M.A. degrees from Western Michigan University (WMU), USA, and M.Sc. degree from Banaras Hindu University (BHU), India all in Physics. He continued his research as a Marie-Curie post-doctoral fellow at Stockholm University, Stockholm, Sweden on beam diagnostics for the DESIREE (Double ElectroStatic Ion Ring ExpEriment) in the project DITANET (Diagnostic Techniques for particle Accelerators – a Marie-Curie initial training NETwork), at the Indian Institute of Science Education and Research-Kolkata, India on high-pressure physics as a Project Scientist-B, and at the University of Electro-Communications, Tokyo, Japan on ion-surface interactions as a Post-doctoral fellow. Throughout his career, Dr. Das worked and collaborated with many researchers, Ph.D., master, and visiting students from different countries. He further visited many countries to discuss research and an international conference participant (UK, Italy, Germany, Greece, Belgium, Bulgaria, Romania, Brazil etc.). He worked at several institutions before assuming his current role at Ajeenkya D Y Patil University. He received the Marie-Curie post-doctoral fellowship in Sweden, Science Academies' Summer Research Fellowship in India, Gowen Frostic Doctoral Fellowship, Department Graduate Research and Creative Scholar Award by WMU, and Leo R. Parpart Doctoral Fellowship by Dept. of Physics, WMU, among many others, throughout his academic journey. He co-authored several research articles in WoS/Scopus indexed international journals, conference proceedings, and scholarly book chapters and co-edited several books published by renowned international publishing houses (IGI-Global, Springer Nature, Nova Science Publishers, Wiley, Scrivener-Wiley, Notion Press). At present, Dr. Das continues to delve into cutting-edge fields, with a keen interest in nanotechnology, UN SDGs, and data science. His multifaceted contributions, spanning teaching, research, and administrative leadership, showcase a dedicated professional who is instrumental in advancing the vision and mission of the institutions he serves.

Oindrilla Ghosh is a Research Scholar hailing from the School of Law at Christ (Deemed to be University) Bangalore, India, who focuses her research on the health of tribal communities. Her work includes Neuroscience on Organizational Behavior publications at IGI Global and Environmental Disasters, of which 40 publications are indexed in SCOPUS and Web of Sciences conference proceedings. She completed her early education at Loreto Day School, Bowbazar, and achieved distinction in her undergraduate (B.A/LL.B) and postgraduate (LL.M) studies at Calcutta University. Having served as an Assistant Professor of Law at Kingston Law College, Barasat, Kolkata, Ghosh has actively participated in numerous National Conferences, International Conferences, UN Global Summits, webinars, and seminars organized by prestigious academic institutions. Her expertise lies in health perspectives, environmental studies, human behavior, and related areas. Additionally, she has conducted various workshops and lectures in educational institutions, and is engaged with NGO's to help the needy

Deepak Gupta is a distinguished academician with over 20 years of teaching experience and expertise in Computer Science and Engineering. He holds a Ph.D. in Computer Engineering and has an extensive research portfolio, including many international journal papers, multiple conference proceedings, and several books. His research interests span machine learning, artificial intelligence, and data mining. Currently, Dr. Gupta serves as an Associate Professor and Head of Department of CSE (Emerging Branches) at ITM Gwalior, MP, India. He has also contributed significantly to the field through patents and copyrights and actively engages as a reviewer, conference chair and editor.

Mayla Khoiriyah completed his undergraduate degree in Accounting at the University of Indonesia in 2015 and earned his Master's degree in Accounting from the University of Indonesia in 2018. From 2019 to present, he has been a permanent lecturer in the Accounting Department, Faculty of Economics and Business, University of Riau. He teaches courses in Financial Accounting, Management Accounting, Cost Accounting, and Financial Statement Preparation Practices.

Erkin Kholiyarov is working in the Department of Information Technology and Exact Sciences at Termez University of Economics and Service, Termez, Uzbekistan.

Kritikka Kunte is a third-year undergraduate student pursuing a Bachelor of Technology in Artificial Intelligence and Data Science at the School of Engineering, Ajeenkya DY Patil University, Pune, Maharashtra, India. With a strong academic orientation toward data-driven problem solving, she has developed a focused interest in the domains of data analytics and data science, supported by both theoretical foundations and applied project experience. Throughout her academic journey,

Kritikka has cultivated proficiency in core programming and analytical competencies, including Python, SQL, and Java, along with essential data science methodologies such as data preprocessing, exploratory data analysis (EDA), and machine learning techniques. She is proficient in industry-relevant tools and platforms, including Advanced Microsoft Excel, Matplotlib, Tableau, and Power BI, to derive insights from complex datasets and present them in a structured and interpretable manner. Her practical exposure includes the successful completion of projects such as Ocean Salinity Analysis, which involved analyzing environmental datasets to identify patterns and trends, and Speech Recognition and Translation, where she explored applied machine learning concepts in natural language processing. These projects reflect her ability to translate conceptual knowledge into functional, real-world solutions. Kritikka has further strengthened her technical profile through professional certifications, including the AWS re/Start Graduate credential from Amazon Web Services, a certification in Software Development, and Python training certified by Google. Her engagement in competitive and collaborative academic environments is demonstrated by her participation in the Smart India Hackathon (SIH) and by securing Second Runner-Up in an inter-collegiate Tableau competition, highlighting her analytical aptitude and visualization skills. With a growing interest in advanced transportation systems and data-centric engineering solutions, Kritikka brings a multidisciplinary perspective to the GHC Hyperloop Project Competition hosted at IIT Madras. She aspires to contribute meaningfully to innovative, technology-driven initiatives that integrate artificial intelligence, data science, and sustainable engineering to address complex global challenges.

Ananya Pandey is a Research Scholar in School of Law at Christ University, Bangalore. She has her research interests in the field of Constitutional Law, Environment Law, Human Rights, Food Security, Intellectual Property Law and Jurisprudence.

Krutika Patre, is an aspiring programmer and technology enthusiast, currently pursuing Engineering in Artificial Intelligence and Data Science. With a passion for learning, she is building experience in a variety of programming languages and technologies, including C, C++, Python, Data Structures (DS), HTML, CSS, and JavaScript, DBMS (My SQL). After learning this programming language, she has created interest in Full Stack Development. She had also attended an Arduino-Based Automation course at Dolphin Labs to improve my software knowledge. There, she learned how to work with sensors, microcontrollers, and circuit design. She has written review paper on Sustainable engineering on build environment. She is doing researching and learning many topics related to AI, Policy and governance and related to my interest. She has taken part in hackathons, workshops, and tech events to explore many fields. She is also working with a group on Hyperloop. Being part of this project has really helped her grow, especially in areas like teamwork, innovation, and systems thinking.

Sinta Ramaiyanti, S.E., M.Ak. is a lecturer at the Faculty of Economics and Business, Universitas Riau. She earned her Bachelor's and Master's degrees in Accounting and has been teaching since 2019. Her research interests include accounting for micro, small, and medium enterprises (MSMEs), accounting information systems, financial literacy, and corporate governance. Sinta actively engages in community development projects that promote financial transparency and digital transformation among local entrepreneurs. Through her academic and outreach activities, she aims to strengthen the role of accounting and governance in supporting inclusive and sustainable economic growth.

Sunil Sankathala is pursuing B. Tech Computer Science and Engineering at Ajeenkya DY Patil University, with a diverse range of interests that bridge technology, sustainability, and innovation. His academic focus lies in computer science fundamentals like programming, data structures, algorithms, and software development. He actively supplements this with hands-on experience in web development and robotics. Beyond the core curriculum, He has a strong research inclination in emerging and impactful fields. His current research interests include Artificial Intelligence in Healthcare, bioplastics, nano bioplastics, e-waste management, and solid waste management—areas where he believes technology can make a meaningful difference in solving real-world problems. He has been publishing research articles and book chapters in reputed national and international journals and books. He is also part of an ambitious Hyperloop project, which involves interdisciplinary collaboration and cutting-edge engineering aimed at revolutionizing transportation. Working on this project has enhanced his skills in teamwork, innovation, and systems thinking. In the tech domain, he has developed proficiency in web development using technologies such as HTML, CSS, JavaScript, and React. His interests in robotics further reflect building smart, responsive systems that interact with the physical world. Throughout his course, he has helped strengthen problem-solving and collaborative skills. He is proficient in languages such as Python, C, C++, MySQL, Ubuntu, Machine Learning and familiar with frameworks and tools like React, Git. He actively participates in hackathons, coding competitions, and tech events to challenge himself and learn from peers. He is also a quick learner and highly adaptable, with an eagerness to stay updated with the latest trends in the tech world. He aspires to become a skilled software engineer and contribute to building innovative solutions that have a positive impact on society. The long-term goal is to work in a dynamic environment where knowledge, grow professionally, and make meaningful contributions to the field of technology. Driven by a spirit of exploration and sustainability, he aims to contribute to technological solutions that address both human and environmental needs. The long-term goal is to become a versatile engineer and researcher, working at the intersection of computer science, environmental innovation, and human well-being.

Devanshi Soni is currently pursuing a B.Tech. in Computer Engineering at the School of Engineering, Ajeenkya D Y Patil University. Her research interests are metal nanoparticles and their applications and the integration of Artificial Intelligence across various domains. Devanshi is particularly interested in exploring how metal nanoparticles can be combined with AI technologies to address practical challenges and develop innovative solutions. She aims to advance research in these fields and contribute to groundbreaking developments that tackle real-world issues.

C.V. Suresh Babu is a pioneer in content development. A true entrepreneur, he founded Anniyappa Publications, a company that is highly active in publishing books related to Computer Science and Management. Dr. C.V. Suresh Babu has also ventured into SB Institute, a center for knowledge transfer. He holds a Ph.D. in Engineering Education from the National Institute of Technical Teachers Training & Research in Chennai, along with seven master's degrees in various disciplines such as Engineering, Computer Applications, Management, Commerce, Economics, Psychology, Law, and Education. Additionally, he has UGC-NET/SET qualifications in the fields of Computer Science, Management, Commerce, and Education. Currently, Dr. C.V. Suresh Babu is a Professor in the Department of Information Technology at the School of Computing Science, Hindustan Institute of Technology and Science (Hindustan University) in Padur, Chennai, Tamil Nadu, India.

Aryan Vasa is a passionate and self-driven Bachelor of Technology (B.Tech.) student specializing in Computer Science Engineering at Ajeenkya DY Patil University, Pune. Currently in his third year, Aryan is committed to building a solid foundation in core technical domains, including web development, data science, and artificial intelligence. With an inquisitive mindset and a strong eagerness to explore diverse fields, he strives to balance his academic journey with hands-on learning and project development. Originally from Jamnagar, Gujarat, and having completed his schooling in Rajkot under the ICSE board, Aryan has always been drawn toward technology, logic, and creativity. He is actively engaged in learning full-stack development while also keeping a close eye on the evolving job market, particularly the shift toward AI and generative technologies. His academic curiosity extends to research in advanced topics such as Generative AI and Digital Synthetic Outputs, for which he is currently writing a comprehensive review article. Aryan has also been a dedicated athlete, having played basketball for over ten years. This experience has helped him develop teamwork, discipline, and a growth mindset. In addition, he enjoys writing analytical and review-based content, merging his technical knowledge with strong communication skills. Committed to personal growth, Aryan maintains a balanced lifestyle that includes regular workouts, general fitness, and a focus on healthy eating. While continuously learning, he aims to contribute meaningfully to India's tech innovation landscape and become a versatile engineer capable of solving real-world problems through thoughtful design and smart solutions. Whether developing web applications, studying emerging technologies, or sharing knowledge through articles and mentorship, Aryan Vasa stands out as a motivated learner and a future-ready technologist.

Index

A

C

D

H

I

L

M

O

P

R

S

T

X

www.ingramcontent.com/pod-product-compliance
Lightning Source LLC
LaVergne TN
LVHW081528300926
849161LV00006B/1342